John Ford in Focus

John Ford in Focus

Essays on the Filmmaker's Life and Work

Edited by KEVIN L. STOEHR *and*
MICHAEL C. CONNOLLY

McFarland & Company, Inc., Publishers
Jefferson, North Carolina, and London

ALSO BY KEVIN L. STOEHR

*Nihilism in Film and Television:
A Critical Overview from* Citizen Kane *to* The Sopranos
(McFarland, 2006)

*Film and Knowledge:
Essays on the Integration of Images and Ideas*
(editor; McFarland, 2002)

Frontispiece: Ford's familiar profile in silhouette, most likely used as a studio publicity image (with permission of Dan Ford, courtesy Lilly Library, Indiana University, Bloomington)

LIBRARY OF CONGRESS CATALOGUING-IN-PUBLICATION DATA

John Ford in focus : essays on the filmmaker's life and work / edited by Kevin L. Stoehr and Michael C. Connolly.
p.   cm.
Includes bibliographical references and index.

ISBN-13: 978-0-7864-3215-8
softcover : 50# alkaline paper ∞

1. Ford, John, 1894–1973 — Criticism and interpretation.
I. Stoehr, Kevin L., 1967–   II. Connolly, Michael C.
PN1998.3.F65J645   2008   791.4302'33092 — dc22   2007036503

British Library cataloguing data are available

©2008 Kevin L. Stoehr and Michael C. Connolly. All rights reserved

No part of this book may be reproduced or transmitted in any form or by any means, electronic or mechanical, including photocopying or recording, or by any information storage and retrieval system, without permission in writing from the publisher.

Cover photograph: John Ford on the set of
The Plough and the Stars, 1936 (RKO/Photofest)

Manufactured in the United States of America

*McFarland & Company, Inc., Publishers
Box 611, Jefferson, North Carolina 28640
www.mcfarlandpub.com*

To our parents, who gave us
the foundation upon which all else is built.

In memory of
Michael Francis Connolly (1897–1970)
and
Norma Isabel Scribner (1921–2006)

and in honor of
Robert and Loretta Stoehr.

Acknowledgments

The editors would like to express our deep-felt thanks and appreciation to the following persons, institutions, and organizations:

Becky and Sean for their kind understanding and constant support.

All of our contributors for their invaluable participation in this project.

Dan Ford for his generous assistance and encouragement, as well as for permitting us to include a chapter from his biography *Pappy: The Life of John Ford*.

Breon Mitchell, director of the Lilly Library, and Saundra Taylor, curator of manuscripts at the Lilly Library, for their courteous assistance in accessing and studying materials from the John Ford Papers archive at the Lilly Library, Indiana University, Bloomington.

The Everett Helm Fellowship Committee at The Lilly Library, Indiana University, for the helpful grant awarded to co-editor Kevin Stoehr in support of his weeklong research visit there.

Saint Joseph's College of Maine for its faculty development grant for co-editor Michael Connolly's research trip to Galway, Ireland.

Kathryn Wilson and the permissions staff at *Esquire* magazine for its permission to use Peter Bogdanovich's tribute to Ford that was published in the magazine's December 1983 issue, 417–425.

Rose Marie Cerminaro at Simon & Schuster for permission to include fragments of the Prologue and Epilogue to Scott Eyman's biography. *Print the Legend: The Life and Times of John Ford*, by Scott Eyman. Copyright © 1999 by Scott Eyman. Excerpts reprinted with permission of Simon and Schuster Adult Publishing.

Lois D. Tobin, director of the Galway Family History Society, for permission to use Matthew Jude Barker's essay that was published in their journal *Galway Roots*, Volume V, 1998, 148–152. Thanks also to Peader O'Dowd for assistance.

Deirdre McGuinness and the folks at the Irish American Cultural Institute for permission to use William C. Dowling's essay that appeared in their journal *Éire-Ireland*, Volume 36, 2001, 190–211. Copyright © 2001: Irish American Cultural Institute, 1 Lackawanna Place, Morristown, NJ 07960. Reproduced by permission of the publisher, the Irish American Cultural Institute.

Kathleen Lloyd, head of the Operational Archives Branch of the United States Department of Navy's Naval Historical Center, for her kind assistance with the Ford Midway interview.

Patricia Marschand, operations administrator, *The American Legion Magazine*, for her friendly assistance with the Ford D-Day interview.

The folks at *Raidió na Gaeltachta* for their permission to use the Maidhc P. Ó Conaola interview that was translated by Ken Nilsen for our collection.

Nora Folan (née Conneely) for her interview with Ken Nilsen, as translated by Ken for our collection.

Margaret Feeney LaCombe and Michael C. Connolly for their photos.

The original John Ford study group at the Maine Irish Heritage Center, including John O'Dea and his staff, David Soule, Maureen Coyne Norris, Howard Vandersea, Jack Dawson, Doug Fuss, and Margaret Feeney LaCombe, along with the two co-editors of this book. Special thanks to John O'Dea for making the resources of the Maine Irish Heritage Center available to us and to Doug Fuss for making Bull Feeney's available for our local Ford-related events.

Jane McPhillips and the Feeney relatives of Portland for their support.

Renée LeBrun (marketing department, St. Joseph's College of Maine) for her kind assistance in enhancing and coordinating photos.

Steve and Judy Halpert of The Movies on Exchange Street, Portland, Maine, for their generous assistance with our Ford Film Festival in October 2005.

Sr. Mary George O'Toole, RSM, of Saint Joseph's College of Maine.

Dr. Kenneth E. Nilsen for his extra legwork in getting two Ford-related interviews in Galway.

Kenneth Thompson, Jr., for his photo of Francis Ford.

Margaret Ellen Majors Feeney, mother of our contributor Margaret Feeney LaCombe, for sharing memories of Portland's Irish community.

Alice Townend of Lille, France, for assistance with photos taken in Galway.

Bartley, Vera, Patrick, and Ned Feeney of Spiddal, Galway, and most especially for sharing photos from their private collection.

Kate Rhein of Saint Joseph's College for help with manuscript preparation.

Claire Foley of Portland, Maine, for her support of all things Irish.

Eileen Burke (née Ward) for her gracious accommodation during Mike Connolly's travels in and around Galway.

Máire and Phelim Murnion of Páirc Thiar, Spiddal, Galway for their accommodations.

William David Barry and Matthew Jude Barker for research suggestions.

Steve Bromage of the Maine Historical Society for his enthusiastic promotion of the study of John Ford in the director's home state.

Juris Ubans for his remarkable coordination of the monthlong statewide John Ford film festival in Portland (1970) and for his continuing encouragement of our project.

Thomas A. Wilsbach of Portland Public Library for his advice and support.

Lindsay M. Reid for her assistance with indexing.

Betsy Rose for her keen eye and attention in assisting with copy editing.

Table of Contents

Acknowledgments	vii
General Introduction *Michael C. Connolly and Kevin L. Stoehr*	1

Part One: Ford's Vision and Importance

Introduction to Part One *Kevin L. Stoehr*	5
A Tribute to John Ford *Peter Bogdanovich*	7
John Ford in the Twenty-First Century: Why He Still Matters *Scott Eyman*	14
Ford and the Romantic Tradition *Charles Silver*	17

Part Two: Life in Maine, Ireland, and Beyond

Introduction to Part Two *Michael C. Connolly*	35
A Bull Is Reared on Munjoy Hill: John Ford's Irish Upbringing in Portland, Maine *Michael C. Connolly*	42
John Ford: A Memorial *Maidhc P. Ó Conaola (Mike P. Connolly), translated by Kenneth E. Nilsen*	68
John Ford and the Feeney Family of Galway and Portland *Matthew Jude Barker*	75
The John Ford Tour *Margaret Feeney LaCombe*	82
John Ford's Arrival in Hollywood *Dan Ford*	93
Reflections on the Battle of Midway: An Interview with John Ford (August 17, 1943)	102

We Shot D-Day on Omaha Beach: An Interview with John Ford
  Peter Martin   111

John Ford's Use of Gaelic in *The Quiet Man*: An Interview with Nora Folan
  Kenneth E. Nilsen   122

Part Three: Ford's Films

Introduction to Part Three
  Kevin L. Stoehr   129

"If You Can Call It an Art...": Pictorial Style in John Ford's Universal Westerns (1917–1918)
  Tom Paulus   131

Beyond the Blessings of Civilization: John Ford's *Stagecoach* and the Myth of the Western Frontier
  Robert C. Sickels   142

John Ford's Festive Comedy: Ireland Imagined in *The Quiet Man*
  William C. Dowling   153

The Quiet Man and the Boxing Film: Allusions and Influences
  Leger Grindon   169

Ways of Knowing: Peter Lehman and *The Searchers*
  Tom Paulus   176

Populist Motifs in John Ford's Films
  Roy Grundmann   187

Heroism, Faith, and Idealism in *7 Women* and Other Films by John Ford
  Kevin L. Stoehr   205

About the Contributors   223
Works Cited   225
Index   231

General Introduction

Michael C. Connolly and *Kevin L. Stoehr*

This book represents a labor of love for its two editors, both of us hailing from director John Ford's hometown of Portland, Maine. Our collaboration began a few years ago while serving together on a planning committee whose goal was the establishment of a local John Ford appreciation society, mainly as a way to heighten recognition of Ford's importance as a filmmaker among those who have roots in this tradition-minded community on the rugged coast of northern New England. We initiated our project under the auspices of the Maine Irish Heritage Center, and we have also benefited from the generosity and resources of the Maine Historical Society. Both organizations have joined with us in paying ongoing tribute to Ford as Portland's second favorite artistic son, the first being the legendary poet Henry Wadsworth Longfellow.

We believe that, deep in his heart and throughout his life, Ford remained as much a Portlander as an Irishman, and these cultural roots emerge in subtle as well as not-so-subtle ways in his cinematic artworks. But it must be confessed, regrettably, that hometown recognition of Ford's greatness as an artist was a long time coming, as has been noted by a few of Ford's biographers. For example, Joseph McBride suggests in his epic *Searching for John Ford: A Life* that some of this late-blooming acknowledgment may have had to do with anti–Irish sentiments in a town where those of English descent had often clashed with or looked down upon those of Irish descent. But even more likely, as McBride also proposes, such tardiness in recognition may have to do with a certain naïveté among many people about the status of film as a genuine art form that has something to say beyond mere entertainment. In most communities across America there are more likely to be statues of politicians and generals, and even of poets like Longfellow, than of movie directors. Ford declared to a friend at one point in his life: "I love Portland; I don't even know if they like me."[1]

During the co-editors' planning for a Portland-based center devoted to the study and appreciation of the life and works of Ford, we agreed to combine our interest in film with our passion for local history, especially the history of the Irish in Maine. This collaboration was the genesis of the book that you now hold in your hands. Since the project began with our efforts to amplify hometown pride in Ford and his cinematic career, it is only natural that the editors' proceeds from the sale of this book will largely go towards continuing the promotion of John Ford in Portland.

Our group of local enthusiasts began to meet regularly at the Maine Irish Heritage Center, which was established in 2001, largely as an effort by the Irish American Club of Maine to locate a permanent home. The venue that the Center chose seemed entirely appropriate: the former Saint Dominic's Church. St. Dom's was Portland's first Roman Catholic Church, established in 1833 by Father Charles Ffrench, a Dominican priest born in Galway, Ireland. St. Dom's was in the heart of Portland's predominantly Irish West End neighborhood, and the church sat only a couple of blocks west of where John Ford's family, the Feeneys, first lived and worked in the city, and where the statue of Ford — dedicated by the city to great fanfare and public attention on July 12, 1998 — now stands at Gorham's Corner. This church was largely built by the contributions and attendance of many of the burgeoning Irish immigrant population who, after the mid–nineteenth-century famine, came to Portland from County Galway and other hard-hit western regions of Ireland. St. Dominic's served the religious and social needs of this community. The church was greatly enlarged and took its present form in 1893, a year before young John Feeney (later taking the name John Ford after he hit Hollywood) was born. Since then, and until it was deconsecrated by the Diocese of Portland in 1998, the church was a focal point for these new arrivals, many of whom were Irish speakers.

When John Ford's parents arrived from near Spiddal in County Galway in 1872 they were active members of this community. Soon after that, the young John Feeney was born in a farmhouse on the sloping shoreline of Cape Elizabeth, not far from the city. He was baptized at St. Dom's and would later serve as an altar boy. The choice of this venue for the Maine Irish Heritage Center as well as for the meetings of a Ford study group was therefore a logical decision. And our subsequent work with the Maine Historical Society, situated next door to the former home of Longfellow in the heart of Portland, was a natural extension of this initial project.

Our group's first Ford-related function was held at the Maine Irish Heritage Center on February 5, 2005, chosen to commemorate the director's birth date of February 1. An audience of more than 100 people gathered to listen to a lecture by longtime Ford fan Howard Vandersea, who had also been the chief organizer of a Ford film festival in July 1998, when the city dedicated the Ford statue. This was the first in an annual series of lectures on Ford's life and work and was followed by a Ford film festival in October 2005.

During this film festival, interviews with two Ford biographers, his grandson Dan Ford and film historian Scott Eyman, were filmed inside St. Dominic's for the PBS *American Masters* documentary concerning the long-running collaboration between Ford and his favorite actor, John Wayne. The church's gorgeous stained glass windows created a backdrop that even Ford, the master of choosing visually striking locations for his movie scenes, would have admired. Several of the contributors to this volume participated in the festival. A local police officer was hired to proudly watch over the display of two of Ford's Best Director Oscars for *The Informer* (1935) and *The Quiet Man* (1952). These were brought to us from their home in California by Dan Ford, who gave a presentation along with Eyman and fellow Ford scholar Charles Silver. It was a marvelous setting in which to hear experts speak of the director's life and artistic significance and in which to view the early and rarely seen Ford silent comedy *Riley the Cop* (1928). The weekend festival also included a talk on *The Quiet Man* (1952) by film scholar Leger Grindon and screenings of such Ford masterworks as *Steamboat Round the Bend* (1935), *My Darling Clementine* (1946), and *Wagon Master* (1950).

This was not the first Ford film festival in his hometown, however. Between November 6 and December 13, 1970, Juris Ubans, director of the Art Gallery and professor of art at the University of Maine at Portland-Gorham, organized a wide-ranging Ford film retrospective. During the five-week program, nearly forty of Ford's film classics were screened at several venues across Maine with the cooperation of the American Film Institute and the sponsorship of the Maine State Commission on the Arts and Humanities. We commend Professor Ubans for this ambitious and inspiring undertaking that was the first in a series of overdue tributes paid to America's greatest filmmaker by fans from his home state.

The second local film festival to honor Ford took place in July 1998 when the statue of the legendary director was unveiled at Gorham's Corner. Portland's then-mayor, Philip J. "Jack" Dawson, had been the principal organizer of this citywide tribute. Classic films by Ford were screened in the auditorium of Portland High School, the very school from which the young Jack

Feeney graduated before heading to Hollywood to join his older brother Francis. (Shortly after this festival, by the way, this venue was renamed the John Ford Auditorium.) Francis "Frank" Feeney had left home several years before and had quickly become a pioneering film director as well as an actor in the earliest days of silent film, replacing his family name with that of "Ford."

A special gala was held in Portland City Hall on one night of this weeklong festival in honor of Ford. At this event, Ford's love of traditional American music was highlighted, as Brian Miller reported for the journal *Classic Images*:

> Both the Navy band and the Choir of the First Congressional Church of Gorham performed. The choir sang the classic folk hymns *Red River Valley, Galway Bay, Battle Hymn of the Republic, Stouthearted Men, Danny Boy, Deep River, Streets of Laredo, Beautiful Dreamer, America, Clementine, Anchors Aweigh,* and *She Wore a Yellow Ribbon*. The Navy Band played a collection of military songs and marches, topped by an impressive rendition of Sousa's *Stars and Stripes Forever*. Of course, many of these songs appeared in Ford's films, and the tribute could not have been more fitting.[2]

Among those celebrating the statue's unveiling on July 12, 1998, were grandson Dan and other family members, along with such actors as Patrick Wayne, Harry Carey Jr., Claude Jarman Jr., and Carroll Baker, all of whom had performed before the camera for "Pappy" Ford. Other special guests and speakers included John H. Dalton, secretary of the U.S. Navy; Janet H. Ramos, chaplain general of the National Society of the Daughters of the American Revolution; and Síle de Valera, Minister of Arts and Heritage for Ireland. One highlight of the ceremony was a prayer of thanks to the director by Billy Yellow, a medicine man and member of a six-member delegation (led by Chief Jefferson Begay) representing the Navajo nation from Ford's beloved Monument Valley. Many of the Navajo people had benefited financially from the filmmaking projects that Ford brought to their remote land, and they gave the respected director the honorary nickname "Natani Nez," or Tall Soldier.

The statue itself, designed and created by New York–based sculptor George M. Kelly, had been donated by Linda Noe Laine, a Louisiana-based philanthropist who had known Ford and his wife, Mary, and who, upon visiting Portland at one point, was admittedly, and understandably, appalled to find that there was no official commemoration of Ford in the city. For example, there was no city-sponsored tour that mentioned Ford-related sites, and there were many Portlanders who did not even know that this famous "director of westerns" hailed from "Down East." Laine subsequently contacted Mayor Dawson, and their plans for the statue and its unveiling were initiated.

The statue portrays Ford sitting regally in his director's chair, pipe firmly in hand and the booted foot of one leg resting sturdily on the knee of the other. This bronze likeness of Ford stares with a ruminating glance across the very part of Portland where his father's saloon once stood, as if searching out the best possible camera shot of nearby Casco Bay. The chair itself is formed of jutting tendrils of stone that echo the landscape of Monument Valley where Ford felt at home. Surrounding the entire statue are six granite pillars, each engraved respectively with facts about Ford's six Oscar-winning films: *The Informer, The Grapes of Wrath* (1940), *How Green Was My Valley* (1941), *The Battle of Midway* (1942), *December 7th* (1943), and *The Quiet Man*.

The present collection of essays continues in this tradition of remembering and appreciating Ford in a way that shines light on both his genius and his place of origin. Anyone who has watched more than a few of his movies recognizes Ford's attuned sense of place as well as his consistent emphasis on the importance of one's roots in family and home.

Notes

1. Joseph McBride, *Searching for John Ford: A Life* (New York: St. Martin's Press, 2001), 27.
2. Brian Miller, "Portland Celebrates Its Native Son: John Ford," *Classic Images* 279 (September 1998).

PART I: FORD'S VISION AND IMPORTANCE

Introduction to Part One

Kevin L. Stoehr

As John Ford biographer Joseph McBride tells us, the greatest of filmmakers—Frank Capra, Howard Hawks, Elia Kazan, Orson Welles, Ingmar Bergman, Akira Kurosawa, Martin Scorsese, Sidney Lumet, and Steven Spielberg, to name but several—have highly praised or acknowledged their debt to Ford.[1] Several of his films—including *Stagecoach, The Grapes of Wrath, How Green Was My Valley, My Darling Clementine, The Quiet Man, The Searchers,* and *The Man Who Shot Liberty Valance*—are consistently rated by film critics and scholars as being among the greatest of American movie classics.

Ford's style of filmmaking has been likened to a kind of visual poetry that flowed from some mysterious source of inner cinematic genius. As Ford scholar Tag Gallagher informs us, legendary Hollywood producer Daryl F. Zanuck chose Ford as the greatest of all film directors because he was able to position his camera in a way that could capture visually that which other directors required dialogue to communicate.[2] Ford could *show* what other directors could only *say*. In 1945, the pioneering Russian movie director and film theoretician Sergei Eisenstein wrote an essay entitled "*Mr. Lincoln* by Mr. Ford," in which he chose John Ford's *Young Mr. Lincoln* (1939) as the American movie that he most wished had his own name attached to it as director. Ford was the first and only filmmaker to have won four Academy Awards as a feature film director, not including two other Oscars that he earned for his work in creating documentaries for the United States Navy during World War II. He received the very first Lifetime Achievement Award from the American Film Institute in 1973, just before his death. Nonetheless, Ford had downplayed any praise of his artistic merit, once saying to interviewer Peter Bogdanovich, the distinguished filmmaker and cinema historian, that he looked upon his film directing as a "job of work."[3]

Scholarship revolving around Ford's life and work did not grow substantially until director and film historian Lindsay Anderson interviewed Ford in the 1950s and wrote about the artistic merits of his films. By the time that Ford died in 1973, Peter Bogdanovich had published various fragments of his interviews with the Old Master in the form of the book *John Ford* (1967, updated 1978). The Anderson interviews were collected along with his commentary and published as a book entitled *About John Ford*, first published in 1981.

After Ford's death there emerged several illuminating explorations of his movies, including Andrew Sarris's *The John Ford Movie Mystery* (1975) and Joseph McBride and Michael Wilmington's *John Ford* (1975). The first authorized biography, written by his grandson Dan and entitled *Pappy: The Life of John Ford* (1979), appeared shortly thereafter. In terms of a scholarly analysis of Ford's films within their respective biographical as well as cultural contexts, Tag Gallagher's *John Ford: The Man and His Films* (1986) provided a panoramic survey of the development of the director's artistic achievement. Since then, we have seen a growing body of literature on Ford's life and work, including dozens of articles and books on Ford's films and the publication of two other major biographies, Scott Eyman's *Print the Legend: The Life and Times of John Ford* (1999) and Joseph McBride's epic and definitive *Searching for John Ford: A Life* (2001). Given the wealth of published material on the director at this point, one very resourceful volume is Bill Levy's *John Ford: A Bio-Bibliography* (1998), which contains an exhaustive listing of all things Ford.

The three introductory essays that form Part One will provide an overview of Ford's overall artistic vision and his importance as a giant in the development of the cinema. They also help to establish the general theme of our collection of essays—the theme of the intersection between Ford's biography and his artistry.

Peter Bogdanovich, in an article that first appeared in *Esquire* magazine in its December 1983 issue, offers a broad-ranging tribute to Ford that provides an overview of the director from a personal perspective. Among other topics, the author discusses his own conversations with the director before his death, Ford's overall significance within the film industry, his relationships with John Wayne and Katharine Hepburn, and his focus on American history in general and the western genre in particular.

In "John Ford in the Twenty-First Century: Why He Still Matters," Ford biographer Scott Eyman reflects on Ford's continuing significance in American culture, and the American film industry by pointing to essential themes in his work and also to the type of evolving moral vision that underlies many of Ford's films. This brief but eloquent tribute to the director provides a view of the general intersections between Ford's biography and artistry.

Film historian Charles Silver, in "John Ford and the Romantic Tradition," examines Ford's personal worldview from a wide-ranging viewpoint and argues that the director's body of work might best be viewed as a cinematic extension of the tradition of Romanticism. While drawing connections between Ford's moviemaking and the works of Romantic literary artists such as Joseph Conrad, the author views many of Ford's films, ranging from the early silents to the later classics, in terms of several major Romantic themes: a passion for Nature, a deep connection with one's home and homeland, and a concern with the code of heroic chivalry.

Notes

1. Joseph McBride, *Searching for John Ford: A Life* (New York: St. Martin's Press, 2001), 707.
2. Tag Gallagher, *John Ford: The Man and His Films* (Berkeley and Los Angeles: University of California Press, 1986), 145.
3. Peter Bogdanovich, *John Ford* (Berkeley and Los Angeles: University of California Press, 1967, Revised and Enlarged Edition 1978), 112.

A Tribute to John Ford

Peter Bogdanovich

Mr. Ford was in bed, as he often was when not shooting, watching TV and half-listening to my attempts at a conversation. Even if the television had not been on, Ford's attitude toward me would have been gruff and lightly sardonic. This was not unexpected, however, since I mainly would talk about his movies, and John Ford never would allow himself to be caught taking any real interest in a discussion of his work or pictures in general. He was seventy-five at the time, 1970, with less than three years to live. I was a thirty-one-year-old director with two movies to my credit, one a documentary called *Directed by John Ford*.

He had been in the film business for over fifty-seven years, fifty-three of them as a director. Only one decade before Jack Ford got into pictures, the film business did not exist, nor the art of movie direction. Ford made 136 pictures, some of which, in the thirty-odd years between 1931 and 1964, earned seventy-two Oscar nominations. They won twenty-three, including six that went to Ford personally. The New York Film Critics voted him Best Director four times. Both achievements still hold the record today.

He had been responsible for creating not only the screen personas of several key stars, most prominently John Wayne and Henry Fonda, but an extraordinary number of America's favorite and most enduring pictures, among them *The Informer, Stagecoach, The Grapes of Wrath, How Green Was My Valley, She Wore a Yellow Ribbon,* and *The Quiet Man.*

Every so often, after being consistently edgy and sarcastic, or soon after a particularly cutting remark, Ford would smile at me in an openly affectionate way. This might start me waxing eloquent again on some scene of his, or asking yet another convoluted or weighty question, and pretty soon he would be insulting me again. "Jesus *Christ,* Bogdanovich! Can't you ever end a sentence with anything but a question mark? Haven't you *heard* of the declarative sentence?"

Most people were intimidated by John Ford. His appearance certainly contributed: grizzled face with one black eyepatch over thick glasses, a short cigar stuck in his mouth, or a portion of a long white handkerchief, which soon turned brown from chewing. His usual expression was either a purposeful, slightly belligerent deadpan or a scowl. Since he always scorned talk of social significance or of art, never discussed his experiences in World War II (in which he had been wounded and decorated), and spoke of himself simply as a "hard-nose director" who enjoyed making pictures as "a job of work," it was difficult to find permissible areas to approach. I mentioned, nervously, that John Wayne's birthday was coming up and that I was thinking of giving him a book.

Without turning from the TV, Ford said loudly, "Hmmm?" Whenever he wanted to

---

This article first appeared in *Esquire*, December 1983, pages 417–425, with photos. It is reprinted here with the kind permission of *Esquire* and the author.

humiliate, Ford would feign deafness and make you repeat several times the thing you just said. So I repeated about Wayne's birthday and the gift I was planning. For a third time, even louder, Ford said: "Hmmm!!?" I nearly shouted the words *birthday* and *book*. Angrily, Ford said, "A what!" I repeated: "*A book!*" Then suddenly, Ford's expression changed completely, becoming reasonable and relaxed. "Oh!" he said and turned back to the TV. He grunted and put a corner of the large handkerchief into his mouth. He chewed meditatively for a few moments before looking at me again and, enunciating precisely, said: "He's *got* a book!" When Ford turned back to the TV, there was the hint of a smile beneath his fixed expression.

Ford's remark was a devastating comment on a man he profoundly loved and had, to the greatest degree, helped to create: certainly, without John Ford, there never would have been a John Wayne. I had known Wayne for five years by then, Ford for seven, and the father-son relationship between them was fairly clear: Wayne loved Ford but was still thoroughly intimidated by him. He was privately both critical and frightened of the Coach, as he called him, or Jack — the man after whom Duke Wayne had most patterned himself. Wayne once told me his response to Ford on *Stagecoach,* the 1939 western that had made him a major star: After Wayne had seen the rushes for the first time, Ford asked how he had liked himself. Wayne shrugged and said, "Well, you know what *that* is—I'm just playin' you...."

There was a similarity in many of their mannerisms, especially the graceful way both gestured with their hands and arms. The famous rolling John Wayne walk was Jack Ford's walk. Wayne's brusque screen character was Ford's in real life. But Ford wasn't six feet four, with a strikingly handsome face and ultramanly physique; off-camera, Wayne was gregarious, warm and outgoing, quick to laugh, strangely innocent. Ford, while I knew him, was much like the older characters Wayne had begun to play in *Red River,* the western he did with Howard Hawks in 1947. Hawks would tell me that over the years Ford invariably was complimented for having made *Red River*; Ford always nodded, smiled modestly, and said: "Thank you very much."

Hawks put it succinctly: "I don't see how a person can make a western *without* being influenced by John Ford." And Hawks (who would never make a western without Wayne) was not being generous; he could as easily have extended the influence to most American pictures, because Ford had long ago become as synonymous with the Great American Film as Jean Renoir had with the Great French Film. Before Orson Welles made his first two pictures, *Citizen Kane* and *The Magnificent Ambersons,* he studied one film exclusively; Welles would tell me he had run John Ford's *Stagecoach* forty times. For *Kane,* he also hired one of Ford's favorite cameramen, Gregg Toland; both pictures owe no small amount to Ford's visual influence.

Although Ford was most famous for westerns, he did not make a talking one until ten years after synchronized sound had arrived. Yet his career had begun in the silent era, and during his first three years as a director, Ford made only westerns, thirty of them (nearly all starring Harry Carey). During the Twenties, he made a dozen more, helping to create cowboy stars out of Buck Jones, Hoot Gibson, Tom Mix, and George O'Brien. The first of his pictures to be a runaway success at the box office was a western: *The Iron Horse,* released in the summer of 1924. For his wife Mary's Christmas present two and a half years later, Ford had a new Rolls-Royce delivered to the front door, with a fur coat on the backseat; the note attached read: "This ought to hold you for a while." He meant it, and gave her no other presents for many years.

The vast majority of Ford's films dealt with historical subjects: the American Revolutionary War and Civil War, the Indian wars, the building of the railroads, the taming of the West, the creation of a new civilization. Yet the early westerns he made depicted incidents and lives then barely thirty years past. Ford not only made movies about the famous marshal and gunfighter Wyatt Earp, but he had known the man (and others of the epoch) well; they told him how it had been.

During the Thirties, Ford guided Spencer Tracy and Humphrey Bogart through their first feature, and Will Rogers through three (including his last), as well as directed a number of popular, highly regarded films, among them *Arrowsmith, The Lost Patrol, Hurricane,* and *The Informer,* which, for 1935, won Ford his first Academy Award as Best Director and his first New York Film Critics prize. Because he had fought against studio indifference and opposition to get the Irish story done, *The Informer* turned Ford into the hero of the critics and the public. He was already married for fifteen years to Mary McBryde Smith — a magnificent, extraordinarily resilient woman, a direct descendant of Thomas More — and they were the parents of a teenage son and daughter, and Ford's reputation as a family man and artist had never been stronger.

At this moment, his personal life was rocked to its foundation. Ford, now forty, fell profoundly in love with a woman of twenty-six named Katharine Hepburn, who also fell in love with him. It happened while the two of them were shooting the film version of Maxwell Anderson's historical drama *Mary of Scotland*. Neither Ford nor Hepburn ever spoke of their affair, but of course the families knew. The attraction between them, the explosiveness and independence of both their natures, can be seen reflected in several of the key romantic relationships in Ford's subsequent pictures, notably in the extraordinarily rich emotional interplay between Maureen O'Hara and Walter Pidgeon as the forbidden lovers in *How Green Was My Valley;* between Wayne and O'Hara in *The Quiet Man, Rio Grande,* and *The Wings of Eagles;* and between Clark Gable and Ava Gardner (who was nominated as Best Actress) in *Mogambo*.

Despite their feelings for each other, Ford and Hepburn came to a difficult and painful conclusion. He was an Irish Catholic, married to a woman he dearly loved, and with a passionate belief in family. The thirteenth and last child of Irish immigrants (his father was a saloon owner in Maine), Ford was now a famous, wealthy, and respected figure in the world. And Katharine Hepburn was already well on her way to the longest and most influential career of any woman in the movies; she had become a top star and won an Oscar after her first Hollywood season, only two years before meeting Ford, and had been nominated again the same year he won his first. Her reputation for integrity and Yankee strong-mindedness matched his. Their first encounters were volatile, but Ford was remarkably gallant and courteous with women, and always pleased with, and refreshed by, a well-phrased and reasoned argument.

Kate Hepburn of Hartford, Connecticut, and Jack Ford of Portland, Maine, were a match made in heaven. But, on the other hand, they both knew how badly their relationship might damage their individual careers and their ability to do what they had evidently been born at precisely the right time to do. They both knew how good they were and how much more they still had to accomplish.

When he and Hepburn decided they could never work together again, they both would have known the degree of happiness they were giving up. The decision, a kind of glorious and idealistic sacrifice, is echoed in most of Ford's subsequent pictures: the burden of duty, tradition, honor, and family is among his central themes.

Eight years later, Hepburn would begin the longest secret love affair in picture history, with another married Irish Catholic father, named Spencer Tracy — a liaison that yielded a handful of memorable costarring vehicles and was not revealed until after Tracy's death. It is difficult not to see a connection between her screen behavior with Tracy and her love not only for him but also for Jack Ford — the truly secret and romantic one.

Ford and Hepburn remained close friends throughout Ford's life; she also had a warm friendship with Mary Ford that continued until Mary died, five years after Jack. In *The Quiet Man,* Ford's single most passionately romantic picture, made in Ireland at age fifty-seven, the Maureen O'Hara character combined the best qualities of the two women who, apart from his mother, Ford most loved; her name in the film was Mary Kate.

Within two years of his and Hepburn's decision, Ford would begin the most expressive, emotionally charged, and poetic series of pictures in American film history. Between 1938 and

1941, while America stayed out of the war, at ages forty-three to forty-six, Ford directed seven profoundly affecting movies. The three release years involved were by far the most productive of quality in Hollywood's entire history; if any one time was the peak for the American screen, it was the years 1939 to 1941, after which the U.S. entry into World War II altered everything. Ford's competition in these years included not only *Gone with the Wind* (which earned thirteen nominations in 1939, against nine for three of Ford's pictures), but a score of other popular and critical milestones, from Capra's *Mr. Smith Goes to Washington* to Lubitsch's *Ninotchka,* from *The Wizard of Oz* to *Citizen Kane.* The Academy nominated Ford each year and he won the last two: the New York Film Critics voted him Best Director all three years. Ford's constant work conveniently managed to prevent him from personally appearing to accept any of his prizes.

This remarkable burst of creativity began, appropriately, with a western; although *Stagecoach* was his ninetieth film, it was not only his first western since the advent of sound, but also his first in thirteen years. Loosely based on a de Maupassant story, *Stagecoach* began the John Wayne myth and established Monument Valley (Arizona/Utah) as Ford's own special country of the West, setting a standard for westerns that only two or three others, including Ford himself, would ever equal or transcend.

His other two films of 1939 starred Henry Fonda: *Drums Along the Mohawk* — Ford's first in color — and *Young Mr. Lincoln.* The director had had to browbeat the actor into accepting the role of Lincoln in their first of seven features together. Fonda recalled Ford demanding: "What do you think you're going to be playing? The Great Emancipator or something?! This is a young jackleg lawyer from Springfield, for God's sake!" The death of Lincoln's early love, Ann Rutledge, and his abiding faith in her spirit reverberate throughout the picture. Ford's other films of this period are *The Grapes of Wrath, Tobacco Road, The Long Voyage Home,* and *How Green Was My Valley.*

In August 1941, four months before Pearl Harbor put America in the war, Ford, age forty-six, went on active duty in the U.S. Navy. With the rank of lieutenant commander (eventually becoming a two-star admiral), he was appointed chief of the Field Photographic Branch, a unit of the OSS, reporting directly to his friend Colonel William ("Wild Bill") Donovan. Though Ford was even more closemouthed about his war activities than he was normally about everything else, he once told a reporter: "Our job was to photograph, both for the records and for intelligence assessment, the work of guerrillas, saboteurs, Resistance outfits.... Besides this, there were special assignments." Except for his work on several war documentaries, Ford would not direct a new picture for nearly four years.

Not long after Ford's death, some of his undercover activities for the government became known through his grandson Dan Ford's biography, *Pappy: The Life of John Ford,* and through director Robert Parrish's autobiography, *Growing Up in Hollywood,* which includes the best personal portrait of Ford yet published. Decorated a number of times, Ford was also given the Purple Heart for injuries sustained during the Battle of Midway, which he personally photographed with a hand-held 16mm camera, even after receiving shrapnel fragments in the arm and groin.

The battles they were filming in Hollywood with Duke Wayne were being lived overseas by Jack Ford. Toward the end of the war, the Navy asked Ford to make a picture (with Wayne) in the line of duty. Typically, Ford chose America's worst defeat, in the Philippines, as the background to what became the finest and most compassionate of American war films, *They Were Expendable.* A deal was struck with MGM and Ford demanded from Louis B. Mayer the highest salary ever paid (at the time) to a director, $400,000, and donated all of it to build a recreation center in Los Angeles for veterans of his naval unit.

The first movie Ford directed after the war was a western. Shot in Monument Valley, with Henry Fonda playing Wyatt Earp and climaxed by a re-creation of the famous gunfight at the OK Corral, *My Darling Clementine* surpassed *Stagecoach* but received almost no special attention. Of the thirty-odd films Ford directed in the last twenty years of his active career, half of them were westerns. Ford had realized that the form he had so greatly influenced, and almost single-handedly perfected into a unique American art, could be the equivalent of the myths or legends of the ancient religions and histories of Europe. As the modern, postwar world became increasingly disheartening to Ford — and less and less interested in his work, especially his westerns — he continued nevertheless to explore the themes that profoundly concerned him.

Unquestionably, these westerns were his most mature and resonant achievements: from the towering cavalry/Indian war trilogy with Wayne, Fonda, O'Hara, and the rest of the Ford family of players — best viewed in this order: *Fort Apache* (1948), *Rio Grande* (1950), *She Wore a Yellow Ribbon* (1949) — to the darkening, increasingly tragic series of frontier stories that began in 1956 with Wayne in *The Searchers* and ended in 1962 with Wayne and Stewart in *The Man Who Shot Liberty Valance,* perhaps the two richest and most complex westerns ever made.

Although Wayne had been a part of Ford's family since 1928 and Ford had not even met Fonda until ten years later, when John Ford went into the war, and after he returned, Fonda clearly was the favorite son. *Stagecoach* had turned Wayne into a box-office attraction virtually overnight, yet all the key male leads in Ford's subsequent pictures had gone to Fonda. After *Fort Apache,* however, Fonda — dissatisfied with most of his other film work — decided to return to the Broadway stage; his first of several huge successes was in the title role of *Mister Roberts,* and he was out of pictures for eight years. In 1954, when Jack Warner hired Ford to direct the film version of *Mister Roberts,* both Marlon Brando and William Holden were proposed for the lead, each of them big names at the time; Fonda was no longer considered a screen draw. Ford said, however, that unless Fonda played Roberts, he would not direct the picture. Fonda was cast. No one told the actor of Ford's intervention.

During the filming, when Ford began to add visual comedy to the script and to beef up the smaller roles, Fonda — having done the play for more than a thousand performances — became indignant, and objected: to him the Broadway text was like Scripture and Ford's additions not only unnecessary but insulting to the integrity of the piece. To patch up the growing rift between star and director, producer Leland Hayward arranged a meeting of the three, he would tell me, "to air their differences." After a few minutes of listening to Fonda's complaints, Ford stood up and socked Fonda on the jaw, sending him to the ground. Fonda would tell me that he had looked up at Ford, age sixty, and realized he could not possibly return the blow. Shortly afterward, Ford suffered a severe gallbladder attack, and Mervyn LeRoy was hired to complete the film. Ford and Fonda did not speak to each other for ten years — not until Ford's daughter, Barbara, told Fonda what her father had done to secure him the Roberts role. The actor called Ford, and though a reconciliation of sorts followed, the two never worked together again.

For Ford's final score of films, John Wayne starred in nearly half, with a range of roles and performances that challenged any Fonda had done. But the shift from Fonda to Wayne had an odd effect on the critical reception of Ford's pictures and on the attitude of the liberal artistic commentary toward Ford himself. Fonda's politics having always been outspokenly Democrat, and Wayne's equally Republican, the assumption was correctly made that Ford's political opinions were similar to, even identical with, his favorite star's. Ford, being resolutely "apolitical," as he would say, made no attempt to convince people otherwise. Referring to Wayne, he would tell a reporter, "I love that damn Republican."

Yet director-writers Joseph L. Mankiewicz and Samuel Fuller each would tell me of the same unpublicized Ford incident they had witnessed, one that helped define his true attitudes. In the early Fifties, while Mankiewicz was president of the Screen Directors' Guild, C. B. De Mille launched a major campaign to demand signed loyalty oaths as a prerequisite for remaining a member of the union. Mankiewicz objected. The De Mille faction began to make insinuations about Mankiewicz's "pinko" leanings, and eventually the situation became so heated in the community and in the press that a special membership meeting was called to decide the issue. Mankiewicz flew in from New York for it, he would tell me, knowing that his career was on the line.

In a record turnout, nearly the entire membership attended. A noisy debate between the sizable De Mille group and the Mankiewicz supporters continued for more than four hours. John Ford, by far the most honored and respected member present, sat on an aisle, Fuller said, wearing his baseball cap and untied sneakers, attentive but without comment or change of expression. Finally, after De Mille's own long, impassioned speech, there was a silence and Ford raised his hand. A court stenographer was present and each person who spoke had to give his name and describe his position briefly. Ford stood and said: "My name is Jack Ford—I make westerns." He then went on to praise DeMille's ability to produce pictures that appealed to the public—more so, Ford said, than anyone else in the room; he turned to look across the hall now directly at De Mille: "But I don't like you, C.B," he said, "and I don't like what you've been saying here tonight. I move that we give Joe a vote of confidence—and let's all go home and get some sleep." Which is what they did.

In his latter years, nevertheless, Ford came to be considered close to a reactionary, because throughout the Fifties and into the Sixties, while the chic American cultural fashion became increasingly irresponsible, antimilitarist, antipolice, and antifamily, Ford continued to make pictures with men in uniform, fighting the chivalrous fight, honoring the women and way of life they protected and cherished. The theme to which he returned most often was the glory in defeat. In each of his cavalry films and westerns, the Indian nations had been treated and portrayed with exceptional accuracy and dignity; the cause of their savagery was always placed squarely on the sins of the white invaders and exploiters. When the old Indian chief in *Yellow Ribbon* cries that he and cavalry officer Nathan Brittles (John Wayne) are "too old" to do anything about the war that is to ensue between their peoples, Brittles' simple response sums up Ford's most essential belief: "…but old men should *stop* wars!"

Plagued by several illnesses and increasingly poor vision, Ford would have realized as he entered his sixth decade as a director that each picture he began could very well be his last. Certainly the final two films he made reflected a desire to deal with subjects he felt had not been sufficiently explored in his work: the Indian's tragic history, and woman's. This last movie was originally titled, appropriately, *Chinese Finale,* but eventually released as *7 Women* (1966): it is among his most revealing pictures but unquestionably the most reviled of his career. Ford's American reputation never recovered from the film's poor reviews and worse business. Though his last years were filled with attempts to make a deal on a new movie—two set in World War II, two set in the Revolutionary War, another about a black soldier—the necessary backing never materialized.

One of the greatest mythmakers in our history had been silenced before his time. But then, the America of John Ford was not the America of the Sixties or Seventies, nor of the directionless Eighties. Is any form less honored today or apparently less "commercial" than the western? Haven't we turned our backs on the only traditions we have ever honored or respected—the chivalrous code of the West, which glorified women and was pledged to defend the hearth and family?

On March 31, 1973, exactly five months before his death from cancer, a frail and emaciated John Ford became the first recipient of the American Film Institute's Life Achievement Award and, in the same televised festivities, the first American filmmaker to receive the nation's highest civilian honor, the Medal of Freedom. President Richard Nixon was on hand, along with the Marine Band, to present the medal. Outside, in front of the building, a protest against Nixon was being led by Jane Fonda.

The irony of the situation was mirrored in one of her father's Ford films: in *Fort Apache*

Fonda had played a tyrannical and glory-seeking martinet whose racist miscalculations — a gross underestimation of his Indian opponents — had led to the massacre of most of his men and of himself: yet at the end, Wayne, playing one of the few survivors and a humanist leader the opposite of Fonda's character, nevertheless confirms the false press and public notion of Fonda as a brave and courageous leader. The morale and spirit of the cavalry as a whole was more important, therefore, than the failings and injustices of a single man. Ford would tell me that heroes were "good for the country," and yet he would show us the truth behind the fake legends.

Richard Nixon could hardly have been John Ford's favorite President — though President Nixon would tell me that his favorite movie director was John Ford. In 1961 Ford had voted against Nixon and for Jack Kennedy. Nonetheless, Nixon was there that night as President of the United States to pay tribute to an American who had served his country in peace and war under several Presidents. The nation and the nation's history were paying tribute for the first time not only to an artist of films, but to one who had for almost sixty years vividly represented the nation and its history, and the kindred histories of other nations, to the peoples of the world.

The last time I saw Mr. Ford, he was again in bed: it was less than three months before he died. I had come with Howard Hawks, and Ford gave us five minutes, throwing the usual banter at me about my incessant questions: "Howard, does he ask you all those damn questions too?" Hawks nodded, grinning. He and Ford and I were pretending that nothing was any different, as though Ford were not pale and weak and ninety-eight pounds and often in excruciating pain. I had entered the room a fraction early and seen Ford assume a casual pose with his cigar. He puffed it nonchalantly until we left. I called him once more from Europe but he couldn't hear me. Kate Hepburn visited him often. The day before his death, Wayne arrived. "Come for the death watch, Duke?" Ford asked. His last words were "May I please have a cigar?" He finished the cigar and, about three hours later, he died.

John Ford in the Twenty-First Century: Why He Still Matters

Scott Eyman

John Ford died more than thirty years ago. John Ford is alive and well.

This in a culture where the average career lasts ten or fifteen years, and the average posthumous reputation is usually extinguished in half that. But the work and, indeed, the reputation of John Ford continue to thrive. In the last seven years, five books have been written on Ford; an American Masters show on the collaboration between him and John Wayne was acclaimed; around twenty Ford films have been released on DVD in America, and more in Europe — everything from the great masterpieces like *The Grapes of Wrath* and *The Searchers* to such B-list but still rich and rewarding Ford as *The Prisoner of Shark Island*.

Why has the work of John Ford continued its hold on the attention of critics and the affection of audiences all over the world, when other directors of the same period, even great directors, have somehow receded into the past? William Wyler was certainly a great director, and ditto George Stevens, but they are remembered for a couple of films apiece. John Ford is remembered for a dozen.

Part of this is because Ford, in the public mind, typed himself. He did much more than direct one kind of movie, of course, but when the average person thinks of John Ford — and how many directors of that era does the average person really think of? — they do not think of *Arrowsmith* or *Mogambo*, but of Monument Valley: of *Fort Apache* or *She Wore a Yellow Ribbon* or *My Darling Clementine* or *The Searchers*.

In retrospect, it can be seen that John Ford told the story of America from the Revolutionary War of *Drums Along the Mohawk*, through the settling of the West and both World Wars, to the dawn of the media age in *The Last Hurrah*. I do not know that he consciously sat down and wrote out a checklist of periods he wished to examine — dozens of westerns, the post–Civil War South, and so forth. I rather doubt it. One of the glories of the studio system was its ramped-up production — a working director could reasonably expect to make two films a year, a tempo that hardly anybody can match today, where every movie has to be built from the ground up. A director with a specific abiding interest in something like American history could reasonably expect to plunge his hands into his favorite soil on a semi-regular basis.

And Ford had the good luck to work for over a decade with Darryl Zanuck, who shared his

---

This tribute to Ford's cinematic vision and continuing relevance is composed partly of material from the Prologue and Epilogue of the author's biography of the director, *Print the Legend: The Life and Times of John Ford* by Scott Eyman. Copyright © 1999 by Scott Eyman. Excerpts reprinted with permission of Simon and Schuster Adult Publishing.

interest in America, and who, moreover, had a great strength in script development, which perfectly dovetailed with Ford's own enormous skill in production and images. Zanuck could set up a picture, massage a script until it was right, and hand it off to Ford, secure in the knowledge that Ford could shoot practically anything, probably including the Napoleonic Wars, in eight weeks.

And there is the specter of John Wayne, the single most dominant representation of America throughout the world, now and apparently forever the image of American masculinity that every succeeding action star has to incorporate or reject. Wayne gave Ford an indomitable presence and Ford gave Wayne intimations of loss and regret that propelled his acting into a third dimension.

The man who was born John Feeney, who became John Ford, always emphasized his Irishness, so commentators and critics followed his lead. But Ford was also that staunchest of New Englanders, a Maine man, with an abiding memory of a New England town, that is to say an ideal community of enduring values. From the town of Portland, Maine, John Ford learned the value of the common people, the beauty of the natural world, and the powerful symmetry that results when the two are joined. He felt the lure of the sea and the unspoken bonds that bind working men together. He saw the wrecks off Portland Head Light, the catastrophe that can result when good men are overwhelmed by fate, and the dignity of the women who quietly waited while their men went down to the sea in ships.

Beyond that, his Maine upbringing had given him a valuable lesson in modesty, for you do not put on airs if you live in Maine; the worst thing a Yankee can be is a snob. In short, from Portland Ford learned the emotional dynamic that would inform practically every film he would ever make.

The roots of his extraordinary talent remain elusive. His childhood had nominal creative input, his adolescence only slightly more so. His sole aspirations were vague longings for a career in the Navy, which was not pursued until middle age. Yet, it was John Ford, more than any director since D. W. Griffith, who instinctively understood the potential of film, who knew how to utilize all the devices intrinsic to the medium. He understood pacing, framing, angles, lighting, composition. Beyond that, he understood character, understood the value of myth, understood people and — this may have been his ultimate secret — he understood the value and mystery of time itself, especially in recognizing the power of the past.

In his work, Ford's Irish melancholy manifested itself in an elegiac sense of loss — for a vanished innocence, for a lost love, for a community, for a home. Many of Ford's films are large-scale, even epic, yet they contain the same warmth, domestic detail and intimacy of his small movies. He had humor, of course, but he also had an intense and sustained gravity and feeling for the dramatic — in landscape and in people. His sense of rapport with the men and women of his movies was remarkable. It is a world of genial humanity — not of cardinal sins, but of venial, hedonistic ones. Ford's deepest moments concern memory and loss.

Ford's vision moved from inclusion — the climaxes of *Stagecoach* and *My Darling Clementine* — to exclusion, where the dances and burials and civilization itself are regarded with the wary eye of the outcast. Ford gently insisted that doing the right thing can and probably will get you killed, that defeat may be man's natural state, but that honor can and must be earned. His men are not leaders so much as loners, and their greatest acts are renunciations. It is no accident that, when Ford made a movie about World War II, he made one about a campaign America lost.

Ford's films can be seen as one cumulative epic of America's national mythology as told by its foot soldiers — the story of the common people. And then there are the westerns. Ford's westerns have the feeling of life. You can hear the timber creak as he combines the theme of the odyssey with his abiding sense of unkempt humanity, the weathering of human wood. Ford's westerns fulfill the essential requirement of anything lasting about America — they are about promise and, sometimes, its betrayal.

John Ford brought the art form to what still seems an ultimate synthesis of character and landscape — pictures superseding words, meanings too deep to be explained, yearnings that must remain unspoken. Most movies are all plot — what happens next? — but Ford's movies are less about what the main character will do than they are about the mysterious question of who and what he actually is.

Ford had several themes that he returned to again and again. The first was the nobility of society's outcasts. The people that can be trusted in John Ford's world are not lawyers or bankers or pillars of society. They're the drunks, the outlaws, the whores, the people who live on the fringes. And the second great theme is the sacrifice that the present has to make to insure the future. This is a theme that stretches from *Straight Shooting* (1917) to *Fort Apache* (1948) to *The Man Who Shot Liberty Valance* (1962) — sacrifices made to build a future that will never be as vital as the rough good times that are replaced. Ford's work is full of a sense of ghost riders on the horizon, watching over the young family they die for — the future of America.

As he aged, Ford managed to show both sides, lay bare all the contradictions of our democracy: politicians are frauds, heroes are fools, and America's image of itself is based on misinformation and wishful thinking. Ford prints both legend and fact, because that is where the peculiar strength of America lies: between idealism and pragmatism, between self-sacrifice and self-interest. For Ford, America and democracy grow out of the encounter between wilderness and civilization, between the palpable and the potential.

John Ford cared nothing for money, little for politics, but a great deal about character and tradition. He believed in America and he believed in the future, even as he mourned the past. In *The Searchers,* Ethan Edwards leaves his feelings for his brother's wife unstated because it would destroy the family; in *The Man Who Shot Liberty Valance,* Tom Doniphon lets Ransom Stoddard have the girl he loves because he knows the lawyer can offer her a world Doniphon can only dream about and would not want anyway. Always, Ford lingered over the man deserted by time and tide, because he knew that it happens to everybody — even famous film directors.

If Ford had never made *The Searchers* or any other western, he would still be regarded as a major director, with a particular gift for repose and astringent wisdom. And the Western would still have a history, but nowhere near as glorious. Ford gave the western a vision and, in Monument Valley, a signature. No other place evokes the West so unambiguously. Ford defined what is American about the Western. Ultimately, John Ford's greatest gift was his ability to combine the epic with the intimate — not just in the same film, but in the same moment, the personal moving side by side with the mythological.

All of this is true, yet none of it is enough. The work of this wild colonial boy flared with a moral imagination equal to the melancholia that marked his life. His instinctive knowledge that things usually end in defeat balanced his idealism and sentimentality. Ford gave the world an America that was a lived experience, a history that can be used. His history became the history of his time, mirroring it, transfiguring it, explaining America to itself.

His films are about the search for a home we can never find again, and form an album of America as it was meant to have been, as well as of the place it really is. Although his films rest easily on the screen, they retain the power to burn through space to a place inside us, an art about memory that makes our own lives more vivid. He shaped a vision for America in the twentieth and twenty-first centuries every bit as majestic and inclusive as the one Jefferson crafted in the eighteenth and nineteenth centuries. It is made up of soldiers and priests, drunks and doctors, servants and whores, and lonely, half-crazed men driven by their need to be alone. The goal is home, the theme is reconciliation. John Ford lives because he is one with Walt Whitman: a primal poet in love with his land. Like Tom Joad, he is all around us in the dark.

John Ford and the Romantic Tradition

Charles Silver

Introduction and Overview

John Ford is a unique figure in the history of the cinema. One of the most distinguished film critics in the United States, Andrew Sarris, in his book *The John Ford Movie Mystery* reflects the fact that there were many facets to Ford's personality and career, some contradictory. What I hope to do here is to examine some of the facets of John Ford which I find particularly interesting and present to you my personal viewpoint on the man whom I consider the greatest of American film artists. Above all, in viewing him as a true artist of the highest caliber, I hope to show that his overall vision is a diverse one but that it is primarily rooted in Romanticism. The Romantic worldview is one that celebrates those very things that make his films so "Fordian": the striving of human passion and the imagination, the sublime power and beauty of nature, the importance of one's origins in a unique culture or homeland, and the code of chivalry practiced by pioneering heroes who hearken back to the knights of medieval myths.

The importance of one's landscape as well as homeland was ingrained in Ford from an early age. Ford's early years, like those of D. W. Griffith, were spent in a very provincial atmosphere, which probably explains why he was never very comfortable with urban life and its more sophisticated and effete lifestyle. He went to college for only a few weeks, if at all, and he tended to be mistrustful of intellectuals and their ideas. The state of Maine where Ford grew up is at the farthest eastern tip of the United States next to the Canadian border. It was commonly called "Down East" in those days, an ironic fact considering Ford's later identification with the American West. At the age of twenty, young Jack Feeney (as he was then known) joined his brother Francis in California where Francis was already an established film director. Francis had adopted the name Ford and Jack soon followed suit.

For the next three years, Jack worked for Francis as a stuntman, actor, and assistant director on Westerns and other adventure films. During the shooting of *The Birth of a Nation* (1915), he appeared as an extra in crowd scenes and began a lifelong acquaintanceship with D. W. Griffith. From this experience he seemed to learn a great deal about Griffith's methods, and Griffith's influence would have reverberations in Ford's career for decades to come. Francis Ford was a leading director of very profitable films for Universal, and his younger brother became known to the studio executives. It was only a matter of time, in those days when filmmaking was very informal, before Jack Ford was given an opportunity to become a director.

John Ford remained an active director for almost half a century. His career can be broken down into three phases or periods. The first and shortest phase (1917–1920) is the one we know the least about, his three years as a director for Universal. It is unfortunate, but the only surviving movie from these years is *Straight Shooting* (1917).[1] We are lucky that at least this one film was rediscovered in Czechoslovakia in the 1970s because it is the first feature-length movie that Ford directed and because there are elements in it which we can clearly identify as Fordian. I am referring here to many of the images and the landscape photography. He had already directed four shorter works, and he was to go on to make over two dozen more films during this Universal period, all of which are lost. Like *Straight Shooting*, most of these starred Harry Carey, the cowboy actor to whom Ford dedicated *3 Godfathers* (1948) and to whom John Wayne pays a moving tribute at the end of Ford's masterpiece *The Searchers* (1956). We will probably never know how typical *Straight Shooting* is of Ford's Universal films, but the one unmistakable fact this film conveys is that Ford was born with a natural gift for photographic composition.

In 1920 the director began the second phase of his career (1920–1936) as a craftsman for the Fox (which later became Twentieth Century–Fox) Studio. Here we are fortunate indeed, for most of these films survive. The path of John Ford's career is without parallel in the American film industry. None of the other great directors was able to survive so long and finally thrive within the confines of a major studio. We have all heard the horror stories associated with the aborted careers of Buster Keaton, Erich von Stroheim, Josef von Sternberg, and, more recently, Orson Welles, all artists whose talent and working methods were incompatible with the American studio system. Griffith himself was forced to become a studio director around the time Ford moved to Fox. He had lost his financial independence and eventually he also found it impossible to go on working. Only Charlie Chaplin was able to be his own boss because of his enormous popularity and his limited number of productions.

Ford worked almost exclusively for the Fox Studio for over twenty-five years, and he gradually rose to be its most famous and successful director. There was a negative aspect to being a trusted house director, however. Ford received many assignments which were neither challenging nor in keeping with his particular talents. It is amazing, for example, that after *3 Bad Men* (1926), the greatest director of Westerns made no films in that genre for thirteen years. Although Ford was gradually perfecting his craft during this period, it was not really until the mid–1930s that his films began to reflect a clear personality, and it was not until 1939, the year of *Young Mr. Lincoln*, *Stagecoach*, and *Drums Along the Mohawk*, that he made his first masterpieces.

During John Ford's earliest days at Fox Studios in the silent era, beginning in 1920, he directed a series of films dealing with life in rural America: *Just Pals* (1920), *Cameo Kirby* (1923), *Lightnin'* (1925), and *Kentucky Pride* (1925). No one of these films is as important individually as their importance as a group. For it was in these films that Ford began an exploration of American cultural values. He was to become adept at portraying American character types in a naturalistic milieu, a genius which would ultimately result in such masterpieces as *Young Mr. Lincoln* (1939), *The Grapes of Wrath* (1940), and *The Man Who Shot Liberty Valance* (1962).

The first genuine flowering of this genius appears in the three very simple films Ford made in the mid–1930s with the very popular comedian/actor Will Rogers: *Dr. Bull* (1933), *Judge Priest* (1934), and *Steamboat Round the Bend* (1935). Rogers had a very strong personality of his own. He personified a rural wisdom, and his popularity reflected the fact that most Americans were then (and to a degree, are still) suspicious of the sophistication of urban, formally-educated America. Rogers was a folk hero in the flesh, bringing up to date the rustic characters Americans admired in literature from James Fenimore Cooper to Mark Twain. Ford lost none of Rogers' distinctive charm and appeal in these films. He placed him in environments which graphically portrayed certain aspects of American life in the present, though they were mostly set in the past. Ford helped Rogers make his best films shortly before the actor's death in 1935, and Rogers helped Ford discover what the director did best — lend a profoundly poetic touch to the American experience.

At the start of the third and most important phase of the director's career, there are extraordinary signs of Ford's newfound maturity and control of his medium in *The Prisoner of Shark Island* (1936). It is, however, with *Stagecoach* and *Young Mr. Lincoln* in 1939 that everything seems to come together. These films are so rich and complex as to justify, from 1939 onward, speaking of Ford's personal vision as one would the vision of Griffith, Renoir, Chaplin, Dreyer, Ozu, and others. The long years of apprenticeship and patiently carrying out the studio's directives were to pay off in twenty-five more years of very individual filmmaking on the highest level of artistic creation. Ford would himself insist that he remained little more than a craftsman doing, as he put it, "a job of work." This can be in part attributed to the fact that American males of Ford's generation found the concept of art a bit too feminine for their taste. Ford did not try to compete with Howard Hawks, Raoul Walsh, and William Wellman in trying to create the illusion of a *macho* personal lifestyle. He tended, however, to make fun of interviewers like Lindsay Anderson and Peter Bogdanovich who inquired about the deeper meanings of his work. This did not, of course, prevent Ford from quoting younger directors like Orson Welles, Ingmar Bergman, and Akira Kurosawa in their honoring him as their hero and teacher.

There is a great irony in the later period of Ford's career when it came to the public's response to his cinematic vision. The more personal and brilliant that his films became, the less that popular critics, his colleagues in the industry, and, ultimately, the audience responded to them. Although he had been America's most honored director — even as late as *The Quiet Man* which won him a Best Director Oscar in 1952 — Ford gradually lost favor after World War II, just as he was embarking on some of his greatest work. Ford finally lost his place in Hollywood, and he spent his last years in enforced retirement. Part of Ford's problem was that he returned to the Western form, and so many of his late masterpieces could not be taken seriously by the rather frivolous American press. Critics of the time thought that any film with John Wayne and horses must be unworthy of their attention. Only the influence of such *auteur* critics as Andrew Sarris, Peter Bogdanovich, and Joseph McBride restored Ford's reputation and that of these timeless works which had been so casually dismissed when they were released. Fortunately, Ford received many honors in his last days, and I think he knew that there was a whole new generation of film enthusiasts who greatly admired him.

Today, Ford's reputation remains secure in the United States, at least among the segment of the population and those institutions that take old films seriously. His movies are revived, written about, and respected for their classic qualities and skills which are increasingly lost in the present trends toward boring television and mindless Hollywood productions lacking in feeling and human values. Nowhere is his presence more honored than in a segment of contemporary American filmmaking where tributes to Ford by younger directors are commonplace. Three recent examples are George Lucas's homage to *The Searchers* in *Star Wars* (1977), Steven Spielberg's use of *The Quiet Man* in *E. T.* (1982), and the very Fordian funeral of Mr. Spock in Nicholas Meyer's *Star Trek II* (1982). While Ford would certainly have appreciated these honors, he probably would not have been very comfortable with the increasing predominance of such space technology movies in an industry which no longer seems to have much room for personal artistry and adult subjects.

The fact is that a phenomenon like John Ford is hardly likely to ever happen again in the cinema. Directors today no longer have the luxury of a long studio apprenticeship in the United States. Television does allow many directors to work regularly, but there is little chance for personal or visual expression. I would argue, somewhat controversially perhaps, that television has yet to produce a filmmaker of truly the first rank.[2] Ford, on the other hand, was able to develop his own methods of work and form a congenial group of actors and technicians who were devoted to him and to their collective enterprise. In having learned to articulate his personal vision in cinematic terms, he was able to borrow the lyricism and feel for characterization of D. W. Griffith and use it to suit his own purposes. He incorporated F. W. Murnau's expressionist visual style into his films, but ultimately discarded the artificial dramatic excesses which would have been inappropriate for his own naturalistic filmmaking. Ford's own brilliant sense of composition, however, was enhanced by Murnau's use of the moving camera, dramatic angles, and depth of focus. Ford made this synthesis of the two great visual styles of the silent period — expressionism and lyricism — into his own inimitable way of looking at the world. Ultimately, the word one must use is poetry, for Ford at his best used his unique genius for imagery at the service of feelings he was trying to convey.

It is helpful to delineate the central values that run through Ford's major work and that are representative of his filmmaking personality. By his major work I am thinking of such films as *Stagecoach, Young Mr. Lincoln, The Grapes of Wrath, How Green Was My Valley* (1941), *My Darling Clementine* (1946), and many later movies. There is much about Ford that is peculiarly American. Although he would probably have laughed at this, I think his work derives in part from the great tradition of American nineteenth century literature — the writings of Whitman, Melville, and Twain, among others. These authors chronicled both the bright and the dark side of the opening up of a new civilization in a land that seemed to have limitless possibilities. By the time John Ford came to Hollywood in 1914, the American frontier, the West, had been officially closed and was being rapidly settled. Ford became deeply committed to American history, and the West provided him with an ample supply of legends and stories to tell, and its landscapes provided his camera with an incomparable beauty to photograph.

The United States is barely two hundred years old as a nation, and this had an impact on Ford's career. For example, when he made his film about Abraham Lincoln in 1939, it was still within the lifetime of some people who had been alive during Lincoln's presidency. In terms of the Western, a number of the historical figures of the frontier were not only still alive when Ford began his career, but they also came to Hollywood to work in the movie business. One of the early films in the Museum of Modern Art archive in New York shows a famous bank robber recreating on film one of his crimes. So Ford knew personally the hero of *My Darling Clementine*, Wyatt Earp, and could supplement historical accounts with Earp's own memories.

The result of this brevity of the American historical experience allowed Ford's recreation of history to have an immediacy and contemporary relevance virtually unparalleled in the cinema. The issues of nineteenth century America remained unresolved in the twentieth century, and many are still problems for our society today. For example, Ford could make a very clear statement on contemporary race relations with *Sergeant Rutledge* (1960). And some of the matters debated at the political convention in *The Man Who Shot Liberty Valance* were debated two years later at the 1964 Republican National Convention which nominated Barry Goldwater for president.

Ford used American history for his own purposes, a trait which should not be confused with falsifying it. Until very late in his life Ford had a very optimistic appreciation of the American experience, and he used his genius as a poet and storyteller to celebrate America and to capture on film a mythological past — a literary tradition going at least as far back as the Greek poet Homer. In his classic heroes, usually played by John Wayne, Ford created the portrait of an ideal American, lovingly superimposed on a spectacular and detailed historical canvas. Ford's tragedy, as superbly expressed in *The Man Who Shot Liberty Valance*, was that as the United States congealed into a modern civilization, it became too small for large and legendary heroes and the heroic values they represented. (Perhaps there is a parallel here with Toshiro Mifune's unemployed samurai in Akira Kurosawa's splendid *Yojimbo* made in 1961, a year before *Liberty Valance*.) The past and its promise began to seem much less relevant in the presence of the Vietnam War with its divisive effect on American society and the prospect of future nuclear catastrophe.

The concept of what is past and lost, however, was far more crucial for John Ford than just in his romantic depiction of a mythological West. In *Judge Priest* there is a very touching scene of Will Rogers by his wife's grave, talking to the long-dead woman. Ford uses essentially the same scene with Henry Fonda in *Young Mr. Lincoln* and again with John Wayne in *She Wore A Yellow Ribbon* (1949). (It was not unusual for him to recycle his own material, each time refining and enriching its texture, just as a ceramic artist might make a pot much like another, but with a slight variation and, perhaps, improvement.) The past — that which had been lost, that which could only be remembered — was Ford's conception of character and human nature. Through memory the past could live again, and, in Ford's films, these memories are deeply felt and vivid, rivaling the reality of the present. Watch Jane Darwell's face in *The Grapes of Wrath* as she must leave her Oklahoma home for California and as she re-examines the souvenirs of a lifetime of memories. These physical objects must now be discarded, but one cannot help being deeply moved by watching her expressions in the flickering firelight as she thinks back over the joys and sorrows of her life. If I had to choose one scene to convey the essence of John Ford, I think I would choose this brief, poignant, and simple moment.

How Green Was My Valley is entirely about memory. What could easily have been just another filmed novel is magically transformed by Ford into a lyrical portrayal of a childhood spent in a loving family, as seen through the eyes of the man who had once been that child. There is a great warmth of feeling which runs through the whole film. It is Ford's most explicit statement of devotion to what one thinks of as the traditional values of home and family. Although Ford himself apparently never had a truly satisfying family life as an adult, *How Green Was My Valley* does seem to echo his own childhood in a large family living in a small Maine town. Many of his heroes tend to live outside the normal social structures, but his films do express an overall belief in the conventional patterns of life. It is, indeed, John Wayne's ultimate self-sacrificing purpose in *The Man Who Shot Liberty Valance* to create an environment in the West where the traditions of civilization, the values of home and family, could take root.

Ford's films show respect for the importance of formality and ceremony. He valued personal loyalty to friends and responsibility for the social commitments one makes. Although he prized individual achievement, there is a strong sense of community in all his films.

He made very few films in which women had major roles, but behind his male heroes often stood very strong women. Jane Darwell in *The Grapes of Wrath* is an excellent example of this. She is the force which holds the family, the community, together in its period of trial. Henry Fonda, her son, goes off to fight for the cause of a just society, while it is the mother who stays behind and bears the true burden. When Ford's cavalry soldiers leave the fort in grand processions, he is always careful to show the women who are left behind. Never does one have the sense that they are frail or weak. It is more a question of each sex doing his or her respective job. It is the great inner strength and endurance of Maureen O'Hara in *Rio Grande* (1950), *The Quiet Man,* and *The Wings of Eagles* (1957) which finally wins out over the hurt and anger of John Wayne, and Ford's great love stories have overtones of a mother-son relationship. In his last film, *7 Women* (1966), Anne Bancroft is as strong and forceful in character as John Wayne in *The Searchers*, sacrificing her personal happiness for the good of the others in her community.

The powerful mothering role of women is something Ford shares with his great Irish-American contemporary, the playwright Eugene O'Neill. While until fairly recently we knew practically nothing about Ford's own youth,[3] I believe the mothers in *Young Mr. Lincoln, The Grapes of Wrath,* and *How Green Was My Valley* must be modeled on his personal experience. Ford's mother was probably typical and resembled O'Neill's very forceful mother whose addiction to morphine is so graphically portrayed in the playwright's brilliant tragedy, *Long Day's Journey into Night*. I also think there is a sense in which Ford's veneration of the past can be viewed as his own personal variation on respect for one's ancestors.

Ford was a Roman Catholic, but he was not a devoted believer in formal religion. In those films where he indulges in obvious religious symbolism such as *The Informer* (1935), *The Fugitive* (1947), and *3 Godfathers*, there is a sense of falseness. Ford's spiritual truth came from human relationships and man's devotion to the land, to nature. Man could achieve fulfillment, in Ford's view, through a sense of inner contentment, a pride in achievement, and a dedication to social responsibility.

With the exceptions of D. W. Griffith and Charlie Chaplin, who were fortunate and managed to do their best work outside the restraints of the American studio system, the obstacles to artistic creation were enormous in the American film industry. The studio executives were tough businessmen interested in providing popular entertainment for commercial return. In those rare cases where the studios consciously aspired to art, the results were generally pretentious and empty. It is extraordinary that the son of a small city saloonkeeper could emerge from such a system as one of the great artists of the twentieth century.

John Ford could never quite bring himself to publicly acknowledge that he viewed himself in this light. Very few of his films were self-consciously artistic, and in his private life his happiest moments seem to have been drinking and smoking cigars with friends like George O'Brien, Ward Bond, and John Wayne. His filmmaking unit of actors and technicians became his family, a family in which he was the father—hence his nickname, "Pappy." How often, standing in the bright sunlight of Monument Valley or chewing on a handkerchief under the klieg lights at the Fox Studio, did Ford consider that what he was doing was artistically profound? That is something we will never know. Perhaps much of his gift was mere intuition and dexterity, his superb eye the equivalent of an expert woodcarver's fingers. For the kind of art he made had much in common with that of folk artisans—simple and expressing very basic values. Ford's creations, no matter how intricate they became, were never abstract or beyond the understanding of the popular audience. His films, in the final analysis, were about feelings, relationships, and people. To appreciate them fully, one must allow oneself to be emotionally vulnerable, to suffer with his characters' tragedies, to celebrate with their triumphs, to identify with them as real human beings. There is no room in Ford's films for such modern theories as audience alienation or theatrical absurdity. He believed very deeply that his films reflected real life. He wanted to make you laugh, and he wanted to make you cry. Most of all, he wanted you to share an emotional experience, and I believe this was at the very heart of the classical cinema.

In Neptune's Hall: Ford and the Sea

> Far as the mariner on highest mast
> Can see all round upon the calm vast,
> So wide was Neptune's hall...
> John Keats, "Endymion," Book III

> ... he was not
> Himself like what he had been; on the sea
> And on the shore he was a wanderer.
> There was a mass of many images
> Crowded like waves upon me, but he was
> A part of all ...
> Lord Byron, "The Dream"

"Down to the sea in ships" (Psalms 107:23). Ford (right) with screenwriter Dudley Nichols, a regular guest on Ford's yacht *Araner* (with the permission of Dan Ford; courtesy Lilly Library, Indiana University, Bloomington).

> ... no matter what [Ford] does, he always wants something he doesn't think he has.
> George O'Brien[4]

> Those first years of his life in Cape Elizabeth were his lost Eden.
> Joseph McBride[5]

Ford was at heart a Romantic artist, as proposed at the outset. A good many Romantic artists have emphasized the influence of one's rootedness in a specific culture and geographical area as well as one's relationship with the natural world of sea, land, and sky. Ford shares in the Romantic emphasis on these themes, and so I turn now to the importance of his roots in a small city on the rugged coast of Maine — as well as to his ongoing connections with the ocean and land, connections that began to form when he was a young boy.

A few hundred feet from the water, Munjoy Hill rises above densely populated northeastern Portland. At its crest stands the Portland Observatory, the last remaining maritime signal tower in America. Climbing the 86-foot tower, one is greeted by spectacular views of the harbor, Casco Bay, and the great Atlantic beyond. The lovingly-restored, red-shingled Observatory, built under the supervision of Lemuel Moody in 1807, was used to give merchants signal of the arrival of vessels sailing in from the corners of the globe. It was also used a century after its construction by young Jack Feeney (later known as John Ford) to dream the dreams of adventure that little boys dream. Perhaps in the tower, like the child who became Joseph Conrad's Lord Jim, "[h]e saw himself saving people from sinking ships, cutting away masts in a hurricane, swimming through a surf with line; or as a lonely castaway, barefooted and half naked, walking on uncovered reefs in search of shellfish to stave off starvation!"[6]

Young Jack would visit the tower for hours from his various still-standing childhood residences just slightly down the hill. From the window of the top-floor bedroom he shared with his brother Patrick on Sheridan Street, the twelve-year-old had a similar, if slightly less elevated view, while doing homework for the Emerson School around the corner.

One can take a short ferry ride across the harbor to Peaks Island where young Feeney spent his summers in a family cottage and rowing a small boat in Casco Bay. (D. W. Griffith had almost accepted a job with a theatrical stock company on Peaks Island in 1908, but he instead chose to go to Biograph and the movies.) On the way to Peaks Island the ferry passes Fort Gorges, built between 1857 and 1865 as an identical twin of Fort Sumter. One may drive just down the Maine coast past the 1791 Portland Head Light to Cape Elizabeth where Jack Feeney was born, a half-mile from the Atlantic.

If one walks today around the old commercial district of Portland harbor, one comes upon a bronze statue of a man seated in a movie director's chair. It is a non-descript neighborhood of mostly aged but still active buildings. Across the street from the statue is a vacant lot, the former site of his father's Feeney's Saloon. On the back of the director's chair, in which a stern-looking, pipe-smoking, bronze fellow sits, is written "Director John Ford," the name by which Jack Feeney eventually became known. It must be confessed, however, that for too long the city seemed blissfully unaware that it spawned possibly the greatest narrative artist in the English-speaking world since Charles Dickens and arguably the greatest of all American artists.

Ford was the second youngest of eleven children (his younger brother, Daniel, died in infancy). He lost a year of school to diphtheria, suffered from poor eyesight, was bookish and artistically inclined, yet compelled to play the dual roles of macho football hero ("Bull Feeney") and brawling saloon-keeper's son, and failed at an attempt to adapt to college. Where would his future lie? Young Jack had worked as an usher in the Gem Theater on Peaks Island when it started showing movies. He loved watching films, and, if the advertisement from the Big Nickel Theater in Ford's high school magazine can be credited, he was exposed to the "Highest-Grade Photoplays": stories from Dickens, Cooper, and other standard authors. He also had an interest in theater and writing. Biographer Joseph McBride attributes the "Bull Feeney" pose to compensating for his sensitivity and interest in the arts.[7]

There would have been a certain kind of logic that, in spite of his thick eyeglasses, he might have followed the examples of similarly situated Romantic young men — James Fenimore Cooper, Richard Henry Dana, Herman Melville, Joseph Conrad — and gone to sea. The year 1914, however, had a war looming on the horizon, and the resonantly-named liner, *The Empress of Ireland*, was to sink in nearby Quebec. He actually did apply to the Naval Academy at Annapolis, but he failed the entrance examination. This adds an extra dimension to his minor early talkie, *Salute* (1929), which he shot at the Academy fifteen years later. He also allegedly had a brief flirtation with an athletic scholarship at the University of Maine, from which he was to receive an honorary doctorate in 1947.

Since older brother Francis Ford was now a large duck in a small Hollywood pond, Jack went west in 1914 to lend a hand with the props. His actual sea experience would mostly wait for another war and for sailing aboard his beloved yacht *Araner* in the Pacific. Sailing and seamanship, however, figure prominently in more than a dozen of the films he was to direct. Ford would never forget his closeness to the water in Portland and Peaks Island, to which he would return from California for many summer vacations. Perhaps he regretted that he could not look

"John Ford knows what the earth is made of" (Orson Welles). Ford on porch steps that most likely belong to his father's home on Peak's Island, Maine. Flowers and gardens were recurring symbols in Ford's films (with the permission of Dan Ford, courtesy Lilly Library, Indiana University, Bloomington, Indiana).

back and muse like Conrad on "my unalterable and profound affection for the ships, the seamen, the winds and the great sea — the moulders of my youth, the companions of the best years of my life."[8]

In Ford's sea films, with rare exceptions, the comfort level of his imagination never really approached that creativity inspired by the West. After he made a post–World War II commitment to the Western, only two of his completed films are even peripherally set upon the water. It is possible that weariness from his war experiences and the gratification found on his 110-foot ketch *Araner* which appears in *Donovan's Reef* (1963), had changed his attitude. Of note, too, is the fact that his first uncompleted attempt at a postwar sea film, *Mister Roberts* (1955), had been terminated by the combined bad memories of a fistfight with erstwhile friend Henry Fonda and a gallbladder attack.

Part of the sea's appeal to both Conrad and Ford was the feeling of escape and simplicity it provided, something Ford was also to find in the Western past. Conrad wrote: "I rejoiced in the great security of the sea as compared with the unrest of the land, in my choice of that untempted life presenting no disquieting problems, invested with an elementary moral beauty by the absolute straight-forwardness of its appeal and by the singleness of its purpose."[9] As did Ford, Conrad viewed civilization as "the frontier of infamy and filth, within that border of dirt and hunger, of misery and dissipation, that comes down on all sides to the water's edge of the incorruptible ocean."[10]

In *Time and Tide*, the great Romantic critic John Ruskin compares the ideal society to a "crew of a ship struggling against the elements on the high seas, all members working to the best of their abilities, sharing the rations, helping the weak and sick, and obeying the captain."[11] Like Ruskin's captain, Ford expressed firm creative authority over a loyal stock company of actors when making films.

In 1934, Ford was commissioned a lieutenant commander in the Naval Reserve. His World War II exploits would eventually make him a rear admiral. Conrad, who had experienced a sudden ascension to captaincy, commented: "I stood like a king in his country, in a class all by myself. I was brought there to rule by an agency as remote from the people and as inscrutable almost to them as the Grace of God...." Becoming a captain had transformed Conrad as magically as Cinderella: "It seemed as if all of a sudden a pair of wings has grown on my shoulders."[12] It strains even a Romantic imagination to conceive of an angelic John Ford, but I think the director could relate to Conrad's proud statement: "It is a great thing to have commanded a handful of men worthy of one's undying regard."[13] Both men could relate to the camaraderie and empathy in adversity engendered by a sea voyage or a long trip to an isolated location, and both appreciated professionalism. Captain MacWhirr's reference to "the work to be done" in *Typhoon* anticipates Ford's recurring references to a film as "a job of work."[14]

It certainly did not escape either man that being at sea or being in Ford's movie company offered substitute filial attachments to them, and just as there is little heterosexual eroticism in either man's work, the isolation in the company of males promotes certain undercurrents of homoeroticism. In *The Secret Sharer* and elsewhere, Conrad's sailors literally cling to each other in a storm, and in Ford's *The Long Voyage Home* (1940), his lovingly-photographed compilation of Eugene O'Neill's sea plays, there is much blubbering and bathos among the sailors.

In this film, Ford comes closest to Conrad in subject matter, portraying a ship full of merchant seamen at the beginning of World War II. Conrad had distinguished his sea stories into two categories: storm pieces (*The Nigger of the Narcissus* and *Typhoon*) and calm pieces (*The Secret Sharer* and *The Shadow-Line*). Ford offers both and adds the additional element of battle. Like Conrad in *The Nigger of the Narcissus*, Ford in *The Long Voyage Home* focuses on the men below deck, not on officers, and Conrad's description of two Norwegian sailors could almost apply to the characters played by John Wayne and John Qualen: "The two Norwegians sat on a chest side by side, alike and placid, resembling a pair of lovebirds on a perch, and with round eyes stared innocently...."[15]

In *The Long Voyage Home*, Ford's inclination toward military decorum is realistically sublimated since, as Conrad says, ""discipline is not ceremonious in merchant ships, where the sense of hierarchy is weak, and where all feel themselves equal before the exacting appeal of the work."[16] The indifferent immensity of the sea and Conrad's deep nostalgia for the passing era of nineteenth-century sailing ships found clear echoes in Ford's lament for the passing of the frontier and its pristine beauty. There is equal loveliness and lovingness in both a Fordian panoramic shot of Monument Valley and in Conrad's elegaic: "There is something touching about a ship coming in from sea and folding her white wings for a rest."[17] Morton Zabel writes of Conrad, "His last five novels turn on themes of surrender, acceptance, sacrifice, the trice with life and fate. They give evidence of the fatigue and compromise that overtook his darker vision and more searching powers before the end."[18]

Ford's "darker vision" is increasingly evident in his final works. The "shadow-line," the title of one of Conrad's works, refers to a passage from youth into greater awareness and its concomitant disillusion. Perhaps much of the wistfulness is evident indecision as to whether to undertake one more voyage. It possibly speaks, too, to Ford's unresolved feelings about his youthful choice to go to the West and not to go down to the sea in ships.

John Ford's sea films, as a genre within his *oeuvre*, with a few exceptions do not measure up to his other achievements, but given what we know of his youthful predilections, his love affair with the *Araner*, and his declaration to Lindsay Anderson that he would be happy to be a tugboat captain, they are worth a bit of closer examination.[19] If nothing else, these films helped Ford define for himself the ritualistic military milieu of one of his supreme accomplishments, the Cavalry Trilogy of *Fort Apache* (1948), *She Wore a Yellow Ribbon,* and *Rio Grande.*

After making Westerns almost exclusively for seven years, Ford first ventured to sea cinematically in 1924 (immediately following *The Iron Horse*) with *Hearts of Oak* (1924), a film that is unfortunately lost. It starred Hobart Bosworth (later Chingachgook opposite Harry Carey's Hawkeye in the 1932 serial version of *The Last of the Mohicans*) as a sea captain who sails along the New England coast and in the Arctic. *The Blue Eagle* (1926) survives in fragmentary form, but it features George O'Brien and Janet Gaynor, the stars of F.W. Murnau's masterpiece, *Sunrise*, made the following year. The typically beefy, good-hearted, and seldom fully-clothed (known off-screen as "The Chest") O'Brien is cast as a kind of "Bull" Feeney at sea. O'Brien had been a naval boxing champion in World War I, and Ford makes full use of his pugilistic skills.

It is with *Salute* (1929), however, that one's sonar first detects personal Fordian undercurrents. *Salute* is set and filmed at the Naval Academy, from which Ford had been rejected in 1914. The film never goes to sea but it dabbles a bit in what makes for a sailor — the ethos and the heroic commitment required. Ford's educational impulse, that which makes the Cavalry Trilogy as much a textbook of disciplined military horsemanship as *Moby Dick* is of whaling, combines actual footage of the parade ground with a histrionic, early-sound rendering of a midshipman's life. O'Brien plays a West Pointer, but two naval upperclassmen are portrayed (uncredited) by men who were later to be central to Ford's art and also drinking/sailing buddies on the *Araner*: John Wayne and Ward Bond. It is a sweet film, more ultimately about football than water, but it must have amused Ford to make an authorized movie about the Academy that had turned "Bull" Feeney down.

Conrad had written of the difficulty of "keeping white" for sailors visiting obscure eastern islands where "unknown to trade, to travel, almost to geography, the manner of life they harbor is an unsolved secret."[20] Several of Conrad's characters succumb to temptation and marry natives, like Willems in *Outcast of the Islands*. Some of the flavor of the temptation of undisciplined culture is evident in the early scenes of both *Men Without Women* (1930) and *The Long Voyage Home*. That these early scenes take place in Shanghai and a Caribbean island respectively does not detract from the point that Ford, a Maine provincial, is taking up the issues of a clash of cultures that would be sweetly resolved in the multiracial lovefest of *Donovan's Reef* (linked with *Men Without Women* by the song "Monkeys Have No Tails" decades and a world war later). The submarine sequences, using what Ford claimed dubiously as the first real submarine in the movies, are much too claustrophobic and static to make for interesting cinema. The storm in the China Sea, scene of Conrad's *Typhoon*, is done with unconvincing miniatures. Frank Albertson recreates his character from *Salute*, Ensign Price, thus making *Men Without Women* a kind of sequel. What is most telling is the film's title, which pointedly describes Ford's professional comfort level for most of his career.

A woman does play a crucial role in Ford's next sea epic, but she is a treacherous German spy who mars the film with a bad performance and a sappy ending. *The Seas Beneath* (1931) is again about submarines, this time during World War I. Here, Ford is beginning to come into his element, showing George O'Brien as Commander Kingsley of a "mystery ship," tricking and attempting to destroy U-boats. The director is clearly fascinated by the strategic killing game, much as Sir Walter Scott was by medieval warfare in the graphic battle scenes in *Ivanhoe*. Again, much of the authentic documentary-style material on shipboard life and submarine maneuvers can be viewed in retrospect as anticipating the Cavalry Trilogy. Chief Costello, whose blarney is much like that of Victor McLaglen's Sergeant Quincannon in those later films, is based partly on Ford's father. O'Brien seems to replicate James Fenimore Cooper's description of John Paul Jones: "[H]is form was muscular and athletic, exhibiting the finest proportions of manly beauty."[21] In *The Seas Beneath*, O'Brien has a benign regality about him, much like Harbor Master Ellis, as described by Conrad in *The Shadow-Line*: "If he did not actually rule the waves, he pretended to rule the fate of the mortals whose lives were cast upon the waters."[22]

By the time of *The Hurricane* (1937), adapted from the novel by Charles Nordhoff and James Norman Hall, authors of *Mutiny on the Bounty*, Ford had largely established his enduring style and his stock company of actors and artisans. Jon Hall and Dorothy Lamour are not particularly convincing South Sea natives, although both would go on to play similar roles in several films; but Ford's racial portrayal appears especially romanticized and benevolent, even a quarter-century before the blissful *Donovan's Reef*. *The Hurricane* makes no attempt to imitate the authenticity of Robert Flaherty's *Moana* (1926), and it fails to approach the profound existentialism and tragedy of Murnau's *Tabu* (1931). At best *The Hurricane* is a step up from King Vidor's comic book *Bird of Paradise* (1932). It does allow him to take a slap at the complacency of the Catholic Church, only two years after *The Informer*, by having priest C. Aubrey Smith proved wrong when he assures the natives that his church will provide sanctuary against the storm. Jon Hall, as an outlaw hero virtually destroyed by the injustices of civilization, is an early exemplar of the Ethan Edwards school of rebellion. The hurricane created by James Basevi's special effects and miniatures and photographed by Bert Glennon (*The Scarlet Empress, Young Mr. Lincoln, Wagon Master*) bids fair to rival those in Cooper and Conrad. "The wind that overturns the world" is Ford's primal depiction of the flip side of Nature's beauty and the director's signal to us that he could make almost any kind of movie, even a disaster film, if so moved.

Ford returned to *Seas Beneath* material with *Submarine Patrol* (1938). He liked it, and the climactic battle scenes received much praise, but Ford had become a major figure as a result of *The Informer* (1935), his trilogy of films with Will Rogers, and *The Prisoner of Shark Island*. In this context, a conventional studio production such as *Submarine Patrol*, whatever its level of craftsmanship, seemed distinctly retrograde. It did contain, however, several instances of creative and experimental filmmaking that demonstrated that Ford was on his way to the masterpieces to follow.

The Long Voyage Home, following on the heels of *Stagecoach, Young Mr. Lincoln,* and *The Grapes of Wrath*, was more in keeping with Ford's newly-attained prestige. Lovely as it is to look at in Gregg Toland's glistening black and white, *The Long Voyage Home* is far too overlaid with O'Neill's pretensions to allow Ford to breathe into it much of his own poetic vision. O'Neill even forces Ford to confront alcoholism as a problem rather than as a basis for humor. Still, for all its self-conscious artiness, one can sense Ford is saying that, a quarter-century later, he has few regrets for the choice he made not to follow in the watery footsteps of Conrad, even if his Romantic respect for the sublime and overwhelming power of nature — here, in the form of the ocean — is evident.

The outbreak of World War II found Ford all over the place as Chief of the Navy's Field Photographic Branch Office of Strategic Services. After his documentaries *Battle of Midway* (1942) and *December 7th* (1943) won Academy Awards, he put himself back in the line of fire to shoot the D-Day landing. Ford had been seriously injured at Midway, but he continued to photograph the Japanese attack. Perhaps Ford felt a need to finally test himself in reality and discovered, as with the hero of *The Shadow-Line*, "such a sense of intensity of existence, the test of manliness, of temperament, of courage and fidelity — and of love."[23]

Returning to his more mundane existence, Ford's best sea film, *They Were Expendable* (1945), came out at the end of 1945, after the guns had stopped. It is a tribute to Ford's personal friend, PT-boat innovator John Buckley. The director also pays homage to his Portland High School English literature teacher, Lucien Libby, naming one of the ships after him. Lindsay Anderson, a Ford scholar and a distinguished filmmaker in his own right (*This Sporting Life, If, O Lucky Man, The Whales of August*), regarded *They Were Expendable* as one of Ford's great masterpieces. Ford used his salary from this film to establish a recreational "Farm" for the veterans of his World War II unit, holding annual quasi-military ceremonies there under his command.

The Wings of Eagles (1957) is ostensibly about screenwriter Frank "Spig" Wead, another Ford naval friend. Wead had penned the screenplay for *They Were Expendable* and had also worked on the script and story of Ford's earlier *Air Mail* (1932). The seagoing scenes in *Wings of Eagles*, however, are not as interesting as the romantic reunion of John Wayne and Maureen O'Hara (memorably paired by Ford in *Rio Grande* and *The Quiet Man*) and Ward Bond's hilarious impersonation of Ford in the form of the director John Dodge.

Finally, Ford returned to his beloved Hawaii for *Donovan's Reef*, his farewell to Wayne. It is a sweet, leisurely, mellow film, much in the mold of *Hatari!* (1962), made by Howard Hawks the preceding year and also with Wayne. There is nostalgia and summing up, reunions with stars of his 1930s movies like Dorothy Lamour and Cesar Romero, and one last little role for the great Mae Marsh, nearly a half-century after *The Birth of a Nation*. It is a film with the brawling spirit of "Bull" Feeney, a movie that takes shots at the New England "Yankees" who hounded Ford's family in Portland. It is a celebration of the beauty of the *Araner*, named for the alleged homeland of the director's beloved mother. In other words, it is a highly personal film that returns to the freewheeling spirit of *Men Without Women* (Australian sailors abandon their dates for a free beer) and *The Seas Beneath*. It is an old man's film about his youth and about that imaginary life that he decided to record on celluloid rather than experience in reality. Ford's sea-oriented films never display the soaring Romantic vision of his Westerns, but *Donovan's Reef* is perhaps a movie that suggests how an ideal life on land or sea should be, a life lived on a lovely island paradise of the mind, surrounded on all sides by the gentle lapping of Neptune's hall.

What the Earth Is Made Of:
Ford, the Land, and the Homeland

> John Ford knows what the earth is made of.
>
> Orson Welles to Peter Bogdanovich[24]

> ...something of which the artist may not be wholly aware, namely the pulsations within him of some kind of infinite spirit of which he happens to be the particularly articulate and self-conscious representative ... pulsations of nature.
>
> Isaiah Berlin[25]

There is no greater poet of the American land and landscape than John Ford. This is in keeping with his overall Romantic vision. In his later Westerns, in *Young Mr. Lincoln* and *The Grapes of Wrath*, and even before that in his films with Will Rogers, Ford captures our spirit and the experience of our folk with richer poignancy and complexity than any other artist. He is our Dostoevsky, our Tolstoy, our Dickens, our Shakespeare. Yet, we cannot ignore the fact that, like Victor McLaglen in *Hangman's House* (1928), he was always a man with divided loyalties; he was a red-white-and-blue American who nonetheless always had a bit of the "green place in his heart."

In Battery Park in New York City, on a small sloping patch of sod not far from the former site of the World Trade Center, there has been fashioned a "replication of an Irish hillside, complete with fallow potato furrows, stone walls, indigenous grasses and a ... fieldstone cottage."[26] This is the Irish Hunger Memorial created by sculptor Brian Tolle. It memorializes the great potato famine that prompted so many Feeneys and others to come to places like New York, Boston, and Portland. It is the mythology of this event and the concomitant British indifference to its consequences that young Jack Feeney imbibed with his mother's milk and later "Bull" Feeney swilled with *Daddo*'s best stout.

Long before he went west, Ford had gone east with his father, directly from Maine to Galway, and savored the lyrical beauty and inspiration of his ancestral home. It was mostly a pastoral Ireland that he experienced and recreated in his films, a Romantic Ireland that owed much to maternal nurturing and paternal saloon blarney. Still, the same humane and poetic eye that gazed back on America and its struggling pioneer people also saw the charm and loveliness of his struggling kinsmen in the other direction, back across the sea.

Although Irish-American characters occasionally appear in Ford's early Westerns, he chose his first non–Western to be his first Irish-themed movie, the now-lost *The Prince of Avenue A* (1920). It starred the former heavyweight champion "Gentleman Jim" Corbett as the son of an Irish mayoral candidate, thus presaging *The Last Hurrah* (1958) by nearly four decades. Irish laborers figure prominently in the historically-correct *The Iron Horse* (1924), and there is some mistily-gauzed Irish material in *The Shamrock Handicap* (1926), but Ford's first full scale foray into recreating "the old sod" comes in 1928 with *Mother Machree* and *Hangman's House*, both starring Victor McLaglen.

Although these films are exceptionally well crafted for Ford at the time, they both show the expressionist influence that F. W. Murnau brought to the Fox lot in *Sunrise* (1927), a film whose production Ford watched with fascinated respect. Some of the pastoral images from the fragments of *Mother Machree* which survive are later recreated in glorious color (and on location) in *The Quiet Man* (1952). The same is true for the horse race sequence in *Hangman's House*, in which John Wayne, the star of *The Quiet Man*, appears as an extra. These early works convey a sentimental, fantasy vision of Ireland, replete even with a harp-playing dwarf, but a tenderness has crept into Ford's work that would have made the "Bull" Feeney of the Universal Westerns squirm in denial. At last, he is beginning to deal with people, his people, us.

John Ford's parents had been born in Ireland, and he always retained a deep sense of identity with that tiny country and its culture. There are three silent films in which Ford explicitly indulges his Irishness. *Shamrock Handicap* is a rather slight film based around Irish horse-racing, but some elements of his great romance of later years, *The Quiet Man*, can be found in it. *Riley The Cop* (1928) seems to me much more personal, full of the broad and charming Irish humor that was to become characteristic of so many of the director's sound films. (J. Farrell MacDonald, the star of *Riley the Cop*, had been acting for Ford since the early 1920s, and he appears as late as *My Darling Clementine*.) The most ambitious of Ford's early Irish trilogy was *Hangman's House*, and, like *Four Sons* (1928), it shows much expressionist influence. It is Ford's first look at the darker side of the Irish experience which was to become the focus of his Academy Award-winning *The Informer*. Both *Hangman's House* and *The Informer* star Victor McLaglen, whom Ford was to make a major star and then turn into a beloved character actor in later years. McLaglen's character here, as an exile from society, has many similarities with that of John Wayne as Ethan Edwards, the most complex of Ford's heroes, in *The Searchers*.

It is in these Irish films that we first start to feel that Ford was beginning to sense the possibilities of the cinema for his own personal expression. There are many ironies connected with Ford's Irish films. One of the most celebrated of these movies, *The Informer*, is particularly un–Fordian in ways ranging from its urban setting to its heavy-handed Catholic symbolism, and with a hero redeemable only through a faith that Ford could not bring himself to convincingly convey. Still, Ford and novelist Liam O'Flaherty mutually admired each other. O'Flaherty dedicated his historical novel *Famine* to Ford, and the director bemoaned the fact that it was too daunting a project for him to turn into a movie at an advanced age.

It is even more ironic that the best of his "Irish" films actually takes place in Wales. *How Green Was My Valley* is at heart the story of a family; it is the story of a large family with numerous elder siblings as perceived and narrated by the youngest, bookish and sickly son; it is the story of John Ford's family. Central to Ford's childhood was his year spent in bed as a result of diphtheria. In the film, Roddy McDowall's Huw Morgan (the surrogate Jack Feeney) communes with the natural world outside his window, reads, or listens as his sister-in-law (Anna Lee) reads to him. In Ford's case, the books included *Treasure Island, Grimm's Fairy Tales*, and several works by Twain, and the reader was his widowed sister.[27] In the film the narrator (Huw grown up) refers to "all the noble books which have lived in my mind ever since," and the camera catches glimpses of the works of Boswell, Dickens, and the very Romantic *Ivanhoe*. Thus, *How Green Was My Valley*, in spite of its Welsh novel origins and setting, and regardless of the director's late arrival on the project, shows itself to be one of Ford's most personal and "Irish" films. The parents, Sara Allgood and Donald Crisp, are clearly modeled on his parents, and the coping of a shy little boy with many older brothers is felt from memory. It is, as Joseph McBride says, "a Feeney family portrait."[28] Ford has taken Richard Llewellyn's novel, a tale of the author's memories, overlaid them with his own, and fashioned an intensely moving poem, a profound elegy to lost youth and family love.

Coleridge had suggested that, "[a]long with friendship, family was the other essential concrete bond on which the generalization of human brotherhood had to be based."[29] If the Romantics looked back to the Middle Ages for a model, they found that establishing the security for family life was a fundamental value. Ford could depict such family life with great beauty in *Grapes of Wrath* or *How Green Was My Valley*, though his heart lay with the resisters, the outsiders, the Romantics. Lord Byron's whole life was lived in rebellion against what he saw as the constraints and deprivations to be suffered by family involvement, perhaps excepting his incestuous relationship with his sister, his rebellion producing great poetry and near-madness. Ford's alcoholic meanness can not be separated from this tension with his soul, this ambivalence toward "the blessings of civilization." Ford's success in his great family-oriented films derived, in part, from imposing his own emotional schematic on the material. As he told Peter Bogdanovich, the displaced Joads were "simple people and the story was similar to the famine in Ireland, when they threw the people off the land and left them wandering on the roads to starve."[30]

The Quiet Man, Ford's great Romantic comedy, stars John Wayne, Maureen O'Hara, and an Ireland remembered and embellished in the director's mind for over a half-century. Dudley Nichols, who wrote many Ford scripts during the 1930s and 1940s (although not always the best), complained in 1953 that Ford's weakness is that he cannot create in his actors the normal man-woman passions, especially the love that is the dark side of impassioned love.[31] But *The Quiet Man* is a film about passion, shot in passionate color in a ravishing Irish landscape. In a traditional sense it is Ford's most explicitly raw Romantic film, rivaling anything in Byron or the Brontës. It is not accidental that O'Hara lures Wayne to the churchyard cemetery to seduce him. André Maurois, in his life of Shelley, reports of Mary Godwin:

> The only place in the world where she felt herself at peace was by her mother's tomb in the churchyard of old St. Paneras. She went there with book in hand every fine day to read and meditate. Shelley, thrilled, asked if he might go with her.[32]

Ford returned to Irish themes in *The Long Gray Line*, *The Last Hurrah*, and *The Rising of the Moon* (the latter shot in Ireland), but less intensely, for he was now racing with old age to complete his canvas of America. The red rocks of Monument Valley eventually transcended the emerald green surrounding Galway Bay.

At the heart of Ford's immensely Romantic admiration for the Old West lay an immense dilemma that reflects a tension in Ford himself, a tension he felt in being separated for most of his adult life from the "homeland" of his family and of his beloved Irish community back in Portland, Maine. Alice, John Paul Jones's fiancée in Cooper's *The Pilot*, tells him: "[Home] is the dearest of all terms to every woman."[33] She stands in for Ma Joad (Jane Darwell), who was uprooted from her home in *The Grapes of Wrath*; for Mrs. Kirby Yorke (Maureen O'Hara), whose plantation was burned by her husband's Union troops in *Rio Grande*; and for little Debbie Edwards (Natalie Wood), who was rescued by her Uncle Ethan (John Wayne) at the end of *The Searchers* and taken to the place from which he is excluded. Home and family are the end products of the westward march of the pioneers, but home and family are something the wanderer of the *Araner* never comfortably found, and the same can be said for many of the heroes in his movies. Ford might have temporarily found a sense of home and family with his stock company of actors and workers in making a film, but its permanent security eluded him as much as it eluded Cooper's Natty Bumppo and Ethan Edwards.

During his self-imposed periods of exile from his family while filmmaking throughout his life, Ford must have occasionally used the passionate power of his imagination to picture himself as being back home with his parents and siblings on the shore of Portland's harbor, amidst those whose ancestral homeland lay just across the Atlantic. Whether reflecting on family and home, or pondering the sublime expanse of the ocean when sailing on the *Araner*, or shooting films about chivalric cowboy heroes who ride across burning deserts against towering mesas, Ford was, if anything, a pure Romantic.

Notes

1. Subsequent to a lecture on Ford that I gave in Tokyo in July, 1983 (from which some of this essay was adapted), two other films have been discovered: *Bucking Broadway* (1917) and *Hell Bent* (1918), along with fragments of a few others from Ford's Universal period.

2. From the perspective of 2007, I might allow that Robert Altman, who also had a long apprenticeship, might be an exception.

3. This has been corrected in recent years by the publication of Scott Eyman's *Print the Legend: The*

Life and Times of John Ford (New York: Simon and Schuster, 1999) and Joseph McBride's *Searching for John Ford: A Life* (New York: St. Martin's Press, 2001).
    4. Darcy O'Brien, *A Way of Life, Like Any Other*, quoted in *New York Review of Books*, 2001, 107.
    5. McBride, *Searching for John Ford*, 41.
    6. Joseph Conrad, *Lord Jim* (New York: Penguin/Signet Classics, 1964), 11.
    7. McBride, *Searching for John Ford*, 60.
    8. Quoted by Morton Dauwen Zabel in "Introduction" to Joseph Conrad, *The Shadow-Line and Two Other Tales, Typhoon and The Secret Sharer by Joseph Conrad* (New York: Doubleday Anchor, 1959, 6.
    9. Joseph Conrad, *The Shadow-Line and Two Other Tales*, 9.
    10. Joseph Conrad, *The Nigger of the Narcissus* in *Great Short Works of Joseph Conrad* (New York: Harper & Row, 1967), 63.
    11. John Ruskin, *Time and Tide, by Weave and Tyne*. In Volume 17 of *The Library Edition of the Works of John Ruskin*, 39 volumes, eds. E.T. Cook and Alexander Wedderburn (London: George Allen, 1905–1912), 372–373.
    12. Joseph Conrad, *The Shadow-Line and Two Other Tales*, 192–193.
    13. Joseph Conrad, "Author's Note" to *The Shadow-Line and Two Other Tales*, 36.
    14. Zabel, "Introduction," 21.
    15. Joseph Conrad, *The Nigger of the Narcissus*, 65.
    16. Joseph Conrad, *The Nigger of the Narcissus*, 69–70.
    17. Joseph Conrad, *The Shadow-Line and Two Other Tales*, 190.
    18. Zabel, "Introduction," 24.
    19. Quoted in McBride, *Searching for John Ford*, 67.
    20. Joseph Conrad, *The Shadow-Line and Two Other Tales*, 155.
    21. James Fenimore Cooper, *The Pilot: A Tale of the Sea* (New York: State University of New York Press, 1986), 63.
    22. Joseph Conrad, *The Shadow-Line and Two Other Tales*, 189.
    23. Joseph Conrad, *The Shadow-Line and Two Other Tales*, 198.
    24. McBride, *Searching for John Ford*, 51.
    25. Isaiah Berlin, *The Roots of Romanticism* (Princeton, NJ: Princeton University Press, 1999), 99.
    26. Roberta Smith, "A Memorial Remembers the Hungry," *The New York Times*, July 16, 2002, E1.
    27. Scott Eyman, *Print the Legend*, 35.
    28. McBride, *Searching for John Ford*, 44.
    29. Michael Lowy and Robert Sayre, *Romanticism Against the Tide of Modernity* (Durham, NC: Duke University Press, 2001), 125.
    30. Peter Bogdanovich, *John Ford* (Berkeley: University of California Press, 1978), 76.
    31. McBride, *Searching for John Ford*, 46.
    32. Andre Maurois, *Ariel: The Life of Shelley* (New York: Frederick Ungar Publishing Company, 1952), 150.
    33. Cooper, *The Pilot*, 364.

PART TWO:
LIFE IN MAINE, IRELAND, AND BEYOND

Introduction to Part Two

Michael C. Connolly

Writing about a local hero is a daunting task for an historian. While constantly searching for the facts and the "truth," one can be inundated by a barrage of stories, anecdotes, personal recollections, myths, and beliefs deeply held by those who, as a popular American saying goes, "shook the hand that shook the hand of the great John L." (Sullivan, in that case, John M. Feeney in this case). In his own work John Ford dealt with this very dilemma, and, at least in the case of *The Man Who Shot Liberty Valance* (1962), we are advised to "print the legend." A popular contemporary television character, Gil Grissom, states in a 2002 episode from the series *Crime Scene Investigation (CSI)*: "That's the conflict of magic — the burden of knowledge versus the mystique of wonder."

Part II of this volume focuses upon selected aspects of Ford's biography and, more especially, his Irish heritage, genealogy, and roots in the coastal community of Portland, Maine, as well as those of the Feeney family in the coastal community of Spiddal, County Galway, Ireland. In "A Bull is Reared on Munjoy Hill: John Ford's Irish Upbringing in Portland, Maine," I explore several early influences on the life of John Ford. I attempt to answer such questions as the following: How did his childhood in Maine, especially Portland, influence Ford and what characteristics in his later life and career can possibly be traced to his childhood environment? Special focal points of the essay include details about Ford's early childhood roots in Portland's Irish community, his family life, his public education, and, finally, his much-ballyhooed high school football career.

In "John Ford: Irish Reflections," Kenneth Nilsen offers his translation of never-before-published interviews by Maidhc P. Ó Conaola (Mike Connolly) that were originally presented on Gaelic Radio (*Raidió na Gaeltachta*) and broadcast in Ireland on October 21, 1973, shortly after Ford's death. The interviewees are Martin Feeney, Martin Thornton, and Lord Killanin, individuals who knew the director well and who reflect on Ford the man and Ford the artist, particularly in terms of their personal experiences of working with him during the production of *The Quiet Man* (1952) in western Ireland.

John Ford's films revolve around the importance of family, memory, and the past, among other themes. Two historians who focus on family, memory, and the past as they relate to the Irish community in Maine have offered detailed views of the ancestral and historical origins of John Ford. Both of these local historians have used unique sources, including municipal and state public records, that will be invaluable to other historians in their future research on Ford. Matthew Jude Barker, in his "John Ford and the Feeney Family of Galway and Portland," gives a brief general overview of the Feeney family origins on both sides of the Atlantic and discusses the importance of Ford's elder brother Francis Ford (Feeney), a pioneering actor and director in the early days of Hollywood. Margaret Feeney LaCombe, a distant relative of the director, provides in "The John Ford Tour" a more detailed glimpse of the Ford/Feeney genealogy in relation to major Ford-related landmarks in his hometown of Portland, complete with several images from her personal collection of family pictures.

Dan Ford is the director's grandson, first biographer, and producer of the television documentary *The American West of John Ford*. His essay "John Ford's Arrival in Hollywood" is a reprint of a chapter from his biography *Pappy: The Life of John Ford*, dealing with Ford's arrival and early work in California, including his work as an actor, stuntman, and assistant director under the mentorship of his older brother Francis. The essay depicts an important transition between the relatively unknown Jack Feeney of Portland, Maine, and the early years of John Ford of Hollywood fame.

Ford was not only a legendary filmmaker but also a heroic naval officer who risked his life to document the Battle of Midway in World War II with his own hand-held camera. In "Reflections on the Battle of Midway," John Ford reminisces in fascinating detail about his experience of this pivotal naval battle, one in which he served the Navy as a documentary filmmaker. The director's footage was used in his Oscar-winning *The Battle of Midway* (1942). This declassified interview with Ford is included with special permission from the United States Naval Historical Center, and it helps to illuminate Ford's longstanding devotion to the American military and his courageous service to the Navy in World War II.

John Ford served his country actively between September 1941 and September 1945. This World War II military service was largely through his work with the Field Photographic Branch of the Office of Strategic Services (OSS) — later known as the Central Intelligence Agency (CIA). The OSS Director, William "Wild Bill" Donovan, presented Ford with the Legion of Merit and the Combat "V" for his work at Midway, Tokyo, North Africa, and other "hot spots," including the D-Day Invasion of Normandy that commenced on June 6, 1944. Twenty years later, in 1964, in an interview granted to Pete Martin, Ford reminisced about what he downplayed as his "small, ant-like part" in this seminal event. It is clear, however, by reading the transcript of "We Shot D-Day on Omaha Beach" that this event and the war generally had an enormous transformational effect on Ford himself, as it did on the nation as a whole. This interview by Pete Martin first appeared in *The American Legion Magazine* in June 1964. Our special thanks go to Patricia Marschand, Operations Manager of *The American Legion Magazine*, for her generous assistance.

The final component of Part Two is "John Ford's Use of Gaelic in *The Quiet Man*: An Interview with Nora Folan," conducted in early 2006 in Spiddal, County Galway, Ireland by Dr. Kenneth E. Nilsen. The interviewee is Nora Folan (née Connolly), and it was conducted in the Irish language, transcribed and translated here by Dr. Nilsen. As a young girl, Nora Ní Chonaola, whose father was quite close to the director, played a small but important part in the filming of *The Quiet Man* (1952) in a region of Ireland not far distant from her own home. Nora helped to coach Maureen O'Hara (Mary Kate Danaher) regarding her short piece in Irish (Gaelic) in the film. In this interview Nora speaks of her own reluctance and of Ford's gentle insistence that she perform this task. Over fifty years later, Nora recalls with vivid clarity some of the small events in what would eventually become arguably John Ford's best known work. This interview is short, playful, and endearing. Ken Nilsen, a true scholar and lover of Gaelic languages and culture, concludes this section with a brief transcription from the start of the interview in its original Irish, for those not familiar with its appearance and form.

One of the recurring themes in the works of John Ford is that of home. Several of the essays deal with this theme both in terms of Portland, Maine, and Galway, Ireland. This theme also became a focus of mine in a summer 2006 visit to Spiddal, County Galway, in search of Ford/Feeney family roots. Sometimes on-site research into a few biographical details can lead

Ford about to depart from Maine after a visit, taking with him an appropriate memento of his beloved home state: lobsters (with the permission of Dan Ford; courtesy Lilly Library, Indiana University, Bloomington).

to an intriguing and illuminating adventure. Armed with biographies, interviews, and leads from Feeneys in Maine and other sources, I was easily able to locate three Feeney relatives still living near the paternal (John Augustine Feeney) birthplace on the western edge of Spiddal, in and near the townland of *Tuar Beag*.

Fortified with this firsthand information I set off to answer the sometimes disputed ques-

Ned Feeney (right), a cousin of John Ford, with Mike Connolly on June 10, 2006, at the Feeney family homestead in Tuar Beag, Spiddal, County Galway (photograph by Alice Townend, courtesy Mike Connolly).

tion as to the birthplace of Ford's mother, Barbara "Abby" Curran. The 1973 *Raidió na Gaeltachta* (Irish radio) interviews of Martin Feeney, et al., translated in this section by Ken Nilsen, seemed to further confirm this site to be on the mainland rather than at Kilronan on Aran (the largest townland on Inishmore [*Inis Mór*], the largest of the three Aran Islands off the coast of County Galway) as had been previously believed by some early biographers and some in the family. I was given further help by the Feeney/Curran family of Derryloughaun West, friends of mine for many years and relatives of the Concannons of Portland, Maine. After further discussions with Pat, Ned, and Bartley Feeney—the latter of whom kindly trusted me with several wonderful personal family images, including a very old film negative of Ford's father during a visit to Spiddal—I was ready to head farther west to trace the origins of Abby Curran.

A mere two miles west of *Tuar Beag* on the main coast road is the townland of Kilroe, its name taken from the Irish *coill rua* meaning "the red wood." Bartley Feeney had conjectured, convincingly to this editor at least, that it would be easy to confuse the place name Kilroe with the place name Kilronan, especially among those not familiar with Irish (Gaelic) or, conversely, as in the case of the young Abby Curran herself, English. At a crossroad, just east of *Coláiste Lurgan* and *Teach an tSrutháin*, I spoke with an older resident, first confirming that this was, indeed, Kilroe West. The exact location of this crossroad is on the main coast road next to a Supervalue store and petrol (gas) station, nearly across from *Abhainn Ruibh* (*Údarás na Gaeltachta*). I felt that the next question would be the crucial one. One wonders at a time like this how one gets from the general to the specific in trying to reach an answer.

When I posed a question to this man concerning the location of Ballynahown the gentle-

Barbara (Abby) Feeney (née Curran) pinning a Mother's Day flower on her son John Ford's lapel. Original staff photograph appeared in *Portland Sunday Telegram* May 12, 1929, page 13A (confirmed by Susan Butler of the Portland Newspapers library staff) (with the permission of Dan Ford; courtesy Lilly Library, Indiana University, Bloomington).

man answered that it was farther along the road, the site of the current TG4, *Teilifís na Gaeilge* (Irish television, channel 4). I knew that this was a correct answer, but it was not the correct one in this particular case. I asked him if there was another such place, closer to this spot. My many visits beginning in 1972 and 1973 to this region known as *Cois Fharraige* (beside the sea) in search of my own ancestral homeland and contemporary relatives had taught me the need for patience and exactness, especially when dealing with the Irish language and Irish place names. The older man, after further reflection, lifted his head. A faint smile on his face and a twinkle in his eyes told me that useful information could be in the offing: "Yes," he said, "the old people used to call a place up this very boreen [small road] by that name." I asked, "Are there any old people still alive there?" "Yes, there is one. Follow me in your car and I'll signal you with my light."

A few minutes later I was knocking at the door of the house of one Matt O'Toole. His son, Mike, after hearing that I was from Portland, welcomed me into the house and escorted me into the back parlor where his father, Matt O'Toole, and his mother were about to have their Sunday tea with two of their children and a new grandchild. Mr. O'Toole, who was fluent in Irish and English, made me deliver my bona fides first. He inquired: "Where are you from? Where are your people from? What are you looking for here?"

Matt O'Toole, most likely in his eighties, had a good deal of relevant information. First, he reported that the Curran family in question had lived just across the road and that although the original house had long since fallen into disuse, the family had recently constructed a new home adjacent to the original homestead. Matt gave his recollection that the property, including the new home, is now in the hands of the Dillon family (originally from Tully, he thought), which had married into the Currans. Matt believed that Mrs. Bríd Dillon (née Curran) was perhaps the closest native maternal relative of John Ford, and that the director had visited this very place himself during past journeys to Ireland. Matt's son Mike took me just across the road to the spot, in all likelihood the very birthplace of Barbara Curran, John Ford's mother. All evidence pointed to this location. Standing on the stone wall one could see Galway Bay just down the boreen and through the faint haze the Burren of County Clare in the far distance to the south. Remarkably, although not unusual in Irish-American family history, this site was roughly four kilometers, barely 2.4 miles, to the west of the very spot where Abby's future husband, John A. Feeney, would have been born!

The Fordian theme of home was in the forefront of my thoughts at that moment. I already felt quite fulfilled, but then, as if to sweeten an already very pleasant experience, Mike O'Toole spoke of the neighbor just above this spot as having relatives, a priest in Portland. I put two and two together and wondered if this could be true. Upon entering the kitchen of this neighbor, another Michael O'Toole, although not a direct relative of the first, there was the only confirmation needed. On the kitchen wall just inside the door hung a perfect image of a young Father Coleman O'Toole, formerly pastor of Saint Patrick's Church in Portland and now serving at Saint Margaret's Church in Old Orchard Beach, Maine. Father Coleman's sister is Sister Mary George O'Toole, RSM, formerly the Superior General of the Sisters of Mercy of Maine and now the Vice President for Sponsorship and Mission Integration at Saint Joseph's College in Standish, Maine, where I have been teaching in the history department for the past twenty-three years!

It is indeed a small world and we are all linked by degrees of connectedness rather than by degrees of separation. Here in *Cois Fharraige* in the summer of 2006, while searching for Feeney/Ford roots and cognizant of the burden of knowledge, I was simultaneously and joyfully confronted by the mystique of wonder. The specific links in this case were forged at first by John Ford's parents, who arrived in Portland around 1872. These links were continued by my own grandparents, Coleman Connolly and Mary Josephine Joyce, from farther west along Galway

Bay, Callowfeenish and Mweenish respectively, who arrived in this same city less than one decade later, along with the O'Tooles and O'Malleys and Coynes from Inverin and the countless thousands of other young, first-generation, male and female migrants from Ireland. We in Portland, Maine, together with those in St. Paul, Minnesota, and over forty million souls elsewhere in America, are still linked by these chains of geography, culture, and, essentially home. For me the discovery of the birthplace of John Ford's mother in a part of Ireland now quite familiar to me was simply the reaffirmation of what John Ford and countless other filmmakers and screenwriters have maintained over the years—"There's no place like home."

A Bull Is Reared on Munjoy Hill: John Ford's Irish Upbringing in Portland, Maine

Michael C. Connolly

> Often I think of the beautiful town
> That is seated by the sea;
> Often in thought go up and down
> The pleasant streets of that dear old town,
> And my youth comes back to me.
> Henry Wadsworth Longfellow
> *My Lost Youth* (1855)

John Ford was notoriously cantankerous, the epitome of a real curmudgeon. He was also famous for exaggerating or even conjuring up stories wholesale, often contradictory to his previous stories, especially if they were about his personal side. But infrequently, almost as if by mistake, he allowed people to catch a glimpse of Ford the person. "My childhood profoundly marked me," he once said.[1] I accept the truth of this introductory quotation and propose to explore in this brief essay the significance of early influences on the life of John Ford.

John Martin Feeney was born in Cape Elizabeth, Maine, on February 1, 1894. Even his date of birth and his legal birth name have, over time, been in dispute. A birth date of February 1, 1895 was often cited by Ford, as were more Gaelicized forms of his name, such as Sean O'Feeney, or Sean Aloysius O'Fearna. Other Gaelic spellings include O'Fiannaidhe, O'Feinneadha, O'Feinneida, O'Fidhne or Feinne.[2] John's older brother, Edward, used the Gaelicized version O'Fearna. None of this is really surprising when one considers that most Irish names in America are attempts to Anglicize unfamiliar Gaelic names, such as O'Conghaile into Connolly, Connelly, Connally, Conerly or even the briefer popular form, Conley. These diverse surname spellings and birthdates have largely been corrected by more recent biographies on Ford. How did his childhood in Maine, especially Portland—Longfellow's town "seated by the sea"—influence Ford, and what characteristics in his later life and career can possibly be traced to his childhood environment? These questions will form the core of this essay.

Essays, journal articles, interviews, and film analyses abound concerning America's most prolific film director and winner of six Academy Awards between 1935 and 1952. These Oscars for Best Director were bracketed by his two most famous works on Irish themes, *The Informer* (1935) and *The Quiet Man* (1952).[3] Major works on the life of Ford the man are less numerous. Four such works include sizeable biographical components.[4]

Irish saying: *Briseann an dúchas tré shúilibh an chait.*
Literal translation: Heritage (culture) breaks out through the eye of a cat.
Popular translation: What is bred in the bone will emerge.

The Feeneys of Portland, Maine were identifiably Irish. John's parents, John A. Feeney (born 1854) and Barbara "Abby" Curran (born 1856), were from Irish-speaking (Gaeltacht) areas of South County Galway. This region is locally referred to as *Cois Fharraige* (beside the sea), and it runs westward from Galway City along the rock-bound coast of Galway Bay. Many of Portland's Irish claim *Cois Fharraige* as their ancestral homeland.[5] Several earlier biographies claim that Ford's mother, Barbara "Abby" Curran, was from Kilronan on Inishmore (*Inis Mór*) in the Aran Islands. More recent works claim that both Abby and John's birth place was *An Spidéal* (Spiddal). The claim for Abby's birth on the Aran Islands has been called "another bit of romantic embellishment," and even Ford recalled that his father "lived at one end of the area and my mother at the other." Possibly one of the most reliable sources for Irish genealogy would be the closest Irish relatives themselves. Fortuitously, Dr. Kenneth E. Nilsen of Saint Francis Xavier University in Antigonish, Nova Scotia, has translated an interview given on *Raidió na Gaeltachta* (Irish language radio network) on October 20, 1973, at the time of the death of John Ford (see "John Ford: Irish Reflections" from a re-broadcast on the program *Ó Na Sceirde Aniar* in this collection, translated by Nilsen). A cousin of John Ford, one Martin Feeney, states confidently that "[Ford's] father was called Seán Mháire from Toorbeg and his mother was known as Barbara Frank from Kylerooa West or Ballynahown as it is known, she was Barbara Curran."[6]

Another prominent connection to Ireland is Ford's omnipresent uncle Michael Connolly (or Connelly), a "Paul Bunyanesque" hero to the young Ford, whose mythic journey from Galway and across America seem more like the wanderings of the ancient Celtic heroes, the *Fianna*. Uncle Mike made alleged appearances in Quebec, among the Black Foot Indians, in the Union Army at Fredericksburg, and at the laying of the Union Pacific leg of the transcontinental railroad before returning home to Galway. Back in his native Ireland, Uncle Mike helped to entice the young John A. Feeney, his cousin and John Ford's father, to try his luck in America.[7] This is a case of Irish chain migration *par excellence*.

Once in Maine by 1872, the Feeneys, Currans, and Connollys were among friends. The last three decades of the nineteenth century saw tremendous Irish emigration to America, and Portland, Maine, was a favorite destination, especially from Galway. By the turn of the century (1900), 41.6% of first- and second-generation immigrants in Portland were the children of Irish-born parents.[8] Within three years of John and Abby's arrival in Portland, these two Irish-speaking Galwegians married (1875) at Saint Dominic's Church in the heavily Irish west end of the city. In 1878 Abby and John became citizens of their new home country. This pattern would be followed by countless others from Connemara, *Cois Fharraige,* and other regions of the west of Ireland that had been hardest hit by the Great Famine (1845–49) and were now in the midst of yet another agrarian disaster (1879–82).[9]

"If there is any single thing that explains either of us, it's that we are Irish."[10]
John Ford to Eugene O'Neill

Like Eugene O'Neill, whose work Ford greatly admired, Ford's Irishness and that of his family were demonstrable. Portland, as with Maine as a whole, was at mid-nineteenth century still a Yankee, Protestant bastion. The Republican party of Hannibal Hamlin of Paris Hill, Maine, Lincoln's first Vice President, was in firm control in this Yankee state and would stay in control well into the twentieth century.[11] The Irish in Maine, as elsewhere in the country, faced a dilemma. Should they attempt to join the majority through assimilation and upward mobility, or should they use their considerable political skills to lead the minority? At least initially the

Saint Dominic's Church, at 34 Gray Street in Portland, is the city's oldest Catholic Church (1833). The first Mass was on November 1, 1830. This enlarged structure was completed between 1888 and 1893. Ford was baptized here in 1894 and served as an altar boy (photograph by Michael C. Connolly).

more rebellious minority group leadership option appeared to be the more appealing choice. Perhaps it was the only option open to them. In Portland, Lewiston, Bangor, and other urban centers in Maine, the Irish could be found leading the minority Democratic Party in Maine.[12] This dilemma of "in" (majority) versus "out" (minority) status could also be witnessed in the areas of religion and labor, among others, where the Irish eventually achieved leadership prominence.[13]

> "Stick to the *Créatúr* (whiskey) the best thing in nature
> for sinking your sorrows and raising your joys."
> (Popular Irish drinking song)

Yet another area where the Irish "in" versus "out" identity was clearly felt was that of alcohol consumption and its prohibition. Remember the one-word interjection uttered by Michilín óg O'Flynn (the shaughran, from the Irish *seachrán*, referred to as the matchmaker in *The Quiet Man*, brilliantly played by Barry Fitzgerald). When forced to ponder on "Amerikay," the land Seán Thornton has recently abandoned, Michilín shakes his head and scoffingly utters, with all the derision his small frame could muster, the word "Pro-hi-*bition!*"[14] Many in Ireland in the 1920s and 1930s were probably equally baffled by such periodic American forays into national self-improvement. That was certainly true of the Irish living in Maine.

The American experiment with national prohibition was largely inspired by the "Maine Law" (1851) sponsored by two-term Portland mayor (1851–1854) and Civil War hero Neal Dow.[15] From the mid-nineteenth century onward Prohibition was intermittently enforced in Portland — often, however, in the breach.

Bootlegging — i.e., the illegal manufacture, transport, or sale of alcohol — was a common means of upward mobility for the Irish in late-nineteenth and early–twentieth-century America. It is somewhat akin to the production of "moonshine" in Appalachia or *poitín* in rural Ireland. The income generated from this illegal sale was nearly as important as the obvious statement of rebellion, resistance, and flouting of authority by these bold practitioners. While seen as vile hoodlums by the larger civilized society, they often achieved an almost mythical importance to their own people, the "outs" or cast-offs living barely on the fringes of civilization. It is no coincidence that many Irish politicians in America started their careers by gaining what is now called "street cred," or credibility, through bootlegging. Many restaurants or grocery stores in Portland at this time were simply fronts for the more profitable trade in whiskey or rum.

In the late 1870s, John Feeney's "store" on 42 Center Street, just below the current Brian Boru Public House (57 Center Street), was most likely just such a saloon in disguise.[16] The role of the publican, both in Ireland and Irish America, was also multifaceted. He was at one time a bartender, a small banker, a political leader, and quite often in the days before psychotherapy, a counselor. Mutual support would be the modern term for this important role in the community. The same skills and personality traits required for running a successful saloon were also needed for being a successful politician. One can hardly watch Ford's portrayal of the Mayor Skeffington figure in *The Last Hurrah* (1958), modeled after James Michael Curley, without witnessing characteristics that would have been apparent in Ford's own father, John A Feeney, or his half-mythical uncle, Michael Connolly.

Mutual support was all the Irish had in the days before civil service reform and the rise of meritocracy. It is informative to recall that the crime for which Mayor Curley served time in prison was taking a civil service exam for a friend. This was clearly illegal (he is called "The Rascal King" by his major biographer), but Curley appealed to his constituents by saying, "I did it for a friend," and they rewarded him by re-electing him while he was serving time. Curley's own epitaph to this criminal episode was, "I'd do it again," which serves as the title of his political autobiography.[17]

It is difficult for early twenty-first-century Americans to remember a time when the Irish were not political powerbrokers, but there was such a time. Maine was a Yankee, Protestant bastion where the Republican Party held sway under such nationally known leaders as Hannibal Hamlin, James G. Blaine, and Portland's own Thomas Brackett Reed. The Irish were the first to infiltrate this white Anglo-Saxon Protestant (WASP) stronghold. Although white, they were neither Anglo-Saxon nor (after the first wave of Ulster Presbyterians in the eighteenth century) Protestant.[18] In Maine, as in New England as a whole, the Irish faced an identity dilemma. Here, as elsewhere, individuals chose one or more paths, sometimes simultaneously. In the case of the Feeneys, they straddled this cultural divide. While John A. Feeney and Uncle Michael Connolly earned a living, at least in part through bootlegging, a later relative, Joseph Connolly, would become a justice of the Cumberland County Superior Court.[19] While some may see this as hypocrisy and a family conflict of interest, the Feeneys and their Irish friends most likely viewed it as a case of upward social mobility—and long overdue at that.

Back to "The Garden"— Inisfree in the New World

One of the most surprising twists in the life of the young John M. Feeney is that he was actually born, not in heavily Irish Portland, but rather in Cape Elizabeth. Today this town is a wealthy suburb of Portland known best, perhaps, as the location of the home (called "Witch Way") of Hollywood stars Bette Davis and Gary Merrill in the late 1950s. After having lived for sixteen years in Portland, mostly in Saint Dominic's parish, a strongly Irish working class west end neighborhood, Abby and John Feeney moved their family (around 1888) to the Spurwink section of Cape Elizabeth. For roughly a decade they lived in this rural seaside paradise that must have reminded them both of *Cois Fharraige*, their region of birth near Spiddal, County Galway. Here they could garden, fish, catch lobster, and watch the waves rolling up on what is now called Higgins Beach in a timeless, familiar, rhythmic pattern similar to that along the north coast of Galway Bay. When one stands today at the John Ford birthplace it is indeed difficult to know which side of the Atlantic one is on.

John A. Feeney, father of John Ford, while visiting family in Spiddal—still a vigorous man late into his life. This photograph existed only in a negative and was nearly lost (courtesy Bartley Feeney).

Pondering the question as to why a large and growing Irish Catholic family would leave the friendly confines of Saint Dominic's parish in 1888 is fascinating. Nearly half of the children were born in the Cape Elizabeth home, including John

Top: View from John Ford's birthplace in Cape Elizabeth, Maine, looking south over the Spurwink River to Higgins Beach and the Atlantic Ocean. The Feeneys lived here between 1888 and 1898 (photograph by Michael C. Connolly). *Bottom:* The Kinsman Homestead in Cape Elizabeth, Maine, the birthplace of John Ford (1894). This is how the shingled farmhouse looks today (photograph taken by Margaret Feeney LaCombe).

Martin who was born on February 1, 1894. Although most historians have written about the tendency of the majority of Irish immigrants in late–nineteenth-century America to settle in urban settings, many immigrants lived in rural America or took up agrarian pursuits as they had largely done before leaving Ireland. One local example of this pattern was the Catholic-sponsored agricultural settlement of Benedicta in southern Aroostook County, Maine.[20]

48   II. Life in Maine, Ireland, and Beyond

The building at 21–23 Sheridan Street, on Munjoy Hill, Portland, Maine, with its wonderful views of Portland Harbor and the Atlantic Ocean beyond. John Feeney lived here from 1906 to 1914, the latter years while he attended Portland High School (photograph by Michael C. Connolly).

Many of the biographies of John Ford assume that the Feeney Family had rented this property while John A. Feeney kept up his businesses in the city — some suggesting that this may have represented a break from the unpredictable liquor trade in what was becoming an increasingly dry city.[21] Recent scholarship by Margaret Feeney LaCombe and Matthew Jude Barker, however, point to records demonstrating that the Feeneys had purchased this parcel of land as early as 1884 and lost it through nonpayment of taxes between 1891 and 1893, after which they likely continued to occupy the property as renters until sometime between 1896 and 1898.[22]

Speculation concerning reasons for this rural interlude aside, the family apparently never really felt as if they fit into the more WASPish community of Cape Elizabeth. Although a Roman Catholic Church had been erected there in 1861, they continued to attend Mass at Saint Dominic's while many other Catholic families would travel to the Holy Cross Church in South Portland. Religion and culture, including language and accent, are cited as factors in their dissatisfaction. As Ford biographer Joseph McBride suggests, "The gains the family had made since coming to America seemed in danger of being reversed. So, largely at Abby's urging, they moved back to Portland in 1898, the year John turned four."[23]

The Feeneys moved back to Portland and there they stayed. Initially the Feeneys took up residence again near the old neighborhood that is today called Gorham's Corner, near the intersection of Fore, Center, Pleasant, Danforth, and York Streets — the present location of the John Ford monument. This time, however, the family would soon move to what was becoming Portland's other Irish neighborhood, Munjoy Hill, located in the Cathedral Parish in the east end of the city. As with Saint Dominic's Church, which served the predominantly Irish working class, the Cathedral of the Immaculate Conception, completed in 1869 in the aftermath of the Civil War and the Great Portland Fire of 1866, served the growing Irish Catholic population on and at the base of Munjoy Hill. Arriving on "the Hill" around 1902, John would have been approximately eight years old. He lived with his family in two houses for more than a decade, at 65 Monument Street (circa 1902–1906) and at 21–23 Sheridan Street (circa 1906–1914).[24] These would be his formative years.

> 'Tis education forms the common mind.
> Just as the twig is bent, the tree's inclined.
> Alexander Pope

Public education has long been the vehicle by which the vast majority of America's youth achieve upward social mobility. This is especially true of the poor and minority (ethnic, racial, religious) communities. American inner-city public schools have historically borne the brunt of this mission, some doing a better job than others—some simply overwhelmed by the enormity of the task. Portland was, and is today, the most diverse city in Maine, a state that until fairly recently was often seen as otherwise largely homogenous.[25] Newly arriving immigrants are always attracted to jobs, and these jobs are found primarily in urban areas. Ports, rails, canals, and other means of transporting goods needed to be built and then operated. In Portland in the late nineteenth and early twentieth centuries, the Irish presented themselves at these sites, ready, willing, and able to work.[26]

The children of these laborers would need an education. Munjoy Hill and the city of Portland offered several excellent choices for public education to the young John Ford. At the turn of the twentieth century the public schools in the east end of Portland included:

North School: Primary grades K–4 and Grammar grades 5–8
Monument Street School: Primary grades K–4
Shailer School: Primary grades K–5
Emerson School: Grammar grades 6–8[27]

While living at 65 Monument Street (1902–06) young John Feeney attended Emerson Grammar School.[28] Records that exist from Emerson School reveal something of the young student in the sixth grade of Josephine O'Connor. His report card suggests "extremely erratic" results with his best grades coming in geography and history.[29]

During his tenure at Emerson School, Feeney contracted a serious case of diphtheria. He was housebound for several months, missing a year of school and largely cared for by his eldest sister, Maime (Mary Agnes), who by this time was herself a young widow. Several biographies credit this health malady as Ford's inspiration for his sympathetic treatment of the sick young child named Huw Morgan in *How Green Was My Valley* (1941).[30]

Evidence exists to demonstrate that the young John Feeney was happy with the family's move to Munjoy Hill and especially to 21–23 Sheridan Street. Later in life, 1966 at the age of seventy-two, Ford said in an interview, "My childhood profoundly marked me.... Until twelve, I did not have a real home."[31] McBride believes that these frequent moves between 1898 and 1906 created a feeling of "rootlessness" in John. "The lack of a fixed address in Portland during that critical period in his early life no doubt helped instill in him the intense feelings about home and wandering that animate so much of his work."[32] John was in residence at 21–23 Sheridan Street roughly between 1906 and his graduation from Portland High School in 1914. This "real home" essentially represented nearly the totality of his teenage years.

Both of the houses the Feeneys occupied on Munjoy Hill in these years, i.e., 65 Monument Street and 21–23 Sheridan Street, represented the upward mobility they were experiencing in the early twentieth century. Substantial homes such as these were housing large Irish-American families. Ford later in life did acknowledge his working-class roots. In a 1968 interview partly on the subject of his film *The Grapes of Wrath* (1940), Ford stated, "I was reared in poverty, so

Emerson Grammar School on Emerson Street in Portland, Maine, is named for Portland's first mayor, Andrew Emerson (1832). John Feeney studied here after 1902 (photograph by Michael C. Connolly).

the picture appealed to me."³³ The periphery of Munjoy Hill, with its stunning views of the harbor (south), the White Mountains (west), the Back Bay (north), and Casco Bay (east), would continue to house Portland's elite well into the new century; however, the Irish and other later newcomers would find their niche in the interior sections, especially along the lower base of "The Hill."

> Study to shew thyself approved unto God,
> a workman that needeth not to be ashamed
> rightly dividing the word of truth.
> 2 Timothy 2:5

This Biblical admonition to study could be found over the stage at the Portland High School auditorium where it greeted thousands of students at school functions. Ironically, the recent renovations for the new John Ford Auditorium have largely, but not completely, obscured these words of scholarly inspiration. Two of the three teachers mentioned most often by Ford later in life as having been influential in his early development were obviously highly regarded by others. Marada F. Adams, the principal at Emerson School, and William B. Jack, the principal at Portland High School, later had schools named in their honor on Munjoy Hill.³⁴

The public schools on Munjoy Hill, together with Portland High School, the second oldest public high school in the country (1821) after Boston Classical English High School, have a long history of dedicated teachers. The challenge then, as now, was how to assist those weaker students in need of remediation without slowing the progress of the more gifted students. Ford seems to especially remember three influential teachers—Adams, Jack, and Lucien Libby—the latter who taught English at Portland High School. They all tried to open doors for him. They all wanted him to further his horizons. They all saw promise in the young son of Irish immigrants, and they each encouraged him to dream dreams.

> Train a child in the way he should go. (*Proverbs* 22:6)

Marada F. Adams taught for fifty years on Munjoy Hill, beginning in 1878 at the North School, then Shailer School, and finally at the newly-built Emerson Grammar School, where she became principal in 1898. When she retired in 1935 she was cited in *Ripley's Believe It or Not* as the nation's oldest active teacher. In that year at the age of eighty-nine, her retirement came after seventy-two consecutive years of teaching.³⁵ Ford, later in life, credited Miss Adams with teaching him about the "basic principles of art." She was the only grammar school teacher singled out by Ford as having such a strong influence on his life.³⁶

In addition to whatever principles of art and vision Miss Adams was able to impart to young John Feeney, there was also the beautiful natural tapestry surrounding him on Munjoy Hill. Munjoy Hill sits at the eastern edge of Portland's natural peninsula. From its naturally rising slopes one can see water on three sides. As McBride states: "With its omnipresent backdrop of the sea and the strikingly varied vantage points of its hilly streets, Portland offered the young John Feeney a rich visual panorama to study and absorb."³⁷

From the southeast-facing windows of his third floor aerie (eagle's nest) at 23 Sheridan Street Ford could clearly see Portland Head Light, which was commissioned in 1791 by President George Washington. Its beacon still lights the way into Portland harbor, one of the North Atlantic's most beautiful naturally-protected ports. The lighthouse inspired Portland's other great artist of an earlier century and a different genre—poetry. Henry Wadsworth Longfellow wrote *The Lighthouse* as a tribute to his hometown sentinel. Probably referring to a vantage point on Munjoy Hill, maybe the Portland Observatory, Longfellow claimed, "Even at this distance I can see the tides, upheaving, break unheard along its base." The poem concludes with this ringing stanza:

Top: Portland Harbor, view from the southeast side of Munjoy Hill — very similar to that seen from the Feeneys' apartment on the third floor of 23 Sheridan Street (photograph by Michael C. Connolly). *Bottom:* Portland Head Light (1791), commissioned by George Washington. One of America's oldest lighthouses, it was very special to the poet Longfellow and to John Ford, who was born in the town of its location, Cape Elizabeth (photograph by Michael C. Connolly).

> "Sail on!" it says: "sail on, ye stately ships!"
> And with your floating bridge the ocean span;
> Be mine to guard this light from all eclipse.
> Be yours to bring man nearer unto man.
>   H. W. Longfellow (*The Lighthouse*)

This same view was available to John Feeney daily from his Sheridan Street perch. To enhance his vision, Feeney, as with Longfellow nearly a century earlier, would have only needed

Portland Observatory (1807) on the crest of Munjoy Hill as depicted in an old postcard (courtesy Margaret Feeney LaCombe).

to walk one or two blocks to what is now the nation's sole remaining maritime signal tower, the Portland Observatory.[38] From this vantage point Feeney could see Mount Washington in New Hampshire's Presidential Range and far out to sea beyond Portland Head. Did he wonder what lay beyond the eastern horizon? If the Irish looked westward across Galway Bay to dream of America, surely this Irish-American boy might have returned their glances and their dreams. Although the stunning views from Cape Elizabeth and Munjoy Hill clearly had a strong influence on Ford's early sense of landscape, actual visits to Ireland profoundly shaped his sense of vision. McBride tells us:

> Nevertheless, Ford told his grandson that the great feeling for scenery that permeates his work as a director was acquired when he visited Ireland as an adolescent. His father made frequent trips home, and took John along when the boy was about eleven or twelve.[39]

The second of Ford's three academic mentors was William B. Jack, principal of Portland High School. Later in life Ford claimed that Jack was "the greatest man he had ever met," and he cited Jack as the one who "set the pattern of his life." Also regarding this teacher's long-term impact on his life, Ford added, "He advised me not to try to go to college, told me to get out of the state, go West and said I had tremendous potentialities. A word which at that time I didn't understand."[40]

Analyzing the world from an American history perspective, Jack gave great credit to the important roles played by various ethnic groups in the development of the American Republic. In many personal and caring ways he signaled to Feeney that he truly cared about him, "giving an insecure young man from an immigrant background the courage and confidence to succeed in the mainstream of American life."[41]

Finally there was Lucien Libby, head of the English Department at Portland High School. Libby is credited with the ability to mix humor with intellect, to grab the attention of even the most disinterested student through his wit, a common language. Once the students were disarmed and at ease, Libby could effectively slip into their minds certain chestnuts of logic or verse.[42] Ford stayed in touch with Libby, especially during his annual trips back to Portland. He would later pay homage to his high school teacher by naming one of the ships in *They Were Expendable* (1945) the *Lucien Libby*.[43]

Bull Feeney, the human battering ram

In John Ford's production of the film *The Man Who Shot Liberty Valance* (1962) there appears the famous line, "When the legend becomes fact, print the legend." One of Ford's major biographers, Scott Eyman, used this as the title of his 1999 study, adding, "Any artist who arouses clean, uncomplicated feelings will almost certainly turn out to be unworthy of serious attention. Human beings are not clean and uncomplicated, and John Ford was a very human being."[44] Ford's biographers are constantly dealing with complex, complicated, and often contradictory data about this man. Possibly nowhere in Ford's young life does this dialectic between myth/legend and reality/fact show itself more clearly than in his football career at Portland High School. One biographer states:

> Johnnie Feeney made the football team in Portland High School. He was known as "Bull Feeney" for his low, blind charges forward to block or tackle. With him in the team were mainly Irish boys, three Italians, and one Jew. These were the fighting children, determined to crash their way ahead. The Yankees felt less need to strive.[45]

Stories abound concerning the young Ford and his powers on the football field.[46] Memories dull with age, and it is only human to recall selectively the details of our youth. What one can say with certainty is that young John A. Feeney (as he was then named) won letters for his play on the 1912 team (record of 3–6–1) and the State Championship 1913 team (record of 8–3–0) during his junior and senior years. The latter team outscored its opponents by 170–18 points. It appears that Feeney, in his 1912 junior year, was backup fullback to George Tabachnick, and, in his 1913 senior year, was backup fullback to John Norton. He did start, however, in four of the eleven games played in 1913.[47] Ford's football prowess, and his sense of "manliness" associated with football, apparently survived his trip out west to Hollywood. In 1928, on the set of *Mother Machree*, in one of his first encounters with Marion Michael Morrison, better known later as John Wayne, and who was then a sophomore attending the University of Southern California on a football scholarship, Ford challenged Wayne:

> "See if you can stop me." He started running at Morrison and slammed into him, then tried to break free. But Morrison had him, not cleanly, but he had him. Then, just as John was breaking free, Morrison kicked the director squarely in the chest and sent him sprawling. There was dead silence on the set. All eyes were on Morrison, whose brief career in pictures was surely at an end. But John simply got up, dusted himself off, and said, "Come on, let's get back to work. That's enough of this bullshit."[48]

A more sober assessment of John Feeney's football career at Portland High School would more closely parallel his academic career. He was a solid athlete on a fine team. Scholastically, he was average at best. During his first two years at Portland High School he was "erratic," earning an occasional B in English, History, French, or Geography. By his final two years he earned only Cs or Ds across the board, apparently otherwise preoccupied with football or the several minor jobs he held in these years.[49] Perhaps he was already thinking about life after high school, and possibly, in his senior year, a little "California dreaming":

> On a weekend in 1914, the inevitable happened. Abby Feeney returned to announce to her family that she had just seen her eldest son, listed in the credits as Francis Ford, in a starring role. They contacted Francis through his studio, and he made a short triumphal visit to his old hometown. Shortly thereafter, some weeks after graduating from high school, John Martin Feeney was on his way to join his older brother in Los Angeles.[50]

Bull Feeney's public house and restaurant, at 375 Fore Street in Portland, is owned and managed by Doug Fuss and dedicated to the Irish and other immigrants who built the city (photograph by Michael C. Connolly).

Portland High School 1913 Maine state championship football team — with John (Bull) Feeney in the back row, far right (courtesy Peter Gribbin).

Closely related to the question of Ford's football prowess is that of whether he went directly from high school to Hollywood, or was there a very brief offer of a football scholarship at the University of Maine at Orono? Joseph McBride reports that while in Orono during the summer of 1914, Feeney was allegedly called "shanty" by a Yankee fellow student and responded by throwing "the plate of stew in his tormentor's face." Scott Eyman largely discounts the entire story and concludes, "it's highly probable that he never showed up in Orono at all."[51] Whichever version is true, it is clear that Ford's college career, if it existed at all, was over in a matter of days. The Portland High School alumni newsletter of November 1914 reported, "John Feeney is closely connected with the Universal Film Company of Hollywood, California.[52]

John and elder brother Francis Ford were apparently not the only Portlanders who were prominent in early Hollywood. A large advertisement in a local newspaper in 1922 lists Portlander Hiram Abrams as President of the United Artists Corporation. This put Abrams in contact with such early film luminaries as Mary Pickford, Douglas Fairbanks, D.W. Griffith, Charlie Chaplin, John Barrymore, and Rudolph Valentino. A graduate of North School (Primary and Grammar), he left Portland High School after the ninth grade and parlayed his small business gains as a local merchant into a lucrative investment in the fledgling film industry. He helped organize United Artists and, as its president, Abrams helped distribute its films in Europe and America.[53] Likewise, Portland-born Charles William Goddard was a principal author of early motion picture serials, including *The Perils of Pauline*.[54] In addition to the Fords, Abrams, and Goddard, at least two other Portlanders had Hollywood careers in these years: Joseph A. McDonough and Timothy L. Donahue, Jr.[55] A nexus between Portland and

Ford (center), upon receiving his honorary doctor of fine arts degree from President Arthur A. Hauck (right), University of Maine at Orono, June 13, 1938. At left is Edville Gerhardt Abbott (with the permission of Dan Ford; courtesy Lilly Library, Indiana University, Bloomington).

Hollywood becomes apparent in the early twentieth century with the two Fords and Hiram Abrams at its center.

> with joy that is almost pain...
> H.W. Longfellow (*My Lost Youth*)

Portland, Maine, has honored two of its most outstanding artists with significant public monuments. The nineteenth century's most popular poet was Henry Wadsworth Longfellow

UNIVERSITY OF MAINE
ORONO, MAINE

THE PRESIDENT

JOHN FORD   DOCTOR OF FINE ARTS
                                                (D.F.A.)

    Born in Maine and educated in the schools of Portland. Beginning in a humble capacity in the motion picture industry, he has achieved distinction as a director, winning numerous awards in this country and abroad for productions that reveal high artistic and creative ability and rare insight into human nature.

    In September, 1914 you came to Orono hoping that you might some day become an alumnus of the University of Maine. Today, because of your notable achievements, it is my happy privilege, with the hearty approval of the very many in your beloved state who admire your work, to welcome you as an honorary alumnus. In behalf of the Trustees of the University of Maine I take pride in conferring upon you the degree of DOCTOR OF FINE ARTS.

Orono, Maine
June 13, 1938

This is a copy of the award speech delivered when President Arthur A. Hauck of the University of Maine at Orono conferred the honorary degree of doctor of fine arts on Ford (with the permission of Dan Ford; courtesy Lilly Library, Indiana University, Bloomington).

Portland High School (1821–present) is at 284 Cumberland Avenue. The second oldest public high school in the United States was John Feeney's home between 1910 and 1914. He played on its 1913 championship football team as "Bull" Feeney (photograph by Michael C. Connolly).

(1807–1882), born along the southern slopes of Munjoy Hill. His birthplace on the north side of Fore Street, near the corner of Hancock Street, would have been very familiar to the young John Feeney who, nearly exactly one century later, lived a stone's throw away at 23 Sheridan Street. There is a wonderful apocryphal story that ties Longfellow in with the Irish immigrants who would have occupied this same city block by the late nineteenth century, just before Ford's arrival in the neighborhood. Longfellow biographer W. Sloane Kennedy informs us:

> The house in which Longfellow was born in Portland is now used as a tenement-house. One day a school-mistress in one of the schools in Portland asked the scholars if any one of them could tell her where the poet Longfellow was born. After considerable cogitation, a little boy shouted out, "I know,- in Patsy Connor's bedroom!"[56]

What did young John Feeney, the son of Irish immigrants, think of his fellow Portlander? Did he ever imagine that he and "The People's Poet" would be in any way artistically linked or jointly honored by significant monuments in their shared hometown?[57]

One other important theme shared by these two Portlanders was that of exile. Although they both visited their hometown often in later life, each maintained a quite separate professional and family life away from Maine — Cambridge, Massachusetts, in the case of Longfellow, and Hollywood, California, in the case of Ford. In addition to frequent visits home, these artists expressed their love for Portland in their own ways and through their own distinct artistic mediums. They would both have shared the diverse, almost conflicting, emotions of the concluding verse of Longfellow's homage to his birthplace, *My Lost Youth* (1855):

The John Ford statue, sculpted by George Kelly, and commissioned by Linda Noe Laine, was dedicated at Gorham's Corner, Portland, Maine, on July 12, 1998 (photograph by Michael C. Connolly).

The statue of Henry Wadsworth Longfellow (1807–1882) is at Congress and State streets, known as Longfellow Square. The statue was sculpted by Franklin Simmons and erected on September 28, 1888 (photograph by Michael C. Connolly).

And Deering's Woods are fresh and fair,
And with joy that is almost pain
My heart goes back to wander there,
And among the dreams of the days that were,
I find my lost youth again.
And the strange and beautiful song,
The groves are repeating it still:
"A boy's will is the wind's will,
And the thoughts of youth are long, long thoughts."

Notes

1. 1966 interview by Claudine Tavernier, "The Fourth Dimension of Old Age," in Gerald Peary, editor, *John Ford Interviews* (Jackson: University Press of Mississippi, 2001), 103. I would like to thank Kate Rhein of Saint Joseph's College of Maine for assistance in preparing this manuscript. I am also very grateful to the following friends who read the manuscript and provided useful criticism: Fidelma McCarron of Portland; Dr. Edward Rielly of Saint Joseph's College of Maine; William David Barry of the Maine Historical Society; Dr. Kenneth E. Nilsen of Saint Francis Xavier University (Antigonish, Nova Scotia); and Dr. Angela Gleason of Princeton University (graduate of Saint Joseph's College of Maine and Trinity College Dublin). All Longfellow quotations contained herein are taken from *The Complete Poetical Works of Henry Wadsworth Longfellow* (Boston: Houghton, Mifflin and Company, 1883).

2. Joseph McBride, *Searching for John Ford: A Life* (New York: St. Martin's Press, 2001), 20. Files on the life and work of John Ford, including his Portland roots, exist at the Maine Historical Society and at the Portland Room of the Portland Public Library.

3. Ford's Oscars, in chronological order of their release dates, were: *The Informer* (1935), *Grapes of Wrath* (1940), *How Green Was My Valley* (1941), *Battle of Midway* (1942), *December 7th* (1943), *The Quiet Man* (1952).

Other Ford films with distinctly Irish themes include: *The Shamrock Handicap* (1926), *Riley the Cop* (1928), *Mother Machree* (1928), *The Plough and the Stars* (1936), *The Long Gray Line* (1955), *The Rising of the Moon* (1957), *The Last Hurrah* (1958).

At the time Ford became incapacitated, circa 1965, he was working on *Young Cassidy*, the story of legendary Irish dramatist and labor activist Sean O'Casey.

4. Dan Ford, *Pappy: The Life of John Ford* (Englewood Cliffs, NJ: Prentice Hall, 1979); Tag Gallagher, *John Ford: The Man and His Films* (Berkeley: University of California Press, 1986); Scott Eyman, *Print the Legend: The Life and Times of John Ford* (Baltimore: The Johns Hopkins University Press, 1999); Joseph McBride, *Searching for John Ford: A Life* (New York: St. Martin's Press, 2001). Also very useful is Bill Levy, *John Ford: A Bio-Bibliography* (Westport, CT: Greenwood Press, 1998).

5. See Séamus Grimes and Michael C. Connolly, "The Migration Link between *Cois Fharraige* and Portland, Maine, 1880s to 1920s" in *Irish Geography* 22 (1989), 22–30.

6. See Joseph McBride, *Searching for John Ford*, 17–19, 22. McBride claims that the exact Feeney compound was the townland of Tourbeg (*Tuar Beeg*— or *Beag*), on *Cnocán Glas* (Green Hill). The house, as is the local tradition, was given a name: *Ard Aoibhinn* (meaning high, pleasant or delightful, blissful, enchanting, place). This author visited this site in the summer of 2006, speaking with three Feeney relatives still living nearby. On pages 47–48 McBride claims that "Abby Feeney could read Gaelic, but, unlike her husband, she was never able to read or write English. She depended on John and her other children to read her the local newspapers." For an analysis of the Irish-speaking community in Portland, Maine see two scholarly essays by Kenneth E. Nilsen, "Thinking of Monday: The Irish Speakers of Portland, Maine," in *Eire/Ireland* 25 (no. 1), Spring 1990, 6–19; and "The Language that the Strangers Do Not Know: The Galway Gaeltacht of Portland, Maine in the Twentieth Century," in Michael C. Connolly (editor), *They Change Their Sky* (Orono, ME: University of Maine Press, 2004), 297–339.

7. Joseph McBride, *Searching for John Ford*, 25–26. See also Tag Gallagher, *John Ford*, 2; Scott Eyman, *Print the Legend*, 30–31; and Dan Ford, *Pappy*, 2–5.

8. *Twelfth Census of the United States (1900)*, Population, Volume I, 876, as cited in Michael C. Connolly, "The Irish Longshoremen of Portland, Maine, 1880–1923," Ph.D. dissertation, Boston College, 1988, 106.

9. See Kerby A. Miller, *Emigrants and Exiles: Ireland and the Irish Exodus to North America* (New York: Oxford University Press, 1985). See also Cecil Woodham-Smith, *The Great Hunger, Ireland, 1845–1849* (New York: Harper and Row, 1962).

10. Joseph McBride, *Searching for John Ford*, 36.

11. In the 1936 presidential election, when only two states voted Republican against the re-election of Franklin Delano Roosevelt, the political maxim, "As Maine goes, so goes the nation," was unceremoniously changed to "As Maine goes, so goes Vermont."

12. This would pay dividends much later for other ethnic Democrats, especially Edmund Muskie who broke the Republican stronghold on the Blaine House (official residence of Maine's governors) in 1954. In the later twentieth century two Irish Democrats would also rise to higher office. Joseph Brennan, whose maternal forebears hail from Callowfeenish in the Galway Gaeltacht, would serve two terms as governor (1979–1987) and two terms as a United States Representative. In 1980, Brennan appointed George J. Mitchell to serve in place of Senator Edmund Muskie, who had been chosen to serve as Jimmy Carter's Secretary of State in 1979. This move propelled Mitchell, eventually, into the powerful position of Senate Majority Leader (1989–1995). Mitchell's Irish ethnicity and judicial temperament were two factors leading to his appointment by President Bill Clinton to serve as Northern Ireland peace negotiator, resulting in the Belfast (Good Friday) Agreement in 1998. See George J. Mitchell, *Making Peace* (Berkeley: University of California Press, 1999).

13. See Connolly, *They Change Their Sky*, 4–10. Every Bishop of the Diocese of Portland from its founding in 1855 to the present has been Irish, with identifiably Irish surnames. See list of all eleven Bishops, including one Feeney (1955–1969), on pages 8–9.

14. Joseph McBride, *Searching for John Ford*, 35.

15. Local and national prohibition data is widely available. For information on the Portland context see Neal Dow, *The Reminiscences of Neal Dow* (Portland: Evening Express Publishing Company, 1898). One century later, in 1998, the Maine Historical Society ran a major exhibition on this issue, organized by Nan Cumming and William David Barry, entitled "Rum, Riot, and Reform: Maine and the History of American Drinking." Jamie Kingman Rice of the Maine Historical Society informed me that an educator's kit for this exhibit is catalogued as M178.5 M284m, or by the title "Rum, Riot, and Reform" in MINERVA.

16. The Feeneys moved to 34 Center Street in the 1880s. *Portland City Directory* (1903) lists the future home of John A. Feeney at 65 Monument Street as his home and his occupation as "saloon." This seems quite blatant in a prohibition city. Courtesy of William David Barry of Maine Historical Society.

17. See Michael C. Connolly, "The First Hurrah: James Michael Curley versus the 'Goo-Goos' in the Boston Mayoralty Election of 1914," *Historical Journal of Massachusetts* 30, no. 1 (winter 2002) 50–74. See also Jack Beatty, *The Rascal King: The Life and Times of James Michael Curley (1874–1958)* (Reading, MA: Addison-Wesley Publishing Company, 1992); James Michael Curley, *I'd Do It Again: A Record of All My Uproarious Years* (Englewood Cliffs, NJ: Prentice-Hall, Inc., 1957); and Joseph F. Dinneen, *The Purple Shamrock: The Hon. James Michael Curley of Boston* (New York: W. W. Norton, 1949).

18. Even on the racial question the Irish were forced to "become white" by differentiating themselves from other non-white menial laborers, i.e., African-American slaves and free blacks. For local examples of this see Michael C. Connolly, "Black Fades to Green: Irish Labor Replaces African-American Labor Along a Major New England Waterfront, Portland, Maine in the Mid-Nineteenth Century," *Colby Quarterly* 37, no. 4 (Dec. 2001): 357–73. For a national discussion of this phenomenon see Noel Ignatiev, *How the Irish Became White* (New York: Routledge, 1995), and David Roediger, *The Wages of Whiteness: Race and the Making of the American Working Class* (New York: Routledge, 1995). For a description of the eighteenth century migration from Ulster into Maine see R. Stuart Wallace, "The Scotch-Irish of Provincial Maine: Purpooduck, Merrymeeting Bay, and Georgia," in Michael C. Connolly, editor, *They Change Their Sky*, 41–59.

19. For more information on Joseph Connolly see Joseph McBride, *Searching for John Ford*, 34–35. McBride (71) later credits Connolly with aiding the Feeneys in relocating the wayward son Francis in Hollywood and getting him back to Portland for a brief reunion in 1914.

20. See Edward McCarron, "A Brave New World: The Irish Agrarian Colony of Benedicta, Maine" in Michael C. Connolly, editor, *They Change Their Sky*, 121–137. Dr. Edward Rielly of Saint Joseph's College (Standish, Maine) and Dr. Kenneth E. Nilsen of Saint Francis Xavier University (Antigonish, Nova Scotia) have drawn my attention to other rural Irish settlements in Iowa, Wisconsin, upstate New York, and Vermont, to name but a few. See also Donald Harman Akenson, *The Irish in Ontario: A Study in Rural History* (Montreal: McGill-Queen's University Press, 1999) that confronts the notion that the Irish were only city-dwellers, and it cites several examples of Irish rural settlements in North America.

21. Regarding the ownership issue, see Joseph McBride, *Searching for John Ford*, 37, where he writes, "Not that they owned it, mind you." Scott Eyman, *Print the Legend*, 33, writes that "the only reason the farm was sold was because the children were growing older and needed the higher quality schools in Portland." Tag Gallagher, *John Ford*, 4, states that the "Feeney family fortunes tended to fluctuate with Maine's dry laws. Around 1898 they were obliged to sell the farm." Dan Ford, *Pappy*, 5, avoids the issue

of ownership and gives as the reason for the family's return to the city "so John could be closer to his saloons."

22. I am greatly indebted to Margaret Feeney LaCombe for sharing the following research with me: "Cumberland County Deeds— Book 514 page 152 John buys Cape Elizabeth farm from Joseph A. and Alice J. Kinsman of Boston for $2400, including assuming a mortgage, on 11/13/1884. Property previously deeded from Nathaniel Jordan to Winter Jordan on 3/18/1822; part of the premises descended from Joseph Kinsman, father of Joseph H. Kinsman, conveyed to Joseph by Winter Jordan in Book 305 page 334. Rufus Kinsman, brother of Joseph H. and only other heir deeded his interest to Joseph 11/6/1880 Book 472 page 461.

"Book 526 page 500 John gets a mortgage from Cornelius Connolly on 12/18/1886.

"Book 589 page 470 Town of Cape Elizabeth seizes farm for nonpayment of taxes on 12/28/1891. John owed $30.36 in taxes in arrears for nine months. Notice of intended sale. Quitclaim deed Book 976 page 433 for Kinsman Farm, 35 acres and two buildings in school district number 8.

"Book 609, pages 104 and 106 Estate of Cornelius Connolly forecloses on mortgage on 12/2/1893 dated 8/16/1886 in Book 528 page 267, property is 33 acres in Cape Elizabeth and marshland, the Kinsman property. Ellen Connolly, widow of Cornelius, published notices of foreclosure in the Maine State Press three times from 11/16/1893 to 11/30/1893. The foreclosure was recorded on 12/2/1893.

"The farm was sold to George W. Chase in Book 976 page 433, but I don't have the date—it was shortly after the town of Cape Elizabeth seized the property. That was the quitclaim deed mentioned above in Book 589 page 470. So probably the Feeneys rented it back from Chase? In any event, we know they continued to live there for several years more."

23. Joseph McBride, *Searching for John Ford*, 40–41. South Portland, formerly a part of Cape Elizabeth, separated on March 15, 1895, and was incorporated as a separate town on December 5, 1898. See *South Portland, Maine: An All American City* (South Portland: Forest City Printing, 1971) 32, available at the Maine Historical Society (M So88.5). A perusal of *Portland City Directories* at the Portland Room of the Portland Public Library confirms that the Feeneys may well have moved back to Portland one year earlier, in 1897. The 1897 *Portland City Directory* states that John A. Feeney resided at 48 Danforth Street and ran a "restaurant" at 517 Fore Street. Just one year earlier, the 1896 *Portland City Directory* listed him as a "farmer" living on Spurwink Road, Cape Elizabeth.

24. 21–23 Sheridan Street is known locally as a "triple decker." Technically #21 would represent the first floor, while #23 would designate the second and third floors. The Feeneys apparently moved from the first floor to the third floor around 1907. Here Ford would reside until his departure for California in 1914.

25. See Connolly (editor), *They Change Their Sky*, for a discussion of other Irish settlements in Maine. Following the Irish, many French Canadians flocked to Maine's mill towns in the late nineteenth century in search of factory work. By the turn of the twentieth century, Eastern European immigrants, including Russian Jews, Poles, and Italians, were also arriving in significant numbers.

26. Michael C. Connolly, "The Irish Longshoremen of Portland, Maine, 1880–1923," Ph.D. dissertation, Boston College, 1988.

27. Joseph McBride, *Searching for John Ford*, 47–50. *Portland City Directory* (Portland: Portland Directory Company Publishers, 1901), 898–900.

28. *Portland City* Directories of 1902 and 1903 found in the Portland Room of the Portland Public Library indicate that John A. Feeney's home was 65 Monument Street and his occupation was listed as "saloon."

29. Joseph McBride, *Searching for John Ford*, 47. The records remain available in the John Ford Collection of the Lilly Library, Manuscripts Department, Indiana University, Bloomington, Indiana.

30. Variations of this story may be found in several sources, including Joseph McBride, *Searching for John Ford*, 48–49. McBride, citing U.S. Navy records, pegs Ford's age at twelve and in the sixth grade at Emerson School in February, 1906. He would miss much of the seventh grade. This fact, taken together with time spent in Ireland with his father, delayed his entry into Portland High School until 1910 (age sixteen), and his high school graduation until 1914 (age twenty). Dan Ford, *Pappy*, 7, gives details but places his grandfather's age at the time of this illness at eight and in the fourth grade at Emerson School. Tag Gallagher, *John Ford*, 4, associates Ford's "sensitivity and love for books with this illness," as with Huw Morgan. Scott Eyman, *Print the Legend*, 35, writes that Ford "would replicate the experience of an ill, fragile child with matchless delicacy in *How Green Was My Valley*."

31. Claudine Tavernier, cited earlier from a 1966 interview, "The Fourth Dimension of Old Age," in Gerald Peary, editor, *John Ford Interviews*, 103.

32. Joseph McBride, *Searching for John Ford*, 42. *Portland City Directories* of 1906 and 1907 list John A. Feeney as a "laborer" who, after 1906, moved from the first floor (21 Sheridan Street) to the third floor (23 Sheridan Street) where the Feeneys stayed in residence for a much longer time.

33. Gerald Peary, editor, *John Ford Interviews*, 125. As was his style, Ford gave an interview in 1969 that contradicted his own claim of childhood poverty. He said to Philip Jenkinson, "We were a comfortable, lower middle class family. We ate better than we do now." See Tag Gallagher, *John Ford*, 2.

34. Marada F. Adams Elementary School, located between Moody, Vesper and Munjoy Streets, replaced the Monument Street School in 1959 and was, in turn, replaced by the East End Community School in September of 2006. The William B. Jack School, located at the north end of North Street and the Eastern Promenade, served as a junior high school from 1943, later becoming a middle school before being replaced by the East End Community School, at exactly the same site, in September of 2006. The names Adams and Jack may be physically gone but are not forgotten. Thanks go to Stephanie Philbrick of the Maine Historical Society for assistance with this data. An 1872 regulation set the primary level at K-4. Grammar schools were usually 5–8 (Emerson appears to be an anomaly by starting with grade 6 at this time). See *School Directory, City of Portland, Maine, 1921 and 1929*. Adams School first appears in 1959 while Monument Street School last appears in 1958 (see *Portland City Directory*, 1958 and 1959). The question remains as to where John Feeney would have attended grade 5 (could it have been Shailer or North School, or was it, in fact, at Emerson School?). There is also the question of whether he ever attended the Monument Street Primary School (formerly located at 25–29 Monument Street between Atlantic and St. Lawrence Street) less than two blocks east of his home at 65 Monument Street. By the mid-twentieth century the public school progression for someone living on the south side of Munjoy Hill would have been Monument Street/Adams School (K-3), Emerson School (4–6), Jack Junior High School (7–9), and Portland High School (10–12).

35. *http://adams.portlandschools.org/pages/schoolinfo.htm* Website consulted on March 31, 2006.

36. Joseph McBride, *Searching for John Ford*, 50. Most of the female teachers, especially prominent in early childhood education, were, by law at first, and later by tradition, single—a large percentage up until the mid-twentieth century never married. See Eileen Eagan and Patricia Finn, "Mutually Single: Irish Women in Portland, Maine, 1875–1945," in Michael C. Connolly, editor, *They Change Their Sky*, 257–275. A review of the teaching staff at Monument Street Primary School and Emerson Grammar School at the turn of the last century (1901) shows that all the teachers were female. At Portland High School (1901) fourteen of the twenty teachers, but neither the principal nor the assistant principal, were female. See *Portland City Directory* (1901), 898–900.

37. Joseph McBride, *Searching for John Ford*, 51.

38. John K. Moulton, *Portland Observatory* (Falmouth, ME: by author, 1996, third edition). This source was kindly loaned to me by my cousins, Nancy and John H. Sherin, Jr., of Mere Point, Brunswick, ME.

39. Joseph McBride, *Searching for John Ford*, 51.

40. From an interview of the director by his grandson, Dan Ford, in the John Ford Collection at the Lilly Library, Indiana University, Bloomington, Indiana. See also Joseph McBride, *Searching for John Ford*, 64.

41. Joseph McBride, *Searching for John Ford*, 65.

42. I know this style well, for hundreds of other Portland High School graduates have witnessed it in the pedagogy of beloved and unforgettable teachers. Though all too often unacknowledged, these teachers live still in the memories of their grateful former students. How many unsophisticated students, without a personal rudder or direction, were brought by wit and intellectual prodding to higher planes by such public school teacher/mentors as Marada F. Adams, William B. Jack, and Lucien Libby; or Miss Florence Vose or Miss Josephine Rand (at Emerson School); or such teachers as Miss Alice Yates or Mr. Leon Berkowitz at William B. Jack Junior High School; or Mr. Howard Reiche or Peter Gribbin at Portland High School—or those carrying on this noble tradition even still?

43. Scott Eyman, *Print the Legend*, 304, 40.

44. "Bull Feeney, the human battering ram," was frequently mentioned in local Portland newspapers covering the powerful Portland High School team in these years, according to Dan Ford, *Pappy*, 8. See also Scott Eyman, *Print the Legend*, 23; also see Joseph McBride, *Searching for John Ford*, 722.

45. Andrew Sinclair, *John Ford* (New York: Dial, 1979), 14.

46. A local newspaper staff sports writer captured the spirit of a reunion of former Portland High School football players, including Ford, in 1955. See Rollie Wirths, "Moving Costs Maine Football Star," *Portland Press Herald*, 31 August, 1955, 13. This article, together with a very pleasant photograph of these six former teammates, was in the possession of Timothy L. Donahue (captain of the 1911 P.H.S. football team and a cousin of Ford). For an amusing aside on the Donahue's public house and restaurant, "a noted Portland rendezvous," see "A Place Called Donahue's" in Harold Boyle, *The Best of Boyle* (Portland: The Guy Gannett Publishing Company, 1980), 46–48. Boyle states that "Tim Donahue was a confidant of John Ford, the Portland-born, Oscar-winning film director, and received an important Federal appointment

under President Franklin Roosevelt." The newspaper archives were made available to me through the kindness of Donahue's granddaughter, Jeanne Whynot-Vickers, Superintendent of Schools (Portland Public Schools). Besides the two cousins, Ford and Donahue, also in the photograph were Oscar "Ski" Vanier, Judge John D. Clifford, Dr. John H. Honan, and Dr. John J. Lappin. "Asked about this group, Ford identified it as the 'Alanna Club.' Pressed for an explanation, he said 'Alanna' is an Irish word meaning 'beloved ones.'" This is, in fact, true. In Irish an endearing way of addressing someone close to you is *a leanbh*, literally meaning "my child" or "my darling." The Irish translation is confirmed by Mrs. Claire Foley of Portland who remembers as a child (Claire Ward of Ballacurra, *Cill Chríost*, Loughrea, County Galway) hearing the following ditty: "Go to sleep, *a leanbh*, till I wet your daddy's tea."

47. This information was largely supplied by retired Portland High School history teacher (and sports archivist) Peter Gribbin of Portland. Gribbin asserts that if these legends were true, "young Feeney would have been another Jim Thorpe." An alternate possible source of confusion is that another Feeney (James H. Feeney, who was one year younger and presumably no relation) was an excellent player over these same years, and even was Captain of the 1914 State Champions, the year after John's graduation. See two works by Peter E. Gribbin, *A History of Portland High School, 1821 through 1981* (Portland High School, 1981); and *The First Century of Portland High School Football* (Portland: Dale Rand Printing, 1989).

48. Dan Ford, *Pappy*, 40.

49. Photocopy of Portland High School academic transcript of John A. Feeney (1910–1914). Again thanks go to Peter Gribbin. His four year class average was 8.419. A classmate at Portland High School, Robert G. Albion, author of several books on sea power and Harvard University oceanography professor, said of Ford, "He seemed about as unintellectual a person as you could imagine. In one class he was told he had no imagination." Joseph McBride, *Searching for John Ford*, 63. McBride analyzes this critical evaluation as resulting from Ford's private nature and "his rough, devil-may-care-façade." Yet another opinion on this matter comes from Tag Gallagher, *John Ford*, 2, who conjectures that the semi-literacy of Abby, Ford's mother, "contributed to her son's ambivalence toward intellectuality."

50. William C. Dowling, "John Ford's Festive Comedy: Ireland Imagined in *The Quiet Man*," *Eire–Ireland* 36 nos. 3–4 (Fall-Winter, 2001): 194–195. This essay is reprinted in its entirety in this collection.

51. Analyses of this intriguing possibility abound. See Joseph McBride, *Searching for John Ford*, 72–73; and Scott Eyman, *Print the Legend*, 44–45. The word "shanty" or "shanty Irish" comes from two Irish words *sean* and *ti* (from *teach*) literally meaning "old house." Today the word shanty is closely akin in meaning to a shack or hut, and it is close in Irish to the word *seantán*. It was then a term of derision toward the poor Irish. On the question of college attendance, in an undated, partially-preserved *Portland Press Herald* article in the collection of Ford's Portland High School football teammate and cousin, Timothy L. Donahue, circa mid–1950s, a staff writer contends, possibly citing Donahue, "The fact is he never went there [Orono] at all, although his father wanted him to have a college education." Again, thanks to Jeanne Whynot-Vickers (original article in her possession). For similar newspaper articles paying homage to one of Portland's favorite sons, see Joseph McBride, *Searching for John Ford*, Sources (724–725).

52. *The Racquet 1863–1914 Alumni Number*, Portland High School, November 1914. A photocopy of this was kindly provided by Peter Gribbin, retired history teacher at Portland High School.

53. Hiram Abrams of Portland (1878–1926) died at the age of forty-eight. It is interesting to speculate as to the extent of his knowledge of, or relationship with, the Ford brothers. According to William David Barry, Francis M. O'Brien, Portland's leading antiquarian book dealer, believed that the Feeney brothers had worked for Abrams locally in a pants press shop. He was said to have begun as a theater owner in Portland, and the *Portland City Directory* (1906) lists him as owning the Portland Talking Machine Company at 418 Congress Street. In Hollywood he was one of the founders of Paramount Pictures Corporation, serving as its second president. He later joined United Artists in 1919, becoming its first president. See Benjamin Band, *Portland Jewry: Its Growth and Development* (Portland: Jewish Historical Society, 1955), 103. See large advertisement in *Portland Sunday Telegram*, July 30, 1922, 7B, and also *New York Times*, November 16, 1926. See "Hiram Abrams" in Harold Boyle, *The Best of Boyle*, 43–44. In this same volume see also "Munjoy Hill Alumni" that deals briefly with John Ford (38–39). Thanks go to William David Barry of the Maine Historical Society for help with many of these references.

54. For Charles William Goddard see *Portland Press Herald*, January 21, 1951, in Maine Historical Society's Portland Obituary scrapbook (Mv P837.4), Volume 12, 105. See also Obituary scrap book, Volume 1, page 9; Volume 8, page 33; Volume 19, page 17; and Volume 28, page 104. Thanks again go to William David Barry of the Maine Historical Society.

55. Regarding Joseph A. McDonough, see Maine Historical Society, Desk Obituaries (catalogued alphabetically). *Portland Press Herald*, May 31, 1944, states that McDonough "left here [at age nineteen] with Francis and John Ford for Hollywood. After some years with the Fox Film Company, Mr. McDonough began his long and successful career with Universal Film." His sister, Mrs. Edward J. Feeney of 11

Sheridan Street, provided this information to the newspaper. Timothy L. Donahue, Jr. was the son of Ford's Portland High School football teammate and cousin, Timothy L. Donahue, Sr. Mr. Donahue, Sr. was captain of the 1911 team that was the first to play against cross-town rival Deering High School in what has become an annual Thanksgiving Day classic. His son was employed by 20th Century–Fox as a budget director from after World War II until his retirement in 1983. See obituaries for Donahue, Sr. (*Portland Press Herald*, March 25, 1957 in Maine Historical Society 080, Book 2, page 108); and for Donahue, Jr. (*Portland Press Herald*, January 24, 1984 in Maine Historical Society 080, Book 12, page 20). Again, thanks go to William David Barry of the Maine Historical Society for assistance in finding both of these references.

56. W. Sloane Kennedy, *Henry W. Longfellow: Biography, Anecdote, Letters, Criticism* (Cambridge, MA: Moses King, Publisher, 1882), 230–231. This source was kindly shared by Matthew Jude Barker of the Maine Historical Society, who also uncovered an early reference to the birthplace of Longfellow in William Goold, *Portland in the Past* (Portland: B. Thurston & Company, 1886), 80. The Longfellow birthplace at 161 Fore Street was demolished in 1955. A stone marker is all that marks this historic spot today. A "drop forge" steel foundry, the Thomas Laughlin Company, operated adjacent to that site (at 143 Fore Street) between 1894 and 1987. In 1967 the name of the company changed to Crosby-Laughlin, a Division of the American Hoist and Derrick Company. Between the years 1978–1987 it apparently went under the latter name exclusively. Thanks go to Abraham Schechter and Margot McCain of the Portland Room at the Portland Public Library for help with this information. In 1987, after ninety-three years of operation, the building's all-too-familiar rhythmic sound was heard no more on Munjoy Hill. At the time of this writing, in the spring of 2006, the city of Portland is going through the permitting and planning stages for a proposed mixed use condominium/commercial development on this site. According to the city planning department, the proposed name for this new complex is "The Longfellow at Ocean Gateway."

57. In 1921 Ford worked on a cinematic production of Longfellow's *The Village Blacksmith*. The Portland connection of both of these artists was stressed by Fox Studios operative Winfield Sheehan, who added, "Every man, woman and child who can speak English throughout the world has read *The Village Blacksmith* and one out of every three people know the entire poem by heart." Scott Eyman, *Print the Legend*, 74. Literally dozens of references exist which refer to Ford as either a "poet" or an "artist," such as that of the famous producer Darryl F. Zanuck, who said of his favorite director, "He was a great, great pictorial artist." (Scott Eyman, *Print the Legend*, 567).

John Ford: A Memorial

Maidhc P. Ó Conaola (Mike P. Connolly), translated by Kenneth E. Nilsen

Translator's note: The following is a transcription of a radio program that was first broadcast on *Raidió na Gaeltachta* (Irish language radio station) on October 20, 1973, several weeks after the death of John Ford. The producer of the program was Maidhc P. Ó Conaola. By pure serendipity the program was rebroadcast on Seosamh Ó Cuaig's program *Ó Na Sceirde Aniar* (From the Windswept West) on *Raidió na Gaeltachta* in December 2005.[1]

The area of Ireland from which John Ford's parents emigrated is on the sea coast of Galway Bay approximately twelve miles west of the city of Galway. The region is known in Irish as *Cois Fharraige*, which means "by the sea." It is the gateway to the western part of Galway known as Connemara. This region was completely Irish-speaking in the nineteenth century when Ford's parents left, and it remains today one of the strongest Irish-speaking areas in Ireland. Irish-speaking districts are referred to as *Gaeltacht* areas.

In the program Maidhc P. Ó Conaola interviews three individuals: Máirtín Ó Féinneadha (Martin Feeney) of Toorbeg, a cousin of John Ford; Lord Killanin (Michael Morris) of Spiddal, a friend of John Ford and former president of the International Olympic Committee; and Máirtín Ó Droighneáin (Martin Thornton) of Spiddal, a distant relative of John Ford who appeared in some of the fight scenes in *The Quiet Man*. All of the interviews have been translated from the original Irish by Kenneth E. Nilsen with the exception of those of Lord Killanin which were broadcast originally in English and are transcribed here.

Interviews

Voice of **Seosamh Ó Cuaig:** The first item we have tonight is a report that was broadcast in the early days of Raidió na Gaeltachta about the movie director John Ford and the presenter of the program back on the twentieth of October 1973, was Maidhc P. Ó Conaola. Now you know that Maidhc P. is from Spiddal and probably some of you know that John Ford's people were from the Spiddal district. Now this is the John Ford who produced *The Quiet Man* and many, many other well-known films. But in any case, Maidhc P. interviewed Martin Feeney, a

---

The reader may note a few minor factual errors in the following interviews due to errors on the part of the interviewees. Except for any errors that have been noted by the translator in his endnotes, the editors have decided to leave the interviews intact without correction or elaboration, due to the fact that they are previously broadcast interviews with the chief purpose of paying personal tribute to Ford.

cousin of John Ford's, Martin Thornton who appeared in *The Quiet Man*, Lord Killanin, and several others.

Voice of **Maidhc P. Ó Conaola**: The first day of February, 1895. The place: Cape Elizabeth, Maine, that is where John Feeney, John Ford, the film producer and director, was born.

Voice of **Martin Feeney**: His father was called Seán Mháire[2] from Toorbeg and his mother was known as Barbara Frank from Kylerooa West or Ballynahown as it is known, she was Barbara Curran. There were five Feeney brothers: his father Seán Mháire, Máirtín Mháire, Peadar Mháire, Nioclás Mháire and Ned Mháire, my father. They were all born up there in the old place and you will see it shortly. We'll go up to see it. I cannot say when he went to America, but it is in Portland that he settled and it is there that he raised his family. Patrick was the oldest son, then Francis or Frank, Éamonn was the third son and John was the fourth, the youngest of the sons. I think there were four sisters but I only know the names of two of them, Mary and Nora. Nora is still in Hollywood. She was a schoolteacher but I do not know if the other one is still living. I don't know if Éamonn or Patrick are still living but I know Frank is not. Patrick was the oldest and was working in Portland, Maine. Now if you would like, we can go up to see the old place.

Voice of **Lord Killanin** (in English): My great-grandmother, Mrs. Martin Morris, died of cholera in the early 1840s and she had just given birth to a boy, George Morris, who was my great-uncle. He was immediately put out to foster parentage at one of the neighboring cottages which belonged to the Feeneys. He was brought up with this family and then about eighteen years later accompanied one of the Feeney boys down to Cove (Cóbh) to see him off to the United States. The boy, a Feeney boy, was John Ford's father. He eventually settled in Portland, Maine where he set up in the bar business, later speakeasy and then bar, again, business. This is my contact with John Ford's family, the Feeney family.

Voice of **Martin Thornton**: I became acquainted with John Ford in 1951 when he came to Ireland to make a picture. It was a January evening, quite cold, that he himself came with Victor McLaglen, Ward Bond, John Wayne and a few other people that I did not recognize. He asked me if I would like to take a boxing part in *The Quiet Man*. I said I would so he arranged for me to go to Cong where the boxing scene was to be filmed. We went to Cong and there would be days when perhaps I would have no boxing or anything to do but I was there for six or seven weeks. Other actors who were there included Maureen O'Hara, a FitzSimons, and other people from Esther Studios in London had parts in it. There were local people in scenes where there was a crowd. Then after about a fortnight I had to do some boxing and then a week after that I had to do some of that boxing again and then after about another week I would have to finish up the boxing scene. It was always the same fight that was being done but a different part was taken each week.

I had heard of John Ford before that because we were related to him. My grandmother was from Toorbeg. She was related to the Ned Mháire family. I am not sure how close it was but we were related. And he himself was aware of that when he came home here. And he had a little bit of Irish because he would say to me when I was boxing, "*Tabhair leadóg eile dhó, a Mháirtín. Tabhair leadóg eile dhó, a Mháirtín. Tabhair leadóg eile dhó. Ciotóg eile, a Mháirtín. Ciotóg eile, a Mháirtín.*"[3] He would be saying that all the time while the fight was in progress.

Maidhc P. Ó Conaola: You have just heard Martin Feeney, a cousin of John Ford, Lord Killanin, and Martin Thornton, the boxer.

Martin Feeney: Here you have, Mike, the place where John Ford's father and all of them were born and raised. It is in a dilapidated condition with the roof and the rafters falling in. It doesn't look very good but this is where they were born and raised, five brothers and five sisters. They all went to America except my father, Ned, and a sister named Bridget who was married here. One of them died crossing the ocean at the time of Free Emigration, a sister of my

Lord Killanin—a man of many parts

father's and of John Ford's father named Nora. It was sailing vessels at that time and they would spend sixteen weeks at sea and they would contract various diseases. But in any case, she is buried on an island. It used to be said that they were thrown into the ocean and maybe they would be if the ship was not close to port. But she is buried on an island, a sister of my father's and John Ford's aunt.

Lord Killanin: John Ford was always interested in Ireland, always interested in politics. He was a great romantic. He told me he had been here during the Civil War and from various friends I have met I believe this to have been so although I could never find out what was fact and what was fiction because this was rather John Ford's way of looking at things.

Martin Feeney: In 1920 around the month of November he came home on a visit for the first time. I do not know if he left from Hollywood or Portland, Maine. He came to see the place where his father was born and raised and he spent a while seeking out the place. He went east to Park, a few miles east of Spiddal because there were a lot of Feeneys there and an old man there told him to come to this village here, Toorbeg, where his father was born. It was quite late when he came with a *sidecar* or a *jaunt* as we used to call it, with an old man named Mike Tierney as driver. But when he realized that he was at the old place, he was in no hurry to leave. It was a cold evening, but it was dry and he left at about eight o'clock to send word to his father that he had found the old place. They went off but things were in a disrupted state at the time with the Black and Tans and as they were approaching the Claddagh Bridge they were stopped and, of course, they probably recognized that he was a Yank. If it were not for that they would be much more.... He gave them no satisfaction because he was not familiar with the state of the country, that the Tans were so bad, and he did not know why they stopped him and were questioning and searching him. But in any case he did not give them the least satisfaction according to Mike Tierney who was driving him. But apparently they took him out of the car and they gave each other a fine thrashing, the both of them. I think he was staying in the Railway Hotel but they sent him straightaway off to Dublin. And whether it was on a plane or a boat, they sent him away. He did not visit again until things had calmed down and we had won our freedom. But he was very much in favor of freedom that evening he was here, like so many of those of Irish descent over there, he was greatly in favor of freedom and of the IRA. But when he came back (in later years) when he would come every year or every half year, he would always be talking about the night that he and the Black and Tans gave each other a thrashing. He was a strong young man at that time, twenty-five years old, and he felt like giving it to them. Of course, they could have shot him, but apparently they did not want to do that because he was a Yank and that would cause them trouble. But that is how the visit went, the first visit.

Maidhc P. Ó Conaola: John Ford did not come home again until 1933. His father was with him this time. It is no wonder that he saw a number of changes in the place since he left, but, of course, he had changed in certain ways also.

Martin Feeney: His hair was grey, he was an old man, and he went to look at all the fields that he had left behind many years before that. He was very interested in the village and the people he had known, although only a few of them were left, but he went to speak to those who were still living. But he was especially interested in the fields and the improvement to the roads.

Opposite top: Martin Feeney (center) of Tuar Beag, Spiddal, a nephew of John Ford's father, visiting with his Portland niece, Margaret Majors Feeney (mother of Margaret Feeney LaCombe) and her son Martin in 1974. This is the same Martin Feeney who was "on the run" when Ford visited Galway in the early 1920s, and also the same person interviewed on Raidió na Gaeltachta after the death of Ford in 1973. His children, including Bartley, Pat and Ned, still live in and around Spiddal (courtesy Bartley Feeney). *Opposite bottom:* Lord Killanin (Michael Morris) is a distant "relative" of the Feeneys through the fosterage of a great-grandfather, George Morris, circa 1840. Killanin's estate was in Spiddal, and he assisted John Ford with *The Quiet Man* and other film projects in Ireland (courtesy Bartley Feeney).

There used to be a poor road going up there when he left but there was a good road at this time. They did not stay long, just a couple of days.

Maidhc P. Ó Conaola: By this time John Ford was well known as a film director. In 1917 he made his first film *Cactus My Pal*. He made another one in 1924 and two in 1930, *Mary of Scotland* and *The Informer*.[4] Victor McLaglen was in that one. He made *Arrowsmith* from the novel by Sinclair Lewis in 1931 and from then on there was no stopping him. In 1939 he made one of the most famous Westerns, *Stagecoach*, and although he made many fine films after that, the experts say that he never surpassed that one.

John Ford had his own style for making a film. Instead of taking all the shots that were to be taken in one place, as most filmmakers do, he would always follow the story and move from place to place until the film was finished. Another thing is that there was always a musician at his side while he directed a film to have a lot of music around him while he worked.

Maidhc P. Ó Conaola: Do you know, Martin, if John Ford was in the War?

Martin Feeney: He told me that he was in the war, the Second World War, 1939 to 1945, at sea in the Navy, and that he was a Second Admiral, as he said. I do not know how long he was in it, but he told me that. I do not know if it is true or not, but that is all I know about it.

Maidhc P. Ó Conaola: John Ford was an industrious worker. The World War was hardly over when he was in full sail again. He made that lovely film about Wyatt Earp and Doc Holliday, *My Darling Clementine* in 1946 and that was followed by other major films *Fort Apache*, *She Wore a Yellow Ribbon*, *Wagon Master*, *Rio Grande*, *The Man Who Shot Liberty Valance*, and *Two Rode Together*. But in the back of his mind, John Ford always had the dream that the day would come when he would make a film in the country in which his father and mother were raised. In 1951 *The Quiet Man* was made. It had been in his head for a long time.

Lord Killanin: In 1937, 1938, I was coming back from China where I'd been the *Daily Mail* war correspondent. I was asked by the *Daily Mail* to stop off in Hollywood and write a few stories. At that time, possibly, Hollywood was, in the eyes of most people on this side of the Atlantic, the United States. My only contact there was John Ford. So I sent him a cable from Japan, and in due course was met by him in his old Rolls-Royce, and it was fairly new in those days, at the station and spent a week or ten days with him. During this time we became great friends. He was some, many years older than me at that time, but we started talking about making films in Ireland and he showed me Maurice Walsh's book which included a short story called "The Quiet Man." We talked about making this film in Ireland and then the war came. During the war, I saw John Ford, who was then in the United States Navy, quite a lot in London and we continued talking about filmmaking and wondered then was it ever going to be possible. Then the war ended and suddenly one day in the nineteen fifties I got a telephone call from Jack, who I'd been in contact with all the time, telling me that the film was off the ground. *The Quiet Man*, as you know, was made in the West of Ireland based chiefly at Cong and Ashford Castle. It had a tremendous success in that it paid for itself in Italy alone. John Wayne came over, Maureen O'Hara and it became one of the great classic films. It wasn't particularly liked in Ireland because it was, in fact, a Western set in Ireland. It had very many Irish-American attitudes towards it. I think in those days we had a few more chips on our shoulders, and I think John Ford in many ways was disappointed that it didn't have the acclaim in Ireland, although it had the financial success that he would have liked.

Martin Thornton: There were a lot of other parts involved in *The Quiet Man*. Some of it was filmed in Ballygloon down at the station. That's where Barry FitzGerald was when Maureen O'Hara arrived and went up on the jaunt and all her baggage was put on it. Barry was like a taxidriver with his jaunt and horse. And then the place where Maureen O'Hara was born was a thatched cottage in Maam that belonged to a Mr. Joyce, but they had it for the making of the film. You would see Maureen O'Hara coming out of the doorway and that is how she met John

Wayne. Then there was another man, Victor McLaglen. He was Maureen's father. He was supposed to give Maureen money and he said that he was not able to give her the money until fair day when he would sell some cows. Well, there was a great crowd at the fair, people and cattle, and John Wayne came along and he wanted to get his money from Victor McLaglen and a big fight started at the fair and that is part of the fighting that I did. I am the one who actually did the fighting, but in the close-up shots it is Victor McLaglen. We were in Maam and we were in Cong and we were in Tuam and in Ballygloon. I would say that he was a man who liked Gaelic a lot because he would be asking me a lot of questions about Gaelic. "*An dorn aríst, a Mháirtín, an chiotóg, an lámh chiotóg.*"[5] And he would say, "*Lá breá, a Mháirtín, cé chaoi bhfuil tú?*"[6] But I do not know if I had started to speak to him in Irish maybe he would not have been able to follow the Irish, but he would use a lot of words in Irish himself. He liked music, also. There was a man there, Paddy Conroy from Maam, from Corr, and he would be there playing music, the old reels and jigs. And whenever Paddy Conroy wasn't playing music, John Ford would say, "*Cá'il Paddy, cá'il an ceoltóir, cá'il an ceoltóir?*"[7] He was able to say *ceoltóir*. "*Cá'il an ceoltóir?*" He liked to listen to music.

Martin Feeney: However it may be that they lost it, and that could easily happen, it was Gaelic that the father and mother spoke to them in the house when they were children. When they started going to school then and growing up they started to lose it. John himself had some Irish, but he had lost it, but he wanted to be able to speak it and he wanted to be a Gael. Irish was the language of the house, why wouldn't it be, one person from this village and the mother from Ballynahown and the father from Toorbeg, you know that they had all Irish. He had a great respect for the language and for the ones that were fighting for freedom, for example Michael Thornton and Edward Walsh and some of those, and Joe Warren, Seán MacGiollarnáth who was in Galway, he was in touch with him. And up there in Mayo when he was working on *The Quiet Man* he was very friendly with Tom Maguire somewhere up by Cong who was the leader of the ambush near Tourmakeady. He was in touch with him a lot also and anyone who had taken a part in the war for freedom, he was greatly in touch with him.

Lord Killanin: The John Ford I knew was basically a very liberal man. He made Westerns where usually the Indians naturally were beaten. He endeavored to redeem himself with a later film called *Cheyenne Autumn*. I remember another occasion with John Ford going to a hotel in Las Vegas with his chauffeur who was a black man. We were not allowed in with the black man. John Ford refused to stay. When John Ford drove away from the hotel, a big hotel, the proprietor came and we were immediately allowed in, including the black driver who stayed with us and ate at our table. This was the typical John Ford. He was a great believer in supporting the underdog although he was very authoritarian.

Martin Thornton: When he had finished the picture he came to me in the pub in Spiddal and asked me if I would like to go to Hollywood. I told him that I would like to. So then he was making arrangements for me to go out and it was in the papers over there that I was going to come out, and my brother who is a priest heard that I was going to go to Hollywood and my brother was well acquainted with John Ford's sisters in Los Angeles where he used to visit them. And my sister who lives in San Francisco knew John Ford's sisters also, and they used to visit each other. So my brother asked him for God's sake to leave me at home and not bring me out to Hollywood, "whatever you do, leave him in Ireland." After a while I received a letter from John saying that my brother was against my going to Hollywood and that was the end of my attempt to go to Hollywood. I suppose the reason my brother was telling him to keep me in Ireland is that I was a bit spirited at that time and he thought that if I got to Hollywood I would be a lot worse. That is why my brother was telling John Ford to keep me at home.

Maidhc P. Ó Conaola: But, of course, you were not spirited.

Martin Thornton: No, I was not spirited, but maybe the people around here thought that

I was, you know. No notice would be taken of that when I was in London. There were people there far more spirited than me but since Spiddal is a bit small maybe a person is more obvious if he is a tiny little bit out of line.

Maidhc P. Ó Conaola: The two townlands, Toorbeg and Knockaun Glas, where the writer Máirtín Ó Cadhain was born, border on each other.

Martin Feeney: Yes, we were talking about him once, talking about Máirtín and once with Máirtín about him. He praised his films greatly, the Westerns, but I cannot say if he met him, but he said that he thought that he was making the best pictures, the Westerns. I don't know if he ever met Ó Cadhain or not, but I thought Máirtín respected him.

Maidhc P. Ó Conaola: It is still too early to evaluate John Ford's work but as Máirtín Ó Cadhain, God rest his soul, said "he made some of the best Westerns and it is certain that they will stand up to the test of time." He showed in a Western that he made in 1966, *Cheyenne Autumn*, that he could be sympathetic to the Indians, and he showed in the film *The Grapes of Wrath* that he made after the war how well he understood the difficult time of the Depression in America. It was instinctive for him to understand, and it wasn't from the wind or the sun that he got that for he had seen hardship and misfortune at home and in the next home, in Portland, and in Connemara at the beginning of the century. When John Ford died a couple of weeks ago, so also died a citizen of the United States and a man of Connemara stock, who had done a man's worth to put Ireland's name on the creative map of the world, and although people might say that the pictures that he made about this country were inaccurate, and I think in a way that they were, one must remember that these films were aimed at the world market and that people only like to see what they want to see, and that Ford went half the way to satisfy them. But in the end, when Ford's work is evaluated properly, it is certain that it will stand on the highest rung of his own profession, film.

Notes

1. I would like to thank Maidhc P. Ó Conaola, the original producer of the program, and Edel Ní Chuireáin, the director of Raidió na Gaeltachta, for permission to translate and publish this transcription of the program.
2. Seán Mháire translates as John son of Mary. In Irish-speaking districts in Ireland where certain surnames are very common it is the custom to name people after their father or more rarely, as in this case, after the mother.
3. "Give him another punch, Martin. Give him another punch, Martin. Give him another punch. Another left, Martin. Another left, Martin."
4. *Cactus My Pal*, a working title, was eventually released as *Cheyenne's Pal* in 1917, and was made to promote the sale of war bonds. *Mary of Scotland* was actually released in 1936 and *The Informer* in 1935. See Tag Gallagher, *John Ford: the Man and His Films* (Berkeley: University of California Press, 1986), filmography, 504 and 523–524.
5. "The fist again, Martin, the left, the left hand."
6. "Fine day, Martin. How are you?"
7. "Where's Paddy? Where's the musician, where's the musician?"

John Ford and the Feeney Family of Galway and Portland

Matthew Jude Barker

John Ford. Sean O'Feeney. Sean Aloysius O'Fearna. Jack Ford. The great Hollywood director John Ford went by many aliases over the years and, in turn, many biographies added to the list, each claiming a different "real" name for the director. Since many studies have incorrectly identified his birth name and birth date, and since almost every biography of Ford contains some inaccuracies or falsehoods, it should be of some importance to attempt to record the origins of Ford and his family while remaining as close to the facts as possible.

John Ford was born John Martin Feeney on February 1, 1894, in a farmhouse on Charles E. Jordan Road in Cape Elizabeth, Maine. His parents were John A. and Barbara Curran Feeney.[1] When John was about one month old he was brought across the Fore River to St. Dominic's Church in Portland, where, on March 1, 1894, Father Edward F. Hurley baptized him. His godparents were Edward and Julia Feeney.[2] St. Dominic's (1822) was one of the oldest Catholic parishes in southern Maine and a second St. Dominic's Church building was dedicated only seven months before the baptism of John Ford.[3]

John Ford's father, John Augustine Feeney, was born in the village of Spiddal (An Spidéal), County Galway, on Dec. 3, 1854, the son of Patrick Feeney or Ó Fienne (an Irish version) and Mary Curran. John's grandparents were Edward and Barbara Morris Ó Fienne, and Nicholas and Margaret Flaherty Curran, all of that region of Galway known as *Cois Fharraige*, a rough, wild, romantic land west of Galway City. The name Feeney was also spelled Ó Fianna, Ó Fidhne, and Ó Fiannaidhe in Gaelic Irish, depending on certain variables.[4]

In 1872, when John Feeney was eighteen, a relative named Michael Connolly returned from America and told John and others of his travels and adventures in the New World. John and Michael spent the next few days talking of the opportunities that awaited a young man in the United States.[5] Michael Connolly was born in Galway in 1846, a son of Patrick and Hannah Hackett Connolly. He married Margaret Feeney, a widowed sister to John Augustine Feeney. Michael and Margaret had several children in Portland, Maine, including Joseph (1874), Patrick (1877), and Mary (1879).

Michael H. Connolly is said to have emigrated to Quebec several years before where, one night, he met a stranger who gained his confidence and got him drunk. He awoke the next day

---

A version of this article was originally published in *Galway Roots, Clanna na Gaillimhe, Journal of the Galway Family History Society West* (Volume V, 1998, 148–152). Since its publication, Joseph McBride's *Searching for John Ford: A Life* (New York: St. Martin's Press, 2001) has proven to be a more definitive work on the director, his life, and his films. The article is published here with the kind permission of *Galway Roots* and the author.

to find himself in a wagon with twenty other men. They were shackled in chains and put to work digging a canal. Michael later escaped and was picked up by a band of Blackfoot Indians who also put him to work. A French trapper secured the young Irishman his freedom. Then Michael was paid $200 by a man named Purvis T. Earl to enlist in the Union Army in his name. He later deserted and ended up in Portland, Maine.[6] Whether any of this is true is not known, but it makes one hell of a story. It is known that Michael H. Connolly, according to his military records, enlisted in the Union Army at Augusta, Maine in June 1862. He was honorably discharged in July 1865 in Savannah, Georgia.[7] As with many aspects of John Ford and his family there are many unanswered questions and stories as well as unconfirmed oral history labeled as "fact."

In any event Michael Connolly put John A. Feeney to work in his saloon in Portland, and thus John entered the shadowy, but profitable, business of liquor sales in a state that had originated many prohibition laws. The first prohibition law in the country was enacted here in 1851, mostly due to Portland Mayor Neal Dow, the "Czar of Temperance." Hundreds of Irish families rose up out of poverty in Maine by selling booze on the sly, and the Feeneys were no exception. In later years John A. Feeney would often be arrested on "search and seizure" charges and would have to pay hefty fines in order to avoid jail.[8]

John A. Feeney entered the United States at Boston on June 8, 1872, and he became ("was admitted") a citizen on September 11, 1880.[9] On July 31, 1875, John, or Seán as he was often called, married Barbara "Abby" Curran, a cousin from a nearby farm in Connemara. She was the daughter of Francis and Bridget Hearney McLaughlin Curran and also came to Portland in 1872. They had eleven children between 1876 and 1898, of whom only six survived infancy. Those born were Mary Agnes "Maime," Delia, Patrick H., Frank T., Bridget, Barbara, Edward Francis, Josephine Cecelia, Johanna, John Martin, and Daniel. John Ford would be the youngest of the children to survive.[10]

By the late 1870s, John A. Feeney was operating a grocery store (which posed as a front for a saloon) at 42 Center Street in Portland's Irish section called Gorham's Corner, a place known for its clandestine activities. An Edward Feeney resided across the street at 43 Center Street and was perhaps the Edward Feeney who was the godfather of John Ford. In 1882 John is listed as a "laborer." Michael "Conley" is also marked as a laborer. The 1880 Federal census of Portland records John Feeney as a twenty-seven-year-old employee who "works in 'Gas House.'" This same source lists his wife "Addie" (sic) as "keeping house."[11]

Throughout the 1880s, John Feeney and his family resided at 34 Center Street. The 1885 *Portland City Directory* records that John A. Feeney operated a saloon at 518 Fore Street.[12] Nicholas J. Feeney, who was John's brother, ran a saloon at 512 Fore Street. In October 1884, John purchased a 33-acre farm near the Spurwink River in Cape Elizabeth from Joseph H. Kinsman of Boston for $2400. Kinsman had inherited it from his father, who had purchased the place from Whitney Jordan in 1861. It was often called the "Kinsman Homestead."[13] John also purchased property near Higgins Beach in Cape Elizabeth and in 1886 mortgaged the Kinsman property to Cornelius Connolly. But Connolly died and his widow Ellen claimed a foreclosure in 1892. Between 1883 and 1895, John is listed fourteen times as either grantor or grantee in the Cumberland County Registry of Deeds. In 1889, the town of Cape Elizabeth taxed Feeney $30 for 35 acres and two buildings.[14]

John is listed as a farmer in the city directories of the late 1880s and throughout the 1890s. He is also listed at 4 Cobb Court in 1891, and by 1895 he was operating a restaurant at 517 Fore Street and had a residence at 49 Center Street, the whole time maintaining his home in Cape Elizabeth. Interestingly enough Nicholas J. Feeney also removed to the Cape in 1886, and was a farmer in the Spurwink district, perhaps near John. John continued his restaurant business until 1899, but in 1897 he moved his family to 48 Danforth Street in Portland. This residence is listed as a saloon by 1901. Many different Feeneys resided at this address at the turn of the century, including Roger, Sarah, Helen, James H., and Edward, son of Daniel, who drowned in 1904, aged sixty-three. A John J. Feeney was a clerk and lived with the Feeneys when they moved to 65 Monument Street, around 1902.[15]

65 Monument Street was the first residence of the Feeneys on Munjoy Hill, another Irish neighborhood in Portland. Once again John opened a saloon here. In 1905 they moved to 21 Sheridan Street, also on Munjoy Hill. John's oldest son, Pat, who had been a clerk at 517 Fore, opened his own restaurant on India Street at the base of Munjoy Hill in 1903, at which he continued to work for a few years.

John A. Feeney succeeded to Mike Connolly's business, and his "dingy restaurant-saloons down near Portland's wharves and warehouses were natural gathering places for the Irish, and John Feeney became a ward leader. He would greet new immigrants, help them settle and find jobs, register them as citizens and voters, and so built himself a political base."[16] It is said that John, through his political connections, helped his nephew, Joseph E.F. Connolly, become a judge. Joseph was appointed a judge of the Cumberland County Superior Court in 1911. He had been admitted to the Maine Bar in 1902.[17]

The city directory for 1907 reveals that the Feeneys had moved to 23 Sheridan Street. In actuality, 21 and 23 Sheridan was one large three-family apartment building they shared with Michael H. Myers and Patrick Mahoney, plumbers, and their families. For a time John's son Edward was a plumber. All three families became close friends.

It was while growing up at 23 Sheridan Street that John Martin Feeney, also called Jack or Johnnie, attended the local schools. He chose Aloysius as his Confirmation name and from then on he always used that as his middle name. And it was at Portland High School that John earned the nickname "Bull" from his rather rough experiences as a running back and defensive tackle for the football team. "He would fight at the drop of a hat, but, you know, he had a great mind and a great sense of humor," one teammate recalled.[18]

As John attended the local schools, his older siblings were already out working. His brothers Edward and Patrick ran cigar stores for several years at various locations, and his sister Josephine became a teacher at nearby North School. In 1914, Pat acquired a fish dealership with his sister Mary, the widow of a fish dealer named John E. McLean who had died in 1909. Pat retired from the fish business in 1947.[19]

Francis Feeney, the second oldest brother, always had a restless spirit and joined the Army when the Spanish-American War broke out in 1898. He deserted and came back to Portland, where he met and married Agatha Della Cole in August 1900.[20] They had a few children, including a son Philip in 1902. But Frank again grew tired of Portland and headed for New York. The rest of the Feeneys did not hear from him for the next several years.

Years later, Frank, under the name Francis Ford, showed up on a movie screen at the Greeley Theater in Portland. Jack Feeney and his mother, who loved the "flickers," recognized him in a movie. Shocked, they eventually located him through a New York agent. Frank had discovered the entertainment world, but before that he had slept on park benches and spent years in vaudeville. Ford was now a top actor-writer-director with his own company at Universal Pictures.

Jack Feeney got a job as an usher at the Jefferson Theater, where Timothy Donahue, supposedly a cousin, was head usher. Ford recalled years later that the first night he worked, the ushers went on strike. He was exposed to more theater at the Gem on Peaks Island, where the Feeneys had a summer home.[21] The 1914 *Portland City Directory* lists Jack as a student, living at home. The next edition reports him having removed to California, where his brother Frank had gone in 1909 following after filmmaker Gaston Méliès. Jack Feeney graduated from Portland High School in 1914. Some sources state that he attended the University of Maine. According to Joseph McBride, he enrolled in the school of agriculture, but after an incident with a "WASP" student, he left the school.[22] John Ford did receive an honorary Doctor of Fine Arts degree from the University of Maine at Orono in 1938. Ford followed his brother Francis out to Hollywood in the summer of 1914, accompanied by his friend, fellow Irish American, Joseph A. McDonough, who eventually had a long and successful career first with Fox and then with Universal Film.[23]

Frank Ford put his brother Jack to work as an assistant and handyman, anything and everything, at $12 a week. Four months later, Jack acted in his first movie, *The Mysterious Rose.* Jack went on to act in several of his brother's movies under the name of Jack Ford. Frank had changed his name to Ford because the car inspired him, he said years later. Another version has it that Frank Feeney once replaced a drunken actor named Francis Ford and the name stuck. In any event, John Martin Aloysius Feeney was now Jack Ford and in 1923, he changed it finally to John Ford.

In November 1915 Francis and John Ford returned to Portland where they filmed two movies. The first, *The Strong Arm Squad,* was filmed between November 26 and 29, 1915 and released February 15, 1916 by Rex-Universal. It starred Francis Ford, Elsie Maison, and Jack Ford as a crook.[24] The Ford brothers also included friends and relatives as cast members in the film, including their parents, brothers Pat and Eddie, their sisters, a niece, Cecil (Cecelia) McLean, William White (a real Irish-American Portland policeman), and Danny Bowen, who played a police chief. In real life, Bowen was head of the Portland Police Department, becoming in 1914 the first Irish-American to become Portland Police Chief.[25] The second movie filmed in Portland was *Chicken-Hearted Jim,* filmed between November 10 and 17, 1915, and released April 23, 1916. This movie also starred the Ford brothers and other relatives and friends. Unfortunately, no copy of either of these silent films seems to have survived.

Jack Ford directed his first movie, *The Tornado,* which appeared in March 1917. He then went on to direct over 150 more movies, including some of the greatest movies of all time. He would make a star of Marion Michael Morrison, also of Irish ancestry. Today this actor is better known to the world as John Wayne.

In the early years, Ford directed eight or more movies a year, all silent. After 1929, all his movies were "talkies," and the number of movies filmed each year dropped significantly. Now there was no stopping John Ford. Many of his movies had either an Irish or Western theme, which would make him famous. The Irish movies included *The Tornado, The Prince of Avenue A., Mother Machree, Hangman's House, The Informer, The Plough and the Stars, The Quiet Man, The Rising of the Moon, The Long Gray Line, The Last Hurrah* and *Young Cassidy. The Informer* (1935) tells the story of Gypo Nolan who betrays his best friend, Frankie McPhillip, for twenty pounds in order to flee to America during the Anglo-Irish War of 1919–1921. The movie was based on the novel by Aran Islander Liam O'Flaherty. Victor McLaglen won an Oscar for his portrayal of Nolan. Ford also received an Oscar for Best Director, the first of six Academy Awards.

It is interesting to note that John Ford was in Ireland during the Irish Rebellion. In November 1921, he visited his first cousin Martin Feeney, who "had been hiding in the Connemara Mountains with the Thornton boys." Ford noted that the Black and Tans, a group of British soldiers and mercenaries who had been called to Ireland to quell the rebels, had burned down many of the houses in Spiddal, which was "shot to pieces."[26]

Francis Ford never made it as big as his younger brother, but he was a star in his own right, in his own day, and in no small way helped and inspired his brother John to become such a great director. Francis abandoned directing in 1927 and for the next twenty-five years he was a character actor in his brother's movies. John Ford said of Francis, "He was a great cameraman ... he was really a good artist, a wonderful musician, a hell of a good actor, a good director — Johnny of all trades — and *master* of all; he just couldn't concentrate on one thing too long. But he was the only influence I ever had, working in pictures."[27] Tag Gallagher wrote, "Frank's superabundance of talents combined badly with streaks of impracticality ... but lacked the stick-to-itiveness that was John's key to success. Frank's passion was variety. He enjoyed many women, through three wives and numerous affairs. And he loved makeup and disguises."[28]

John and Frank's brother Eddie also moved to Hollywood where he was an assistant to his famous brothers. He directed one film by himself in 1920, and then went on to become an assistant director to his brother John. Eddie changed his name to O'Fearna, mistakenly believing that it was Irish for O'Feeney. One Ford assistant said Eddie and John always fought, even though Ford thought he was indispensable. "This goes back to the days in Maine when Eddie and the others ran a saloon and they used to kick Ford out of there and wouldn't let him drink. Ford never got over this."[29]

John Augustine Feeney, the father, passed away in June 1938, at the age of eighty-four. He suffered a stroke at his Peak's Island home. Over the years he had made frequent winter visits to California to see his children. His wife Abby had died in 1933. John A. Feeney's funeral was held at his son Pat's home at 92 Sheridan Street.[30] He was interred in the family lot in Calvary Cemetery, South Portland, where today one can still see the large Celtic cross marking the plot. His children had loved and respected him dearly. Francis Ford recalled that "Father was the greatest actor that ever lived. When he told a story of the elves and banshees and fairies, it was like a real experience."[31]

John Ford often returned to his boyhood home, always slipping in and out without notice. He and his wife Mary were made life members of the Harold T. Andrews Post of the American Legion in 1948. Twice he entertained Maine's delegates to American Legion conventions at his California ranch.[32] From June 26–29, 1958, the Harold T. Andrews Post celebrated the 40th Annual State Convention of the Legion in Portland. A large celebration was held at the Eastland Hotel, and on June 27, 1958 John Ford addressed the assembly. A booklet put out at the time was dedicated in memory of Legionnaire Francis Ford, "From Members of the Harold T. Andrews Post, No. 17, Residing in Southern California." These included John Ford and his wife, their son Patrick, Francis Ford, Jr., and the three children of Eddie O'Fearna.[33]

Another daughter of Galway emigrants, Mary Moran Costello (1896–1993), graduated from Portland High School with John Ford. She told this author that she hosted a class reunion at her home in South Portland one year and everyone was pleasantly surprised when John Ford showed up at the reunion, unannounced.[34]

Francis Ford died in Los Angeles in 1953 and was survived by three children. Pat Feeney died in Portland in 1964, survived by two children. Eddie died in 1969 and was survived by three children. Their sister Josephine, who had been a teacher in Hollywood for decades, was the last survivor of the Feeney siblings, and she died in Beverly Hills in 1985, aged ninety-three.[35]

John Ford was honored by the American Film Institute with its first Life Achievement Award in March 1973. President Nixon "appeared to wheel Ford around, present him with the Medal of Freedom, and promote him to full admiral."[36] The country did not forget that while filming a portion of the Battle of Midway, Ford suffered a concussion and three of his men were killed. He had been given the Purple Heart at the time.[37]

John Ford, the great Irish-American film director from Portland, Maine, passed away in his sleep on August 31, 1973, at his home in Palm Desert, California. He was seventy-nine years old and was buried in Holy Cross Cemetery, Culver City, California. He had suffered from cancer the last few years of his life.[38] Survivors included his wife, the former Mary McBride Smith, his sister Josephine, his children, Patrick Michael Roper Ford (born 1921) and Barbara Nugent Ford (born 1922), and two grandchildren.

On July 12, 1998, a John Ford monument was dedicated at Gorham's Corner in Portland near where his family once resided and near the site of his father's saloon. The gift was made possible by the Linda Noe Laine Foundation. Laine, whose father was James Albert Noe, a former governor of Louisiana and a friend of Ford, donated $10,000 in May 1996 to cover preliminary design costs. A Ford Film Festival ran a week prior to the dedication at Portland High School. Finally, twenty-five years after his death, his hometown recognized and honored him. In 2002 an Irish pub and restaurant opened up at 375 Fore Street in the Old Port section of Portland and the owners named it *BULL FEENEY'S*, after John Ford's high school football nickname. More recently, in October 2005, the Maine Irish Heritage Center, located at the old St. Dominic's Church, hosted a symposium on John Ford, his life, and his films.

Notes

1. Cape Elizabeth Vital Records, 1745–1896, transcribed by Eleanor Murray, 1935, from original records. Collections of the Maine Historical Society (hereafter MHS) (Mv C17.3 2003).
2. Copy of baptismal record obtained by the author, 1996. The original record is now in the custody of Sacred Heart/Saint Dominic Parish, corner of Mellen and Sherman Streets, Portland, Maine.
3. "History of St. Dominic's Parish," in Michael and Marilyn Melody, editors, *St. Dominic's: 175 Years of Memories, 1822–1997* (Portland: Smart Marketing, Inc., 1997), 19. Available at MHS.
4. Edward MacLysaght, *More Irish Families* (New York: Barnes & Noble, 1960), 105.
5. Dan Ford, *Pappy: The Life of John Ford* (New York: De Capo Press, 1998), 2.
6. Dan Ford, *Pappy: The Life of John Ford*, 2.
7. Military records of Connolly were obtained at the Maine State Archives by Herbert Adams, 1996.
8. For two representative liquor indictment cases involving John A. Feeney see *Daily Eastern Argus*, January 14, 1882 and October 4, 1892. In the latter case, Feeney was fined $200 for a liquor "nuisance" and was ordered to pay the fine or spend six months in jail. Available through the microfilm collection at the Portland Public Library.
9. Original naturalization record of John A. Feeney found at the Maine State Archives, Augusta, Maine. See also *Cumberland County Naturalizations Index, 1787–1906*, Court House, Portland, Maine (available at MHS, 929.3 C91). See John A. Feeney, page 00024 (Number 82, Box 513).
10. See the genealogical account by Margaret Feeney LaCombe in this collection.
11. *Federal Census of 1880*, Enumeration District 52, Portland, Cumberland County, Maine, 37.
12. *The Portland Directory and Reference Book for 1885*, 292.
13. Cumberland County Registry of Deeds, Vol. 514, 152. (142 Federal Street, Portland, Maine)
14. Cumberland County Registry of Deeds, Vol. 589, 470.
15. This information was garnered from the Portland City Directories, Maine Historical Society.
16. Tag Gallagher, *John Ford: The Man and His Films* (Berkeley: University of California Press, 1986) 2.
17. See obituary, *Portland Evening Express*, 2 October 1939.
18. Joseph McBride, *Searching for John Ford: A Life* (New York: St. Martins Press, 2001) 60, 63.
19. This information was garnered from the Portland City Directories, Maine Historical Society.
20. *Portland Vital Records*, Volume 8, Page 438 (originals at Portland City Hall, these taken from a microfilm copy at the Maine Historical Society). They had two known children, Philip, born in 1902, and Arthur S. Feeney, born in 1907. Arthur, who had been born in Bridgeport, Connecticut, died in Portland at two months of age. These same records list Frank's occupation at this time as a tailor.
21. Tag Gallagher, *John Ford*, 5.
22. Joseph McBride, *Searching for John Ford*, 72–73.
23. Joseph McBride, *Searching for John Ford*, 76; also see obituary of Joseph A. McDonough, *Portland Press Herald*, 31 May 1944.
24. Filmography of Ford's work, with each of the films he starred in, directed, produced, or helped write, with production and release dates as well as cast members, can be found in Tag Gallagher, *John Ford*, 501–546. Also see *Portland Evening Express*, 20 November 1915, 2.
25. See obituary of Daniel L. Bowen, *Portland Press Herald*, 11 August 1945.
26. Tag Gallagher, *John Ford*, 29.
27. Tag Gallagher, *John Ford*, 8.
28. Tag Gallagher, *John Ford*, 10.

29. Tag Gallagher, *John Ford*, 31.
30. See obituary, *Portland Press Herald*, 23 June 1938.
31. Tag Gallagher, *John Ford*, 2.
32. See *Maine Sunday Telegram*, 8 June 1958.
33. See "Fortieth Annual State Convention, American Legion," from collections of Matthew J. Barker, who received a copy of the booklet from his grandfather, Thomas F. Gillan, Esq., who had been in charge of legal affairs for the convention. Copy at MHS, see Ethnic Vertical File, "Irish Americans in Maine: Ford (Feeney) Family."
34. Interview by Matthew J. Barker of Mrs. Mary W. Moran Costello (spring 1989). Also see *School Report of the City of Portland, 1914* for a list of the members of the Class of 1914, Portland High School. (Collections of the Maine Historical Society)
35. See obituary of Josephine C. Feeney, *Maine Sunday Telegram*, 27 January 1985.
36. See *Portland Press Herald*, 31 March 1973; see also Tag Gallagher, *John Ford*, 454.
37. Tag Gallagher, *John Ford*.
38. Tag Gallagher, *John Ford*, 454–455. See also obituary, *Portland Press Herald*, September 1973.

The John Ford Tour

Margaret Feeney LaCombe

We don't know exactly when the Feeneys came to Tuar Beag, Bohoona, Spiddal, County Galway, but they have lived there at least 200 years (some say 400) in this coastal town in western County Galway.[1] Edward Feeney married Barbara Morris in Spiddal before 1814, and they raised their family in a two room stone house on the landward side of the coast road about one-quarter mile up the narrow road (boreen) from the main road. Edward Feeney and his wife Barbara were dead before Griffith's Valuation of Ireland enumerated heads of households in 1856, and they may have died from the Great Hunger of 1847, or from natural causes. Their children survived the Famine, and starting in the early 1850s some of them emigrated to the United States via New York and Boston to Portland, Maine. Son Patrick Feeney remained behind on the Feeney land with his wife Mary Agnes Curran. Here his son, John Augustine Feeney (John Ford's father) was born on December 3, 1854.[2]

The exodus from Spiddal was primarily economic, a way to get ahead in the world. The Feeneys had weathered the Great Famine of 1847, although according to Maureen Langan-Egan, "the people of Spiddal were barred from any relief under plans to raise money for road construction, as the small head-rents payable to the landlord were inadequate security for loans, as the chief rents were payable to a widow up to 1852, under the terms of a settlement."[3] In those days most of the Irish were allowed only to rent their land, not to own it, so these work-for-welfare schemes were financed through the landlords' coffers.

The first to emigrate were Daniel Feeney and his wife Bridget, who was also a Feeney by birth. Evidence suggests that Bridget Feeney, not her husband Daniel, was the child of Edward Feeney and Barbara Morris, and therefore she was John Ford's great-aunt Bridget.[4] Daniel Feeney emigrated in 1852 or 1853, with his wife and children arriving a little later on December 1, 1853 on the Bark *Clarence* in New York.[5] They settled in Portland where she died of cholera in September 1854. Bridget was buried in the Western Cemetery in the west end of Portland in the Catholic Strangers' Ground along with the earlier Famine-era immigrants.[6] They were among the many Feeneys, Lydons, Currans, and Foleys from the Spiddal area who arrived in Portland in the mid-nineteenth century.

Daniel Feeney remarried and bought a house in Gorham, Maine, one of Portland's outlying towns, where he had many more children before he died there in 1897. John Ford and his parents were friendly with the children from both marriages. They visited John Ford at his California home and were given rides on his sailboat, the *Araner*. Edward Feeney, son of Daniel and Bridget, lived in the same building as John Ford's parents at 43 Center Street in the late 1870s, and again in 1900–1901 at 48 Danforth Street. Edward's grandson, Daniel Joseph Feeney, became the Catholic Bishop of the Diocese of Portland 1955–1969.[7]

The Feeney family homestead ruins in Tuar Beag, Spiddal, the birthplace of John Ford's father, John A. Feeney, now used to house Ned Feeney's greyhounds (photograph by Alice Townend, courtesy Mike Connolly).

The next of the Feeneys to emigrate were John Feeney and his wife Mary Lydon Feeney before 1860. They lived in Portland, then Gorham, before moving back to Portland where they lived on both Center Street in the heavily Irish neighborhood known then and now as Gorham's Corner, and on nearby York Street. Center Street was one of five streets that converged at Gorham's Corner, and it would have been Portland's equivalent to New York City's Five Points district.

Only one of the children of John Feeney and Mary Lydon reached adulthood. The other children died young and were buried with the first husband of Ford's aunt Margaret Feeney in Calvary Cemetery in South Portland.[8] Some of Mary Lydon's brothers and sisters also emigrated: the brothers and brothers-in-law took jobs building the Grand Trunk Railroad line from Portland to Montreal. A railroad strike stranded them and others in Greenwood, Maine. They settled there, creating the still-named Irish Neighborhood section, where they had to contend with the occasional bear attack, and where they were eventually buried in a small cemetery in the woods.[9] Mary's brother, Bartley Lydon, married a Curran, probably related to John Ford's mother Barbara "Abby" Curran.

When John Ford's father, John A. Feeney, emigrated to Portland in June 1872, he was greeted by a support network of family and friends from Spiddal. John A. Feeney's sister, Margaret Feeney, had preceded him. It is her first husband who is buried with the children of her uncle and aunt, John and Mary Lydon Feeney. Margaret Feeney emigrated in April 1863 on the

Heowatha from Galway to New York. She married John Maloney in 1867 at St. Dominic's Church.[10] John died in 1869 at age twenty-seven of lung fever.[11] A widow and boarding house owner, Margaret next married Civil War veteran Michael Henry Connolly from County Galway. This is the Michael Connolly, sometimes spelled Connelly, who features so prominently in all the major biographies of John Ford. According to family lore, he is the person who almost single-handedly convinced John Ford's father to join him in Portland.[12] Connolly operated a saloon at 42 Center Street at the corner of Fore Street, and this is where John Ford's father, John A. Feeney, worked and lived when he first arrived in Maine.[13]

Bridget (Delia) Feeney (sister of John A. Feeney, and of Ned, Nicholas, Peter and Martin) and Patrick Connolly. These are the grandparents of the Feeneys from Saint Paul, Minnesota (courtesy Bartley Feeney).

Margaret and Michael Connolly's son, Joseph E. F. Connolly, was a Portland lawyer and County Superior Court Justice. Connolly was socially conscious of the anti–Irish prejudice and the devastations that poverty was wreaking on the lives of the ever increasing numbers of Irish emigrants to the city. He used his position to rule that children should not be forced into the almshouse with their parents, but should instead be placed with private families of their own religion. Judge Connolly was the force behind instituting a system of probation so that the families of offenders would not be thrown into poverty by the incarceration of a father or mother. He also strongly supported the creation of city playgrounds and public bathhouses, and, in addition, prepared wills for a majority of the Irish in Portland.[14]

John A. Feeney soon met his cousin Barbara "Abby" Curran from Ballynahown, Kilroe West, Spiddal, County Galway.[15] She had emigrated in April 1873 through New York on the ship *Greece*, and was

Ned Feeney (brother of John A.) and his wife, Helen (Eibhlín Ní Chualáin), seated, and his sister, Bridget Feeney, standing (courtesy Bartley Feeney).

processed through the Castle Garden immigration office. She came to Portland and worked as a maid in Portland's Falmouth Hotel.[16]

Abby arrived in Portland three months after the Portland wedding of her half-sister Bridget Costello to John Coyne of Spiddal in January of 1873. Another half-sister Hannah Costello who married John O'Toole of Furbo, County Galway, gave birth to her first child in April 1870 in Boston, so it appears that the Costellos and Currans were emigrating as early as 1870. Abby's half-sister Mary Costello married Stephen Kilmartin who was her boss at the Falmouth Hotel.[17] He was a source of job patronage for many County Galway Irish who found jobs at the hotel. The Falmouth was "a six-story, 200-room hotel ... described as the finest this side of New York City when dedicated in June 1868."[18]

John Augustine Feeney and Barbara "Abby" Curran were married on July 31, 1875 at St. Dominic's Church in the west end of Portland.[19] They baptized most, if not all, of their children there. It is said that John Ford was later an altar boy at St. Dominic's, the first Catholic Church in Portland (1833), built by and sustained mainly by Irish immigrants.

Judge Joseph E. F. Connolly, son of Margaret Feeney and Michael Connolly, who became Cumberland County Superior Court Justice and initiated many reforms for the Irish and the poor of the city. He died in 1939 (courtesy Margaret Feeney LaCombe).

In 1880 John Ford's parents were living at 53 Center Street and John A. Feeney was working at the gas house, located on Beach Street near the end of York Street, just west of the then new bridge to South Portland.[20] He later operated a "blind pig" near the gas house. To avoid prohibition laws, an operator of a bar, instead of selling liquor, would charge an admission fee to enter his rooms to see an attraction, like a blind pig, and then serve "free" liquor.[21]

From 1883 to 1885 the Feeneys lived at 34 Center Street. During these years the Feeneys also lived in a farmhouse with almost forty acres on the Charles Jordan Road in Spurwink, Cape Elizabeth, where John Ford was born on February 1, 1894. John A. Feeney bought the house from Portland property investor Cornelius Connolly, who held the mortgage on the property. The Feeneys lived at the oceanfront farm from 1878 to 1896, while maintaining rooms in Portland. When Cornelius died, his wife requested immediate payment of the mortgage and it is unknown whether Feeney was able to comply or whether he instead rented the property from her until 1896, their last year at the Cape Elizabeth house.[22]

Opposite top: Falmouth Hotel (1868–1958), at 214 to 220 Middle Street, was one of Portland's finest and largest hotels and the source of much employment for the newly arrived Irish, especially female domestic workers (courtesy Margaret Feeney LaCombe). *Opposite bottom:* Saint Dominic's Church, at Gray and State Streets, the religious center for Portland's west end Irish Roman Catholics. This is an early sketch of the Church and rectory as they probably appeared to the Feeneys (courtesy Margaret Feeney LaCombe).

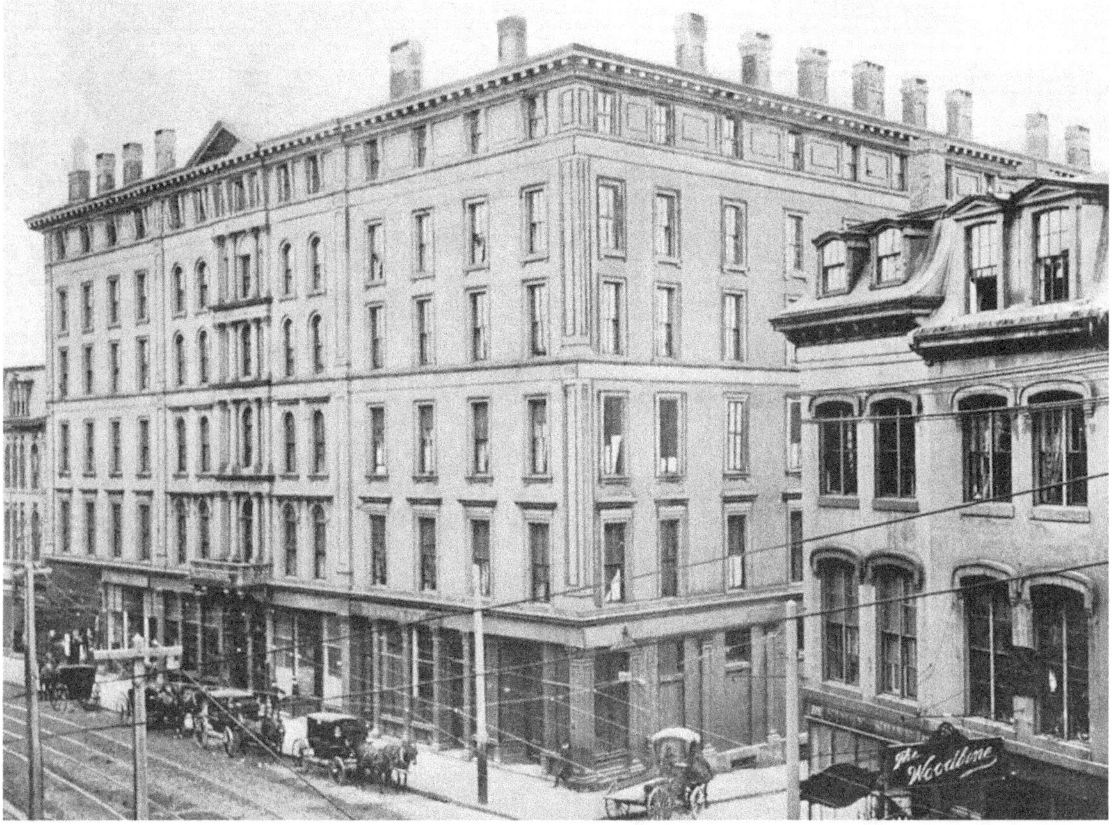
The Woodbine

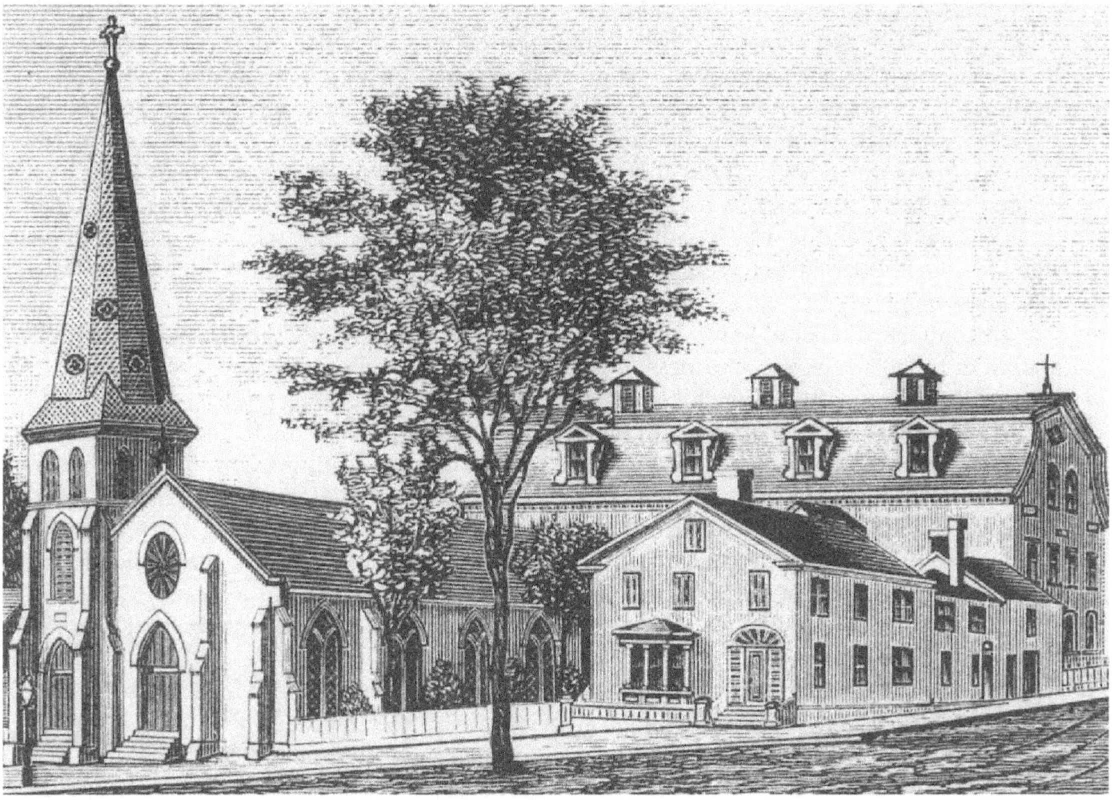

The extended Feeney family in Saint Paul, Minnesota, in 2001. These sixty-five descendants of Bridget (Delia) Feeney and Patrick Connolly possess names today such as Richardson, Vogl, and Boo (courtesy Bartley Feeney).

John A. Feeney owned a saloon at 518 Fore Street on the corner of Center Street in Gorham's Corner until 1899. No photo of this building apparently exists today. John Feeney's brother, Nicholas Feeney, lived with John's family in Portland and Cape Elizabeth, having emigrated on June 16, 1873 through Boston on the ship *Atlas* when he was twenty years old. Nicholas owned a Gorham's Corner saloon across the street from those of his brother and of his brother-in-law Michael Connolly.[23] Both Nicholas and his brother John A. Feeney appear frequently in Cumberland County Court dockets for liquor law violations, along with distant relatives such as Patrick C. Nugent and James C. Cady.[24] Nicholas Feeney returned to Ireland by 1888 with his wife Mary Curran, also from Spiddal, and opened a small grocery store on William Street West in Galway city.[25]

By contrast, another of John A. Feeney's brothers, Martin, lived the American dream. Emigrating in the 1870s, he was a witness in 1879 for his brother Nicholas' marriage in Portland. Perhaps he decided, after seeing his brothers' legal troubles in running saloons, that he would try his hand at railroad work. He appeared in St. Paul, Minnesota in the 1880 census, living in a popular boarding house owned by a possible cousin, Hannah "Auntie" Concannon Connors, from Saliahoona, Spiddal, who had emigrated through Portland, Maine, as did her brothers. Starting as a laborer for the Great Northern Railroad, Martin worked his way up to foreman. He then invented a device used in trains, a coal catcher, which made him wealthy. Friends and relatives emigrating in a steady stream from Spiddal often stayed at John A. Feeney's house in Portland before boarding the train for Martin Feeney's house, or their brother Peter's house, both in St. Paul, Minnesota.[26]

When John A. Feeney registered to vote in 1895 he gave his address as 49 Center Street, and from 1897 to early 1899 he had a saloon at 48 Danforth Street, although he still had a "restaurant" at 517 Fore Street as well. All of these were in Gorham's Corner.[27] The Feeneys in 1902 moved to 65 Monument Street on Munjoy Hill in Portland's east end. John A. Feeney opened

Portland's waterfront fishing wharves — the source of gainful employment for many, including the Feeney family — from a postcard (courtesy Margaret Feeney LaCombe).

a saloon/restaurant at 14 India Street that same year when John Ford was eight. John Ford's brother, Patrick, worked at the restaurant until 1909 when their sister's husband, John McLean, died, leaving a bereft widow and a wholesale fish market to be run. Patrick became a co-owner of the business and managed it at least until 1930. The Feeneys thus had a steady supply of inexpensive fish.[28]

In 1905 the Feeneys moved less than two blocks to 21–23 Sheridan Street, also on Munjoy Hill, where they lived until 1917.[29] In 1907 John A. Feeney had a restaurant at 196 Federal Street, west of Exchange Street.[30] In 1911 John Ford's brother Edward opened a cigar store on Fore Street.

Young John Ford's playground was the Eastern Promenade with its breathtaking vistas of ocean and the islands and ships in Casco Bay. Children still burrow under the cast iron fence to climb the small cliffs up and down to the railroad tracks below. With each walk around the Promenade, or down the hill to school, the children passed historic cemeteries and sites of old forts from colonial days. Boys liked to fish from the piers and throw rocks at the wharf rats. There were so many children on the Hill that it was easy to raise a quorum for street games, and on a hot day, when parents' patience was tested, they could send the children uptown to the library or the small Museum of Natural History on Elm Street, the Longfellow House museum, or the art museum, all of which were free to the public. There was winter sledding on the hill descending from the four-sided monument engraved with Portland's various historic names through the centuries. For the price of a nickel, they could sit in the "cheap seats" at the many theaters downtown and see vaudeville acts and plays. They could take the ferry to Peaks Island and to the Gem Theater there, or to explore the old forts.

Though a small city, Portland was the largest city in Maine and offered a degree of culture and entertainment. In the heyday of the port, up to the early 1920s, Portland was the winter terminus for Montreal and Canadian grain, when the St. Lawrence River was frozen.[31] Ships full

A postcard of Fort Allen Park and the Eastern Promenade on the eastern point of Portland's peninsula looking across the harbor and out to sea (courtesy Margaret Feeney LaCombe).

of emigrants docked at the port, and Russians, Swedes, Poles, Irish and Italians, among others, embarked onto the streets at the bottom of Munjoy Hill, to board trains at terminals on India (east end) and St. John Street (west end).[32]

John Ford attended Emerson Grammar School. He graduated from Portland High school in 1914, and today the school auditorium is named for him. It is the second oldest site of continuing high school education established in the United States.[33]

With the ocean before him, and ships and trains waiting to take him anywhere he desired, Ford chose to leave his native town to follow his brother Francis to Hollywood in July 1914. His options in Portland were limited, had he stayed. Like the other Irish and their descendants in Portland, he could have opened a small restaurant or cigar store, worked for the gas company, as a longshoreman, for the railroad, for the fish packing companies, for the canning companies or hat makers, or he could have become a tailor like his brother Frank, before Frank ran off to New York. He could have become a fisherman, or studied at the local business college to become a clerk or bookkeeper. He could have read law like his cousin Joseph E. F. Connolly. He could have attended teachers' college, or run for office and built a political career, calling in chits from his father's and cousin's connections. Ford's cousins followed all of these paths, but John Ford instead boarded a train to California with friend Joseph A. McDonough. McDonough became an assistant director at Universal Studios, and John Feeney became John Ford.

John Ford's parents moved from Sheridan Street by 1917 and lived at 91 Atlantic Street with their widowed daughter Mary Feeney McLean.[34] By 1930 John and Abby Feeney bought a suburban home at 1609 Forest Avenue near the Riverside Trolley Park, across from the Bailey Cemetery. Ford's parents usually wintered in Hollywood with their sons, and summered at their Peaks Island cottage on Maple Street. Relatives lived in cottages around the corner from them on Winding Way. Ford visited there regularly in the summer.

John Ford's mother, Abby Curran Feeney, died in 1933, and his father, John A. Feeney, died in 1938. They and other family members are buried in the older section of Calvary Cemetery in South Portland, in section N, lot 311–312, near the Sisters of Mercy lot. John Ford died in 1973 and is buried in Holy Cross Cemetery, Culver City, California, along with his brother Francis Feeney Ford. Today the John Ford statue sits in Portland's old Irish neighborhood of Gorham's Corner.

Notes

1. Dan Ford, *Interview with Josephine Feeney*, in the John Ford Collection, Lilly Library, Indiana University, Bloomington, Indiana.

2. John Feeney naturalization information, Index to New England Naturalization Petitions, 1791–1906, microfilm roll F453-F626, New England Historical and Genealogical Society, Boston, MA.

3. Maureen Langan-Egan, *Galway Women in the Nineteenth Century* (Dublin: Four Courts Press, 1999), 112.

4. For example, none of the Tuar Beag, Spiddal Feeneys had children named Daniel. Irish naming patterns call for some sons to be named after brothers and uncles. If Daniel Feeney was one of the Tuar Beag Feeneys, then his brothers and nephews should have had sons named Daniel, and they did not.

5. Castle Garden website, http://www.castlegarden.org.

6. Microfilm, Cumberland County Vital Records Pre-1892, Roll 36, Farrington-Finch, Maine State Archives, Augusta, Maine.

The Feeney family gravestone, front view, in the old Calvary Cemetery in South Portland, Maine, was the burial site of John Ford's parents and other relatives (photograph courtesy Margaret Feeney LaCombe).

7. http://www.portlanddiocese.net/about_feeney.html.

8. Section H, Lot 69, old Lot 584, Calvary Cemetery, South Portland, Maine.

9. See "Little Ireland in the State of Maine," *Portland Sunday Telegram*, Portland, Maine, 16 Oct 1910, microfilm, Portland Public Library. See also Margaret Joy Tibbetts, "The Irish Neighborhood," in the *Bethel Courier* 5, no. 1 (March 1981) in the Maine Historical Society. Thanks go to Michael C. Connolly for this reference, and to Stephanie Philbrick of the MHS for assistance in locating the reference.

10. St. Dominic's Church Parish Records, Volume 5, page 169, presently stored at Sacred Heart / St. Dominic Parish, 80 Sherman Street, Portland, Maine.

11. Roll 19 Portland Maine Vital Records, Deaths, Maine Historical Society, Portland, Maine.

12. Portland Maine Marriage Index 1748–1883, Maine Historical Society. See also St. Dominic Church records.

13. See for example Tag Gallagher, *John Ford: The Man and His Films* (Berkeley: University of California Press, 1986) pages 2 and 31. Also see the essay by Matthew Jude Barker in this volume.

14. "Former Justice Joseph Connolly Dies," *Portland Evening Express*, Portland, Maine, October 2, 1939, pages 1 and 11.

15. Co-editor of this book, Michael Connolly, confirmed this location on his trip to Spiddal, County Galway in July 2006. See his introduction to section two of this volume regarding this discovery.

16. Joseph McBride, *Searching for John Ford: A Life* (New York: St. Martin's Press, 2001) 24.

17. Ibid.

18. "Falmouth Hotel to Close Nov. 1, Says Management," *Portland Sunday Telegram*, Sunday, October 26, 1958, page 1.

19. St. Dominic's Church Parish Records, which are presently stored at Sacred Heart/St. Dominic Parish, 80 Sherman Street, Portland, Maine.

20. Portland Maine City Directories, Tower Publishing, Portland, Maine. Copies located in the Maine Room of the Portland Public Library, and also at the Maine Historical Society, both on Congress Street, Portland, Maine.

21. E-mail to author from Ford cousin, Joseph Majors, 2004: "John Ford's father ran a 'blind pig' somewhere close to the foot of Beach Street hill but I expect that building would be long gone with all the traffic lanes *et cetera* that attend on the Vaughn Street Bridge ... the Feeney/Fords once lived next to, or across from, the Fraternity House down by Fore Street, and I think it also served as a "blind pig" for a time. I don't think Sheriff Emerson Doughty ever closed any of these and, according to Irish folklore, never did close one where 'political contributions' were frequent and generous."

22. Cumberland County Registry of Deeds, County Courthouse, Portland, Maine Book 514 page 152: John A. Feeney buys the Cape Elizabeth farm from Joseph A. and Alice J. Kinsman of Boston for $2400, and assumes a mortgage, on November 13, 1884; Book 526 page 500: John Feeney obtains a mortgage from Cornelius Connolly on December 18, 1886; Book 589 page 470: Town of Cape Elizabeth seizes the farm for nonpayment of taxes on December 28, 1891; John A. Feeney owed $30.36 in taxes in arrears for nine months. Notice of intended sale; Book 976, page 433: Quitclaim deed for Kinsman Farm, 35 acres and two buildings in school district number 8; Book 609, pages 104 and 106: On December, 2, 1893, the estate of Cornelius Connolly forecloses on a mortgage dated 8/16/1886 in Book 528 page 267. The property comprises thirty-three acres in Cape Elizabeth and marshland, called the Kinsman property. Ellen Connolly, widow of Cornelius, published notices of foreclosure in the Maine State Press three times from November 16, 1893 to November 30, 1893. The foreclosure was recorded on December 2, 1893.

23. Portland Maine City Directories, Tower Publishing, Portland, Maine. Copies located in the Maine Room of the Portland Public Library, and also at the Maine Historical Society, both on Congress Street, Portland, Maine.

24. Cumberland County Maine Court records on microfilm at the Maine State Archives, Augusta, Maine; 1881 Nicholas J. Feeney, appellant, court docket #338, sale of intoxicating liquors, and docket #339, appeal of sentence for keeping an open shop on the Lord's Day; 1881 John A. Feeney, docket #343, similar charges; January 1882 term, John Feeney, docket #79 and docket #80 for drinking house and tippling shop; January 1883 term, John Feeney, docket #90; May 1883, Nicholas J. Feeney docket #179 Sept 1883, John Feeney, docket # 279, 280, 290, 298, 327, 338, 356; Nicholas J. Feeney, docket # 334, appealing a July 1882 decision.

25. Death Certificate for Nicholas Feeney, May 18, 1904, Galway 2, District Galway, County Galway, #367, General Register Office, Dublin, Ireland.

26. Obituary of Martin Feeney, *St. Paul Pioneer Press*, St. Paul, Minnesota, Saturday, October 8, 1927, page 15.

27. Portland Maine City Directories, Tower Publishing, Portland, Maine. Copies located in the Maine Room of the Portland Public Library, also at the Maine Historical Society.

28. Ibid.

29. Ibid.

30. Ibid.

31. *http://en.wikipedia.org/wiki/St._Lawrence_and_Atlantic_Railroad*. See also Michael C. Connolly, "Nationalism Among Early Twentieth-Century Irish Longshoremen in Portland, Maine" in Connolly, editor, *They Change Their Sky: The Irish in Maine* (Orono: University of Maine Press, 2004) 277–296.

32. Portland newspaper accounts of those days tell of heart-wrenching tales, like those from Ellis Island, of people who were denied entrance to the United States by customs officials because of eye infections or disease or lack of traveling money, or who arrived in Portland on their way west to find no one waiting to meet them.

33. *http://portland.portlandschools.org/content/mainoffice/history.htm*.

"Portland High School was the third public high school to be established in the United States, and today remains as the second oldest continuing high school in existence."

34. Portland Maine City Directories, Tower Publishing, Portland, Maine. Copies located in the Maine Room of the Portland Public Library, also at the Maine Historical Society.

John Ford's Arrival in Hollywood

Dan Ford

Arrival

John stepped off the train in Los Angeles on a July day in 1914, and as he rode out Sunset Boulevard in his brother's big open car, he smelled scrub oak, sweet eucalyptus, and dusty pepper trees for the first time. Pastels blurred by the periphery of his vision, faded red Spanish tiles, white stucco walls with bougainvilleas spilling over. Los Angeles in 1914 was a place of bright sun, strong shadows, dry heat, and a sense of the desert just over the hills.

The car rattled over the dirt roads and dust boiled up behind it. Francis, wearing riding breeches, jodhpur boots, and a shirt open to the waist, drove expertly and fast. He carried a riding crop and smoked cigarettes and seemed the very epitome of sophistication to his younger brother. Sitting beside Francis was a handsome woman in her early thirties. She had quick blue eyes, a wide sensual mouth, and was dressed in an efficient brown suit. Her name was Grace Cunard; she was Francis' friend, business partner, and lover.

In 1914 Francis Ford was beginning to make his mark as an actor-director of western shorts. John went to work for his brother as an all-around assistant, and the experience and training he got is difficult to imagine in the Hollywood of today. In those pre-union days, John was able to work in every area of film production. He played bits, did stunts, and learned about cameras, smoke pots, explosives, and how to do horse falls with running Ws. He learned about timing, cues, breakdowns, and budgets. By 1916 he was an assistant director at Universal Studios, owned by Carl Laemmle, the diminutive German-born tycoon. To take advantage of his brother's name, he started calling himself Jack Ford. He was in on the ground floor of a budding new industry.

During his first years in Hollywood, John shared a room at the Virginia Apartments, located at 6369½ Hollywood Boulevard, with Hoot Gibson. A former drifter, rodeo cowboy, and veteran of the Wild West shows, Gibson was now a bit player at Universal.

On March 15, 1915, accompanied by much fanfare, Carl Laemmle moved Universal to its present site in the San Fernando Valley. Every employee, including the entire Francis Ford Serial Company, stood by as Laemmle cut the ribbon and walked onto the lot.

The new studio was called Universal City. With its western, New York, and Hong Kong "streets," it was the first truly modern studio. There was one enormous stage that could accommodate thirty-six film companies. Because there was no sound, they could all work at the same time; a comedy scene would be shooting on one set, a barroom brawl on the one next to it.

This is a reprint of the chapter "Success" from Dan Ford's biography *Pappy: The Life of John Ford* (New York: Da Capo Press, 1998). It has been included with the generous permission of the author. The editors have made only minor stylistic alterations and have added header titles for major sections.

R. L. "Lefty" Hough is a crusty, colorful man whose trademarks include a baseball cap cocked back on his head and four-letter words spewing out the side of his mouth. He began in motion pictures in 1915 as a carpenter with the Francis Ford Serial Company, stayed with John as a prop man and assistant director, and eventually became a production head at Fox, a job his son holds today. He remembers the heady atmosphere of Universal City in 1915.

"It was a very exciting place in those days—something was always going on. An elephant would get loose or a tiger would get out and everybody would run for cover. At one time there were forty companies, shooting at Universal, and there were five thousand people on the lot. Whenever one of the other companies would hire a lot of extras, Francis, Jack, myself, and a cameraman named Harry Grant would sneak out and photograph their crowd scenes. Then Francis would go back and write a picture around what we had photographed. If it was a group of Civil War soldiers, then he would write a Civil War picture. If he'd photographed a crowd of Indians, then he'd write a western.

"In those days there were so many companies working at Universal that the sets were all built back to back. One time we were working on a western street and there was a colonial home built behind it. There was an actor by the name of Phil Small, one of those guys who used to lay around on a pillow. He had a woman director named Lois Webber. They were doing a Southern story with girls in big crinoline skirts. They were the first outfit ever to have music on the set: violins, organs and all that sort of stuff. The Ford outfit was making a western on the other side. One day we blew up a bank that was attached to Small's colonial home. There was a huge explosion and this colonial house came down on their laps, musicians, organs, big hooped skirts and all. It's a wonder we didn't kill somebody. Oh, it was a hell of a mess."

Francis Ford

Although Jack often worked as an actor with the Francis Ford Serial Company, he showed little promise in that area, being neither expressive nor handsome. He did, however, show some promise as a writer and was constantly submitting scripts to his brother.

But it was the men with the megaphones—the directors—that Jack Ford admired most. In 1916 the big names were Thomas Ince, Sidney Franklin, Alan Dwan, Tod Browning, and the master of them all, D. W. Griffith. Griffith was then breaking up the static narrative of the stage play with the close-up, the dolly shot, the fade, and the dissolve. He was inventing the new language of film.

From the very beginning, Jack Ford showed an aptitude for directing. By 1916 he was an assistant director in charge of large groups of extras and cowboys. He took control naturally and with ease. Most of the early movie cowboys were veterans of the Wild West shows. Just barely removed from the real thing, as a group they were mean, stupid, and cruel, respecting only rattlesnakes and live ammunition. These were the men Jack Ford had to keep sober and get to the set on time. Then he had to run them through their scenes. Alan Dwan, who by then was already a prominent director, recalls how Jack Ford did it:

"Jack Ford was a leader and he could handle men. He used his own language when he lined the cowboys up. There wasn't any 'Please step over this way.' It was, 'Come on, you bastards, get in line and shut up.' He was only twenty years old, but there was no doubt about who the boss was.

"He was a natural director. He wouldn't just say to a bunch of cowboys, 'Come over the hill and yell.' He'd give them all specific pieces of business. He'd say, 'You there, when you ride over the hill, throw your hat up in the air; you over there, get shot and fall, and you, I want you to get shot at the top of the hill but make it all the way down before you keel over.' He'd pick those things out for himself. He directed the crowd scenes and he was starting to make a name for himself. He wasn't directing principals, but he was directing."

Throughout 1916 and 1917, Francis ground out two-reel serials. Their plots were primitive by today's standards, but they were the usual fare for their time. There was *The Broken Coin*, a fifteen-episode serial in which Francis and Grace Cunard search for two halves of a coin because it has a map to a buried treasure on it. There was *The Lumber Yard Gang*, in which detective Phil Kelley (Francis Ford) chases Dan McLean (Jack Ford). There was *Peg o' the Ring, The Bandit's Wager,* and *The Purple Mask.*

Francis was a man of many talents. He was an excellent actor, a sure-handed director, and a fluid, graceful writer. But Francis wanted to be his own boss, to have full control of his pictures, and in 1917 he left Universal to go into independent production. He opened his own studio, The Francis Ford Serial Company, on Beachwood Drive, between Sunset and Santa Monica boulevards. The day he moved in, Francis posed for photographers, straight-backed and proud, his arms crossed in front of him. He was a man at the peak of his powers.

Francis found his new freedom intoxicating and worked from sunup to midnight, grinding out serials of every description. He wrote them, directed them, and starred in them. But he was a creative man, not a factory manager; an artist, not a businessman. The added responsibility of running a studio proved too much for him; he spread himself too thin, and the quality of his work suffered. Within a year he was back at Universal as an actor-director under contract.

Because it divided the European market in two, World War I gave a tremendous boost to the American motion picture industry. British films could not be seen in Germany, and the varied and excellent German films couldn't be seen in the Allied countries. American films, however, were distributed throughout Europe, and during World War I Hollywood became the world center for motion picture production, a position it never relinquished. But America's isolation ended in April 1917, when the country entered the war. Everyone John had grown up with seemed to be getting involved, as suggested by a 1917 letter to John from his sister Josephine: "The old crowd seems pretty much broken up. There was no draft in Portland. The enlistments were so large and above the quota that they took no one. Fat Riley from the West end is in France with Jimmy Walsh and have already been fired on. Bet they wish they were back 'doing' Congress Street...."

Unlike many of his contemporaries, John never served in World War I. Because of their propaganda value, motion pictures were declared an essential industry, and he was given a deferment. The expansion of the American movie industry during the war gave John the opportunity he was looking for. In 1917 he directed his first film, a two-reel short called *The Tornado*. He wrote it, directed it, and worked in it as an actor. Then, with the breakneck speed with which he would lead his entire life, he followed it with another two-reeler called *The Scrapper*. Jack Ford had made it — he was now a director. In September 1917, he signed a contract with Universal that called for "The Universal Film Manufacturing Company" to "employ the employee as director in and about the business of producing plays and scenes for moving picture films." His pay was $75.00 a week. Along with his contract he received a memo from the Universal front office containing the following list of things not wanted in the company's pictures:

"Stories dealing with the ruin of young girls. Black jacking. Excessive smoking. Fake wallops in fight scenes. Cowboy stories which get over the idea that cowboys are either always drunk, getting drunk, drunk fighting, or looking for a fight. Stories requiring inserts and long explanatory titles. Maudlin displays of patriotism. Insanity. Hunchbacks. Mugging in close ups. Rats. Snakes. Kittens. Pie slinging contests. Preachments. Propaganda. Drinking scenes. Bar room brawls. Sissies. Heavy dames. Men, especially policemen and detectives, who are constitutionally incapable of removing their hats when entering a room in the presence of ladies or in any other way showing the least sign of impoliteness."

In three hectic years John Feeney, a lace-curtain Irishman from the State of Maine, son of a saloonkeeper, had become Jack Ford of Hollywood, California, director of action-packed western films. He was twenty-two years old.

Harry Carey

Francis Ford was John's first great teacher and his first great professional influence, but it was John's teaming with silent star Harry Carey that paved the way to his eventual success. Ford and Carey made twenty-three films together, and when their partnership ended John Ford was a first-rate action director.

Harry Carey's widow, Olive Golden Carey, is one of the senior members of the old "John Ford stock company." I've known her all my life and look on her as part of my family. Crusty, outspoken, and profane, a genuine character with plenty of salt, she is part gypsy, part circus, part carnival, and all Hollywood. In her own inimitable way, she remembers how Harry got started in motion pictures and how he got teamed up with John Ford:

"Harry was from New York, and his father was a judge in White Plains. He wanted to follow in his father's footsteps and went to law school at N.Y.U.. In those days there was a whorehouse down in the village called Madam Moran's, and one day Harry got stiff and stole Madam Moran's picnic drawers, those big things with ruffles and lace, and put them up on a flag pole. They expelled him from school for that.

Francis Ford, the older brother of John, who was the first to change his surname from Feeney to Ford. He was a successful silent film actor and pioneering director and, after 1914, mentor to John Ford in his early years in Hollywood (courtesy Kenneth E. Thompson, Jr.).

"Harry drifted around for a while then, playing semi-pro baseball and working here and there. Then he went back to law school and graduated in the same class as Jimmy Walker, but he got pneumonia and never did take the bar examination. While recuperating, Harry started reading a lot of western history and became an absolute nut on the subject. He read someplace that no play that actually had a live horse on stage had ever failed, so he decided to write a western melodrama with a horse. It was called *Montana*. He got some dough together, took it out on the road, and it cleaned up. After touring the country, Harry joined D. W. Griffith's American-Biograph when it was still in New York and came to California with Griffith in 1913. I met Harry two years later when I went up to San Francisco to make a movie for O.A.C. Lund. Harry was the leading man, and I fell for him like a ton of bricks. We got married right away. After that, he came down to Universal and signed a contract for $150.00 a week.

"Harry was working with a director named Fred Kelsey and they weren't getting along. Jack Ford was on the lot working for Francis, and one day he came over to the set. Harry and Jack got to talking. Jack was so responsive that they just clicked, that's all. That started the whole damned thing. Harry went to Laemmle and said he wanted Jack to be his director."

Jack Ford and Harry Carey went to work grinding out two-reel, or twenty-minute, western shots. Most of the shooting was off-the-cuff, often as not, with no script, only a rough continuity that John had blocked out. Then in July 1917, they wrote a feature-length script called *Straight Shooting*. They presented the idea to Universal, but the studio told Carey and Ford to stick to their two-reel format. The two men had nothing to lose but their shirts, so they went ahead and made the picture as a feature without Universal's knowledge. To get enough raw stock John claimed that he had accidentally dropped his film in a stream and needed another 4,000 feet. When they finished, they presented Universal with a ninety-minute feature, a *fait accompli*. Incensed at their insubordination, the studio wanted to cut *Straight Shooting* back and release it as a two-reel short, but Irving Thalberg, Carl Laemmle's executive assistant, intervened. In August 1917, it was released as a feature-length film and was an immediate hit.

In 1965, a print of *Straight Shooting* was uncovered in Prague. It is the oldest John Ford film known to exist.

Straight Shooting was surprisingly sophisticated for 1917, with its strongly defined plot, real rhythm, and subtle bits of characterization. Many aspects of the film suggest that John had carefully studied the work of D. W. Griffith. There is one sequence where the cattlemen assemble their forces, salute their leader, and ride into ranks that exactly copies a parallel scene, the assembly of the Klansmen, in *The Birth of a Nation*.

With the success of *Straight Shooting*, Universal scheduled a whole series of Harrey Carey features, and the Ford-Carey team went to work turning out a feature-length western every six weeks. Billed by Universal as "Harry Carey's and Jack Ford's Just Plain Westerns," they had titles like *The Secret Man, Three Mounted Men, A Woman's Fool, The Phantom Riders, A Scarlet Drop, Hell Bent, Roped, Riders of Vengeance,* and *Bare Fists*. They used all the basic dime-novel western plots: sin towns with corrupt sheriffs, stories about gold or silver mines, railroad right-of-ways, and gun runners or whiskey peddlers stirring up the Indians. There were family feuds, range wars, cattlemen vs. sheepmen, and cattlemen vs. farmers. If all else failed, there was always the classic standby: a hero's search for his father's murderer.

For young Jack Ford this was a time of hard work and of growth. Working twelve hours a day, seven days a week, he learned invaluable lessons about story, construction, exposition, and plot. Every day there was a new light effect or camera angle to try, and with every picture his characteristic style emerged. The Harry Carey westerns, made with small budgets and under great pressure, forced John to shoot quickly with a minimum number of setups, to keep the camera stationary, and to use simple shots rather than opt for intricate compositions. Working under this kind of pressure taught him the greatest lesson of all: to find the beauty in simplicity. In the dry alkaline canyons around Newhall, where most of these films were made, John was drawing the blueprints for an entire career.

Even during these early years John showed an inclination for working with familiar and congenial collaborators. On the Harry Carey pictures, he formed bonds with actors J. Farrell McDonald and Mollie Malone, cowboys Vester Pegg, Cap Anderson, and Duke Lee, and cameramen Jack Brown and George Schneiderman.

Perhaps the most fascinating character in this group was a thickset man with a handlebar mustache named Edward Zachariah "Pardner" Jones, a great marksman and trick-shot expert who, as one of Wyatt Earp's deputies, had helped his "pardner" Earp sweep the pimps, dicemen, and gamblers of Tombstone.

But of all John's professional and personal relationships, the one with Harry Carey was by far the most important. Carey was a boss, a teacher, and a Dutch uncle. Ollie Carey remembers them together: "They were working in Newhall, around Placerita Canyon, and we were spending so much time out there that we decided to move to Newhall. We rented a little joint and all lived together. There were six of us: Jack, Harry, myself, George McConigal, Pardner Jones, and Teddy Brooks. We had this funny little three-room house, but Harry and Jack wanted to be pioneers, so we had to sleep in the alfalfa patch in bed rolls.

"At night they would sit around this little tiny kitchen with a wood fire going in the stove and drink Mellow Wood. They would talk, talk, talk, late into the night and Jack would take notes. They molded the whole thing between them and the next day they'd go out and shoot it. Every once in a while Universal would decide they needed a story department so they'd hire some writers and send us these *terrible* scripts. Harry and Jack would take one look at them and say, 'Christ, that's horrible,' then throw them away and go back to their own stuff. They had a strange and funny relationship. Harry was eighteen years older than Jack, had graduated from law school and had been in pictures for about ten years, but Jack still held his own. Harry started out as the dominant one, but Jack was catching up awfully fast."

The Harry Carey pictures established John as a first-rate action director and gave his career a dramatic upward turn. His salary went from $75 a week in 1917 to $150 in 1918 and $300 in 1919. Adopting the *de rigueur* life-style of a Hollywood director, he bought a 1916 peacock blue Stutz with a long hood, high fenders, enormous wheels, and a canvas top. He dressed in jodhpur boots, khaki twill riding breeches, and hunting jackets that he bleached white with gasoline.

But if John's salary had doubled and doubled again, it was nothing alongside Harry Carey's, which went from $150 a week in 1917 to $1,250 in 1918 and a staggering $2,250 in 1919. The discrepancy between John's $300 and Carey's $2,250 became a point of real tension between the two men, since John couldn't help but feel that he was entitled to more of the spoils of their success.

With his new affluence Harry Carey adopted one of the most flamboyant lifestyles in Hollywood. He bought a 3,000-acre ranch near Newhall and built an adobe ranch house with walls three feet thick, high beamed ceilings, a tile roof, and massive fireplaces. Carey's ranch was like the backlot of a movie studio. There were chuckwagons, covered wagons, stagecoaches, and corrals filled with Appaloosa ponies. He even brought sixty Navajo Indians from their Arizona reservation and had them live on his ranch. They built hogans, raised sheep, and brought their life-style intact to California. On Sundays, in a small canyon near his ranch house, Carey staged Wild West shows and invited his friends to come out, sit in the shade, sip warm whiskey, and watch the trick roping, the bronc riding, and the bulldogging. The Carey ranch was a western showcase, a place where Harry Carey, western actor, could live out his fantasies, bridging the gap to the "real" West. But Carey's lifestyle, like his salary, aggravated the tensions between him and his young director.

In the summer of 1919 John and Carey undertook their most ambitious film together, an adaptation of Bret Harte's "The Outcasts of Poker Flat." Then, in November 1919, they made *Marked Men*, based on a Peter B. Kyne short story called "Three Godfathers." It was their last picture together.

Success and Marriage

The following month John was loaned to the William Fox studios to direct two Buck Jones westerns, *Just Pals* and *The Big Punch*. This was exactly the opportunity that he had been looking for. Fox was a bigger studio than Universal and made a more sophisticated product. When John's contract at Universal expired a few months later, he became a contract director at Fox, at a salary of $600 a week.

Since stepping off the train in 1914, John's rise had been nothing short of meteoric. In six years he had risen from his brother's stunt double to a leading action director, and although he was still a long way from realizing his future greatness, by 1920 Jack Ford was a prominent man in the Hollywood community.

But success is sometimes more difficult to deal with than failure, and if there were a recurring problem, a dominant theme, weaving through this period, it was John's difficulty in dealing with success. Jealousy, competition for money and recognition, had undermined the Ford-Carey relationship. Most important of all, it brought on an identity crisis as John began to molt his Irish skin and replace it with an American coat. For the first time in his life John felt rootless and lost.

On Saint Patrick's Day, 1920, at a party given by director Rex Ingram, Jack met a woman with long dark hair, delicate bone structure, and fine classical features. Her name was Mary McBride Smith. John was completely taken with her elegance, style, and natural good humor. It was a wild, hot-blooded time for courtship. The Volstead Act had been passed in October 1919, and America was discovering just how thirsty it really was. No longer afraid of being branded with Nathaniel Hawthorne's scarlet letter, women were throwing off their corsets, smoking cigarettes, and dancing the Hesitation Waltz. It was the era of speakeasies, hip flasks, tin lizzies, white mule, bathtub gin, Al Capone, Bugs Moran, Valentino, and Theda Bara. From radios and victrolas came the sultry sounds and jungle rhythms of a hot new music called "jazz."

John and Mary had a whirlwind romance. They went for long drives out to the beach in his open Stutz and ate quiet dinners at the Ship's Café on the Venice pier. They went to all the speakeasies: the Clover Club on Sunset, Lucy's on Melrose, and the Little Mill down in Watts. On July 3, 1920, John and Mary were married. Their first home was a bungalow at 2253 Beachwood Drive in Hollywood. The following October they moved to a stucco house perched precariously on the side of a hill, at 6860 Odin Street, in the "Majestic Heights" section of Hollywood. They paid $14,000 for it, and Mary furnished it with conservative wooden furniture. In April 1921, Mary gave birth to an eight-pound, ten-ounce son whom they named Patrick, after John's older brother. It was an unabashedly Irish name, chosen as though to reaffirm John's roots, to implant the future with the seeds of the past.

On the surface, it looked like an ideal match. Mary was bright, sharp, cynical, strong enough to stand up to John and to live with his boundless energy, while still being supportive of his career. But deeper down, there were some very basic differences between the two. Mary had North Carolina Presbyterian blue-blood roots. She was a direct linear descendent of Sir Thomas More and traced her family in America back to the seventeenth century. A number of Mary's uncles and cousins had gone to Annapolis and West Point; an uncle, Rupert Blue, was the Surgeon General of the United States; and Mary's father was a wealthy Wall Street speculator. Mary had money and family, and John was very much aware of both. Although he wouldn't have admitted it, he had married above himself.

Back to His Roots

While class consciousness continued to be a problem for John, rootlessness did not. During these years a bloody revolution was being fought in Ireland, as Irish nationalists, Sinn Féin, largely financed and encouraged by the Irish community in the United States, struggled to break away from British rule. "The Troubles," as they were called, were of great interest to John, who studied the papers for news of Dáil Éireann, of Patrick Pearse and De Valera. John's father was a generous backer of Sinn Féin, and the cause of Irish nationalism brought the two back into contact. The Troubles gave father and son things in common that they hadn't had in years.

Family portrait: Son Patrick, left; daughter Barbara, center, standing; father John, right; and wife, Mary, sitting (with the permission of Dan Ford; courtesy Lilly Library, Indiana University, Bloomington).

John became so caught up in the Irish Revolution that in the fall of 1921 he decided to go to Ireland and get a firsthand look at the war. On November 19, 1921, he boarded the *S.S. Baltic* in New York and sailed for Liverpool. During the trip he wrote Mary a chatty account of his travels. It reads in part:

"Dear Old Fruit, on board S.S. Balls-tic. I am going to keep a sort of diarrhea for you about happenings on board—(with the proviso, of course, that I am able). We are just leaving. I am glad you are not on the wharf with that throng of handkerchief waving maniacs.... We are approaching the Statue of Liberty. What a sight. It recalls the old saying of the cheapskate who would not pay a nickel to see the old gal piss over the Brooklyn Bridge. Will write more later. Adios.

"5:30 PM: Darling, I am sorry to say that I am slightly skunked. Yes Sir! Burned! I also have hiccups. Mary, how I wish you were with me. Gosh, we would have had such a wonderful trip. It's really wonderful on our boat. I have spent the entire afternoon in the *BAR* drinking Bass Ale and feel quite wonderful (except for the hiccups). Honey, the first opportunity we get you and I and Pat shall take a sea trip because every night I think how Mary would love this. I think that after Emmett [Fox Director Emmett Flynn] and I finish our contracts, I shall persuade him to take Jean and then we all can take a trip around the world. How I wish you were with me....

"As soon as I landed in Liverpool I left for Ireland. The boat I traveled in across the Irish Sea carried Michael Collins and Arthur Griffith, the returning Sinn Féin delegates with Lloyd George's proposals to Dáil Éireann. We were only twenty minutes from Holyhead when we cut a fishing schooner in two and sank her. Three of the crew were drowned and although we cruised around for an hour we found no bodies. The shock of the impact was terrible. When we struck, the boat shivered and rocked for quite a while before she straightened out....

"At Galway I got a jaunting car and rode to Spiddal and had a deuce of a time finding Dad's folks. There are so many Feeneys out there that to find our part of the family was a problem. At last I found them.... Spiddal is all shot to pieces. Most of the houses have been burned down by the Black and Tans and all the young men had been hiding in the hills.... Cousin Martin Feeney (Dad's nephew) had been hiding in the Connemara Mountains with the Thornton boys. I naturally was followed about and watched by the Black and Tan Fraternity. Tell Dad that the Thornton house is entirely burned down and old Mrs. Thornton was living with Uncle Ned's widow while his sons were away...."

The trip to Galway was one of the most important experiences in John Ford's life. Its significance goes far beyond the making of contact with relatives. The Martin Feeney to whom John's account refers was an IRA cell leader with a price on his head, hiding from the Black and Tans, the British military police. Martin Feeney is still alive today, a man in his mid-eighties with reddish cheeks, wispy white hair, and a farmer's rough hands. He recalled for me how his cousin John sought him out in the hills to give him food and money. The British, he says, knew who John was and were hoping he'd leave the country before he got involved in any "incidents." He also says that his cousin [John] was repeatedly stopped and questioned by the Black and Tans and was at one point "roughed up pretty well" by them. After two weeks in Galway John was picked up by the British, put on a boat bound for England, and told that if he ever returned to Ireland he would be imprisoned.

This trip helped resolve the identity crisis that had grown out of John's success and his marriage. John had found a facet of himself that he would never forget — his Irishness. In Martin Feeney's words, "He has been back many times since then, and although he was rich and famous he never felt he was above us. He felt that we were his people and this is where he really belonged."

Reflections on the Battle of Midway: An Interview with John Ford (August 17, 1943)

John Ford: This is Commander John Ford, USNR. I am in command of the field photographic branch of the Office of Strategic Services. This is a photographic branch among other things. Most of the people in our outfit — officers and men are from Hollywood. They are writers, directors, some actors, but mostly technicians, electricians, cutters, sound cutters, negative cutters, positive cutters, carpenters, and that sort of thing.

About 1932 my old friend Admiral Frank Scofield, who at that time had the flag in the fleet and Captain Herbert Aloysius Jones ("Baldy" Jones, as he is known to the Navy) got me to return to the Naval Reserve and to organize a photographic [movie-making] section. He thought at that time that in the future, the future emergency, it would be of value; so I came back and organized this outfit. I was called into active service in August, 1941, and started planning. Before Pearl Harbor we had gone to Iceland, and made a complete [film] study there, a complete [film] study in Panama. After Pearl Harbor I was asked by the Secretary of the Navy and the Secretary of War to go to Honolulu and give a factual photographic [film] account of the action there. So I left with a crew about January 4, 1942 and arrived there about twelve days later and got to work.

We found Pearl Harbor at that time in a state of readiness. Everybody had learned their lesson from Pearl Harbor. The Army and the Navy — all in good shape, everything taken care of, patrols going out regularly, everybody in high spirit — was courageous, [in a] spirit of hope [that] I have ever seen. I was particularly interested in our new blue jacket [US Navy enlisted men]. He was a man of unlimited education, background, he had evidently left a good trade. He was a fighting man. In a few months I was to see what a good fighting man he was.

The first task force I went on — I was called by Admiral [Chester W.] Nimitz [USN] on the phone. I knew him quite well, [and] he said, "Throw a bag together and come out here and see me." So I left immediately and went out to Pearl Harbor [and] saw him. He told me to report to Admiral Bagley. I left there immediately and went down to the Harbor, got into the speedboat and caught a destroyer that was leaving. Got on board while it was in motion, while she

---

These are the recollections of Commander John Ford, United States Naval Reserve (USNR), concerning his experiences making combat motion pictures under battle conditions. Ford commanded the OSS Field Photographic Branch during World War II. His footage of the Japanese attack on Midway was the basis of his subsequent Oscar-winning documentary film *The Battle of Midway* (1942). This adapted interview has been included with the kind permission of the United States Department of the Navy's Naval Historical Center in Washington, D.C. The co-editors have made only minor stylistic alterations and stayed as close as possible to the adaptation and transcription by the original editors, capturing the spontaneous flow and occasionally fragmented course of the original interview material. Bracketed items are editorial insertions by the original editors.[1]

was underway. Hadn't the slightest idea what I was doing, where I was going. I found out when I got on board that the destination was Midway.

After we had been out a couple of days, we picked up a flotilla of PT [high-speed wooden motor torpedo] boats—I think we picked them up at French Frigate Shoals—refueled them, and gave them food. It was the first time I had seen the PT boys. And that, gentlemen or ladies, whoever is listening, that is really an outfit, that is really a wonderful group of boys. I have nothing but the utmost admiration for them. We proceeded then to Midway. I think at the time there was some report of some action impending some place or some movement in the seas, [since] everything and everybody was on KV [a form of alert].

I proceeded to make a pictorial [film] history of Midway. I photographed the Gooney Birds, I photographed the PTs and all that sort of thing. I didn't believe much in the impending action, if it did come I didn't think it was going to touch us. So I worked, spent about twelve hours a day in work, had a good time up there, a wonderful station. On June 3rd, my friend, Massy Hughes, Commander Massy Hughes, asked me to take the [aircraft] patrol with him the next day. He said (he speaks in a southern accent), "Well, it looks like there is going to be a little trouble out there—" To resume, Massy Hughes, he says, "Well it might be some trouble tomorrow, you and I are too damned old for this war anyway, so we better take the easy dog leg." That was the northeast triangle [segment of the aerial patrol route]. So we got aboard, took off, it was very, very cloudy weather, didn't see anything for a long time, finally the radar picked up something, [and] we presumed it was one of our task forces. About sixty miles off we saw through a rift in the clouds as we started to go over, we suddenly saw a couple of cruiser planes coming for us. Taking a quick look, we realized they were Japanese. We hadn't any idea that we had seen their task force so Massey did a quick bank, got up in the clouds, stayed there for a while, finally ran out of clouds. We got down to about three feet from the water and really got some speed out of that old PBY (twin-engine patrol bomber seaplane, known as "Catalina"). At one time he said he thought he was doing about eighty-nine miles an hour. We managed to get back.

It's too bad we just saw the task force for a moment, it was so far away, otherwise I might have gotten a good picture of the disposition and so forth, but we did get a pretty accurate, just in a flash, we got a pretty accurate view, you could tell pretty much what was there.

The next morning—that night we got back and evidently something was about to pop, great preparations were made. I was called into Captain Semard's office, they were making up plans, and he said, "Well, now Ford, you are pretty senior here, and how about you getting up top of the power house, the power station, where the phones are?" He said, "Do you mind?" I said, "No, it's a good place to take pictures." He said, "Well, forget the pictures as much as you can, but I want a good accurate account of the bombing." He said, "We expect to be attacked tomorrow."

And he told me to do the best I can, get out, lay out my phones. I had some wires, two phones with the wires leading to the command dugout, and then I had a sea phone, stationed those, got everything ready. Tried them out, went to bed that night, upstairs, got a bedroom there, went to sleep and early the next morning everybody had breakfast. There were about eight Marines in the power house with me. I think the alarm (of course, I haven't any notes)—but the alarm went off, I imagine around 6:20. So everybody took their stations and Midway became sort of a deserted island.

I imagine the Japs when they attacked thought they had caught us napping, there was nothing moving, just a lazy sort of a tropical island. Everything was very quiet and serene. I had a pair of powerful binoculars with me and finally spotted the Japanese planes. I picked them out to be Zeros [Japanese fighter-bomber planes], by what in picture identification we thought would be Zeros. They evidently were. The first flight I saw there were about twelve planes. They

Ford in naval uniform, most likely instructing a camera class for members of his OSS Field Photographic Branch aboard his yacht *Araner* (with the permission of Dan Ford; courtesy Lilly Library, Indiana University, Bloomington).

were coming at about 10,000 feet, so I reported this to the command post, told them that the attack was about to begin. Everybody was very calm. I was amazed, sort of, at the lackadaisical air everybody took. You know everybody sort of took to the line of duty as though they had been living through this sort of thing all their lives.

Suddenly the leading Jap plane peeled off. As he peeled off, evidently the Marines [fighter planes] who had left earlier got the rear plane which went down in flames. I photographed that, but my eyes were sort of distracted by the leading plane, the leader of the [Japanese aircraft] squadron who dove down to about five thousand feet, did some maneuvers and then dove for the airport. We have all heard stories about this fellow who flew up the ramp on his back, but it was actually true. He dove down to about 100 feet from the ground, turned over on his back and proceeded leisurely flying upside down over the ramp. Everybody was amazed, nobody fired at him, until suddenly some Marine said, "What the Hell," let go at him and then shot him down. He slid off into the sea.

But by this time, of course, everybody had been watching this fantastic thing and by that time Hell started to break loose around there, and, of course, the high altitude bombers started to come in. The Zeros evidently—what I took to be Zeros had evidently some sort of small caliber bombs. They started to plaster the ramps or the airfield. They did a very neat job. They went up and down and got the outside area. They didn't touch the field itself—I imagine their idea was to land there later that day themselves. They didn't drop any bombs on the landing mat itself, but did a thoroughly good job of dropping (I would say) 200 pounders [bombs] up and down outside. Of course, I mean the [American] planes had all been pretty well scattered and they didn't get any and, as I was saying, about this time the high altitude [Japanese] bombs started dropping. This I reported to Captain Semard. Forgot to try to count [Japanese] planes and [do] photography. I got a pretty good estimate, I estimated about, that I saw with my own eyes, I would figure there was from fifty-six to sixty-two planes.

By this time the attack had started in earnest. There was some dive bombing at objectives like water towers, [they] got the hangar right away. I was close to the hangar and I was lined up on it with my camera, figuring it would be one of the first things they got. It wasn't any of the dive bombers [that got it]. A Zero flew about 50 feet over it and dropped a bomb and hit it, the whole thing went up. I was knocked unconscious. Just knocked me goofy for a bit, and I pulled myself out of it. I did manage to get the picture. You may have seen it in [the movie] "The Battle of Midway." It's where the plane flies over the hangar and everything goes up in smoke and debris, you can see one big chunk coming for the camera.

Everybody, of course, nearly everybody except the gun crews were under ground. The Marines did a great job. There was not much shooting but when they did it was evidently the first time these boys had been under fire but they were really well trained. Our bluejackets and our Marine gun crews seemed to me to be excellent. There was no spasmodic firing, there was no firing at nothing. They just waited until they got a shot and it usually counted.

The planes started falling, some of ours, a lot of Jap planes. It seems when you hit a Zero plane, it almost immediately goes into flames. At least that was the impression I got. One [Japanese] fellow dove, I think he was going to [attack] the clubhouse. He dove, dropped a bomb and tried to pull out and crashed into the ground. The place that I was manning, I didn't realize, the power house, but they evidently tried to get that. I think we counted eighteen bombs, some big, some 200 pounders, some 500 pounders, that dropped around that. I would say that the Jap high [altitude] bombing was bad. I don't know whether they hurried or not, but they were not hitting their objective. Of course, incendiaries set fire to the wooden buildings. It seemed as though they were doing a lot of damage, actually they were buildings that had been used since the Pan American [Airlines, which had previously had a trans-Pacific seaplane fueling outpost] gave up there. They hit an oil tank, but it was an old unused oil tank that hadn't any oil in it and then there was a fake plane in the center of the field and they really wasted a lot of time blowing that up. They strafed [machine-gunned] it and finally dropped a 200 pounder [bomb] on it. They really — they lost about three planes trying to get that fake plane, as it came into a cone of [American] fire that was pretty dangerous.

During this, I suddenly saw the PT boats which were circling around, open up [begin firing]. They did a tremendous amount of damage. The Japs couldn't figure what the Hell they were and they really gave the place a wide berth. I would say the PTs were responsible for about three planes and they drove the fighters and low bombers — they pretty well drove them off, because that thirteen boats out there were [with] those multiples 50s [.50-caliber heavy machine guns], that is too much fire power, they put up an awful blast.

The raid wasn't over, still a few bombs dropping now, but of course, you couldn't restrain the bluejackets. I mean they would run out when a plane would fall. There was about fifty bluejackets around it [the crashed Japanese plane] trying to haul the Jap out of the plane, getting souvenirs, and you would see some ensign or j.g. [lieutenant junior grade] screaming, "Get the Hell back there" and the fellows would look and they would go back. They were all pretty jolly about it.

The Marines with me — I took one look at them and I said, "Well this war was won." They were kids — oh, I would say from eighteen to twenty-two — none of them were older. They were the calmest people I have ever seen. They were up there popping away with rifles [Marines at that time were armed with bolt-action M1903 .30-caliber rifles], having a swell time and none of them were alarmed. I mean the thing [a Japanese bomb] would drop through, they would laugh and say, "My God that one was close." I figured then, "Well, if these kids are American kids, I mean this war is practically won."

I was really amazed, I thought that some kids, one or two would get scared, but no, they were, they were having a time of their lives. Each one of the eight claimed he had brought down a [Japanese] plane with rifle fire. They certainly fired enough at them, they had a good time. Of the eighteen [Japanese bombs] dropped around the power house, one finally grazed the corner off and filled the place full of smoke and that caused these kids to start looking for me. They came in and bandaged me up and said, "Don't go near that Navy doctor, we will take care of you, this guy over here, Jones, is a swell doctor." Talking right under fire like that, it was very interesting.

Well, finally the attack was over and we went around counting heads. What made it unfortunate, they made one hit on a dugout, that a Marine detachment was in on Sand Island, I think they killed about sixteen men there. Of course there were quite a few casualties, dead and wounded, but that was a lucky hit, and that was just too bad. Otherwise the bombing didn't mean anything. As we know now, I guess it's no secret, Midway was not really protected at the time, I mean, it was sort of a peacetime station. We had very few 20 mm [anti-aircraft guns], had no 40 mm's [anti- aircraft guns] and even at that time there were quite a few 30 caliber machine guns there, which strangely enough they did very, very effective work. The Marine gunners and our Navy gunners were really excellent, I have never seen a greater exhibition of courage and coolness under fire in my life and I have seen some in my day. Those kids were really remarkable, [and] as I said before, I figured, "Well, this war is over, at least we are going to win it if we have kids like that."

There are no incidents that I can report, I mean there is nothing particularly. Oh, I did see, I did see one of our kids jump in a parachute, I think it was a Marine flyer. It was quite a distance away and I had, that is, I couldn't photograph it. I had to look at it through my [field] glasses. This kid jumped and this Zero went after him and shot him out of his [parachute] harness. That was observed by about eight people. The kid hit the water and the Jap went up and down strafing the water where he had landed [and] even sunk the parachute [and] filled that full of holes, which I thought wasn't very chivalrous at the time. I only prayed to God that I could have gotten a picture out of it. That was verified. A lot of people did see it.

Pretty soon the Marines [fighter pilots] started back, a lot of them badly shot up, some had to make emergency landings on the field. And, well, we all went about our job, taking care of the wounded and getting things ready and putting out fires, which was very, very quickly done. Then, of course, after that, I mean things were exciting for the next two or three days. Planes kept coming in and going out. We got reports of the [naval] battle and the submarines came in and after the battle, after a few days we went back to the peaceful routine.

That night, I forgot to say, a [Japanese] submarine came in and started shelling the island. He came up, I imagine, about a mile away and I heard the first rumble and I ran out there and saw him fire. He fired about six times. I think he was firing at the airfield but his shots were way over. One Marine five-inch [coastal defense artillery gun] let go and I am positive he got a hit on the submarine because there was a yellowish greenish flash out there, and from then on we didn't hear any more from the submarine.

It was very amusing — a very amusing incident occurred there, this Marine Sergeant was sound asleep, really tired and one of the kids ran up and said, "Hey, Sergeant, wake up, wake up, God Damn it, we are being attacked," and he [the Sergeant] started pulling on his mattress. And he said, "Where, where, what is it?" And he [the young Marine] said, "A submarine," and he [the Sergeant] said, "Oh, shaw!" and went back to sleep.

Interviewer: Commander, I understand you must have been very busy, because they gave you a citation for the reports you sent in, and you yourself said you were quite busy taking pictures.

Commander Ford: Well, evidently the reason that Captain Semard and Captain Logan Ramsey sent me up there, they figured I was a motion picture man and naturally should have a photographic eye so I made a pretty good choice, because I knew what I had to do and that was to count planes which I immediately did. One of the Marines stood by me and checked and we double-checked, and so I think that my count of the [Japanese] planes was official. As far as the citation was concerned I think it was more for being wounded in an exposed position and not leaving my post. Well, Hell, you couldn't leave your post, there was no place to go.

But my report was pretty good and as I say I have a photographic eye and we are used to that sort of thing, reporting, taking battle scenes, and mob scenes and notice every detail and that's why I probably would notice a lot more than the layman who is not trained for that sort of thing. Like the chap that did the flying upside down and was noticing the Jap that shot that kid out of his harness. Things of that sort immediately photograph themselves on my memory.

Interviewer: Commander, from your account I take it there were no planes on the ground except that decoy plane you spoke about?

Commander Ford: No, they [the American planes] had all pulled off early in the morning. The PTs had flown back to French Frigate Shoals. After all these [Japanese] planes were picked up coming in the radar, they were picked up on the radar and so we had about, I think, nearly a half-hour's warning. Of course, the Marines took off about twenty minutes before [Japanese] planes arrived and as a matter of fact, as we know, they attacked the first five planes coming in and did a Hell of a good job. So there was nothing on the ground for them [the Japanese attackers] to hit, so I presume when the Japs came, they thought the planes were on the ground well dispersed to the side of the field, covered with camouflage. That's why they did such a good job of blasting that portion of the field. They did a very good job of systematically plastering both sides of the runway. Oh, there was one other plane on the ground, that was Captain Semard's duck and that caused them a lot of trouble. They blew that up. But the thing that really caused them the trouble was that fake plane. I mean they really went for that thing. I imagine they have put that in use since so it is pretty well exposed.

Interviewer: Did anyone get the Jap that had strafed the man, our man in the parachute?

Commander Ford: That I can't say, Sir, I don't believe so, because he went to the clouds later on. I would like to meet him myself some day, Sir.

Interviewer: So would I.

Commander Ford: You're asking about the African invasion. We were in England, assigned to Admiral Stark's staff there, requested by the Army to cover this operation, for them. They evidently hadn't enough cameramen at the time. And, of course, we wanted to go along to cover it from our own Navy standpoint.

We left Greenwich [in England] about noon one day. [We had] a very interesting journey up the Clyde [in Scotland] to see these ships in full daylight pulling out, [and] the factories along the side started their horns a'tooting and people yelled and screamed, and I sort of had the premonition then: "Well, the thing is about to start, I think we are going to take over this war." Seemed like old days.

It was the first emotion I had seen displayed in this way on the part of the [British] civilian population. It was really quite a wonderful sight if you know the Clyde. It's not very wide and as we ploughed, its banks were lined with people, factory whistles blowing and a few people out with flags. I remember particularly one, someone, had a small American flag waving it like the dickens there. It was quite an inspiring sight. The outfit I was with was mostly — well I should say about 85% British, parachutists, commandos, different combat units, then we had a signal corps unit under a Colonel Dobbs, which was a very, very good unit.

We proceeded out, continued down the coast, headed around Ireland, and down the — I think we went due west for about a day and a half and then suddenly we went south and made for Gib[raltar]. Strangely enough, there was nothing seen all the way down. We didn't, I mean we might just as well have been on a pleasure cruise. Lovely weather, sun was shining, everybody stripped down and getting tanned. [We] hit Gibraltar one night and proceeded to go through it [i.e., the Straits of Gibraltar]. Nothing happened at all, didn't even pick up Italian submarines. [We] got there [and] loaded into L.T. [tank landing craft] boats and went ashore. I had a particularly easy time. Our landing wasn't contested at all. As a matter of fact, I didn't hear it, but there was a report that a very indignant French official came down, the French always came down[,] and bawled somebody out for being three hours late or something. I didn't know anything about that, I didn't see it so I don't know, but that was the report that was going around.

I remember one funny incident happened, we were groping around in the dark, I had my camera equipment and I ran into a fellow and we started talking. He said, "What are you doing?" I said, "I'm a photographer, I don't know what the Hell I am doing here in the middle of the night trying to photograph." He said, "What about me? I'm a psychiatrist." So that was that.

Then we came in — there was a lot of sniping going on and they [the Allied forces] took over the town. I think everything went according to plan very beautifully. It is more interesting. We left Algiers with these tank landing craft, with the 13th Tank Landing Regiment and we went up the coast to Bone, we traveled at night, hide up in the daytime. Usually about half an hour after we would leave a port, the German planes would come over and blast Hell out of the town, evidently looking for us. By that time we would be sneaking along the coast. We saw a flight of Italian planes near sundown, [but] they just couldn't quite figure out what we were. We had no protection with us, [but] we had a fishing schooner that is acting as a guide, a fishing schooner with an auxiliary motor. Of course, the tanks had the machine guns pointed up. These Italians, I don't imagine they quite knew what we were and so they didn't make an attack.

We landed at Bone. Of course, there was no opposition there, some aerial activity. The Germans were making sporadic [air] raids there. About every hour or so they would come over in waves of ten to twenty-five and, but I thought their bombing was very bad. They would come over and let go and try to get away and the place was jammed full of shipping and occasionally they would hit a French fishing smack or a tugboat or something, but they never seemed to get these landing craft that the tanks were on. I thought their bombing was bad, they would do a lot of damage in the town, burn down a lot of places.

From there we proceeded with the 13th right on through as far as Medjez el Bab, where we contacted the enemy. We stayed with them [the 13th Tank Landing Regiment] a couple of weeks. It was very, very interesting. My Chief Petty Officer, Ronald J. Pennick, Jack Pennick, who was quite a well-known picture actor, happened on an old Marine pal. He [Pennick] was with the Peking [Peking, China, U.S. Marine] Legation Guard in 1912. He's been with me for twenty years. He did a good job, proved he was a good soldier, did quite a stunt up there, was decorated by the Secretary of the Navy with the Silver Star, for gallantry.[2] We saw quite a bit of action. Finally, by that time, the Signal Corps cameramen started to arrive so we were ordered out, came on back. I think the experiment of learning how to use landing craft was very good. I think it was a good thing we went in there because we found out the deficiency of a lot of the stuff. They take the personnel barges in and you couldn't get off quickly enough, the next wave would beat them out so they were just helpless, starting to broach. I think they have fixed that since then, I know the one we went in on, I sat alongside the kid [the coxswain who steered the landing craft] and told him to ride it like a surfboard. He jammed her right up on the beach so we did all right. But it was a great experiment. I think it helped our ultimate success in Tunisia and Sicily. [That is] the experience these lads got out of handling these boats.

Interviewer: Commander, in the first landings were our soldiers—did they have full marching order equipment? Did they have them on then or were they light so they could take care of themselves in the water?

Commander Ford: Well the outfit, of course, the men that I landed with were British and they were in very, very light battle gear, very light battle order. Their stuff came from the ships later. I understand a lot of the boys got weighted down with the equipment. As I said, we had no trouble, our fellows landed in, I think the British refer to as, light battle order. They are in battle dress and carried canteen, rifle, ammunition, but no overcoats or blankets, or any heavy gear of any kind. They were pretty mobile when they landed.

Interviewer: The general system is to land the personnel at one point and the equipment at another. Is that right, Sir?

Commander Ford: I don't know.

Interviewer: I noticed some of the later operations, they reported that they do that. Commander, I don't recall that you mentioned the name or type of the ship that you were on when you went down the Clyde.

Commander Ford: Well, I forget the name of the ship, she was one of the—she was a Duchess boat. Wasn't the *Duchess of Athol*, or *Duchess of Richmond*, I forget what it was. She was one of the old Duchess boats that runs from—run from Montreal to England, some very fine boats. Food was especially good, accommodations were good, it was a very, very neat boat. I can't remember the name of the boat, I have been on so many. I would have to refer to my diary, to my notes on that. There were quite a few Duchess boats. As a matter of fact, I think they were three or four in that particular convoy. All boats are similar types, I would say passenger ships from eighteen, oh, about fourteen to eighteen thousand tons.

Interviewer: You were in some action there on land?

Commander Ford: You mean at Algiers—Tunisia? Oh, yes. Yes, we were there about three weeks under heavy dive bombing and artillery firing all the time, [German Luftwaffe] Junkers 88' [bombers] and that sort of thing.

Interviewer: How did the marksmanship of the Germans compare with the Japs?

Commander Ford: I thought they were pretty much on a par. You were referring to their bombing, Sir?

Interviewer: Yes.

Commander Ford: I thought their bombing was pretty bad. Of course, those dive bombers, the German dive bomber, has a lot of guts, they would come right on through and try to do their stuff. But I thought their bombing as a—generally was bad. It seemed to be hurried, they tried to do it and get away with it. But I don't think they had the precision that our fellows had. I know the only thing that interested me, when they piled all our gear on the center of the of the field one day and I asked Pennick, "Well, where's our stuff?" And he said, "In that pile." And I said, "Good heavens they are going to take that for an ammunition dump." He said, "Aw, well, that's just what I told 'em." Just then it went up, that was the best shot they [the Germans] made. We lost all our gear. But their bombing is hurried, I don't think it compares with ours, only that's my own opinion, Sir.

Interviewer: Commander, these pictures that were taken at Midway, and Africa, where do they eventually end up? I mean, is there any arrangements made so that these pictures can be taken care of for future generations?

Commander Ford: Oh yes. That is very thoroughly and systematically done. Those [motion] pictures are censored, sent on to a common library for the services and processed so that they will be preserved for centuries. Very, very well taken care of. Each picture will reach its proper destination eventually.

Notes

1. These de-classified reflections were adapted by their original editors from Commander John Ford, USNR, interview in Box 10 of World War II Interviews, Operational Archives Branch, Naval Historical Center, Washington, D.C. The de-classified document, entitled "Narrative by Comdr. John Ford, U.S.N.R., Photographic Experiences from Pearl Harbor, December 7, 1941," is dated as follows: "Recorded: August 17. 1943." This document was provided with the generous permission of the Naval Historical Center by Kathleen M. Lloyd, Head of the Operational Archives Branch.

2. Chief Petty Officer "Jack" Pennick, USNR, was a well-known character film actor whose body of work spanned the period from silent films to the 1950s and included many John Ford films, including Ford's classic World War II drama *They Were Expendable* (1945).

We Shot D-Day on Omaha Beach:
An Interview with John Ford

Peter Martin

Who saw D-Day in Normandy twenty years ago? No one man really saw it, for its stage was as big as the world and its actions were as big as history.

While Nazi Germany held all of France after the fall of Dunkirk on the English Channel in 1940, we amassed huge forces in England. In an operation called *Overlord* we committed them to the perils of the sea and the German-held invasion beaches of the French Normandy Coast, starting at the base of the Cotentin Peninsula at 0015 hours on the morning of June 6, 1944.

Since Dunkirk, millions of men and women had lived, worked, suffered, prayed, died—so that this invasion of Hitler's fortress would come off. The British had licked their wounds, and rallied behind the indomitable spirit of their Prime Minister. They clawed away at Hitler's air force as the Luftwaffe tried to pound their island soft for a German invasion. On the Continent, a valiant and vigilant underground army somehow endured, risking torture and firing squads for themselves and their families and friends to hamstring the German occupation forces in a thousand secret ways.

After June 1940, the fight grew more difficult as, one by one, the remaining European nations joined Hitler or were crushed by the weight of his military forces. Hungary, Romania, and Bulgaria allied themselves with the Nazis. Only Yugoslavia and Greece resisted. In April and May 1941, they in turn fell before the German Wehrmacht. In all Western Europe only Sweden and Switzerland [and the Irish Free State] remained neutral. Then suddenly in June 1941, Hitler turned eastward, invaded Russia, and England gained a new ally. Two months later the U.S. Congress, prodded by President Roosevelt, voted lend-lease aid to save Britain from a collapse boded by her African defeats and shipping losses to U-boats.

The Japanese attack on Pearl Harbor on December 7, 1941, brought our own country into World War II. The year that followed was the darkest of the entire war for the Allies. In the Pacific the Japanese captured everything in sight. They were even on the frightening verge of invading Australia. In Africa, Rommel's *Afrika Korps* swarmed into Egypt like the plague of locusts Joseph said would best Pharaoh. Soon it would be within striking distance of the Suez Canal. In Russia, German armies, penetrating the Caucasus, attacked Stalingrad. During most of 1942, U-boats were sinking Allied ships in the Atlantic faster than they could be built and launched!

But General Montgomery, with the help of lend-lease tanks and equipment, stopped Rommel in October at El Alamein; and the Russians held at Stalingrad. The following month, our

This article first appeared in *The American Legion Magazine*, June 1964 (14–19, 44–46). The editors have made only a few minor stylistic alterations to the original article.

armies under General Eisenhower invaded North Africa to help the British and Free French defeat the *Afrika Korps*. By May 1943, this was accomplished. Meanwhile, in February, the Russians had fought the Germans to a standstill at Stalingrad, mounted a huge counteroffensive and captured nearly a third of a million Nazi troops.

With each victory the Allies gained new momentum. From Africa we launched our attack on Sicily, then Italy. That country surrendered in September 1943, though the German forces there did not! It was on June 5, 1944, *one day before D-Day,* that Rome was captured. Not until the war's end in 1945 was northern Italy mopped up with finality.

With the invasion of Italy under way in 1943, and the submarine menace declining in the Atlantic, the Allies began to establish the huge base of operations in England that would make it possible for us to invade Fortress Europe across the English Channel.

Throughout the rest of 1943 and early winter of 1944, preparations continued at a frenzied pace. The Russians were impatient at the delay, for the Western invasion of France would ease German pressure against them in the East. In England the race was against time and tide. Unless the invasion took place during early June, H-hour could not be triggered and set for the prized combination of early dawn and the lowest tide. Without this combination, thousands of underwater obstacles and mines would not stand exposed to be avoided or destroyed by the invading landing craft and troops.

Somehow, by an effort that now seems incredible, almost two million men were assembled in England. On D-Day, some 160,000 managed to get ashore on the French Coast. This was a day for which the world had waited anxiously for years. Hearts skipped beats and fingers were crossed around the world while the ebb and flow of events on the Normandy beaches were in question. Failure would throw the free world into gloom. The answer to the question "What now?" in case we were hurled back was one that people hoped they would never have to provide. All that first day, until word came that our troops had begun to plunge inland, hearts pounded while millions clasped their hands and bowed their heads in prayer.

Despite the fears of *Overlord*'s planners (and possibly *because* of them), Allied casualties on D-Day, June 6, 1944, were much lighter than had been anticipated. The Allies lost between 10,000 and 12,000. Of these, approximately 6,600 were American, the rest British and Canadian. German casualties were a third of the Allied total, though by the end of June they reached about a quarter of a million, including prisoners.

Nobody who was there really saw the operation. The anxious people all over the world who pieced together the news reports with bated breath saw more of it; the intelligence officers putting bits of information together for the high command and the heads of the contending nations saw it. The Army historians saw it later as they wrote the Normandy invasion into the Army's huge history of World War II. But the participants didn't see it. Each saw his own little acre; his own piece of treacherous, churning water; his own sweep of beach; the bluff ahead that he had to mount against the fire from that house, that cliff; his own comrade who just fell on the sand.

The very first forces ashore were troops of our 82nd and 101st Airborne Divisions who dropped on the Cotentin Peninsula behind Utah Beach the night before. They saw little of the mighty world drama; in the dark, they even had to find one another out by ear, snapping five-and-dime cricket toys as signals. The crew of the old battleship *Texas* stood with the offshore armada to give heavy artillery support for the landing waves. Though it was daylight, they saw but a part of the invasion. Little spotting planes, droning low over the coast, were the *Texas*' eyes to tell it via radio where to fire.

There was one man there on Omaha Beach whose sole mission was to see the invasion for the world, and for history. He was John Ford, the movie director and producer. What did it look like to him?

Ford ... has had a career studded with top cinema awards for such films as *The Quiet Man,*

The Informer, The Grapes of Wrath, How Green Was My Valley, The Long Voyage Home, Stagecoach, and *Tobacco Road*. After painting motion picture classics with film, he was one of those given the assignment of preserving on movie film the history of the Normandy invasion for posterity. He drew Omaha Beach as his "location" and as a result didn't see Utah Beach at all. But on Omaha, the acting was real enough and so was the shooting.

This winter I found a tired John Ford back in California between takes of a movie he was directing in Wyoming. He'd talked very little about D-Day in the last twenty years. "What is there to tell?" he asked at first. "My story is in the film we shot! Millions of feet of it!"

Finally he said that the real-life drama he remembers most vividly of all in his film-making career was the tragedy and triumph of D-Day. "Not that I or any other man who was there can give a panoramic wide-angle view of the first wave of Americans who hit the beach that morning," Ford said. "There was a tremendous sort of spiral of events all over the world, and it seemed to narrow down to each man in its vortex on Omaha Beach that day. My group was there to photograph everything we could for the record. In the States, as *Overlord* got under way, the film *Going My Way* with Bing Crosby and Barry Fitzgerald was a smash hit. I had nothing to do with it, but the title was somehow appropriate when I remembered what we were starting in Normandy."

Ford was head of the Photographic Department of the Office of Strategic Services under General "Wild Bill" Donovan. The cameramen in his unit were attached to the Coast Guard and trained for every sort of action. They could drop by parachute, land with raiders, commandoes, infantry. They knew about amphibious landings. All Ford had to do was name it. They could do it. He'd hand picked his group of helpers. They were a superb team. Ford was told to head that team up and get both color and black-and-white footage of the invasion of Omaha Beach from start to finish.

He was in London when Wild Bill gave him the word. Ford (as well as practically everybody else) knew the invasion would start soon. He and his outfit had been in the British Isles for quite a while readying themselves for their part in it. Two high-ranking officers talked out of turn at parties about the impending invasion. Ike broke them both back to pre-war rank — one major general to a lieutenant colonel — and shipped them to the United States with a devastating reprimand.

Ford's team had been alerted for several days. There had been no passes for the men. They loaded $1 million worth of camera gear on the destroyer *Plunket*. By June 3 they were set. They went off in convoy on the night of June 4, only to be called back. Bad weather off the French Coast. The next day, June 5, was even worse, but there was a good chance for a Normandy landing in spite of the bad weather. The meteorological experts reported the weather would let up for a while in France, long enough to get the landing started. As it happened, the "bad weather" was the worst Channel storm in forty years. D-Day, originally set for June 5, was postponed in the middle of a raging gale. Hundreds of ships that had set off for their rendezvous the day before headed back to port. Others flopped around blindly at sea, waiting, their crews and the troops aboard furious, seasick, underfed, weakened by the storm. Finally, at 0415 hours, June 5, while winds of near hurricane force snarled, the meteorologists told Ike and his staff that they would slacken the following morning, and stay fairly clear for thirty-six hours. Ike polled the staff. Some said yes; others were doubtful. Finally there was a silence and everyone waited tensely for Ike to make the decision as Supreme Commander. Later it was said by some that he deliberated between fifteen and twenty seconds, others stated that he took two minutes, even as many as five minutes, before looking up and saying, "Let's go ... I don't see how we can do anything else."

Jack Ford says, "When we did start we were the last ship out in our huge convoy. There were more than fifty other convoys, some bigger than ours. Nobody was quite sure just how many ships there were in all, at least 4,000 though, I heard later. Nothing like it ever in the

English Channel, not even the Spanish Armada, 356 years before. I went below for a minute or two and suddenly our flotilla was switched about and we were headed in another direction, which put the old *Plunket* in the lead. I am told I expressed some surprise at leading the invasion with my cameras. What I'll never forget is how rough that sea was. The destroyers rolled terribly. Practically everybody was stinking, rotten sick. How anyone on the smaller landing craft had enough guts to get out and fight I'll never understand, but somehow they did; and well, too. We hadn't heard President Roosevelt's hastily scheduled radio address a few hours earlier about Rome having been taken by the American and British forces pushing up the Italian peninsula. I did read later that he gave no hint about *Overlord*, saying only of the three Axis capital cities: 'One down and two to go.'

"The *Plunket* dropped anchor close inshore off Omaha Beach about 6 A.M. Things began to happen fast. It was extreme low tide and all the underwater obstacles put there by the Germans stuck out crazily like giant kids' jackstraws with mines and shells wired all over them. There were demolition teams on the first landing craft that were supposed to blow such things out of the way for the landings to follow. As the first landing craft started past the *Plunket*, I could see the troops bailing with their helmets, stopping to heave their guts out every few throws. In the closer LCMs and LCVTs I could even *hear* them puking over the noise of motors and waves slapping flat bows all the way to the beach.

"I remember looking with pride at the battlewagon *Texas* anchored to our left," Ford told me. "She was one of our old, old battleships, not new like the *Wisconsin* or the *Arizona*. I was listening on the radio to TBS, the talk-between-ships. The *Texas* had artillery observers both ashore and in recon planes overhead who spoke back to them and gave directions about knocking out certain points of German defense on the coast. Of all the rounds the *Texas* fired she only missed once. The only trouble was that for some reason nobody, not even we, expected the flight overhead of all our little L-4s and L-5s-observations planes; and we apparently shot most of them down ourselves. Poor fellows. As a result we were short on observers for a couple of days until we got more on shore. I heard later that U.S. plane production was being cut back that same month. And the Government apparently had just cancelled a contract for 800 cargo planes after the Budd Manufacturing Co. had built only four of them. If we hadn't gotten ashore that day, a hell of a lot of plans would have gone down the drain. They must have been awfully sure of success back in Washington.

"The fog and mist cleared away shortly and it became full daylight. The cloud cover didn't go away, however. When our fleet of heavy bombers went in to clobber the beaches, they bombed blind through solid cloud and their bombs fell way inland. That was another mess. They had been supposed to blanket the beaches, the Nazis' machinegun nests, observers' posts, big gun emplacements. This would explode a lot of mines in the sand, make convenient craters in which our men could take cover at first, and stun or knock out a lot of enemy gunners. I expect they planned to scare them, too. The Germans opposite us were supposed to be Russian or Polish 'volunteers' and service troops. Unhappily, when our bombs missed the troops opposing us they turned out to be a tough infantry division that had been moved up for rest and training without our intelligence finding it out. When they finally opened up with fire power, it was tragic what they did to us.

"Everyone had held his breath while the naval bombardment was going on. We wondered about the complete absence of return fire. Not a shot from shore all the time our landing craft headed in. When our fire lifted just below our first LCVTs began to blow up on the obstacles, we thought they were going to make it without any opposition from the coast. Then the Nazis opened up and hellish fast, too.

"Troops were jumping over side into the water so they wouldn't have to wade through streams of machinegun fire when the bow ramp dropped. Then some of the tanks with flotation gear started going by. I saw two take direct hits, or hit mines. Others had their canvas flotation gear punctured and sank like stones. I don't believe more than one or two climbed out on the beach near us. The tanks were supposed to give mobile, close-in artillery support while our men were getting past the sea wall to knock out the pillboxes and machineguns, but they didn't have a chance. Neither did the LCMs bringing in bulldozers and more tanks. They really caught hell. Later I heard that only three bulldozers out of thirty or forty made it. I also remember seeing landing craft swing out of control and smash against obstacles where they touched off a mine and blew sky high. On a later day, much later, I discovered that it was this very week that the first U.S. shipyards were getting ready to lay off hundreds of men as wartime orders slackened.

"At one point, just before we went ashore with the second wave, our ship, the *Plunket*, was banging away at a stone building just behind the beach. I said to the captain, 'I wouldn't think the Germans are stupid enough to stay in there. It's too prominent. I bet if you raised your guns and fired at that little house back up there, you might stir up something.' He fired a couple of shots at it, and by God, the place spewed German troops like a hornets' nest. It erupted.

"The objective of my outfit was simple — just take movies of everything on Omaha Beach. Simple, but not easy. The skipper of the *Plunket* loaded us into DUKWs. About mid-morning they went off shoreward. I remember watching one colored man in a DUKW loaded with supplies. He dropped them on the beach, unloaded, went back for more. I watched, fascinated. Shells landed around him. The Germans were really after him. He avoided every obstacle and just kept going back and forth, back and forth, completely calm. I thought, *By God, if anybody deserves a medal that man does.* I wanted to photograph him, but I was in a relatively safe place at the time so I figured, *The hell with it.* I was willing to admit he was braver than I was.

"The discipline and training of those boys who came ashore in the later waves of landing craft, throwing up and groaning with nausea all the way into the beach, was amazing. It showed. They made no mad rush. They quietly took their places and kept moving steadily forward. Anyone can have hindsight, there is no trick to that, but it is still hard for me to realize that back home in the nightclubs 'Pistol-Packin' Mama' was making the audiences sing, clap and stomp.

"From the *Plunket* I recall vaguely seeing a landing craft off to my right hit a mine and suddenly go up, and another tangled in an underwater obstruction swinging around in crazy, uncontrolled circles. Most of the kids on board got off and waded ashore. Once I was on the beach I ran forward and started placing some of my men behind things so they'd have a chance to expose their film. I know it doesn't make it blazingly dramatic, but all I could think was that for the most part everything was all so well coordinated, fitted perfectly, went beautifully. To my mind, those seasick kids were heroes. I saw very few dead and wounded men. I remember thinking, *That's strange,* although later I could see the dead floating in the sea. I also remember being surprised at how much closer the *Plunket* looked from shore, much closer than the shore had looked a few minutes earlier from the *Plunket*! Thoughts are funny things; they wander. I recall wondering how our troops in the Pacific felt. A couple of weeks later they invaded Saipan to establish airfields for the B-29s.

"My memories of D-Day come in disconnected takes like unassembled shots to be spliced together afterward in a film. I can't remember seeing anybody get wounded or fall down or get shot. I passed men who had just been hit. I saw one group get out of a landing craft and make a rush to their assigned positions. As they rushed they passed two men on the ground who had been hit. They glanced at the two for a minute. They knew that the medical corpsmen would reach them right away. One of the two who had been wounded managed to rise and stagger to cover. The other had to be dragged. It was a good thing that the previous month the U.S. pharmaceutical industry had produced a record-breaking 100 million units of the new wonder drug penicillin. The Army had the highest priority. It needed it.

"To tell the truth, I was too busy doing what I had to do for a cohesive picture of what I did to register in my mind. We stayed on our job and worked that day and for several other days and nights, too. When you concentrate on a job the way we did, there was no time for sightseeing. I was reminded of that line in *The Red Badge of Courage* about how the soldiers were always busy, always deeply absorbed in their individual combats. In this awful seesaw, the people who were actually there on the beaches only saw the thing the way I did. In my case, it is the extreme example of the narrow view of the participants, because my staff and I had the job of 'seeing' the whole invasion for the world, but all any one of us saw was his own little area.

"At first when our outfit hit the beach, we ran for cover. Then we made for the hills, pausing to expose film footage here and there. I'm not sure of the name of the main town just back from the coast — Colleville-sur-mer? If I'm right, that means Colleville-On-the-Sea. After that the Germans made their first stand. Actually, I had expected that we'd meet much more resistance from the Germans on shore, but after all it was a surprise attack. As we began silencing or capturing their guns one at a time, the fighting in our immediate sector slackened and no German reinforcements appeared.

"The Germans thought our landing craft were going to zero in on Pas de Calais, 240 miles northeast, Europe's closest point of land to England. The Air Force had run all kinds of diversionary movements over that spot and in considerable strength. Our bombers had plastered Calais for weeks. As a result, the Germans were concentrated there. I read later that Hitler had said that we would land where we did, but Rommel disagreed with him. Later each changed his mind and accepted the other's opinion. But since the net result left them still on opposite sides of the fence, that didn't help them very much. Hitler held back his Panzer reserves to meet the expected attack on Calais until it was too late for them to counterattack before we had a foothold. In addition, Allied paratroopers who went in the night before D-Day had captured roads and bridges so far inland that it made it difficult for a counterattack to be assembled and set in motion. The German High Command had recently ordered the word 'catastrophe' eliminated from all military reports and the German vocabulary in general. As I recall it, the only counterattack launched on D-Day was against the British. But the B.E.F. had been able to land their tanks and anti-tank guns so they stopped the Germans cold just inland from the beach on their way to Caen.

"At any rate, it turned out that Rommel was in Germany for his wife's birthday. I guess we can be damn grateful he wasn't at headquarters in LaRoche-Guyon when we landed. God knows it was terrible enough without him. We'd heard from a British woman, interned by the Germans and repatriated a week earlier, that the German people were supposedly terrified of being invaded. German newspapers were publishing conflicting reports every day, guessing at dates and locations of the Allied landings. The German troops sure didn't act terrified!

"As I think back on it now, I doubt if I saw — really saw — more than twelve of our men at one time. Looking back, I saw the *Texas* and the heavy cruisers still firing. At the end of that day when I listened to the TBS, the only battlewagon I listened to was the *Texas*, but the others probably had records just as good. It's amazing how accurate they were, and how effective the observers were on shore. They were Navy radiomen and they pinpointed just about everything.

"Omaha Beach had cliffs that had to be climbed straight up from the edge of the sand. The plan was for the Rangers to mop up the Germans on top at the fringe of the cliffs. Those Rangers swarmed up ropes. Somehow they got up those cliffs. I was there, but I don't really know how they did it. I think they shot the ropes with grapnels upward with special rocket guns. I was told later that the ropes got soaked in the rough seas coming in and were so stiff some rockets couldn't shoot them to the top, and the Germans leaned out and dropped grenades on the attackers as they shinnied up the rope. I only remember that vaguely as a part of all that went on around me. I was busy concentrating on my immediate job, and looking after my unit.

"How would I describe my job?" John Ford said, when I asked him. "Unofficially, I was in charge of cinematography, but in all honesty I was really more or less a logistic officer. It was up to me to see that everybody who should have a camera had one. I take my hat off to my Coast Guard kids. They were impressive. They went in first, not to fight, but to photograph. They went with the troops. They were the first ones ashore. They filmed some wonderful material. Fortunately, most of them came through well. There were a few casualties. I lost some men. It is a coincidence that one of the cameramen who works for me today—his name is Archie Stout—had a son in my outfit. He was one of the two photographers who rode ashore on a Phoenix concrete breakwater. He rode his Phoenix all the way over from England photographing everything in sight. He did a fine job riding that big box. He got a Silver Star for it. Later, he was to be flown back to England to sign his papers for a commission for which he certainly qualified in every way. On his way, even before he'd left France, a lone German fighter popped out of nowhere and shot him down. He's buried there in a cemetery where the landing was. That cemetery was a new one and Stout's was one of the first graves there. I've been back to it several times to leave flowers.

"I think it's amazing that I lost no more, when you consider how much some of them were exposed to fire, although I wouldn't let them stand up. I made them lie behind cover to do their photographing. Nevertheless, they didn't have arms, just cameras, and to me, facing the enemy defenseless takes a special kind of bravery. When a man is armed with a gun he's probably much braver than if he doesn't have one.

"In action, I didn't tell my boys where to aim their cameras. They took whatever they could. Once they got ashore they just started photographing our troops in different groups rushing to their assigned places. Not that they rushed wildly, they rushed with a definite purpose. After they got ashore, they made for a certain objective. There was no panic or running around. I've often wondered why they didn't run faster. Probably they weighed too much with all their equipment on. They hurried, but there was no frantic dash, just a steady dogtrot.

"I remember meeting Col. Red Reeder on the beach. I knew him well and I met him a long time later when I went to West Point to do a picture, *The Long Gray Line*. On D-Day, Red was sitting with one leg smashed so badly it had to be amputated. 'Got any orange juice?' he asked me. I said, 'Orange juice! What the hell would I be doing carrying orange juice? How about a shot of brandy?.' We had been issued little bottles of brandy in case anybody needed it. Doggedly he said, 'No, I want orange juice.' I said, 'Colonel, I'm afraid that's something I can't get you, but I can help you get back to our ship which is close in. Once there you can get some aid.' He said, 'No, I just want some orange juice.' Red and I had a laugh about that long afterward at West Point. In a moment of crisis, people get funny fixations. I asked him, 'Why didn't you take that brandy?' He said, 'I don't know. It's the first time in my life I ever refused a drink of hard liquor. All of a sudden I was pure. As a matter of fact, I don't even like orange juice.' He was in shock, and as I've said, they had to cut off his leg in an emergency operation.

"The film my men took was processed in London, in both color and black-and-white. Most of it was in Kodachrome. It was transferred to black-and-white for release in the news weeklies in movie theatres. All of it still exists today in color in storage in Anacostia near Washington, D.C. My cutting unit was in London, too. They worked twenty-four-hour watches, picking out the best part of the film that had been shot. I'm sure it was the biggest cutting job of all time including the cutting done for the recent picture *Cleopatra*. The cutters worked four-hour shifts—on four, off four. Allen Brown, the producer, now a captain in the Reserve, was in charge. There were literally millions of feet of film. When Brown's unit saw something they liked, they pressed a button, and put clips on that portion of film. When they cut the stuff all they did was cut at the places marked by those clips. It saved a lot of time. Very little was released to the public then-apparently the Government was afraid to show so many American casualties on the screen. After all, even *The New York Times* best-seller list that summer had only six 'war books' on it out of a total of thirty.

"As I've said, I don't think I ever saw more than a dozen men at one time on that beach. That's all my eye could take in. For that matter, I don't think anybody on the beach saw more than twenty at the outside. After all, they all were attacking in small groups. They were trained to do that. The first wave consisted of about 3,000 men, and not all of them got ashore alive. Numerically, that wasn't so many really.

"I don't remember just when we reached our first inland village, but I do remember that on my way there our troops ahead were smoking out a nest of Germans on the edge of the town. They had no artillery support, so they sneaked up with flame throwers. It turned out that the house held five Germans and three female French collaborationists.

"As I remember it now, the shells the *Texas* fired must have been twelve-inch jobs. They made a big sound, but the odd thing was how they looked. They gave off yellowish smoke—and instead of rupturing the ear drums of listeners they made a dull boom. Sixteen-inch guns shattered ear drums, but the twelve-inch ones went boom like an explosion going off inside of a mine. The sixteen-inch guns were murderous. You had to stuff your ears with cotton if you were too near them. They tell me Omar Bradley used cotton. He must have been on one of our big battlewagons. I didn't see him, but I did see young Teddy Roosevelt near Utah Beach on D-Day plus three or four. We had met in Scotland where my unit trained nearby. I thought him a fine man. He didn't last very long after he landed.

"He was the principal founder of The American Legion back in 1919. While he was alive he did twenty men's jobs and was awarded the Medal of Honor. He didn't know that because a heart attack killed him on July 12. He just kept going up and down Omaha Beach with the walking stick under his arm, very neat, very presentable, getting things done, directing traffic, giving orders to the men running up to him. His boss, Terry Allen, who was in charge of the First Division, was a lot of man, too. That was twenty years ago and even now I don't know too much about what an Army general's job is, but when I met Terry and Teddy, the impression I got was that they were both good men doing efficient jobs.

"My unit shot motion pictures of the whole Operation Mulberry, too—the construction of the man-made harbor facilities designed to handle 8,000 tons of supplies a day. In the end it handled more. A fleet of old ships was brought across the Channel and purposefully sunk, nose to tail, in a row offshore. This bit was named Operation Gooseberry. It began on the second day. Those ships caught quite a bit of German artillery fire. Each time we sank one the Germans reported to Goebbels that another enemy vessel had been sunk by glorious German fire. On D-Day plus three, by the time the Nazis figured out what was happening, most of those ships were in position and the first of the big concrete Phoenix breakwaters was being pushed into position and sunk. There was an outer line of floating steel breakwaters, too. Finally came the three piers running from the beach straight out to deep water. These were called Whales, and LSTs came right up to them and unloaded in less than an hour. The operation was a triumph for an idea conceived by Britain's Lord Louis Mountbatten. Two years earlier he had made the revolutionary suggestion of taking our own seaport along with the invading forces instead of trying to capture the heavily defended French ports. The other brass hats laughed at him at first—though never to his face.

"That was quite an improvement over beaching LSTs, unloading and floating them off twelve hours later to fetch another load, which is what was done until the Mulberry harbor was finished on D-Day plus ten. They called the operation Mulberry because the mulberry is sup-

Ford (left) and Chief Petty Officer "Jack" Pennick, USNR. Pennick was a cameraman in Ford's OSS Field Photographic Branch unit and a character actor in many of the director's films. In his interview on D-Day, included in this collection, Ford identifies his wife Mary as a member of the Harold T. Andrews American Legion Post in Portland, Maine (see sign in photograph) (with the permission of Dan Ford; courtesy Lilly Library, Indiana University, Bloomington).

posed to be the fastest growing tree. I never did figure out any of the other code names. Maybe that's why the secret was kept so well — no one else could either.

"A few days later, on the nineteenth and twentieth, when a gale hit and destroyed practically everything, I had some of my unit station themselves on one of the Phoenix caissons. It was blowing like hell and I was out in a small boat picking them up. As I was heading in, somebody yelled at me from an old English ferryboat, a sidewheeler, one of the decrepit old Brighton excursion boats. I could see it was a chief petty officer yelling, 'Hi, Jack! Hi, Jack!' I looked at him, waved and asked, 'Who is it?' Then I recognized Ian Hunter, the actor, who afterward worked with me in *The Long Voyage Home*. Hunter played the English officer in that film. He was as surprised to see me as I was to see him. He yelled, 'What are you doing here?' I yelled, 'Damned if I know. What are you doing?' Hunter said, 'Damned if I know either.' It was a brief encounter because I was concerned with getting my boys off and ashore. The gale messed up the painfully assembled and constructed Mulberry harbor. Landing craft of all kinds broke loose and piled into docks and breakwaters. My photographers got plenty of footage of that 'for historical purposes.' It was as bad a Channel storm as the first one, if not worse. It was weeks before the harbor was straightened out, though supplies continued to get ashore somehow. That is the best I can do twenty years after D-Day. This is the first time I've ever talked about it.

"I would like to say to *The American Legion Magazine* readers that I am a lifetime member and so is my wife, Mary. We were both given our silver lifetime membership cards in 1955. Mary was a nurse in World War I. She is a member of the Harold T. Andrews Post in Portland, Maine. I'm not much of a joiner. The Legion is the only organization I belong to. We're proud of it, and proud of the American soldiers we have known over the years.

"One other thing. I guess it's the only Hollywood attribute I share with stars: John Ford isn't my real name. My real name is Sean Aloysius Kilmartin O'Feeney." Ford paused while we both thought about D-Day in Normandy and all over the world.

There is small doubt that the preparation for and the launching of *Overlord* was the most important military movement ever made by this country, with the possible exception of the marching, re-marching and bloody dying of men wearing blue and gray near a small sleepy town in Pennsylvania called Gettysburg. Even there only our soldiery was involved; not our Navy, our Marine Corps, our planes, our Coast Guard, all blended into one mighty spearhead of men as they were on Utah Beach and Omaha Beach, with the British and Canadians on more beaches to the east. And although the world stood on tiptoe, its hands cupped around its collective eardrums for the first word of how we did there, in its crazy, natural, sometimes silly and inconsequential way life went on elsewhere.

The day before Operation *Overlord*, a fairly important thing took place as Rome fell and Allied troops marched into it. In China, squadrons of new super-fortress B-29s were being readied for their first attack on Japan (the first U.S. raids since the Dolittle "30 Seconds Over Tokyo" group had made its gallant gesture two-and-a-half years before). Just about that same time, a famous name in show business was singing in New York with Mary Martin. Eddie Cantor sang: "We're Having a Baby, My Baby and Me." [On one of the early shows the network eliminated the sound throughout the entire second verse. At the last minute it felt that the lyrics needed censoring.]

In Vincennes, Indiana, Mrs. Lyndon Eberly and her daughter, Helen, heard on the radio that their soldier, Sgt. Richard Eberly, twenty-one, had been one of the first to be landed by air in France. The Eberlys were praying. At 3:30 A.M. in Marietta, Georgia, the bell of the Methodist Church began to peal; by 4 A.M. every church was lighted, and in every church people prayed. Aloud or in their hearts, plain men were not ashamed to say what General Eisenhower said in his Order of the Day to his men: "Good luck, and may the blessing of God go with you."

In Japan, German correspondents in Tokyo writing for their newspapers revealed much that was not meant for U.S. eyes. When the Japanese Government closed all theaters, newspapers complained: "The hard-working population cannot live on patriotic speeches and moral sermons alone."

The invasion of France was the Seventh Front. Maps were bought in large volume by civilians anxious to know where their friends, sons, husbands and families were located. In Great Britain at Lewisham, Mrs. Edith Robinson, thirty-two, had quadruplets and the news caused hardly a ripple. This was the fifth set born in Britain in a year, the third set born to wives of servicemen, the second set to wives of R.A.F. men.

Like 135 million of his countrymen, Franklin Roosevelt spent the week waiting for invasion bulletins. As the scanty news trickled in, the President, like his fellow citizens, took it steadily, neither optimistically, impatiently nor fearfully. But the nation's eyes were on the coast of France. What happened in the hedge-rowed fields and the coastal swamps and beaches and in the ancient towns of Normandy was all important. But the people's look at the war was farther, far beyond Normandy.

Since then Jack Ford has made many motion pictures, and what he regards as "my small, ant-like part in *Overlord*" has been hazed over by the passing years. Sometimes he thinks the events he remembers most vividly concerning those explosive days have to do with a small priest standing by a roadside before his squat Norman church, waving a tiny American flag, the kind that may be purchased in any five-and-dime store around Independence Day.

"Off to the right there was a little church," Ford said. "Its little priest stood about five-feet-four. He had a little American flag in one hand and a big jug of calvados in the other. To us, that's apple brandy. As our troops went by he dipped into it for them. Then he'd pour out another drink. When he ran out of brandy he gave them red wine. After that he served cider and last water. The water was appreciated as much as the brandy. As our guys streamed by and saw this little priest and the American flag, a lot of them asked his blessing and took a drink. My memory of that little man with his white hair is burned on the inside of my skull. He'd been saving that flag for a long, long time.

"When I went back there three years later," Ford went on, "he was still there and I talked to him. By that time I had more boys buried there in that little priest's cemetery. In spite of my bad French and the priest's bad English, we talked up a storm. The priest kept talking about what he called 'jour de dea.' It was as close as his tongue could get to 'D-Day.' Perhaps no man's tongue can get closer. It was a day for dying and a day for victory."

John Ford's Use of Gaelic in *The Quiet Man*: An Interview with Nora Folan

Kenneth E. Nilsen

My name is Nora Folan but I was a Connolly before I married and my father was a Connolly. He was a cousin of John Ford's because my grandmother and John Ford's father were sister and brother. John Ford was my first cousin once removed. My grandmother was Bridget Feeney and John Ford's father was John Feeney. They were sister and brother and they were born in Toorbeg, about a half mile west of Spiddal, in a nice little thatched cottage and I think it is still standing but I have been gone from there now for fifty years. I live further west on the road.

They were always great friends, John Ford and my Dad. He was very friendly with my Dad. My father was called Mikeen. And he told me, "*Mikeen is my favorite cousin.*"[2] He liked him very much because my father had a *jaunt*[3] and a horse long ago and he used to go west to Connemara with the *jaunt* with *spalpeens*[4] and people like that, you know, and into Galway.

But John Ford kept coming now and then, whenever he felt like it. Nothing could keep him from coming. He would come over (from America) the way we would go into Galway. But then he came over that year 1951 and I was not married at the time and my Dad was not very well at the time. The poor man had started to have Alzheimer's. And John Ford said he was going to make this *film* but none of us knew at that time what a *film* was. And he said that he had Maureen O'Hara over from America and that she would have a part in which she would have to say her confession in Irish and he said he wanted me to go with him to Cong where the *film* was to be made so that I could say the words in Irish for Maureen O'Hara but that I would not be in the picture. Maureen O'Hara would be talking to Ward Bond who was fishing in the lake. And that is how it happened. It was only a couple of words but I had to spend six weeks going there.

But I turned him down at first. I said I wouldn't go because I was too shy and I couldn't keep up in English with the *Yanks*. I knew that Americans would be working with him and I said I would not go. So he came over a second time from America a month later and said I had to go. And I said, "I won't go. I don't have the kind of English the Americans have and I wouldn't be comfortable in such a situation."

Finally there were two Feeney girls, of the same family, relatives of his father, who were attending the teachers' training college in Tourmakeady. They had been attending for about a

---

Nora Folan (Ní Chonaola) was recorded in Irish in Spiddal, Ireland, at the home of Séamas Ó Cualáin, on February 5, 2006, by Kenneth E. Nilsen,[1] who also translated the interview.

Set of **The Quiet Man** (1952) near Cong, County Mayo. In this photograph are Francis Ford (with white beard), Bridget Feeney, Nora Conneely (later Folan), Maureen Feeney, Barry Fitzgerald (with derby hat), Etta Vaughn (stand-in for Maureen O'Hara), and Micheál O'Brien (from Spiddal, and the Abbey Theatre) (courtesy Bartley Feeney).

year. So I said to him, "If you let me take those two Feeney girls with me, I'll go." "Yes, you can," he said. And he let me tell Bridget and Mary Feeney to accompany me. And he sent a car every morning and the driver had lodgings nearby and the car picked us up at Creggduff where I was from, just on the other side from Toorbeg and we left at half past seven every day for six weeks and went down to Cong with nothing to say but "*Chuir mé faoi ndeara do mo fhear céile codladh i mála codalta.*"[5] That's all there was. And I had to say that and be ready all the time to say it. But I wasn't to be seen in this film, you know, because I was standing behind her in the trees, as it were.

Well then he asked for a shawl, you know, the Connemara shawls, the *Galway Shawl* they call it and we had a beautiful new shawl, of my mother's, because that is what we were wearing at the time. There were no coats. And he wanted a *bawneen*[6] and my father had a *bawneen*, maybe you don't know what a *bawneen* is and he wanted a pair of tweed trousers and we had a brand new pair of those from my father. Well, we gave the newest one anyway, one that had no dirt on it. He took those with him down to Cong and used them until the *film* was finished and then the shawl was taken to America and he sent it back to me a good while later because the *film* was not completely finished. And he wanted to take me to America but I refused and refused and I said, "I won't go. It's no use for you. I am not going to America." And I did not go to America. I was too shy and I was afraid that I couldn't handle American English. And I did not go to America at all.

But he was very satisfied. There would be days that he did not like when the weather wasn't good. And one day when a crowd of people from the university in Galway came out to Cong to see the *film* being made they were speaking Irish and he was very interested in the Irish language and he said to me, "What do you think of them?" "They are fine," I said. "*They haven't*

On location making *The Quiet Man* (1952): John Ford, far left; Maureen Feeney, Patrick Ford; Nora Folan (née Conneely) and Bridget Feeney (with the permission of Dan Ford; courtesy Lilly Library, Indiana University, Bloomington).

the blas,"[7] he says. "Well," I said, "they couldn't have the *blas* because they do not have it from the cradle." I had to say that in English however I put it, I don't know. But he gave in to that. But anything he would see he would make me say it in Irish. There was a bicycle there, a woman's bicycle and there was a little basket tied onto the back of it, the way they used to have it, and he took me over to tell them the word for basket, the ones who were attending university and here I had never left home, I didn't know anything. And he was embarrassing me because I was afraid that I was not good enough for these people, you know.

But the shawl, the bawneen and the trousers went over to America. The bawneen and the trousers stayed over there but he sent the shawl to me because the shawl was very valuable and still is and I still have it. It was a new one. It was beautiful all right. Maybe if you saw the *film*, she has it on in the *film*, Maureen O'Hara.

But he came to see the house where his father was born and raised. He was there often. And he took two of his brothers there. Francis, if you saw the *film*, he has a beard and an Aran cap on. He was making films before John started at all, I think. And there was another brother with them. So he took them up to see the place where his father was born. And Maureen O'Hara was there too. It was a Sunday. And they drank tea and that is what he wanted to have served, tea. I do not know if the brothers liked it but he liked tea in the old house. I was up there. I was preparing the tea along with the woman of the house, the wife of Martin Feeney, another cousin of his. Martin Feeney and John Ford and Mikeen, my father, were three cousins.

But he was very taken by it and very satisfied with it. Lord Killanin was with him and he probably had been thinking that the film could be made in Spiddal but there wasn't enough

Maureen Feeney, Maureen O'Hara, and Nora Conneely (who later married Tom Folan and now lives in Kilroe, near Tí Chualáin) in 1952 (courtesy Bartley Feeney).

space up at his place. John Ford had a lot of big *caravans*, one for make-up and so on. He had a long line of them as you would see at a *circus*, coming one after the other for a quarter of a mile going into Cong, going to the Maam Valley where there was a nice little thatched cottage belonging to a Mr. Joyce. The poor fellow and his wife and son were all nice. And it was probably John Ford himself and Lord Killanin who found that place but I am not sure of that. They traveled around until they found a suitable place and they thought this house would be. They fixed up the house beautifully. They put thatch on it, put in a new door and windows. They put *whitewash* on it and it was beautiful in the picture. They put flowers on the outside of the windows and flowers on the path and they painted the little gate that opened onto the garden. They made it beautiful for the picture and that is the place where he himself and Mary Kate Ann, that is Maureen O'Hara, they were going to live in that little house.

When he had completed *The Quiet Man* he was very poor. He had no money left because he was paying the people quite well. He was giving a pound and ten shillings to everyone every evening and everyone was coming in. For instance, there was a wedding scene with all the local people and a fair scene and people were poor at the time and they got the same amount we were getting. When he was finished with *The Quiet Man* I heard he was quite low in his finances but then he did well with it over in America. But when he finished it in Ireland I do not think he had much to spare. I never asked him about it.

But he was very natural. He had a special feeling for his father's relatives. I would think that he would kiss the ground where his father was born. His father, his father. His father was lovely but I was very young at the time that the father came to Ireland. He was a very nice, polite man. He was so easy-going and he would give you a kiss. He was so natural. He came to the old place where he was born and raised. He liked it.

Then John Ford brought John Wayne over from America. And one summer evening at ten o'clock, the day before the filming began, I had been out working on the bog and I had no shoes on. And who should come but John Ford with a big car and John Wayne inside. They came right into the house and I had to start looking for my shoes. I had been working out on the bog all day. I said to my brother's wife, "Where are your shoes? I'll put them on." I couldn't get them on. They were too small!

So he brought him in and he and John Wayne drank tea and he thought the tea was excellent. And my father was sitting by the fire but the poor fellow, his mind was failing. John Ford had a great fondness for my Dad but my Dad's mind was failing and he wasn't saying anything. Ford thought that he could talk to my father as he had always done because he got along really well with my Dad. The very first time he came to Ireland he took my Dad out to Connemara in a car hired out from Galway. And he took pictures of everything he saw in Connemara. At one point they met two little lads coming from school, with little jackets on them and little shorts pants down to their knees and their little bags under their arms with their little school books. And he fell in love with them. "Oh, Mike," he said, "aren't they lovely!" And he took a picture of them. And my father hardly knew what a camera was at that time.

He was extremely interested in the Gaeltacht and the Irish language. He wanted children to have names in Irish. The Feeneys were fortunate in naming the two oldest sons Éamonn and Bartley because that is what their grandfathers were called. His heart and soul were in the Gaeltacht, Connemara and Spiddal. He had no aloofness.

But that is how he came to me in the first place because he knew my father. We were on the main road and the house where his father was born was a bit up the lane. He liked this house because it was right on the main road and he used to have great conversations with my father. I didn't want to do this. I wasn't used to doing anything like it but I was reluctant to turn him down. So he sent the other two girls along with me and we spent six weeks lying on the hillside, traveling back and forth between here and Cong with nothing to do. He used to say, "The Spiddal girls do not have a lot to say," because we were too shy. We would not say anything, you know. We would be staying back out of the way of the Yanks, you know. He would say, "The Spiddal girls are very quiet." But he was satisfied. We would not go anywhere or say anything for fear that it would not be right. We were not pushing our way but just staying still and quiet.

Everyone used to get lunch on the hillside. There was a big caravan there. But two days he told them to have the Spiddal girls get their dinner in the castle. We went in and tried to act properly. We were unsophisticated, you know. We weren't used to such things. The other two girls were going to college but I had only gone to secondary school.

I do not know why he chose me. I suppose it was because of my father. I did not want to refuse him because he was so nice. But it was difficult.

Maureen O'Hara has written a book but I do not think that she mentioned that she was in the Feeney house and that she drank tea there. And she was on television and she did not say anything about the shawl or about me or anything. I was with her quite a bit and I took pictures with my own little camera. And it was John Ford's sister who gave me the camera. She was with him when he brought his father over. She stayed in Galway and left the camera with us. And I didn't know much about such things at the time but I took it with me to Cong and took the pictures.

Appendix

The interview I had with Mrs. Folan was conducted in the Irish language. Below is a short excerpt of the beginning of the interview in its original language:

Nóra Ní Chualáin a' t-ainm atá ormsa ach ba Conghaile bhí orm sul má phós mé agus ba Conghaile é m'athair agus ba colceathar é do Sheán Ford, mar mo mhamó agus athair John Ford ba deirfiúr agus dearthair iad. Is colcúigear dhomsa John Ford. Is colceathar do mo athair é agus sin é an fáth a bhfuil mise i mo Chonghaile agus an chuid eile muintir Fhéinneadha, Bríd Ní Fhéinneadha bhí uirthi. Seán Ó Féinneadha bhí ar athair John Ford. Agus ba deirfiúr agus dearthair iad agus rugadh iad ar a' Tuar Beag, taobh thiar den Spidéal, tuairim's leath mhíle taobh thiar den Spidéal agus teach ceann tuí, teachín deas ceann tuí. Agus tá, sílim go bhfuil sé ina sheasamh fós ach tá mise imithe as le leath chéad bliain. Tá mé goil níos faide siar a' bóthar.

Bhí siad an-chairdiúil ariamh agus bhí Seán Ford an-chairdiúil go deo le mo Dheaide. Dúirt sé liom, Mikeen a bhí ar mo Dheaide, agus dúirt sé, "*Mikeen is my favorite cousin,*" agus bhí an-suim go deo aige ann mar bhí *jaunt* ag mo Dheaide fadó agus capall agus bhíodh sé a' goil siar Conamara leis a' *jaunt* le spailpíní agus daoine mar sin, bhfuil fhios agat, is a' goil Gaillimh, isteach Gaillimh.

Notes

1. I would like to express my gratitude to Mrs. Nora Folan for permission to publish this translation of our interview. I am also indebted to Séamas Ó Cualáin for arranging for me to meet Mrs. Folan and for his kind hospitality.
2. Words in italics are in English in the original.
3. "a jaunting car"
4. itinerant farm workers, *spailpín* in Irish
5. I made my husband sleep in a sleeping bag.
6. Irish *báinín*
7. *Blas* in this context means "proper accent."

PART THREE: FORD'S FILMS

Introduction to Part Three

Kevin L. Stoehr

Part Three is composed of a diverse set of essays by film scholars who explore theories of why many of Ford's movies have sparked such interest, debate, and enjoyment. They range from analyses of particular movie scenes to surveys of selected films according to relevant themes. All of these essays share the common goal of attempting to situate Ford's films within a broader cultural and intellectual context.

In "'If you can call it an art...'": Pictorial Style in John Ford's Universal Westerns (1917–18)," Tom Paulus argues for a theory of influence that addresses the seminal roles of D. W. Griffith and John Ford's older brother Francis on his developing style. Most importantly, the essay considers the rarely mentioned influence of European "pictorialist" traditions of staging and lighting on Ford's early work. The author examines three extant films from Ford's early Universal period of silent filmmaking: *Straight Shooting* (1917), *Bucking Broadway* (1917) and *Hell Bent* (1918).

In his essay "Beyond the Blessings of Civilization: John Ford's *Stagecoach* and the Myth of the Western Frontier," Robert C. Sickels analyzes Ford's landmark western—a film that helped to revitalize and reshape the genre—in terms of the tension between modern civilization (a movement toward urban industrialized society) and wilderness (a sense of nature as being untamable to some degree). Sickels centers on two very different conceptions of the Old West, that of a frontier existing to be conquered by the forces of Eastern expansionism and that of a frontier lying always somehow beyond the manipulative reach of humans. The author also discusses the movie's focus on the theme of social prejudice and explains the importance of natural landscape for Ford, in this case, that of Monument Valley.

Our focus next shifts to two essays that deal specifically with one of Ford's most popular movies, *The Quiet Man* (1952). In "John Ford's Festive Comedy: Ireland Imagined in *The Quiet Man*," William C. Dowling explores this classic film in terms of its play upon various stereotypes of the Irish people and in terms of its echoes of Shakespearean romantic comedy. While many viewers have grown to love Ford's movie for its quaint depiction of rural folk and their antiquated customs, not to mention its beautiful color photography and bawdy comedy, many view the movie as depicting the Irish in a negative, even oppressive light. Dowling seeks to counter these criticisms and argues that the film has long served as a mirror for Irish cultural anxieties. He suggests that certain scenes previously interpreted as patronizing or chauvinistic actually echo ancient Irish social rituals.

Leger Grindon, in his essay "*The Quiet Man* and the Boxing Film: Allusions and Influences," offers an analysis of *The Quiet Man* by considering it in relation to the boxing film genre and more particularly in comparison to a series of boxing films from the early 1950s that featured the boxer after he leaves the ring, including *From Here to Eternity* (1953), *On the Waterfront* (1954) and the teleplay "Requiem for a Heavyweight" (1956). Finally, the essay discusses the influence of Ford's boxing flashback in *The Quiet Man* on the design of boxing sequences in Martin Scorsese's *Raging Bull* (1980).

We return to the Western genre with Tom Paulus's essay "Ways of Knowing: Peter Lehman and *The Searchers*," in which the author considers one of the dominant voices in Ford criticism. The author confronts Peter Lehman's psychoanalytic investigation into Ford's style with a neo-historical approach that explores possible stylistic variation within the dominant paradigm of the classical Hollywood cinema. The essay discusses notions of auteurism in relation to Ford, counters Lehman's assumptions about the director as a "repressed" or "unconscious" author, and takes a more pragmatic view of the problem-solving process of filmmaking in the studio era.

In "Populist Motifs in John Ford's Films," Roy Grundmann examines the ways in which populism, and primarily its focus on the relationship between individual and community, is expressed in selected films by Ford, including *Young Mr. Lincoln, She Wore a Yellow Ribbon*, and *My Darling Clementine*. The author attempts to show the impact that America's cultural heritage had on Ford and to analyze the ways in which populist ideas and themes are translated by Ford into cinematic narrative and visual composition. As a focal point, Grundmann examines one specific motif that is present in many Ford classics, the recurring scene in which a hero delivers a soliloquy at the grave or deathbed of a loved one.

Concluding the section and the book is an analysis of Ford's final feature movie, but within the broad-ranging context of recurring themes from Ford's entire career of filmmaking. In "Heroism, Faith, and Idealism in *7 Women* and Other Films by John Ford," I provide an analysis of Ford's final but underappreciated movie in the context of his entire career by connecting themes, scenes, and characters in this film with those in lesser known works by Ford, including *The Lost Patrol, Arrowsmith, The Fugitive, 3 Godfathers*, and *Wagon Master*. Major themes discussed include religious faith, heroism, and the limits of idealism.

"If You Can Call It an Art…":
Pictorial Style in John Ford's Universal Westerns (1917–1918)

Tom Paulus

In her essay on the initial formulation of the classical American film style in *The Classical Hollywood Cinema*, Kristin Thompson suggests that by 1917, the year in which Ford's first feature film, *Straight Shooting*, was released, the system was complete in its basic narrative and stylistic premises.[1] Thompson's understanding of the "classical style" of American filmmaking rests on the integration of these principles in the feature film: the classical Hollywood cinema is a distinctly narrative cinema in which setting and lighting, spatial arrangement and the cutting together of shots in a continuous, unobtrusive manner, all contribute to the viewer's absorption in a causally motivated and temporally consistent narrative with psychologically based characters. The coalescing of classical norms then occurred within a set of institutions, the studio system and the trade press, which turned them into normative principles.

Although Ford's extant features from the teens—*Straight Shooting* (August 1917), *Bucking Broadway* (December 1917), *Hell Bent* (June 1918), all westerns featuring Harry Carey as "good badman" Cheyenne Harry—clearly belong to this tradition, there is also a sense that in these films narrative and style are not always fully integrated in the manner suggested by the classical cinema's "invisible" style. Around the time Jack Ford got his start at Universal, a fierce debate was being waged, not just in the industrial press but in the op-ed columns and prestigious journals like *Harper's Weekly*, on the issue of whether motion pictures were an art form or a corruption of the classical texts and the older forms from which they often drew. Arguing for the former position were directors like D.W. Griffith, Maurice Tourneur and Herbert Brenon. One of the contexts of the debate was the relationship between motion pictures and the legitimate stage, which, as Nicholas Vardac has shown, had moved to the very threshold of cinema in its "photographic realism" made possible by new mechanical and electrical effects. The main American figure in this tradition was David Belasco, the theatrical impresario famously associated with spectacular settings and aesthetic lighting effects. Although the industrial press had started to champion an American cinema as a distinctive medium superior to theatre, a company like Famous Players-Lasky still held closely to a theatrical line associated with Belasco's prestige and success. Wilfred Buckland was part of the Belasco crew that director Cecil B. DeMille brought to Hollywood. He was one of the first art directors, a new function in moviemaking by the mid-teens, responsible not just for the technical supervision of set construction but also for advising the director and cameraman on matters of *mise en scène* (i.e., visual composition) and chiaroscuro lighting (i.e., dramatic contrast between brightness and darkness). Buckland was an electrical expert in stage lighting who provided his director with spotlights, and contributed to developing the low-key lighting style known as "Lasky lighting," but referred to by DeMille, in a rhetorical strategy typical of the "movies as art" debate, as "Rembrandt lighting."[2]

While the legitimate stage and the new stagecraft of Gordon Craig and European designers like Max Reinhardt were shaping the look and ambition of films produced at Famous Players-Lasky, John Ford was making pictures for a studio, Universal, that was a model of standardized organization and cost-efficient production. "Prestige" pictures that could settle the debate in favor of movies as art were furthest from the mind of studio president Carl Laemmle, a propagator of Taylorist ideas of scientific management who designed his Hollywood factory— Universal City, the first major studio complex to open in Southern California in 1915—to roll out short films, serials and modest features meant to be taken together as a program aimed at the subsequent-run circuit. Then there is the enduring image of the neophyte filmmaker who, as it were, rolled into directing: in Ford's case the creation myth narrates how young Jack Ford, then working as a combination prop man-stuntman for his brother Francis, was drafted by Laemmle personally to direct a couple of western scenes for a crowd of visitors at Universal City's opening ceremonies after the director who was scheduled to work that day failed to show up because he was suffering from a hangover.[3] There is no doubt some anecdotal truth to these stories, and they do entertainingly evoke the catch-as-catch-can days when the movies were still young, but they do tend to deflect attention away from the well-organized mass production system that was the U.S. film industry by the mid-teens, certainly at a studio like Universal. Writer Dudley Nichols' assessment to Lindsay Anderson that Ford's films "poured out" during this period, and that Jack and Harry Carey worked up their stories, then shot them during the balance of the week,[4] does not take into account, for instance, the required continuity script, a highly detailed shooting outline that had become normal practice in filmmaking by 1914 (according to Ford, he would have a screenwriter bang out an after-the-fact continuity script to keep the front office happy).[5]

Even so, Ford and Harry Carey were left relatively free to shoot their pictures on location, mostly not too far from Carey's ranch near Saugus, a freedom resulting from their low production budget. Ford's westerns cost between $10,000 and $15,000 to make, and the economy began with the director's salary: Ford started directing features at $35 a week in early 1917. This was substandard even for a bread-and-butter company like Universal, but, as William Everson has pointed out, it did free the director somewhat from assembly-line requirements.[6] This (relative) freedom Ford put to use in order to, in Eileen Bowser's phrase, "refine the product."[7] Although the Ford-Carey features were often hastily put together (as is evident from the often sloppy editing which has mismatched shots), they have a respectable level of production polish and were not "low-grade," as, for instance, the films released under Universal's Red Feather label were. One area where they distinguished themselves from the string of westerns mass-produced as stock-in-trade at Universal and elsewhere was in the quality of the photography. When "effects" lighting in the Lasky/Rembrandt mode was not yet a growing tendency, Ford and his cameramen Ben Reynolds and John Brown were using source lighting for naturalistic effect, simulating the effect of a match being lit or a burning fireplace. Low-key lighting was also used here to enhance moods, most strikingly in two scenes from *Bucking Broadway* in which Ford and Brown use shading effects to suggest their heroine's mood of terror and depression in the presence of the villainous Thornton. Such lighting effects stand out in a western since they were more frequent in films produced on the East Coast, where interiors were shot entirely in blacked-out studios, than in California, where until about 1919 films were generally lit by daylight that was then controlled in one way or another.

Although the studio sets used in Ford's Universal westerns were still rudimentary, they do display the new interest of film producers in verisimilitude and depth: sets were becoming three-dimensional and were constructed according to pre-construction diagrams. This allowed the director more leeway in staging than had previously been the case with flat painted backdrops. Even the flats of pioneer homes constructed on location were L-shaped to emphasize layers of depth in the frame, mainly through doorways in the back. The bigger sets in Ford's pictures, constructed on the back lot, display not only the new tendency to design large and deep, but were also dressed with an eye towards realistic detail. None of Ford's early westerns credit their technical director or stage manager, and it is hard to imagine Laemmle okaying an art director even for his "Special Attraction" westerns. Nevertheless, the coordination of photography, staging and set design evident from these films shows how theatrical staging and lighting trends were having an effect even at Universal. Although we can be certain that it never was Laemmle's intention to rival Zukor and Lasky, or Goldwyn, in adhering to theatrical models, the contracts of technical directors like Frank Ormston, Edward Langley (who briefly worked with the great cinematographer Alvin Wyckoff at Lasky and would be the art director on many of the Douglas Fairbanks spectacles at United Artists), and especially Richard Day (who would design the sumptuous sets for Von Stroheim's films at Universal) show that Universal was certainly not adverse to the general trend of hiring theater personnel to design their pictures.

Wilfred Buckland consistently argued for the elevation of the position of the stage manager or technical director to that of art director, and although he never openly joined the "movies as art" debate, he was most vocal in suggesting the Hollywood comparison of setting and lighting design with painting. "Pictorialism" in the context of Hollywood films of the teens meant, therefore, the influences of painting and stagecraft. Ford was both stagestruck and an amateur painter: in his hometown of Portland, Maine, he was an usher at the Jefferson Theatre during his high school years, where he acquired an instinctive familiarity with all aspects of stagecraft and saw many a Belasco play, like *The Warrens of Virginia* and *The Girl of the Golden West*, and, as a kid, wanted to be an artist after watching Winslow Homer paint at his studio at Prout's Neck. The realization that *movies*, even *westerns*, could be, if not art, at least *authentic*, was no doubt inspired by the critical acclaim of the one and two-reel westerns his older brother Francis was making for Thomas Ince and the New York Motion Picture Company.

After a short stint as a prop man for the New York stage and some minor roles on Broadway, Francis "Frank" Ford began his career as a film actor with the G. Méliès Company, one of the first companies to transfer its operations out West, then left it in April 1911 to star in the "101" Bison westerns Thomas Ince was producing for the New York Motion Picture Company. Bison was the brand name, while "101" was a label named after the film company's use of the personnel, animals and equipment of the Miller Brothers' "101" Ranch Wild West show and rodeo, located in Oklahoma but wintering in Santa Monica with their own film production unit. After a legal battle over stock, Universal acquired the Bison-101 brand in late 1912, leaving the New York Motion Picture Company (NYMPC) to reorganize its production of westerns under the new brand names of Broncho (Frank's own unit) and Kay-Bee (after NYMPC incorporators Kessel and Baumann). After starring in most of the early Broncho and Kay-Bee productions and directing about half of them, Frank, along with star actress Grace Cunard, left Ince and NYMPC to take over the Bison unit at Universal. With the Bison productions, praised in the trade press for their craft and artistry and distinguished from the regular style of "Indian and Cowboy pictures," Laemmle gained immediate prestige and a taste for multiple-reel westerns.[8] When Frank and Grace Cunard started their successful *Lucille Love* serial in the wake of similar efforts at Kalem and Pathé, his unit was entrusted to Henry McRae. McRae was the director with the hangover who failed to show up to entertain the crowds at Universal City's inaugural celebration, leading to Jack Ford's opportunity to direct a scene for Laemmle. In that same inaugural year, Frank's growing desire for independence from studio control definitively soured his relationship with Laemmle, and Jack Ford took over the Bison brand, for which he directed his first two-reel pictures.[9]

Judging from his extant work at Universal, as a filmmaker Francis Ford shows the influence of his theatrical background in the way he relies more on staging, on moving his actors around, often in depth, than on editing. Ford fully makes use of the new features of theatrical set design, especially the fact that room sets were now constructed in rows and another full-sized room could be seen at the back of the main set (in John Ford's *Straight Shooting* a particular room-behind effect is created by showing the second space through flapping saloon doors). The depth compositions that characterize Frank's films with Ince, shot on location in the picturesque Santa Ynez Canyon with lengthy takes from high atop a hill or mountain, can also be said to have come with the territory, as they seemed the only way to do justice to the wide open spaces of California (Eileen Bowser suggests as much).[10] Still, a company like G.M. "Broncho Billy" Anderson's Essanay, which had gone West even earlier than the New York Motion Picture Company, was using *shorter* shots to explore the dynamic potential of the wide open spaces. Also, Frank made good use of the limitations imposed by flat-drop sets built on location: he expands deep space by placing a door at the rear of the set, through which can be glimpsed a landscape of real trees and vistas. This type of framing can be seen with some regularity in John Ford's westerns.

The open door at the back of the location set also produced an artistic lighting effect which Eileen Bowser has called the "open door effect": strong contrast lighting is obtained without artificial light by shooting figures in an unlighted room against the fully day-lit exterior seen through an open door.[11] The result is a silhouetted figure in the foreground that emphasizes the brightness of the vista behind. The Bison-101 pictures, shot by cameraman Ray Smallwood (who would later photograph Nazimova at Metro), also feature other types of pictorial silhouette lighting, especially in their impressive final tableaux that were highly praised by the trade press, like the low-angle extreme long shot from *The Indian Massacre* (March 1912) in which an Indian mother stands silhouetted on a bare hilltop before the platform that bears her own dead child, or the low-angled shot that ends *Blazing the Trail* (April 1912) that shows unmarked graves in the bottom half of the frame and riders and mourners silhouetted high up against the horizon.

Similar pictorial skyline silhouette compositions can be found in John Ford's *Bucking Broadway*: a day-for-night shot that shows Cheyenne Harry and his sweetheart Helen Clayton riding past the herd, or a high-angle deep landscape shot of Helen's father, Ben Clayton, and her suitor, Captain Thornton, surveying the herd at dusk. Most often, however, the silhouette effect is an actual "open door" shot usually achieved with natural light. (A shot in *Bucking Broadway* of Cheyenne framed in an open door showing the hotel lounge as another spatial area where two big-city hustlers are waiting to scheme against him, is the only example I have found of an "open door" effect achieved in a darkened studio.) When Cheyenne jumps on a train in *Bucking Broadway*, he is framed in silhouette in the back door of a railroad car; in *Hell Bent* we see a group of villains escaping through an open window bordered by panels of darkness; and in that same film the "open door" effect is combined with a skyline silhouette in an extreme long shot of Cheyenne flanked by canyon walls. In all these examples the silhouette effect is pure pictorial embellishment, but there are also cases in which it serves more expressive narrative ends: a beautiful side-lit doorway shot from *Bucking Broadway* perfectly captures the melancholia of the aging patriarch, Ben Clayton, who saw his daughter run off with the wrong man, while in *Straight Shooting* open door framings enhanced by silhouettes of Cheyenne and cowhand Sam Turner stress their desire to be taken into the household of Farmer Sims. Here the lighting creates the dramatic mood of the scene, as in Frank's Kay-Bee production, *The Army Surgeon* (November 1912), in which an equally conflicted hero is backlit by the light of the dying sun behind him.

Barry Salt has traced the origin of silhouette shots in French, Danish and especially Italian films of the early teens, made available in the United States through the American branches of European companies like Gaumont, Nordisk and Cines, and he also mentions the influence of still photography in this respect, in the United States especially from the "Secessionist" photographers grouped around Alfred Stieglitz's famous gallery at 291 Fifth Avenue.[12] The Photo-Secession photographers, who had their first collective exhibition in 1902, anticipated the "movies as art" debate by aiming to prove the status of photography as an art form, worthy of the traditional visual arts from which they drew their inspiration. It is safe to assume that any influence from the Photo-Secession on the photography of the westerns that were being produced in Santa Monica and the San Fernando Valley, was filtered first through Stieglitz's New York neighbor, D.W. Griffith. A *New York Times* movie review of October 10, 1909 (the first ever in its pages), compares the shade effects created by Billy Bitzer and Arthur Marvin in Griffith's *Pippa Passes* (August 1909) to the photographs of Stieglitz, Brady, and White. In his biography of D.W. Griffith, Richard Schickel notes the irony in the cross-reference, since Stieglitz famously revolted against the school of photography that found its ideals of lighting in Rembrandt, while the movie people, including Griffith, would shortly begin publicizing their "Rembrandt" lighting.[13] No matter, since Griffith's model was neither Stieglitz nor Rembrandt, but the spectacular stage of Belasco. What came closest to the spectacular stage in the early teens, were imports: French *films d'art* and Italian epics. The latter featured not only "Rembrandt" type lighting but also the kind of panoramic long shots, which Griffith started calling "distant views" in his famous 1913 self-advertisement in the New York *Dramatic Mirror*.[14] These "distant views" would serve him well in capturing the wide open spaces of California when the Biograph Company began wintering there in early 1910.

Griffith's influence on Ford's early features, as William Everson reminds us, is dominant, even in duplicating specific plot points and compositions: the famous scene from *Straight Shooting* of Molly fingering her dead brother's dish was probably inspired by Mae Marsh and her baby's shoe in *Intolerance*, while the gathering of Thunder Flint's horsemen and the ride to the rescue that follows is a clear nod to the gathering of the clans in *The Birth of a Nation* (a sequence in which Ford participated as an extra; he was the hooded Klansman with the glasses, riding with one hand to hold the hood up so he could see).[15] The Griffith influence goes beyond mere homage and extends to narrative structure, editing and *mise en scène*. Although all three extant Universal features have a conventional "rescue" pattern of crosscutting (or "cutbacks" as crosscutting was known at the time) for their fast-cut finales, their Griffithian editing patterns also appear quite archaic in a period of increasing reverse-angle cutting. They are characterized by frontal scene dissection (cutting in to a closer shot along the camera axis), and show a general disregard for screen direction. The parallels I want to draw to Griffith, however, are less related to editing than to shot composition and framing, specifically to "pictorial" aspects of Griffith's imagery where, again, we need to understand "pictorialism" in its Hollywood meaning as betraying an influence from both stagecraft and painting.

The first Biograph expedition to California at the beginning of 1910 had a dramatic effect on the landscape and atmosphere of Griffith's films: the diversity of California locations allowed for a type of pictorial composition developed in sea pictures shot in Santa Monica, like *The Unchanging Sea* (May 1910), *Fisher Folks* (January 1911) and *Enoch Arden* (June 1911), where the inspiration came from late nineteenth-century paintings of women at the shore watching for distant ships, created by such painters as George Inness and Winslow Homer. But most striking were the mountains and open spread of the plains, which allowed for the use of panoramic long shots to emphasize the spectacular, a technique borrowed both from the Italian epics and from American landscape painting. In his cultural reading of Griffith's "Eastern" framing of the Western landscape, Scott Simmon has pointed out that the high-angle long-distance shots the director started taking from the top of a California hill (often Santa Monica) looking down into a California canyon, were not so different from similar "prospect" shots from high atop a hill in earlier Biograph Westerns filmed in the wooded surroundings of the Palisades cliffs in New Jersey or Cuddebackville in New York, like *Comata, the Sioux* (August 1909) and *The Red Man's View* (December 1909).[16] The main difference lies in the sometimes striking depth of field that creates planar tension between background and foreground in the California-shot westerns like *Ramona* (May 1910), in which Henry Walthall as a noble Indian is framed in the foreground in high angle on the edge of a cliff while his village burns in the far distance. For the typical "Ramona" shot, Simmon argues, Griffith essentially transferred conventions from Hudson River landscape painting to the California setting.

The "distant view" and "Ramona"-type shot features prominently in the Bison-101, Broncho and Kay-Bee productions: both *Blazing the Trail* and *The Invaders* (November 1912) contain beautifully composed long shots and high-angle prospect shots of Indians on a cliff watching either wagon trains or surveyors below. These conventions had become integral to the western genre when John Ford started his career, but the director and his cameramen came up with eye-catching variations: in a virtuoso shot from *Hell Bent* we see the stage crash and tumble off a ridge in extreme long shot; as the stage falls down the rock face, the camera dollies slightly back to reframe the shot and allow us to see the debris blocking the way of the team of horses who have turned into the path below. The second shot of *Straight Shooting* is a slow iris-out on a full shot of Thunder Flint on horseback, gradually revealing his position high atop a hill, surveying his herd grazing below. To accentuate the depth of the shot, Ford has Flint ride down to the middle ground where he converses with two of his men before exiting middle frame right. The first images of *Bucking Broadway* are similar shots of foreman Buck Hoover looking over his herd and cowboys from a prospect point. This film also has a beautiful shot of Ben Clayton and Captain Thornton silhouetted against a sea of cattle in the background and a more modern variation, consisting of a cowboy who sits on a fence in the long shot foreground and observes a motorcar approaching in the far distance.

In the latter shot, a fence, a favorite compositional element of John Ford's found throughout his work with different cinematographers, is used as a framing device, a way to expand the depth of the composition. A natural frame, selected to best represent a natural scene as it is, was another technique developed by Hudson River landscape painters like Thomas Cole and Asher B. Durand, who also placed trees, overhanging branches, bushes, outcrops of rock and (tiny) human figures in the foreground to draw our gaze into the monumental background. The climactic sieges of *Straight Shooting* and *Hell Bent*, especially, have this kind of shot composition. The siege of the villains' hide-out in *Hell Bent* is preceded by a high-angle view through overhanging foliage, showing the arrival of the seized stagecoach, while in *Straight Shooting*, whisked away in a flurry of "switchbacks" to Cheyenne and Black-Eyed Pete's bandits riding to the rescue, Ford composes a foreground shot of two silhouetted cowboys framed by an overhanging branch, containing the encircled Sims house in the distance. This shot repeats an earlier mode of depth framing, exploiting planar tension between background and foreground: in the foreground, framed by trees, hired gun Placer Fremont shoots at innocent youth Ted Sims in the background; after a cutaway to a long shot view of Ted falling, Ford returns to the biplanar composition and has the villain (still in extreme long shot) turn to the camera and sneer.

Scott Simmon calls this type of foreground framing combined with deep staging the "Claude Lorraine" convention, pointing to roots of American landscape painting in the work of the sixteenth century French artist. Tom Gunning has emphasized the theatrical effect of the Claude landscape, in which powerfully vertical trees crowned by fan-like foliage serve as *coulisse* (the flats that conceal and naturalize the off-stage space of the wings) that draw the viewer's gaze into a recessive arrangement of space.[17] The "Claude" composition can be found in several of Griffith's films from 1908 onwards, shot in the East, like *The Girl and the Outlaw* (August 1908), as well as in the West, like *The Lonedale Operator* (March 1911). From our Ford westerns, the repeated high-angle view, framed by an overhanging branch, of cowboys firing at the encircled Sims house in the recessive depth, can be seen as an embellished "Ramona" shot in which a natural frame of trees or branches serves as a proscenium arch: it includes two Claudean compositional elements—the *repoussoir*, a darker element framing the foreground, setting off the landscape's glowing central depth, and *staffage*, unimportant figures with backs to the viewer facing into the scene.

Other examples from our three early features further illustrate Ford's pictorial compositions, in which trees, boulders and fences frame and balance the shot. The pastoral setting where Cheyenne gives Bess a puppy as a token of his love in *Hell Bent*—a scene reminiscent of Thomas Worthington Whittredge — has all three compositional elements neatly arranged: a break in the fence frames Cheyenne and Bess in the foreground, while our gaze is drawn into the background by the scattered boulders and twisting brook. In *Bucking Broadway* two huge erratic boulders, one on each side of the frame, are the *coulisses* in the scene of Cheyenne's earliest encounter with Helen. Recessive depth is activated here when Harry's attention is drawn by his cowboy buddies approaching in the far distance, while a picturesque long shot of Helen perched on a fence against a blurry mountainous landscape introduces her first tryst with the villainous Captain Thornton.

Ford's most unforgettable composition is a graveyard setting from *Straight Shooting*. Here the final verticality of Sweetwater and Joan Sims's bodies on opposite sides of Ted's grave, marked by a pile of boulders, is contrasted to the hesitant horizontality of the primitive wooden cross on the grave, the leaning trees in the background, and Sam Turner's solitary mourner. This scene, possibly inspired by the closing moments of William Hart's *Hell's Hinges* (February 1916), or indeed by any of Francis Ford's closing tableaux from the 101-Bison films, exhibits Ford's talent for making a dramatic point by moving his characters in a static frame: while the heartbroken family members escorted by a repentant Cheyenne move further to the background and exit the frame through the gap between the left and middle trees, Sam Turner is isolated in the middle ground between the middle and right trees. In contrast to this subtle use of movement in the frame, the beginning of the scene is almost completely still: Ford holds the beautifully composed static long shot of the mourners almost as a *tableau vivant*, as an image pregnant with introspective emotion, but at the same time reminiscent of painted laments.

The tableau has a long history in the pre-classical silent cinema, appearing in films as early as Lumière, that derived from the theatrical tradition of "Living Pictures," in which actors could be posed to recreate a famous painting. That Ford was familiar with this tradition is shown by the initial scene of *Hell Bent*, which opens with the author of the story admiring a Remington picture, *The Misdeal*, which then comes to life after a dolly-in as an "acting tableau" in the next shot. The convention is jokingly employed in the context of a popular western: American moviegoing audiences would more readily recognize a Remington than a classic master. The tableau also has a use beyond the frame compositions that a painter or an art historian would recognize. We earlier referred to the closing scenes of *The Indian Massacre* and *Blazing the Trail* as instances of the tableau. In these cases the tableau functions to bookend the picture, like a frontispiece: a shot epitomizing the subject matter is placed at the end of the film, or (as was more often the case in early filmmaking) at the beginning. Ben Brewster and Lea Jacobs give even more functions of the cinematic tableau: besides providing a summary of a situation or final resolution, the tableau could also function as allegorical commentary or to punctuate important moments in the narrative.[18] In *A Corner in Wheat* (December 1909), Griffith and Bitzer employ the tableau both in its original function as a painting brought to life, in this case Millet's *Angelus* and *The Sowers*, and as allegorical commentary in a much-debated totally motionless shot of men waiting for a breadline to open.[19] There is certainly nothing in our Ford films that even comes close to the use of a tableau as allegorical commentary with no movement for the entire duration of the scene, but we do find examples of the cinematic tableau that allows for limited forms of figure movement within the shot used to punctuate important narrative or dramatic moments, like the burial of Ted Sims at the midway point of *Straight Shooting*, a moment that also signals Cheyenne's change of faith. This moment is meant to heighten expression to such a degree that the narrative stops dead in its tracks.

As a powerful instrument of expression to underline the already heightened moment Ford and Carey use the "pose" and the look directly at the camera. The "pose"— identified by a slight pause in the actor's movement, a "hesitant calm," that expresses the character's interior state — is associated with what Roberta Pearson calls the "histrionic code" of film acting. Pearson uses the term to describe film acting at Biograph in the period between 1908 and 1912.[20] She opposes the "histrionic code," theatrical acting in which the actor palpably acts and strikes conventionalised poses (i.e., early Griffith), to a "verisimilar code," a system of more restrained gestures and facial expression (which evolved out of a broader range of camera distance and continuity editing) aimed at creating realism and psychologically complex characters (i.e., later Griffith).[21] Brewster and Jacobs adhere to Pearson's argument that the evolution from one code to the other should not be seen as clear teleological progression, and stress that appeals to realism — the standard of authenticity and verisimilitude according to which the western especially was judged — do not necessarily preclude an emphasis on attitudes and posing. What they call "pictorialism in acting" is based on the kind of posing aimed both at expressiveness and restraint and can be observed throughout the later (post–1912) Griffith.

The "pose" Harry Carey strikes is that he grasps his right arm. This gesture is almost always accompanied by a look directly at (William Everson would say "beyond") the camera, something which Barry Salt claims had been largely eliminated from American dramatic films by 1914.[22] Although lingering on an actor's face to express a psychological state was an integrated convention of the classical continuity style by 1917, Ford and Carey actually pause both the actor's movement and the flow of the narrative in a way that comes close to Brewster and Jacobs' "hesitant calm." Such moments of intensity, which Richard Griffith calls "soul-fights," make conspicuous dramatic use of the pause, even of immobility, to draw the spectator close to the emotional core of the action.[23] Griffith mentions Ince's Civil War drama *The Coward* (October 1915), directed by Reginald Barker under the Kay-Bee label, as an instance of the "soul-fight," combining theatrical pose and psychological realism, but one can find traces of it in earlier Francis Ford pictures (like *The Army Surgeon*), and in Ince's later features with William Hart, all constructed around a central moral dilemma. William Everson credits early Danish features directed by Benjamin Christensen and August Blom in 1913–14 with having pioneered the "thinks" look at the camera: in these films, Everson claims, actors are given time to think and reflect, instead of being at the mercy of a narrative that propels them from one scene to the next.[24] Everson mentions another Ince/Barker feature, *The Italian* (January 1915), as a fully realized American instance of an acting style that projects intensity of thought by seeming to play "beyond the reaches of the camera."[25]

The "acting tableaux" we find in John Ford's Universal features, the compositions in depth with foreground-background tension, the complex blocking and framing devices, all look back to a tradition of what Ben Brewster and Lea Jacobs call "stage pictures." The presence of such "overdetermined images," as Tom Gunning describes certain imagistic moments from Griffith's early films at Biograph, must not be seen as contradicting but rather as broadening the conception of the classical Hollywood cinema as displaying an unobtrusive, "invisible" style based in editing.[26] By the mid-teens the influx of stars, directors and technical experts from stagecraft was still widespread — even Laemmle was making room in his release schedule of 1915 for a line of "Broadway Features" with theater imports like Jane Cowl, Nat Goodwin, Florence Reed and … Harry Carey—but at the same time the trade press had started to champion an American cinema as a distinctive medium superior to theater, and stage pictorialism had started to seem remote from the normalized narrative cinema aimed at a mass audience.

By the late teens only Famous Players-Lasky and companies with strong European ties like the World Film Corporation were still holding to the theatrical line. Still, leading filmmakers of the day, like Griffith, Tourneur, Ince and DeMille, all with backgrounds in the theater, were — somewhat paradoxically perhaps—presenting their plea for the standing of movies as a distinctive art by analogizing the cinema with the stage. One of the reasons for doing so was that by modeling themselves after stage-directors like Belasco or Gordon Craig, they could pitch the film director as a creative genius who was responsible not solely for coaching the actors but for the whole artistic package. This is what Griffith achieved in his *New York Dramatic Mirror* advertisement. The advertisement heralded Griffith as being responsible for "revolutionizing Motion Picture drama and founding the modern technique of the art."[27] What it did not mention was that many of Griffith's representational strategies that lasted him well into the classical era were hardly revolutionary and had their roots in stage pictorialism. This holds equally for Tourneur who, despite a sophisticated feeling for montage, always kept a sense of an invisible proscenium in the films he directed, creating proscenium-like foregrounds even on his outdoor pictures to "theatricalize" the action. Clarence Brown, who was Tourneur's editor and assistant director until 1921, remembered how the crew used to carry branches and twigs around on exteriors in case Tourneur needed a foreground.[28]

And the same can be said about Thomas Ince, whose films with Francis Ford of the early teens, despite their being based almost completely on the spectacle of landscape, are extremely theatrical, both in the way action is staged in depth rather than edited and in the theatrical effect of the "Claude" landscape. (Scott Simmon calls the style of Kay-Bee's *The Invaders* "archaic even for 1912").[29] The same visual framework is largely maintained in Ince's films with his new star, William Hart, another former Broadway actor whose predilection for historical detail and scenarios of moral conflict was clearly inspired by Frank's work at NYMPC (and by G.M. Anderson's "Broncho Billy" character, the original "good badman"). And it is evident, amid a flurry of Griffithian "switchbacks" and fast-cut action sequences, from John Ford's Universal westerns.

Following from this suggested direct line from Griffith to Ince and Francis Ford and William Hart to John Ford, my final point relates to the question of how filmmakers of the period were made aware of the "norms" of stylistic structure. Kristin Thompson argues that how-to columns, books and trade journals were perhaps the most important source for the normalization of a classical American film style.[30] I would say that we should not automatically equate commentary with filmmaking practice. If normative codes propagated at the time of Ford's début in feature-filmmaking were largely dissociated from the aesthetics of the stage, this was because Hollywood movies were being pitched as a distinctive new kind of mass entertainment. It does not automatically follow that pictorialism was no longer a valid stylistic choice. As long as they held to the basic rules of storytelling, filmmakers were left relatively free to "overdetermine" their images. This was especially the case if they were their own producers or if they worked for a studio, like Paramount, that nurtured artistic ambition as a means to differentiate their product. This was not the case at Universal, although Laemmle clearly saw something in *Straight Shooting* that inspired him to release it as a "Special Attraction" and promote it as the greatest western ever made. Second, in light of recent attempts by film historians to focus more on the norms than on individual filmmakers traditionally considered major, the question of direct influence, now seen as narrowly "art-historical" in focus, has become skewed. Griffith is now generally accepted as weirdly idiosyncratic and as having changed production practices and filmic techniques only in limited ways.[31] But should we therefore disregard his obvious stylistic influence on a director like John Ford, who, despite his reputation as one of the foremost classical American filmmakers, might not give the best impression of the norms either?

Talking to Peter Bogdanovich about his apprenticeship in the early teens at American Film (another major independent company, like NYMPC, whose output during the early teens was almost exclusively made up of westerns shot in California), Alan Dwan, who directed Francis Ford and started John as a prop man at Universal, says, "I had to learn from the screen. I had no other model. We picked up and manufactured what technique we could, watched the other fellow [...] The only man I ever watched was Griffith, and I just did what he did. I'd see his pictures and go back and make them at my company." Dwan learned from Griffith — about backlighting, side-lighting and composition — because "there weren't any other noted people."[32] To John Ford, there were two noted people: Griffith and his brother Francis. Ford told Peter Bogdanovich about Frank: "[H]e was the only influence *I* ever had, working in pictures." On Griffith, he said, in a much quoted phrase: "Griffith was the one who made it [motion pictures] an art," to which he quickly added, in a move typical not only of his own self-effacement but of the general conception of Hollywood movies, "if you can call it an art."[33]

Notes

1. Kristin Thompson, "The formulation of the classical style, 1909–28" in David Bordwell, Janet Staiger and Kristin Thompson, eds., *The Classical Hollywood Cinema: Film Style and Mode of Production to 1960* (London: Routledge, 1996), 157.
2. On DeMille coining "Rembrandt lighting" see Sumiko Higashi, *Cecil B. DeMille and American Culture: The Silent Era* (Berkeley, Los Angeles and London: University of California Press, 1994), 27.
3. Joseph McBride, *Searching for John Ford: A Life* (London: Faber and Faber, 2003), 88–9.
4. Lindsay Anderson, *About John Ford* (London: Plexus, 1999), 33.
5. Peter Bogdanovich, *John Ford* (Berkeley and Los Angeles: University of California Press, 1978), 40.
6. William K. Everson, *American Silent Film* (New York: Da Capo Press, 1998), 108.
7. Eileen Bowser, *History of the American Cinema: Volume 2: The Transformation of Cinema 1907–1915* (Berkeley, Los Angeles and London: University of California Press, 1990), 235.
8. Richard Abel, "The 'Imagined' Community of the Western, 1910–1913" in Charlie Keil and Shelley Stamp, eds., *American Cinema's Transitional Era: Audiences, Institutions, Practices* (Berkeley, Los Angeles, London: University of California Press, 2004), 131–143.
9. On Francis Ford's Bison films and John Ford's debut at Universal see Scott Eyman, *Print the Legend: The Life and Times of John Ford* (New York: Simon & Schuster, 1999), 40–56.
10. Eileen Bowser, *History of the American Cinema*, 162.
11. Bowser, *History of the American Cinema*, 239.
12. Barry Salt, *Film Style and Technology: History and Analysis* (London: Starword, 1992), 71–72.
13. Richard Schickel, *D.W. Griffith: An American Life* (New York: Limelight Editions, 1996), 141.
14. Tom Gunning, *D.W. Griffith and the Origins of American Narrative Film: The Early Years at Biograph* (Urbana and Chicago: The University of Illinois Press, 1991), 270.
15. William K. Everson, *American Silent Film*, 252.
16. Scott Simmon, *The Invention of the Western Film: A Cultural History of the Genre's First Half-Century* (Cambridge and New York: Cambridge University Press, 2003), 38–43.
17. Tom Gunning, "Landscape and the Fantasy of Moving Pictures: Early Cinema's Phantom Rides" in Graeme Harper and Jonathan Rayner, eds., *Cinema and Landscape* (Detroit, Michigan: Wayne State University Press, 2007), 2.
18. Ben Brewster and Lea Jacobs, *Theatre to Cinema: Stage Pictorialism and the Early Feature Film* (Oxford: Oxford University Press, 1997), 48.
19. Tom Gunning, *D.W. Griffith and the Origins of American Narrative Film: The Early Years at Biograph*, 249.
20. Ben Brewster and Lea Jacobs, *Theatre to Cinema*, 101.
21. Roberta E. Pearson, *Eloquent Gestures: The Transformation of Performance Style in the Griffith Biograph Films* (Berkeley, Los Angeles and London: University of California Press, 1992), 38–51.

22. Barry Salt, *Film Style and Technology*, 136.
23. Griffith quoted in Eileen Bowser, *History of the American Cinema*, 93.
24. William K. Everson, *American Silent Film*, 61. See also Tag Gallagher, *John Ford: The Man and His Films* (Berkeley, Los Angeles and London: University of California Press, 1986), 19.
25. William K. Everson, *American Silent Film*, 61.
26. Tom Gunning, *D.W. Griffith and the Origins of American Narrative Film*, 233.
27. Quoted in Roberta E. Pearson, *Eloquent Gestures*, 10.
28. Kevin Brownlow, *The Parade's Gone By...* (Berkeley and Los Angeles: University of California Press, 1968), 140.
29. Scott Simmon, *The Invention of the Western Film*, 67.
30. Kristin Thompson, "The formulation of the classical style," 232.
31. Thompson, "The formulation of the classical style," 158.
32. Peter Bogdanovich, *Alan Dwan: The Last Pioneer* (New York: Praeger, 1971), 25.
33. Peter Bogdanovich, *John Ford*, 40.

Beyond the Blessings of Civilization: John Ford's *Stagecoach* and the Myth of the Western Frontier

Robert C. Sickels

Like most Westerns, John Ford's *Stagecoach* (1939) takes place in the period between the end of the Civil War in 1865 and the closing of the American frontier, which Frederick Jackson Turner's Frontier Thesis establishes as no later than 1890. Turner's thesis asserts that not only American expansion, but also American democracy and American character, can be traced directly to the existence of the American West. Simply put, "The existence of an area of free land, its continuous recession, and the advance of American settlement Westward, explain American development."[1] Like Turner, Ford believed that the harsh but beautiful Western landscape helped shape American character.

However, Turner also describes the frontier as "the meeting point between savagery and civilization," an idea which has been attacked, and rightly so, as the "ethnocentric perspective of a bygone era."[2] Ford's take on the frontier, although at times equally ethnocentric, is somewhat different from Turner's. He sees the West not so much as a meeting point of savagery and civilization, but as a place where individual freedoms, needs, and desires conflict with the stifling rules of an ever encroaching "civilized" society. Ford saw the Western frontier as an ideal locale to visually portray the conflict of what Leo Marx calls the "machine in the garden."

Although made nearly seventy years ago, Ford's *Stagecoach* is still remarkably relevant. This is because the conflict between the myth of an agrarian Western frontier and the reality of America's industrialization remains omnipresent in our everyday lives. Even though we really do not want to give up our cars, phones or computers, we still cling to our sentimental dream of a pastoral existence on the frontier, far beyond "the blessings of civilization." Accordingly, one wonders if in America's supposedly free society there is room for individuals who do not readily fit into the socially dictated class system. If not, what is to be done with them? Ford uses the backdrop of the American West to cinematically pose and answer this still culturally pervasive question.

As is characteristic of Ford's relatively early films, in *Stagecoach* our hero, the Ringo Kid (John Wayne), is something of a simpleton who lacks formal education, but who possesses an idealized pastoral logic. Ringo sees complexity in nothing as his thought process is black and white; there are two ways of looking at every issue, the right way and the wrong way, and, of course, Ringo, the possessor of what Mark Twain would call "corn-pone" logic, is always on the right side of the fence. Simply put, the encroaching forces of Eastern "civilization," as symbolized by certain characters and towns in the film — most obviously and effectively the town of Lordsburg — are "bad" as they will ultimately result in a kind of social homogenization in which the individual freedoms valued by the stereotypical Western characters will be pushed aside in favor of conformist adherence to the social order. In *Stagecoach*, Ringo sees the character flaws of all the Eastern figures and has the guts to call a spade a spade when he sees one, regardless of the consequences. However, in the post-frontier social order there will be room for neither an agrarian Western hero like Ringo nor the love of his life, the saintly prostitute Dallas (Claire Trevor). Nevertheless, *Stagecoach* ultimately validates the American pastoral myth, as it is informed by a kind of optimistic hope; Ford's heroes ultimately can not live in an Eastern society, but they can still peaceably escape its confines and retreat to the frontier periphery, where they will be allowed to live as they choose with no interference from dehumanizing industrialization and urbanization.

Stagecoach is essentially a "B" Western, rife with stereotypes, that follows the structure of what would later be known as a "road movie." However, Ford was fully aware of the stereotypes, the use of which, as Richard Slotkin observes, "allowed him to take advantage of genre-based understandings—clichés of plot, setting, characterization, and motivation to compose an exceptional work marked by moral complexity, formal elegance, narrative and verbal economy, and evocative imagery."[3] The second the credits begin to roll and the opening image hits the screen, viewers are presented with what will be the central conflict throughout *Stagecoach*. We see a stagecoach, representing civilization, speeding over a dirt road against the massive real-life backdrop of Monument Valley. The machine has surely crossed into the garden, but this garden is not your run of the mill vegetable patch. It is both awe inspiring and intimidating. When we see it in films now we think of it as a cliché, but Ford was the first to film in Monument Valley. Ford's use of Monument Valley in *Stagecoach*, as well as in nine films to follow, provides an alternative insight into the progressive myth-ideology associated with Turner's frontier thesis, which so many of us, indoctrinated since childhood by countless Westerns, grew up believing was gospel truth. Monument Valley is beyond the concepts of manifest destiny and Teutonic migration. Its fierce buttes and wide plains are not to be settled or conquered; their visual impressiveness suggests they are untamable. The valley shapes the personas of its residents, not the opposite.

Immediately after the shot of the stagecoach come fairly quick, contrasting cuts back and forth between shots of the cavalry riding through the valley and shots of what we quickly learn must be Geronimo's Apaches doing the same. The music accompanying the cavalry is meant to be inspiring, clueing us in to the obvious: the cavalry are "good," exemplary representatives of the society they are sworn to protect. Accompanying the Apaches is what any fan of the Western knows is "Bad Indian" music: the pounding of drums that invariably accompanies natives on the warpath. The film cuts to the cavalry camp, where we are privy to a telegraph being sent to the troops via Lordsburg. It is cut off after one word: "Geronimo." The forces of savagery have succeeded, for a time, in disrupting the colonizing progress of civilization. Interestingly, in the context of Ford's films, Eastern society plays a similar role to that of native Americans, in that its spread forever disrupts the idealized pastoral lifestyle Ford romanticizes. The main difference, of course, which Ford's films usually fail to recognize, is that Native Americans were there first, while Easterners are "spreading" like a plague.

After the set up we are taken to the town of Tonto, in which we meet eight of the nine members of the ensemble cast. Each of the nine is an immediately recognizable Western movie stereotype, meant to represent a particular class, culture, or combination of both. Ford knowingly uses stereotypes in order to invite

> viewers to accept the film as a folk tale or fable rather than as a serious attempt at historical realism. But Ford's deliberate play with type-casting categories is a way of invoking the memories that such

movie-stereotypes contain, the framework of associations with earlier stories that defines each character's meaning and mode of action.[4]

The stagecoach pulls into town and stops, at which point the passengers get out. We are introduced first to the driver, Buck (Andy Devine), and his passenger, Lucy Mallory (Louise Platt). Buck is an oaf: well-intentioned, good-hearted, not the sharpest knife in the drawer, but a lovable rube nonetheless. He is an unsophisticated denizen of the Western frontier. In contrast, Lucy Mallory is the cultured woman from the East. In much of Ford's work, the East represents all that is corrupt and stifling in "civilization." It is in the West that the true new Canaan is found on the top of a dusty Western hill. Time and again in his films Ford used the cliché of the woman from the East — or the man, as in the cases of *My Darling Clementine*'s (1946) Doc Holliday and *The Man Who Shot Liberty Valance*'s (1962) Ransom Stoddard. We are shown immediately that Lucy is outside her element. When she asks Buck if there is any place in town she can get some tea, he replies, "Yes, ma'am, you can get a cup of coffee at that hotel over there." "Tea" connotes civilization and is more than a little effete. Tea has yet to come to Tonto, but it will. With the arrival of women like Lucy Mallory, or Clementine Carter for that matter, the arrival of tea can not be far behind.

We are next introduced to Sheriff Curly Willcox (George Bancroft). In classical Hollywood Westerns there are two kinds of sheriffs: good or bad. It is not until much later that we get the moral ambiguity associated with the onslaught of moody revisionist Westerns, ambiguity which in itself becomes another kind of stereotype. Curly is plainly a good, just sheriff. It is in his office that we first hear about the plight of the Ringo Kid, who has busted out of jail and is looking for the Plummers, whose bogus testimony framed him for a crime he did not commit. The sheriff, like many a movie sheriff before and after, obviously sympathizes with the Kid, with whose father he once rode. The Kid is rumored to be headed for Lordsburg, where the Plummers are known to be. The sheriff, wanting to keep the Kid from being killed, tells Buck he'll ride shotgun on the coach to Lordsburg.

Next we meet the town banker, Henry Gatewood (Berton Churchill). If anyone in the central cast of characters is truly all bad, it is Gatewood. Bankers are the ultimate symbol of the triumph of civilization over nature. For example, the thousands of small farms foreclosed on during the dust bowl years of the 1930s were done so by nameless "banks," a story Ford would delve into much more deeply in *The Grapes of Wrath* (1940). Banks are a concrete symbol of the way in which the encroaching East displaced and/or controlled previously independent or free aspects of life on the Western frontier. Eastern money men increasingly came to own the West in the years following the Civil War; banks were perhaps the largest flywheel in the machine that ultimately plowed the Western garden. The Westerners had but two choices: join the new urban order or get the hell out of Dodge. In Henry Gatewood Ford has given the nameless, faceless institutional machine a face, which must have been particularly resonant for an audience still not fully recovered from the Depression. Gatewood is representative of society's upper crust, the product of supposed good breeding and gentility. When he says, "What's good for the banks is good for the country," we can not help but recognize him as a comic book figure of capitalist evil. The fact that Gatewood almost immediately steals a $50,000 payroll deposit only reinforces the audience's distaste.

Next we are introduced to two of the three societal outcasts, Dallas (Claire Trevor) and Doctor Josiah Boone (Thomas Mitchell). Both are being displaced by the new social and economic order. Dallas is the whore with a heart of gold. Yes, she sells it for money, but only because she has to survive; she really does not much like it. When we first see her she is being escorted out of town by the Ladies' Decency League. Ford cuts to Doctor Boone, who is being kicked out of his place of residence for lack of payment. Doc Boone is the lovable but wise fall-down drunk, a Western stereotype used time and again by Ford. Dallas and her escorts cross paths with Doc Boone. She tells him they are forcing her out of town and that she does not want to go. He tells her not to worry and that they have no choice but to go, as they are the "victims of a disease called social prejudice." Though standard stereotypes, Doc and Dallas are indeed representative Westerners in that they are who they are. They do not try to conform to societal standards in order to fit in. In a free society people should be allowed to live the way they choose, provided they are not hurting anyone else, but that is never the case. The loudest faction, although often in the minority, decides what is right and wrong and forces its mandates on those who can not defend themselves. Once on the stage, the passengers are told that Apaches are on the warpath and that there might be some danger. Dallas sets her jaw, stares out at the Ladies' Decency League, and says, "There are worse things than Apaches."

Lastly, we are introduced to Peacock (Donald Meek) and Hatfield (John Carradine). Peacock is the answer to Doc Boone's prayers: a whiskey drummer with a valise full of "samples." He is also recognizably "good" from the first. He is effeminate and meant to be comic relief just as much as Doc Boone is, but he is always a sympathetic character. Conversely, Hatfield is a Southern gambler who fought in what he calls "the war of the rebellion." He is known to have shot people in the back. Nevertheless, in keeping with the code of Southern chivalry he decides to go on the stagecoach in order to protect Lucy Mallory, who is what he calls "an angel in a jungle," an allusion to the Eastern characters' perception of the West as "uncivilized."

Once all the various characters have been introduced, they board the stage and the trip to Lordsburg begins. In many ways the journey's structure is somewhat akin to that of Huck and Jim in that the story alternates episodically between the coach, which is like the raft on the Mississippi, and the stops along the way to Lordsburg. As soon as they leave town they pass through a fence which is symbolically like the banks of the Mississippi in that it keeps "civilization" in just as much as it keeps "nature" out. They are leaving the rigidly drawn boundaries of civilization and heading out into the great Western frontier. But the natural world into which the stagecoach heads is very different from that of the Mississippi, just as the vessel in which the characters ride is different from the raft. In Ford's films, Monument Valley has come to be more than just a place outside of civilization; it is the frontier in all its glory, a place so visually different from any other in the world that it lends authenticity to the notion of the Western landscape as a shaper of character. As Slotkin writes:

> Monument Valley has become so well established as a "typical" landscape, emblematic of "the West," that it is difficult for modern audiences to recognize that in this film (and in his subsequent Westerns) Ford is *inventing* the Valley as a cinematic (and American) icon. The Valley is in fact as unique a landscape as can be imagined. The "monuments" are huge red monoliths of volcanic stone shooting up out of rubble-piles, shaped like open hands or towered skylines or phallic spires, surrounded by the flat plane of a barren rocky desert. In *Stagecoach* it is the landscape's visual oddity that gives it authenticity—this is not a landscape anyone could invent or build in the San Fernando Valley. Its peculiarity effectively represents the alien quality of the Frontier—which had been in its time as uncanny a place for pioneers as a moonscape might be.[5]

People will never get this amazing landscape to conform to their notions of civilization. They must mold their personas to that of the land in order to survive; they must be tough, hard, unyielding, and unforgiving. Only then will they escape the stifling confines of civilization and be able to live a pastoral reality on the frontier and on their own terms. Ford's choice of Monument Valley as the setting for *Stagecoach*, as well as many other Westerns, visually reinforces and enhances the conflict between the agrarian (natural) and the industrial (civilized) at the root of both *Stagecoach*'s narrative and the frontier expansionism celebrated in so many Westerns.

While his passengers are on the road to the first stop, Dry Fork, Ford establishes the visual pattern for the film when the stagecoach is in motion. He alternates between wide panoramic shots of the coach looking tiny as it moves against the magnificent backdrop of Monument Valley, a two-shot of Buck and Curly talking atop the stage, and, inside the stage, close-ups of each individual as he or she speaks. Even though the natural world dominates the film as the stage rides through it, inside the stage the individual characters carry on their social roles. It is as though the stage, since it is encapsulated, serves as a microcosmic and mobile version of an idealized America. Over the course of the film the stage functions as a nascent republic on the edge of the frontier, containing a heterogeneous cast of characters whose very diversity symbolizes the democratic experiment that the Westward movement was ideally thought to be. Obviously Ford does this for effect, but it must be noted that the stage, unlike Huck and Jim's raft, is enclosed, thus keeping societal roles in place.

Prior to arriving in Dry Fork, the stage runs across the Ringo Kid, standing roadside, looking magnificent with his saddle slung over his left shoulder and his rifle, which he spins with graceful aplomb, in his right hand. As contemporary viewers we can not help but think of Wayne, regardless of the particular character he is playing, as "The Duke." As historian Anne Butler writes:

> More than any other medium, film is responsible for the image of the West as a place locked in the nineteenth century and defined by stark encounters between whites and Indians, law and disorder. Although social trends have altered the content of Western films, the strong, silent man of action — epitomized by John Wayne — remains the central figure.[6]

John Wayne has come to stand for a particular kind of American, one who takes no guff and fights for what he knows is right, which often appears to be what is best for America as well. This is true for no other reason than we cannot imagine John Wayne, who in his own life was far from an angel, leading us down the wrong path. The myth of John Wayne is firmly ensconced in the collective American psyche. That myth begins with this shot of him as "the Ringo Kid" in *Stagecoach*.

However, John Wayne was a firmly established "B" Western movie star in 1939, but that is about all. Literally hundreds of actors were better known than he. But *Stagecoach* and Ford changed all that. Walter Wanger, the film's producer, urged Ford to cast Gary Cooper and Marlene Dietrich as Ringo and Dallas, but Ford did not want established stars and instead convinced Wanger that John Wayne and Claire Trevor were right for the parts.[7] He did so because the casting of Cooper and Dietrich would have meant that audiences would bring preconceived notions to the film. They were not only stars, but "personalities" as well (especially Dietrich). In casting relative unknowns Ford was able to ensure that audiences would be enthralled by the story and not by the visual presence of big stars.

For Wayne, *Stagecoach* was the film that began his march towards cultural immortality. Ford saw Wayne as emblematic of the kind of hero he wanted in his films, and he was also able to get better work out of Wayne than did any other director (with the notable exception of Howard Hawks in *Red River* (1948). But this is perhaps because Ford cast Wayne in roles that he thought were perfect for him. In films after *Stagecoach* Ford did not cast Wayne solely because he was a sure box-office draw; he cast him in roles tailored to Wayne's particular talents. In later films such as *The Searchers* (1956) and *The Man Who Shot Liberty Valance* (1962), Ford cannily played on Wayne's cinematic iconography and increasing chronological age to recreate him as a far more complex, embittered figure than he portrays in earlier films. Ford's re-creation of Wayne's persona would not have been nearly so effective had not Wayne first played simpler Fordian characters like the Ringo Kid and the heroes of the Cavalry Trilogy.

After Ringo's dramatic entrance, the stage pulls into its first stop, Dry Fork. Here we see a gigantic gate pushed open and the stage safely returns to civilization. The gate is quickly shut behind it, so as to keep the unknown and unwanted out. The passengers quickly find that the cavalry they thought would be waiting for them has been ordered to move on and is already gone. They also find that the cavalry which has been escorting them to this point must move on without them. They have literally reached a crossroads and must now convene as a group to decide what to do.

After entering a large hall, Curly calls for a vote. Even at a dusty outpost in the heart of the valley, people try to form a kind of democratic social order. One would think the vastness of their surroundings would render the idea of order useless, as their societal roles are rendered equally insignificant in the face of the undiscerning natural world with which they are surrounded. Nevertheless, Curly calls for a vote. But it is not the vote of an ideal society; it is a vote that places emphasis on how each person is viewed by his or her peers. Curly immediately establishes that he votes to move on to Lordsburg as it is his duty to do so. He then says that since Ringo is his prisoner, due to the Kid's outlaw status as an escapee from jail, Ringo also votes for Lordsburg. He then states that Buck is the driver and therefore has no choice but to drive them on. So Curly basically casts three votes, all in favor of his own opinion. The "criminal" has no rights and the hired hand is nothing more than the equivalent of kitchen help with no more say in his destiny than a criminal. Curly then asks Mrs. Mallory for her vote. She is in pursuit of her husband and votes to press on. Curly then begins to ask Peacock, at which point Ringo jumps in. "Where's your manners, Curly?" he asks. "Aren't you going to ask the other lady first?" The others are shocked at his insinuation that Dallas, a prostitute, should be grouped with Mrs. Mallory, a "lady." We know for sure that Ringo is good at heart and we love him for it, and so does Dallas, who blithely says that she can not go back so she might as well go on. Ringo's simple idea of social order coincides with that of the sympathetic audience, but would the audience be in accord with him outside the confines of the big screen? It is unlikely. Ringo's vision of a fair society where all are treated equally can only exist in a fantasy land, a place where the machine has not made its way into the garden, and never will.

The group, aside from Peacock, decides that they will press on, and so, that being decided, they gather around a table to eat before resuming their journey. Dallas makes the faux pas of sitting next to Mrs. Mallory, who acts as though she has been physically assaulted. Hatfield, ever the gentleman, leaps to her rescue, asking her if she might not want to sit by the window, "where it's cooler." All recognize Dallas's mistake save Ringo, who naively thinks it is he who has offended Mrs. Mallory's sensibilities. Ringo says, "I guess I must have the plague." Thinking Dallas will be likewise offended, he begins to move, but she pulls him down, telling him it is okay. Ringo thanks her for her generosity, not realizing that it's he who is being kind. He smiles and says to her, "I guess you can't break out of prison and into society in the same week." Ringo is representative of America's pastoral impulse; he is guided by an unerring sense of right and wrong and believes there is a place where he can just "be," a mythical frontier where he will be unfettered by societal expectations and allowed to live life on the land without answering to anyone save himself. Although Americans know such a place only exists in the movies, we can not help but identify with Ringo as his unrealistic belief in America's pastoral myth coincides with our own, at least in our role as movie-goers.

The journey resumes as the stage heads for Apache Wells, the last stop before Lordsburg. During this ride we are once again privy to some of the finer moments of Dallas and Ringo's budding romance, which not only endears them to the audience, but further heightens the class conflicts aboard the stage, which continues to serve as a societal microcosm. First Dallas notices Mrs. Mallory's obvious discomfort and tells her that she can rest her head on her shoulder if she wants. It is apparent that Mrs. Mallory would like to do so, but as a "lady" she just can not consort with a prostitute and so turns Dallas down. Shortly thereafter Hatfield offers a canteen of water to Mrs. Mallory. She accepts his offer, at which time he produces a silver cup from inside his coat, fills it, and gives it to Mrs. Mallory. Once again, Dallas is snubbed, and once again Ringo gallantly comes to her rescue. He secures the canteen for her, but Hatfield disdainfully retrieves his cup, not wanting a whore to drink from it. Ringo good-naturedly smiles and hands Dallas the canteen, saying, "Sorry, no silver cups...." With a smile, Dallas drinks straight from the canteen.

The class conflicts that permeate *Stagecoach* are more than representative of America in the 1880s. Audiences in the late 1930s were still reeling from the sting of the Depression. Class differences have always been present in America, but the recognition of the haves and the have-nots had never been more heightened than during the Depression. Although the similarities between Ford's depiction of American society in the 1880s and the actualities of American life in the 1930s were largely incidental, 1930s audiences could not help but see it as reflecting the society of their own times. Though similarities to 1930s America are not the key to the narrative, audiences' identification with the film nevertheless helped to make *Stagecoach* an even greater success than it would have been otherwise.

After the canteen scene, we once again see a giant gate open wide as the stage arrives at Apache Wells. But this stop is very different from the stops that came before. It is somehow wilder, more representative of the frontier than it is of the civilized human landscapes that characterize the two main towns in the film, Tonto and Lordsburg. It is not whites who inhabit Apache Wells, but Mexicans and Apaches, who are presented not as people but as "savages." In fact, almost the first thing we hear upon the group's arrival is Peacock, eyes wide and bulging, saying "Savages!" in a frightened and excited tone as he sees the outpost's denizens. Chris (Chris Pin Martin), the outpost's proprietor, says that they are not savages, but his wife's "people." He informs them that he married an Apache woman in the hopes that it would keep the outpost safe from Apache attacks.

Shortly after arriving, Lucy Mallory faints. We find out, much to our surprise, that Lucy Mallory, despite being physically thin and never having mentioned it, has come full term in her pregnancy and is about to give birth. The characters, however, do not share in our surprise, and set themselves to preparing. For Doc Boone, this means sobering up, so he begins to drink coffee, black, and lots of it. While waiting for Lucy to commence giving birth, Dallas and Ringo get a chance to be alone together, at which time he proposes, despite having just met her and not knowing that she is a prostitute. He has a farm in Mexico, just over the border. It is "a nice place, trees, grass, water...." In Westerns the frontier is almost always devoid of trees, grass, and water. As Tompkins writes, the "land is defined by absence: absence of trees, of greenery, of houses, of the signs of civilization, above all of water and shade."[8] However, that is exactly the point; the frontier is a virgin land that can theoretically be sculpted into whatever form its settlers choose to give it. But Ringo is well aware that the small outposts through which they keep passing are merely the beginning of the onslaught; civilization is coming to the West and Ringo wants no part of it. Instead he dreams of retreating to his mythical land across the border, on which he can be with Dallas and raise his family in peace and on his own terms. He wants to live a pastoral existence as a Jeffersonian yeoman farmer. Of course, being a repressed Fordian hero, he never actually asks, "Will you marry me?" (nor does he ever say "I love you"); instead he just asks Dallas if she will come with him. If anybody ever needed to return to a pastoral existence it is Dallas, who has been victimized mercilessly by society. She not only agrees to go with Ringo, but offers to help him escape. Despite one being a convicted felon and the other a long-time whore, they appear in this film as babes in the woods, and we find ourselves rooting for their success.

As Mrs. Mallory finally begins to give birth, Doc Boone and Dallas each has a chance at moral redemption. However, this stereotypical situation is treated very differently by Ford than it might be by another director. Doc Boone sobers up enough to deliver the baby without a hitch.

As a result, he gains not only the respect of the others, but a newfound self-respect. In fact, when Gatewood asks Doc if he will join him in a drink, Doc disgustedly says, "No thanks," and tosses his drink out. This is standard Western fare. On the other hand, Dallas stays up throughout the night and tends both to Lucy and her newborn child. In most films she would be recognized by the others as the truly good person she is, but in *Stagecoach* Ford chooses to keep her forever on the outside looking in, at least when in "civilized" company. Lucy recognizes Dallas's decency and kindness, and when they finally do get to Lordsburg Lucy says to Dallas, "If there is ever anything I can do for...." But she never finishes the sentence. Lucy has returned to society. In spite of knowing better, when she is in town Lucy has no choice but to play her role, which is to adhere to the standards set by the women of the Decency League. Even if there is something she can do for Dallas, she will not do it; we know it and so does Dallas, who tersely answers "Sure!" According to the conventions of the genre Dallas should be redeemed for her "sins," but she is not—at least not in the eyes of the "civilized" passengers.

The child is born without difficulties and is promptly nicknamed "Little Coyote" by the others. This name, although hokey, is not without significance. As previously mentioned, Apache Wells is more wild than the other stops along the way. It is closer to the omnipresent threat of the Apaches and seems somehow more akin to the harsh surrounding landscape than were the other stops. Accordingly, "Little Coyote" is emblematic of the wildness into which the child has been born. He is literally a babe in the woods, a child of nature, and "Little Coyote" is an apt reminder of this. He is born without the prejudices that go along with the social structure of cities, but we quickly realize that the wildness he represents will be taught out of him. As the child of Lucy Mallory, he will be raised to disdain those who are not his social equals, even though without them it is doubtful he would have made it into the world alive.

Shortly thereafter Chris's wife reinforces the stereotype of Natives and Mexicans as "savages" by helping the vaqueros at the outpost to steal the coach's fresh horses. At this point, Ringo and Dallas come to a crossroads. Ringo, with Dallas's help, is about to escape when he sees smoke on the horizon, which means that the Apaches are on the warpath. Ringo must make a decision: should he make his escape to his farm in Mexico and lead the life of a yeoman farmer, or should he join civilized society as represented by the microcosm of the stagecoach passengers? In him we see a still central conflict of American society: the battle between our sentimental desire for pastoralism and our more pressing need to succeed in an ever increasing urban reality. Ringo decides to stay and help the others to reach Lordsburg, even though he can never fit into their society.

Between Apache Wells and Lordsburg the stage is attacked by Geronimo and his band of warriors. However, shortly before this happens, Doc Boone astutely reveals the lay of the human landscape awaiting the various passengers in Lordsburg. With a sample bottle of Peacock's whiskey in hand, he surveys his fellow passengers one by one and smiles as he raises the bottle to them and says, "Ladies and gentlemen, since it's most unlikely that we'll ever have the pleasure of meeting again socially, I'd like to propose a toast ... to your health!" They have established a kind of uneasy but tolerable peace out of necessity. Doc knows, however, that the peace is merely transitory and that if they reach Lordsburg, each will resume his or her "proper" place in society. Prefiguring the disruption of their peace are the Apaches, one of whose arrows hits Peacock in the chest just after Doc Boone makes his toast. And with that the chase is on.

On the one hand, *Stagecoach* contains among one of the most exciting Cowboy and Indian chase scenes ever filmed, while on the other it is somewhat anticlimactic. As in most Ford films, the conflict is established immediately, with the resolution coming very late. In the meantime, we have become wrapped up in the lives of the characters, to the point of almost forgetting about the Apaches, even though they are alluded to throughout the narrative. Hatfield is killed, and Buck and Peacock are injured. In fact, it looks as though the day is lost, but at the last moment we hear the distant sound of the cavalry's bugler, soft at first, but steadily increasing in volume. The cavalry, which in Ford's later Cavalry trilogy will become his strongest symbol of the keepers of order in an urban society, saves the day. We cheer and we love their arrival, despite its implausibility.

Upon arriving safely in Lordsburg, Gatewood is arrested for theft, Lucy joins her husband, and the rest assume their societal roles. It is here that Dallas returns to prostitution and Ringo must return to jail. Fortunately, Curly is a classic "good" sheriff who sympathizes with his charge. When Ringo asks if he can walk Dallas home, Curly agrees, going so far as to give him a rifle, even though it has no bullets. Ringo, in classic John Wayne fashion, reveals that he has saved three bullets, which is all a guy like him needs to take care of the three Plummers who had framed him and sent him to prison. Curly wishes him luck and sends him off to meet his destiny.

Their ensuing walk though Lordsburg is a symbolic condemnation of towns. As Tompkins points out:

> There is a tremendous tension in Westerns between the landscape and town. The genre pulls toward the landscape — that, in a sense, is its whole point. But because there's so much emphasis on getting away, town also exerts a tremendous pull — otherwise there would be no reason to flee.[9]

The town is the cradle of Eastern urbanization, and accordingly it has its benefits: stores, saloons, restaurants, women, etc.. But a town, by its very nature, must be structured in an orderly fashion as decreed by an elite minority. A town is no place to live a life on one's own terms, especially if one wants a life on the land. Pastoralism is impossible in a town and living in one, in the conventions of the Western, only makes one want to flee to the frontier. As Ringo and Dallas walk arm in arm towards Lordsburg's red-light district, they do it against a backdrop of increasing decadence. With the rounding of every corner the prostitutes become more visible, the saloons are seedier, the lurid, debauched laughter gets louder, and the faces in the night held by the camera only in brief passing become more pallid and washed out. The town, supposedly the ultimate achievement of industrial civilization, seems to breed nothing but decay. As Ringo says, "This is no town for a girl like [Dallas]."

Upon arriving at Dallas's new "home," the dim light of recognition finally goes on in Ringo's head. In seeing the broken down walkway that leads to the poorly lit, nearly windowless house, he at last realizes that Dallas is a prostitute. Of course this does not matter to him, for he has recognized that she, like he, has a heart of gold. He leaves her there to go off and fight the Plummers, but not before telling her to go to his farm across the border, his frontier oasis, and wait for him to return from prison. In typical Fordian underplay, we do not even get to see the complete shoot-out. We hear the shots and we know that Ringo has accomplished his mission of vengeance.

As a man of honor, Ringo returns to Curly and turns himself in. As a parting request he asks Curly to see that Dallas gets to "my place across the border," which Curly solemnly promises he will do. Curly and Doc ask Dallas if she would like to ride to the outskirts of town with Ringo. She steps up onto the buckboard, and Curly and Doc whip the horses into motion, setting Ringo and Dallas free to pursue their dream life out on the frontier. Doc smiles and says to Curly, "Well, they're free from the blessings of civilization," and with that the two men head back to town for a drink. *Stagecoach*'s ending is stereotypical as far as Westerns are concerned, but very different in its ultimate social commentary. The stagecoach has not only acted as a physical carrier in a journey across the landscape of the American West, but has also served to navigate and comment on the social landscape that came about as a result of the shift in American society from agrarianism to industrialism. The stuff on which America was founded — freedom, democracy, justice — has become lost in the onslaught of "civilization." The frontier is dead, but we still fantasize about its existence, assuming that it is there, just outside the city limits and easily obtainable by way of our sport utility vehicles. But, as Ford knew and illustrates throughout his work, industrialism and technology are both the contents of Pandora's box.

Westerns often celebrate that time before the contents of the box had fully manifested themselves in American society, but even in a film as seemingly simple as *Stagecoach*, Ford realizes that in America the frontier is a place eternally beyond the rainbow. As Slotkin writes:

> [T]he "progress" achieved through the journey's ordeal belongs only to the isolated individual — it has no social realization, no historical home. Democracy, equality, responsibility, and solidarity are achieved only in transit; they exist — they are *visible* — only in the midst of the narrative, only during the pursuit of the goal. When the goal is reached they dissolve, and social order lapses into habitual injustice, inequality, alienation, and hierarchy. Our only hope is to project a further frontier, a mythic space beyond the frontier, a mythic space beyond the Western landscape and American history — whose possibilities have been thoroughly used up.[10]

However, despite realizing that the possibilities of the Western landscape are, as Slotkin claims, "used up," Ford nevertheless panders to our desires by sentimentally idealizing its existence. Ringo is allowed to escape, with Dallas in tow, to his place across the border.

Even though *Stagecoach* offers no metaphorical synthesis of the machine and the garden, it is still not as cynical as Ford's later work. Tag Gallagher asserts that

> ... no other Ford Western gives a more cynical verdict of the notion of the West as synthesis of nature and civilization. In *Liberty Valance* (1962), for contrast, Ransom Stoddard spends a lifetime to figure out what everyone in *Stagecoach* already knows: that civilization is corrupting. The idealism, progressivism, and enlightenment shared by virtually everyone in *Liberty Valance* is absolutely absent in malodorous Lordsburg and Tonto — dirty, sleazy, full of mean, intolerant, aggressive people.[11]

Although Gallagher is right concerning the lack of a synthesis of nature and civilization, he misses the optimism of the film's ending, which is a kind of happy celebration. Yes, the folks in *Stagecoach* know civilization is corrupting, but they have not yet conceded that it is inescapable, which in *The Man Who Shot Liberty Valance* is the realization that ruins not only Ransom Stoddard (Jimmy Stewart), but the Ringo Kid's cinematic descendant, Tom Doniphon, also played by John Wayne. Whereas Ringo and Dallas simply leave Lordsburg behind, Tom, who wants to live on a farm outside the confines of Shinbone's boundaries, ignominiously loses his girl to Stoddard, the Easterner, and is forced to live out his final years anonymously in Shinbone. Despite the fact that Ringo and Dallas are going to a land outside of history, a pastoral place that probably never existed anywhere save in the collective American mind, they *do* in fact escape urbanization.

In *Stagecoach* the chances of a fully realized, ostensibly integrated society are nil. The social forces which determine people's respective places are just too strong, and those who do not fit into any of the socially viable roles are not allowed to stay in the community. However, the fact is that Ringo and Dallas, the outcasts, do not want to live in an Easternized town anyway. What separates *Stagecoach* from Ford's later work is that Ford himself, at the time *Stagecoach* was made, was still hopeful about the possibilities of American life. Accordingly, even though they can not live in the constricting confines of a town, Ringo and Dallas still have the option of retreating to the frontier to live an ideal pastoral life.

In *Stagecoach* Ford appeals to our preconceptions, however erroneous, of what in our best dreams we envision America to be. Although Ford's films have been assumed to offer a reconciliation between Western pastoralism and Eastern industrialism, this is not the case in *Stagecoach*. My reading of *Stagecoach* suggests, rather, that although he does not attempt to metaphorically reconcile Western pastoralism with Eastern urbanism, Ford's narrative nevertheless finds a way to keep his characters, and his audience, optimistic that there is a frontier awaiting us all — a simple place outside the confines of the dehumanizing landscapes of our industrial reality, a magic place where our sentimental pastoralism is not only a dream, but a fact. In this crucial respect, *Stagecoach* is the most optimistic of Ford's Westerns.

Notes

1. Clyde A. Milner, in Clyde A. Milner, Carol A. O'Connor, and Martha A. Sandweiss, eds., "America Only More So," in *The Oxford History of the American West* (New York: Oxford University Press, 1994), 4.
2. Clyde A. Milner, "America Only More So," 4.
3. Richard Slotkin, *Gunfighter Nation: The Myth of the Frontier in Twentieth-Century America* (New York: Atheneum, 1992), 303.
4. Richard Slotkin, *Gunfighter Nation*, 304.
5. Richard Slotkin, *Gunfighter Nation*, 305.
6. Anne M. Butler, "Selling the Popular Myth," in Milner, O'Connor, Sandweiss, eds., *The Oxford History of the American West* (New York: Oxford University Press, 1994), 793.
7. Tag Gallagher, *John Ford: The Man and His Films* (Berkeley: University of California Press, 1986), 146.
8. Jane Tompkins, "The Language of the Western," in Leonard Engel, ed., *The Big Empty: Essays on the Land as Narrative* (Albuquerque: University of New Mexico Press, 1994), 285.
9. Jane Tompkins, "The Language of the Western," 299.
10. Richard Slotkin, "John Ford's *Stagecoach* and the Mythic Space of the Western Movie," in Engel, ed., *The Big Empty: Essays on the Land as Narrative*, 279.
11. Tag Gallagher, *John Ford*, 161.

John Ford's Festive Comedy: Ireland Imagined in *The Quiet Man*

William C. Dowling

Introduction

In late 1951, as his film *The Quiet Man* was being edited into final form, director John Ford sent a cautiously optimistic telegram to his friend Lord Killanin in Dublin: "The Quiet Man looks better and better. There is a vague possibility that even the Irish will like it."[1] Though *The Quiet Man* would be enormously popular in America, its portrait of rural Irish life in the 1920s striking a chord of deep sympathetic response among moviegoers of all religious and ethnic backgrounds, Ford's hopes for a similar response in Ireland were in vain.

"It was not very popular here at first," Killanin would recall years later, "and there were strong objections to the line from May Craig, 'Here's a fine stick to beat the lovely lady.'"[2] Initially, as Killanin's remark suggests, it was the film's portrayal of the tempestuous relationship between Sean Thornton (John Wayne) and Mary Kate Danaher (Maureen O'Hara) that met the strongest resistance. "To this day," says Margaret Niland, a local woman who was there when *The Quiet Man* was filmed in County Mayo, "I still don't like that bit where he drags her across the fields.... That scene is not so nice because I think it does the Irish down."[3]

Today, it is *The Quiet Man*'s picture of a premodern or preindustrial Ireland — an older society of dowries, cattle fairs and donnybrooks — that more often draws the objections of Irish commentators. A common move is to portray Ford's image of Ireland — "a never-never Golden Age," as Harlan Kennedy describes it, "a time of simple pastoral integrity"[4] — as a mode of cultural imperialism, with Hollywood perpetuating various Irish stereotypes whose origins lay in long centuries of English political domination. Along with outright falsity, remarks James MacKillop, the sins attributed to *The Quiet Man* include "sentimentalism, condescension, cliché, and gimcrackery."[5]

Taken together, Kennedy argues, such qualities add up to a view of "Irishness" that is "not less patronizing and oppressive than the collar-and-lead colonialism long exercised by Britain."[6] In recent years, as Irish Studies has attempted to make a place for itself in an Anglo-American postcolonial discourse driven by identity politics, this has become more and more the standard line. Thus, for instance, Lance Pettitt's recent *Screening Ireland* approaches *The Quiet Man* from a perspective deriving less from film study or Irish history than from the "postcolo-

This article appeared previously in *Eire–Ireland: An Interdisciplinary Journal of Irish Studies*, 23:1 (2001), 190–211. Copyright © 2001: Irish American Cultural Institute, 1 Lackawanna Place, Morristown, NJ 07960. Reprinted by permission of the publisher, the Irish American Cultural Institute. We have made only slight stylistic changes to the original which was published during the fiftieth anniversary of the release of *The Quiet Man*.

nial" theorizing of such writers as Homi Bhabha, Gayatri Spivak, Ania Loomba, and Edward Said.

In Ireland, a sense that American cinema represents a threat to Irish cultural independence is nearly as old as the republic. "We cannot be the sons of Gael and citizens of Hollywood at the same time," wrote one Irish nationalist in the 1930s.[7] This is the spirit in which so much contemporary Irish filmmaking has defined itself specifically in opposition to *The Quiet Man*'s image of Ireland as, in Luke Gibbons's phrase, "a primitive Eden, a rural idyll free from the pressures and constraints of the modern world."[8]

The truth about Ireland is therefore to be sought in the bleak social reality that *The Quiet Man*'s pastoral idyll hides from sight, as in what Terry Byrne describes as the "mind-numbing and desperately depressing" existence of the characters in Joe Comerford's *Traveller* (1978),[9] or the rural poverty portrayed in Pat O'Connor's *The Ballroom of Romance* (1982), or the squalor of the Dublin squatter society—drug addicts, dealers, prostitutes, pimps—in Cathal Black's *Pigs* (1984).

Even a commercially successful film like Roddy Doyle's *The Commitments* (1991) is taken to provide a modicum of truth in what might be called the Corpo flat realism of the scenes taking place in Dublin's public housing projects: "an alternative body of imagery," as Gibbons calls such material, that can be seen as addressing "the realities of Irish life."[10] As Gibbons's phrasing suggests, his sympathies are on the side of the new Dublin realists against what he describes as the straitjacket of stereotype. Yet Gibbons has also, virtually alone among Irish commentators, grasped the sense in which *The Quiet Man* has for nearly fifty years been serving as a mirror for Irish cultural anxieties, provoking reactions having very little to do with the film itself. His essay "Romanticism, Realism and Irish Cinema," which goes some way toward taking *The Quiet Man* seriously as a work of the artistic or cinematic imagination, anticipates several points I want to make in this essay.

Nonetheless, my attempt will be to get entirely beyond the matter of "alienating images"[11] of Ireland, as Gibbons calls them. For my argument will be that John Ford saw in "Ireland" something like the imaginative resource that Yeats found in Irish myth—"a symbolic language," as Yeats himself once puts it, "reaching far back into the past"[12]—and that *The Quiet Man* is far closer to Shakespearean romantic comedy, and to the premodern world of village festivity and pagan ritual we glimpse in its immediate background, than to anything in recent Irish culture.

My argument will be, ultimately, that the power of *The Quiet Man* is the power of cultural myth.

Ford the Irishman vs. Hollywood

The making of *The Quiet Man* has itself become a myth, a story about Ford's long struggle against the Hollywood studio system to make a film that, though it had intense personal meaning for him, was seen as having no commercial potential. From the time in 1936 that Ford bought the rights to Maurice Walsh's *Saturday Evening Post* short story "The Quiet Man" as well as to the expanded version included in Walsh's collection *Green Rushes*—this is the version that, adding such characters as the *shaughraun* (matchmaker) Michaeleen Og Flynn, would become the basis of Ford's film—he tried to interest producers and studio heads in this tale of an American prizefighter who, having killed an opponent in a boxing match, returns to his ancestral homeland in hopes of finding peace.

In 1935, when Ford had made *The Informer* on a Hollywood sound stage and a very tight shooting schedule, the making of a Hollywood film for personal or artistic reasons was still possible. By 1945, when Ford returned to Hollywood after three years as head of a wartime Navy

The Quiet Man (1952): The director's older brother Francis Ford, far left; John Wayne, Maureen O'Hara, and Barry Fitzgerald, far right (with the permission of Dan Ford; courtesy Lilly Library, Indiana University, Bloomington).

photographic unit, the idea had become virtually unthinkable. "You're in Ireland and we're in America," wrote Ned Depinet, an RKO distribution head to whom Ford showed the screenplay of *The Quiet Man*, "and I'm not going to pay for that."[13]

Yet Ford's own career warns us against taking the struggle to make *The Quiet Man* as any simple allegory of artistic integrity versus the profit motive. For the key to Ford's genius as a director was precisely his ability to turn the constraints of the studio system to artistic advantage. He had learned his trade in the ruthless economic competition of the silent film industry and had come of age as a director of sound films under Darryl Zanuck at Twentieth Century–Fox. Such Ford masterpieces as *The Grapes of Wrath* (1940) and *How Green Was My Valley* (1941) were produced under what are sometimes called the assembly-line conditions of the Hollywood system.

A genuine appreciation of the artistic possibilities made available by the system may be heard in Ford's insistence, in an interview with Jean Mitry, that "it is wrong to liken a director to an author." "He is," Ford would say, "more like an architect, if he is creative. An architect conceives his plans from given premises— the purpose of the building, its size, the terrain. If he is clever, he can do something creative within these limitations."[14]

On the other hand, one hears throughout Ford's career a note of longing for a more pure or personal mode of artistic expression. "There's nothing surprising about the difficulty of doing things you yourself believe in the movies," he said in a 1936 interview with *New Theater* magazine, "when you consider that you're spending someone else's money. And a lot of money. And he wants a lot of profit on it."[15] Ford's long association with Dudley Nichols, a screenwriter whose political sympathies lay with the radical left, is partly to be explained by their shared sense of being involved in a sort of guerilla warfare against the studio system as a machine relentlessly geared to the maximization of profits.

"Another 16-inch shell into the MGM glamour empire," Nichols jubilantly wrote Ford after seeing the final cut of *The Long Voyage Home* (1940), a film he and Ford had adapted from four one-act plays by Eugene O'Neill. This is the context in which the project of making *The Quiet Man* would come to symbolize for Ford and members of his film "family"—most importantly, John Wayne and Maureen O'Hara—a struggle for artistic expression against the commercial imperatives of the Hollywood glamour empire. A major clue to *The Quiet Man*'s portrayal of Ireland lies in its importance to Wayne and O'Hara and other members of what is sometimes called the John Ford stock company. For the stock company served Ford throughout his career as a surrogate community or extended family able to protect him as an artist from the otherwise destructive commercial pressures of Hollywood. In the numerous interviews and reminiscences left by its members, it is true, no one speaks in direct terms about the way Ford's film family insulated him from commercial pressure. They tend to talk instead about the set of a Ford movie as something very like a magical space, a sphere sustained by complex rituals and ceremonies to which newcomers—always at the risk of an explosion from the mercurial Irishman sitting in the director's chair—had to be introduced in whispers. Yet all seem to have understood, as their long loyalty to *The Quiet Man* as Ford's "Irish project" makes clear, that the magical sphere he created around himself was for Ford the equivalent of an imaginary Irish village or family, with its rituals and jokes and loyalties and feuds, held together by the testy and wholly unpredictable presence of Ford himself as *paterfamilias* or head of the clan.

The story of how Ford came to Hollywood has become a legend. He grew up as John Martin Feeney in the Munjoy Hill section of Portland, Maine, the son of Irish-speaking parents in a Irish Catholic immigrant community. His older brother Francis, a handsome scapegrace driven out of Portland by a bit of local scandal, had lost touch with the family for several years, drifting into an acting career in the fledgling film industry in Los Angeles, where he had emerged as an important director as well as a successful leading man.

Meanwhile, back in Portland, their mother Abby, who as a native Irish speaker had never learned to read and write English, was an enthusiastic fan of the new silent films being shown at the Empire Theater. On a weekend in 1914, the inevitable happened. Abby Feeney returned to announce to her family that she had just seen her eldest son, listed in the credits as Francis Ford, in a starring role. They contacted Francis through his studio and he made a short triumphal visit to his old home town. Shortly thereafter, some weeks after graduating from high school, John Martin Feeney was on his way to join his older brother in Los Angeles.

Virtually from the moment of his arrival, Ford set about establishing the private world within filmmaking that would sustain him through a long Hollywood career. Within an astonishingly short time, he had surpassed his brother Francis's reputation as a gifted director, demonstrating a special talent for making the two-reel westerns that were a staple of silent film production. As has often enough been remarked, part of his genius lay in translating the cultural values of his parents' rural Ireland to an American setting. Ford's westerns, as Luke Gibbons has observed, "are often vitalized by an infusion of Irish themes—collective violence, family ties, rituals of solidarity, a longing for community."[16]

What is less often remarked is that these same rituals of solidarity, meaningful only within an established community, were central as well to the way Ford actually made his films. Here lie the origins of the John Ford stock company: the major stars—Harry Carey in the silents, Wayne and Ward Bond and Victor McLaglen and Maureen O'Hara in the period of sound—

who appear over and over in Ford's films, the grips and prop men and stuntmen who moved with Ford from production to production, the writers (Dudley Nichols, Nunnally Johnson, Frank Nugent) and cameramen (Gregg Toland, Joe August, Winton Hoch) who show up again and again in the credits to his films.

In reminiscences by members of the Ford stock company, even the smallest of these rituals of solidarity assumes a mythic importance. Consider, for instance, the accordion playing of Danny Borzage, who would greet the arrival on the set of each principle player with a theme drawn from a film they had done with Ford — "Red River Valley" for Henry Fonda, "Wagons West" for Ward Bond, "Marquita" for John Wayne — and softly fill in the background between takes with Ford favorites like "Bringing in the Sheaves."

Borzage's presence on every Ford set for over forty years has a great deal to do with the emotional quality of Ford's films. "Upon arriving on the set," recalls Harry Carey, Jr., "you would feel right away that something special was going to happen. You would feel spiritually awakened all of a sudden.... This feeling has never happened to me again on any set." And Carey, like everyone else, remembers Borzage's music as an essential part of the mood: "He certainly was not a particularly good accordion player, but his music moved you. It wouldn't be a Ford set without his sounds of plaintive sadness that pulled at your heart, that made you feel, 'Thank God I'm here to do a scene for that Old Man by the camera.'"[17]

The Quiet Man assumed symbolic importance for members of Ford's film family not least because it incorporated so many of these rituals into its own story. Those who have objected to the film as a hopelessly sentimentalized picture of Irish society — "a tourist's vision of Ireland," as MacKillop says[18] — have, for instance, been especially hard on the music in the story, as though it portrayed the Irish as a happy-go-lucky people always ready to break spontaneously into song no matter how terrible the tribulations of poverty and history.

A favorite example in condemnations or dismissals of *The Quiet Man* is the scene in Cohan's pub where the company learns that the tall American stranger in their midst is Sean Thornton, come home from the steel mills of Pittsburgh to his ancestral village of Inisfree, at which point an accordionist strikes up "Wild Colonial Boy" and all join in a rousing rendition of the song. Yet this scene is not in any simple sense about Ireland. It is at some level, as reminiscences like Carey's remind us, about the real community from which *The Quiet Man* had emerged as a work of cinematic art, for whom Danny Borzage's accordion was a constant reminder of mood and purpose. At such moments *The Quiet Man* is gazing through or beyond its Irish story to a deeper relation between ritual and community.

The story of how *The Quiet Man* at last came to the screen does read like a fable of Hollywood greed versus artistic integrity. Its villain was Herbert B. Yates, a former tobacco magnate whose Republic Pictures specialized in cheaply-produced westerns — the typical shooting schedule was seven to fourteen days — and whose only major asset was a contract with John Wayne, who after having been lent to directors like Howard Hawks and John Ford was emerging as a major star. Unable to get out of his contract with Yates, Wayne attempted to improve his own lot by bringing Ford to Republic.

The result was a draconian deal: Ford would make three films within a two year period, none to exceed $1.25 million in budget. The lure was *The Quiet Man*, a project that Yates detested — he described it to John Wayne as a "phony art-house picture"[19] — but that he agreed to let Ford make if the first of the three films turned out to make a profit. With the recent success of *Fort Apache* and *She Wore a Yellow Ribbon* behind him, Ford chose to begin with a western. Wayne was already under contract at Republic. Ford borrowed Maureen O'Hara from Fox and shot *Rio Grande*. It was a box office success, and the Ford film family was, at long last, ready to move on to *The Quiet Man*.

The shooting of *The Quiet Man* has lingered as a local legend in County Mayo and environs, one suspects, because it was so obviously a celebratory occasion for members and relations of Ford's extended film family. To permit Ford to make the film within the rigid budgetary limits imposed by Herbert Yates, John Wayne agreed to work for a greatly-reduced fee. Wayne brought his four children along on location, and Ford gave them parts in an important scene in the film. Ward Bond and Victor McLaglen, veteran stalwarts of the Ford stock company, played major roles as the unsaintly parish priest Father Lonergan and the blustering squireen Red Will Danaher.

McLaglen's son Andrew was assistant production manager. Maureen O'Hara played Mary Kate Danaher, the fiery-tempered Irish girl with whom Wayne falls in love over the objections of her bullying brother. O'Hara's own real-life brothers Charles and James FitzSimons play the former IRA commandant Forbes and the young priest Father Paul. Barry Fitzgerald is the irrepressible shaughraun Michaeleen Og Flynn, his brother Arthur Shields the Protestant vicar Mr. Playfair. And Ford's own brother, Francis, whose early success in silent films had given Ford his start as a director, plays the white-bearded village elder Dan Tobin.

The Quiet Man is often described as Ford's homecoming to Ireland, and to a degree this was so. A reporter from the *Connaught Tribune*, for instance, was suitably astonished to hear the Hollywood director drop into Irish in an interview, unaware that Ford's parents were from the Gaeltacht (Irish-speaking region), or that Irish had been spoken in his home in Portland, Maine.[20] But the real homecoming of Ford and *The Quiet Man* company was not to Ireland but to Inisfree, the wholly imaginary village in which the story takes place. It is Inisfree that embodies the sense of community and shared ritual that had permitted Ford and his film family to create their own magic space in a Hollywood presided over by the likes of Herbert B. Yates, for whom the entire meaning of a film was its box office receipts.

This is the space Federico Fellini would later have in mind in describing Ford as someone "who has made out of motion pictures a fairy tale to be lived by himself, a dwelling in which to live with joyous spontaneity."[21] The subject of *The Quiet Man* is in this sense not Ireland or the Irish but the survival of art in a time in which "the filthy modern tide," as Yeats called all those forces of modernity hostile to mind or spirit or imagination, has swept away all but a few fugitive traces of a world once coherent and whole.

The Green World

The Quiet Man has a great deal in common with Shakespearean comedy. The resemblance was remarked upon almost immediately by Lindsay Anderson, the English film director who remains the most perceptive critic of Ford's work. Like Shakespeare, Anderson wrote to Ford in 1953, referring to both *The Quiet Man* and Ford's next film *The Sun Shines Bright* (1953), Ford had succeeded in creating a world that was "all harmony and reconciliation," exactly like "one of those late untidy magical comedies—*Winter's Tale* or *Cymbeline*."[22]

His observation holds obviously true at the level of plot, where Ford's famously digressive style of film narration bears a marked resemblance to what Anderson calls the untidiness of Shakespeare's later comedies. At the deeper level of comic structure, however, *The Quiet Man* bears a far stronger resemblance to the comedies Shakespeare wrote in the period between *The Taming of the Shrew* and *As You Like It*, with their characteristic movement — as Northrop Frye once said, thinking in particular of the Forest of Arden in *As You Like It*—"out of the world of experience into the ideal world of innocence and romance."[23]

This comic structure was brilliantly analyzed in 1959 by C.L. Barber in *Shakespeare's Festive Comedy*, which isolated in these plays what Barber calls a "saturnalian pattern" derived from holiday games and customs that had survived from an earlier pre–Christian culture, and in many cases from pagan rituals already archaic when Aristophanes was writing comedies in ancient Athens.[24] Thus it is, on Barber's account, that Shakespeare's romantic comedies are so filled with allusions to English village games—"morris dances, sword-dances, wassailings ... mummings, disguising, masques"[25]—associated with the procession of holidays—"Shrove Tuesday, Hocktide, May Day, Whitsuntide, Midsummer Eve"[26]—that for long centuries had governed the rhythms of the European medieval year.

Their essence is caught in Barber's notion of a saturnalian pattern, *Saturnalia* having been the Roman festival during which normal social hierarchy was inverted and masters waited on their servants. The point of the pattern lies precisely in the principle of ritualized disorder called misrule or the-world-turned-upside-down, a moment of collective freedom from the rule of an unvarying obedience to authority that might otherwise threaten to become intolerable.

An important point in Barber's analysis is that the rule of authority reversed or inverted during the holiday interlude need not be that of social hierarchy merely, but may be that of a rigid moral or religious code demanding an unreasonable purity of motive and behavior. Thus it is, for instance, that a valuable source of information about the holiday games and customs of Shakespeare's day comes not from the village merrymakers but from their Puritan critics, who correctly saw in them a survival of pagan rituals in which the ordinary rules of continence and sexual morality were temporarily suspended.

A particular object of Puritan detestation was the May Day customs associated with "bringing home the May," in which young men and women went into the woods together—a certain amount of sexual dalliance being expected and tolerated—to return with the Maypole, a slender sapling set up in the center of the village to celebrate the return of spring. "They strew the ground round about," wrote the Puritan Phillip Stubbs disgustedly in a polemic entitled *The Anatomy of Abuses*, "bind green boughs about it ... and then fall they to dance about it, like as the heathen people did at the dedication of the Idols."[27] As Stubbs and his fellow Puritans clearly understood—it is what Stubbs means to get at in talking about "Idols" and "heathen people"— the green boughs strewed around the Maypole were survivals of an ancient fertility worship for which the rebirth of nature in springtime bespoke a mystery of regeneration—Dylan Thomas's "force that through the green fuse drives the flower"—so powerful as to temporarily sweep away conventional morality. The archetype of the May Day ritual as it existed in Shakespeare's time, no doubt, was the Bacchic ritual of the ancient Greek and Roman world, in which drinking and sexual license combined to create something like a complete suspension of ordinary social rules.

A strong element of Bacchic release survived, at any rate, in the Elizabethan customs that permitted a great deal of drinking and verbal and physical bellicosity during the period of holiday license, usually under the direction of a Lord of Misrule chosen to preside over the festivities. Barber quotes in this connection Sir Thomas Urquhart, who describes this personage as "the King of Misrule, whom we invest with that title to no other end, but to countenance ... Bacchanalian riots and preposterous disorders."[28]

The point of the saturnalian pattern in Shakespearean comedy, as in the holiday games and customs to which the plays so frequently allude, is the revelation that the ordinary or workaday world, which seeks to present its claims to sober morality in exclusive and unconditional terms, is after all no more than one possible world among others. This is the point missed by Puritans like Phillip Stubbs, who treats the very idea of common holidays, or time taken out from work or business and devoted to festivity, as an offense to God and man.

In a work like Stubbs' *Anatomie of Abuses* we are already very close, as Barber points out, to that emergent social and economic order described by Max Weber's famous essay on the Protestant ethic or by R.H. Tawney in *Religion and the Rise of Capitalism*, "a world of isolated, busy individuals, each prudently deciding how to make the best use of his time."[29] Against this, Shakespearean comedy counterposes the vision of an earlier social order in which individual life had taken on meaning within the communal existence expressed in May Day or Hocktide ceremonies of misrule, which is why the festive comedies so often give the effect of "a group who are experiencing together a force larger than their individual wills."[30]

The comic structure of *The Quiet Man* is very close to this Shakespearean pattern. The major difference is that in Shakespeare the symbolic opposition between the world of sober morality and that of holiday freedom is normally made internal to the play. Thus, for instance, in *As You Like It* the Elizabethan opposition between Stubbs' Puritan values and those of the May Day merrymakers is reproduced in the opposition between the court, ruled over by the usurping Duke Frederick and his followers, and the Forest of Arden—the green world, as it is usually called by scholars of Renaissance literature, representing "a region defined by an attitude of liberty from ordinary limitations."[31]

In *The Quiet Man* the green world is Ireland, or at least the version of Ireland that Ford locates in the imaginary village of Inisfree, counting on his audience to recognize the Yeatsian or poetic overtones of the name. The opposing world that corresponds to Stubbs' Puritan values, on the other hand, especially as these have led in modern times to a dissolution of community in the name of a relentless economic individualism, is that absent or distant America from which Sean Thornton has returned to Inisfree.

The Quiet Man's story revolves around a deep underlying tension between the opposing world views of Inisfree and twentieth-century America. This is posed at the beginning of the story as a problem about romantic love and traditional marriage customs, originating in the overwhelming romantic attraction between Sean and Mary Kate, which corresponds in the film to the overpoweringly "natural" forces set loose in Elizabethan May Day revelry or the green world of Shakespearean comedy.

Early in *The Quiet Man*, for instance, this sense of release gives us the scene where Sean impulsively kisses Mary Kate, and where she slaps and then a few moments later kisses him just as impulsively in return, as the wind howls about the windows and bangs the shutters of an as-yet-untenanted White o' Morn cottage. Later in the story, the same overflow of barely-controlled romantic passion sets in motion the jubilant "escape" of Sean and Mary Kate from the fussy propriety of Michaeleen Og Flynn in his role as *shaughraun*, ending in the famous thunderstorm scene in the graveyard where wind and rain rise up as if in response to the elemental force of the attraction between the lovers.

The great puzzle of Inisfree thus becomes, for an altogether mystified Sean Thornton, how so powerful a passion can be blocked by mere custom or tradition, here represented by Red Will Danaher's refusal to let his sister marry the American stranger. For in America—where, as Sean once plaintively says, all a man has to do is honk his horn outside the house and the girl comes running out—brothers or parents or family or community have no part in such matters. A painful undercurrent of pure emotional bafflement always runs just beneath the comic surface of *The Quiet Man*, at times coming very close to tipping the story over into personal heartbreak.

Nowhere is this possibility more obvious than in the scene where an uncharacteristically grave Michaeleen Og Flynn must explain to Sean Thornton that in Ireland his proposal of marriage to Mary Kate means, by itself, exactly nothing: "This is Ireland, Sean, not America. Without her brother's consent, she couldn't and wouldn't." The near-tragic undertone of the scene lies as much in the heartbroken dignity of Mary Kate's speech before she runs upstairs—"Sean Thornton, I thank you for the asking"—as in the image of her tear-stained face watching at the upstairs window as her lover departs.

A major complication in this context is Mary Kate's independence of spirit. For had Sean Thornton simply had the misfortune to fall in love with a woman weakly submissive to social demands, there would be a problem for him but none for the story. But Mary Kate Danaher is, as we see almost from the beginning, the very opposite of such a woman. The resemblance between *The Quiet Man* and Shakespeare's *The Taming of the Shrew* has been noted often enough.

It is nowhere more obvious than in those scenes where Mary Kate responds to any hint of male domination with a fearless physical defiance: aiming a ferocious blow at Sean Thornton when he presumes to kiss her in the White o' Morn scene, threatening her brother with a heavy piece of crockery when he moves as if to chastise her physically—"You do," she says, "and there'll be a fine wake in the house this night"—or taking a wild roundhouse swing at Sean, to the great delight of the onlooking villagers, in the "dragging" scene. Mary Kate is, like Shakespeare's Kate, a barely-controlled elemental force, and a central question posed by *The Quiet Man* is why she then chooses to submit herself to custom or tradition.

The Quiet Man will resolve this problem by giving primary importance to a relation between marriage and property that was a survival from early or pre–Christian Irish law. The film brings into view a pagan Ireland—the world of the *fine* or kinship group and its all-embracing claims on the individual—that serves much the same purpose in Ford's story as do the holiday customs of May Day or Hocktide, with their insistent reminders of an earlier pagan Europe, in Shakespeare's romantic comedies.

Conrad Arensberg and Solon Kimball's *Family and Community in Ireland*, a classic sociological study revealing how marriage and kinship in rural Ireland are shaped by a body of custom and tradition dating from early Irish law, serves as an especially useful guide to the way *The Quiet Man* invokes this earlier social order. For their study was among the small group of books that Ford ordered to be sent to his screenwriter Frank Nugent—others included an English-Irish dictionary and Liam O'Flaherty's *Land*—as preparatory research for writing the final shooting script of *The Quiet Man*.[32]

Family and Community in Ireland describes rural Irish marriage as a transaction between families or kinship groups in which property functions much more as a symbolic medium of group consolidation or alliance than as a medium of exchange in the modern sense. It is precisely this conception of property that Sean Thornton, as a newly-returned American, is initially unable to grasp, just as he is unable to grasp the notion of community or collective solidarity that explains Mary Kate's otherwise mystifying insistence that he claim her dowry from her brother.

For behind Mary Kate's insistence, as behind the rituals of marriage negotiation reported in Arensberg and Kimball's study, lies the older notion of kinship alliance described in studies like Alwyn and Brinley Reeses' *Celtic Heritage*:

> In medieval Ireland and Wales, the most highly esteemed form of marriage was a contract between consenting kin-groups—marriage "by gift of kin" ... —and between partners of comparable status, with proper arrangements about marriage payments.... The approved union, even among common people, was a "match" negotiated by two families.[33]

In *The Quiet Man*, of course, there can be no consent between families, for Sean Thornton's parents are dead and he has no siblings. (Thus the men of Inisfree, who recognize his ancestral right to "Thornton land," will assume the status of a surrogate family or kinship group in relation to Sean, taking his side in the quarrel with Red Will Danaher and even fighting for his rights in the wedding night sequence where Danaher refuses to bestow on his sister the furniture she inherited from her mother and grandmother.)

But the underlying issue in the conflict between Sean and his bride is a breakdown of custom that she feels as a matter of deep personal shame and he finds wholly unintelligible. So long as Mary Kate has married a husband in "American" terms—that is to say, as a union of two isolated or unattached persons operating in a social void—she will remain a woman in exile from her own community, an unintegrated figure cut off from communal life and values. She will also remain, in terms of ancient Irish law and custom, an unequal partner in her own marriage.

The notion of marital equality here, though it has been mistaken in feminist commentary on *The Quiet Man* for gender equality of the modern sort,[34] goes back once again to a notion of balance or equality between kinship groups. Property serves in this instance as a symbolic medium for establishing what Nerys Patterson calls the "legally defined degrees of relationship according to which a woman was more or less vested with rights in her husband's household and *fine*."[35]

There were seven orders of marriage or connubium, with the highest being *Lanamnas comthinchuir*—"connection of equal, or joint, property," as Patterson explains, in which the term for property has "a general meaning of equipment, and also a special sense of household goods," and in which the marriage property was contributed by both partners—and the next, already far inferior in the rights to which it entitled the woman within the household, the *lanamnas fir for bantinchur*, "a relationship in which the woman was supported on the property of the man."[36] The latter is what Mary Kate has in mind when she tells Sean that without her dowry she is only the servant she had always been in her brother's house.

In *The Quiet Man* Mary Kate's insistence on her rights of dowry culminates in the scene where, her brother having been at last shamed into handing over her fortune, she moves in perfect concert with Sean, throwing open the door of the threshing furnace as he picks the banknotes up off the ground and throws them into the flames. Here we witness not simply the immolation of the banknotes, but of Sean's false (or American) understanding of property, and thus of his earlier misunderstanding of Mary Kate's motives as having been, as he once bitterly puts it, "mercenary."

In terms of an older body of Irish custom or tradition, Mary Kate's inequality in their marriage is immolated as well. In a film filled with unforgettable moments, the inexpressible jauntiness of Maureen O'Hara's walk as the crowd divides and she strides off toward their cottage, a woman at last perfectly reintegrated into her own community and at peace in her marriage, is among the most unforgettable.

Yet the threshing fire scene is a mere prelude to the great donnybrook episode that follows, for which everything else in the story has been in a manner of speaking a preparation. The donnybrook sequence expresses in nearly pure terms a standard theme in Ford's films, the idea that the communal energies released in innocent or ludic violence have a power to redeem community, purging old antagonisms and widening the circle of social acceptance to include even those previously banished to or left on the outside.

Here *The Quiet Man* is closest to Shakespearean festive comedy, a resemblance wholly attributable to the sense of saturnalian or Bacchic release, or what we earlier heard Sir Thomas Urquhart, speaking of the village revels of his own and Shakespeare's time, call Bacchanalian riots and preposterous disorders. As in Shakespeare, moreover, the mood of festive or holiday release is meant to include the audience, who, as Barber says in relation to plays like *Love's Labour's Lost* and *A Midsummer Night's Dream*, "have gone on holiday in going to a comedy."[37]

Only the Reverend Mr. Playfair, a compulsive collector of sports memorabilia, knows about Sean's having killed a man in the ring, leading to his vow never to fight again. The tremendous drive of the donnybrook sequence, its sense of an accelerating rhythm so powerful that it can only end by sweeping along every member of the community, derives from the way this secret functions as a taboo or ritual blockage, a source of behavior that even Sean's strongest supporters among the villagers find mysterious or unaccountable.

It is Mr. Playfair, himself a featherweight boxer during his college days, who at last succeeds in making Sean understand why his refusal to fight Red Will Danaher will lose him his wife's love. "It's an old custom, and a good custom," says Mr. Playfair about the dowry, thus opening the way to release of the pent-up energies that culminate in the donnybrook. Yet even Mr. Playfair is not permitted to see what the film's audience has seen: the nightmare flashback in which Sean, floored by Red Will Danaher's punch during the earlier wedding parlor scene, is in his groggy state visited by a vivid involuntary memory of killing his opponent in a professional boxing match.

The prize fight flashback is a technical tour de force. Its pitiless lighting and intercut close-ups combine to produce an effect that is on one level harshly "realistic"—this in direct and calculated contrast to the romantic or pastoral mistiness of Hoch's Technicolor photography in the outdoor Irish scenes—and on another surreal or hallucinatory in the manner of those Bosch or Grunewald paintings where leering faces seem to jump out at the viewer from an unnaturally flattened perspective.

Commentators on *The Quiet Man* have usually taken the flashback as an explanation of Sean's failure to understand his wife's attitude toward her fortune. He killed Tony Gadelo, he says bitterly to Mr. Playfair, for money: "lousy money, a piece of the purse." It is a revelation not only about prizefighting but about the power of money in a country where human values have been eroded or dissolved by a remorseless economic individualism. From that perspective Sean persistently mistakes the meaning that her dowry has for Mary Kate—"Money!" he exclaims at one particularly explosive moment: "Is that all you Danahers ever think about?"—a view of money or property that, quite as much as any simple objection to violence, lies behind his resolve not to fight Danaher.

The nightmare flashback involves a much harsher condemnation of American economic individualism than Sean Thornton, whose thoughts are focused entirely on the death of his opponent, will ever be asked to understand. The truly nightmarish element in the flashback sequence is not the death of Tony Gadelo—that is, as the gentle Reverend Mr. Playfair remarks, "just one of those things," the sort of accident that might happen in any sport involving strong physical contact—but the press photographers, figures updated from Bosch or Grunewald, who climb through the ropes once the ringside physician has pronounced death.

With hats on their heads, cigarettes dangling from their lips, eyes weary with cynicism, they fire flashbulb after flashbulb at the corpse on the floor—now, at last, with a towel mercifully draped over its face—and then at the stunned, stupefied, half-comprehending agony of Sean Thornton watching helplessly from his corner. By morning, we understand, their pictures will be splashed over the sports pages of mass circulation newspapers in an America where death and personal agony are important mainly as they can be used to sustain advertising revenues.

The Quiet Man's great countermovement toward a vision of innocent or ludic violence begins in the scene by the riverbank where Mary Kate switches into Irish while describing her unhappy marital situation to Father Lonergan. The scene is itself a comedy of ludic violence: Father Lonergan's battle with the great salmon he has been trying to catch for ten years, which, after a great deal of splashing and shouting and thrashing about, the fish wins.

But the ceremony of Mary Kate's confession in Irish, the Gaelic speech of that older Ireland that predated the coming of Christianity, is wholly serious as it signals a break or rupture in cultural time. Though the Reverend Mr. Playfair has tried to prepare him by pointedly remarking that he considers Sean now to be "in training" for the fight with Danaher, it will take Sean Thornton some hours yet to understand that he is operating in an altered social dispensation.

Yet from the moment that Mary Kate switches from English to Irish, the rules governing life in Inisfree will be those of an earlier Irish society where property has no meaning outside communal values and where, within a closely-related context of festive or Bacchic release, certain ritualized forms of violence or abuse have a power to regenerate community. The culminating theme of redemptive violence begins in the "dragging" scene in which Sean Thornton forcibly marches Mary Kate the five miles from the Castletown train station to her brother's fields. As we have seen, the episode drew a great deal of angry comment in Ireland when *The*

Quiet Man was released. In subsequent years, as Anglo-American film criticism has been more and more influenced by feminist ideology, it has assumed the same virtually unmentionable status as the ride of the Ku Klux Klan in Griffith's *Birth of a Nation*.

Yet the villagers of Inisfree understand, as does Mary Kate Danaher herself, that the dragging scene is not some gratuitous display of male violence, but a ritual of community meant to put right the violated kinship relations that Sean Thornton, with his American understanding of property and marriage, has until this moment utterly failed to grasp. It is a ritual meant as well to reintegrate Red Will Danaher, who as a gombeen man or acquisitive purchaser of other people's property has throughout the film displayed proto-American tendencies toward what C.B. Macpherson labeled the ideology of possessive individualism.[38]

The Quiet Man is closest to early Irish custom in the dragging scene, which directly echoes various marriage rituals meant to dispel antagonisms between kinship groups through what the Reeses in *Celtic Heritage* call "displays of mock hostility." Thus, for instance, "in parts of Ireland, on the day of bringing home the bride, the bridegroom and his friends would ride out and meet the bride and her friends at the place of treaty. Having come near to each other, the custom was of old to cast short darts at the company that attended the bride, but at such a distance that seldom any hurt ensued; yet it is not out of the memory of man that the Lord of Howth, on such an occasion, lost an eye." In Wales, the meeting of the two parties led to a "mock scuffle," whereupon the bride's party rode away with the bridegroom and his friends in pursuit. When he catches her, the bridegroom " leads her in triumph and the scene is concluded with feasting and festivity.'" In Ireland, the same source reports, "the ride of the bridal party is termed 'dragging home the bride.'"[39]

In *The Quiet Man*, where Sean Thornton and Mary Kate have earlier gone through the formalities of a legal wedding ceremony, the plot demands that this be played out on a delayed basis. But the point remains the same: their marriage can be made "real" within its community only through a cleansing ritual of innocent or ludic violence. The ritual quality of the dragging scene in *The Quiet Man*, which as Ford conceives of it is inseparable from its comic character, is signaled throughout by the hilarious counterpoint of elaborate politeness, suitable to the drawing room or Sunday parlor, with the knockabout physicality of the march across the meadows. Thus the villagers and train crew, for instance, madly on the run to catch a view of Sean and Mary Kate as they start on their epic walk, nonetheless pause momentarily to tip their hats or curtsy to the visiting Protestant bishop looking wonderingly on from his car.

And thus Mary Kate, when she loses her shoe, not only has it retrieved for her with an air of ceremonious courtesy by the station master, but finds a moment in the mad physical whirl to acknowledge his gallantry with a gracious "I thank you kindly, sir." Even in the most famous line in the scene, "Here's a fine stick to beat the lovely lady," commentators have tended to overlook the way the graciousness of "lovely lady" underscores the theme of innocent or ludic violence. In a setting where violence is so obviously and inevitably moving toward an ultimate reconciliation, the speech is in effect the village woman's way of welcoming Mary Kate Danaher back into her own community.

In purely formal terms, the signal of the donnybrook as entry into the world of saturnalian release is the punch with which Sean Thornton floors Red Will Danaher at the end of the threshing furnace scene. Sean throws the banknotes into the fire, ducks with a professional boxer's contemptuous ease the wild roundhouse right Danaher aims at his jaw, then delivers a short, explosive counterpunch to the midsection that crumbles Danaher to the ground. This is the moment that Mary Kate, with the triumphant air of a woman who has at last seen her world come right, exits the scene as the crowd parts before her.

Yet the festive or Bacchic nature of the scene is fully signaled only some moments later in the sequence, when Michaeleen Og Flynn spontaneously assumes the role of Lord of Misrule,

John Wayne leads Maureen O'Hara (both in foreground), along with a procession of villagers, in Ford's 1952 classic *The Quiet Man* (with the permission of Dan Ford; courtesy Lilly Library, Indiana University, Bloomington).

firing a pistol into the air to abruptly put a stop to what has rapidly been turning into a joyous free-for-all. This is, he announces in the tone of someone who expects to be obeyed, a private fight, in which third parties have not been invited to participate. He then adds, altogether less hopefully, that when the main bout resumes it should be conducted according to Marquis of Queensbury rules.

As the donnybrook sequence gathers momentum, betting on the outcome gradually becomes an activity equal in importance to the fight itself, supplying a mode of vicarious participation that serves to channel the energies and emotions of the entire community into the common drive toward saturnalian release. Michaeleen Og Flynn's busy and officious role as bookmaker is in this sense an extension of his role as Lord of Misrule, giving him direct control over a donnybrook carried out in the symbolic terms of odds and wagers rather than physical conflict.

Indeed, by the end of the donnybrook episode betting will have carried the all-embracing saturnalian spirit far beyond the village limits of Inisfree, as when a local policeman takes a call from his supervisor at distant headquarters about the reported "riot" in Inisfree. ("What did he say?" a policeman standing by asks the policeman who took the call. "He said to put five pounds on Danaher's nose.") At the end of the day, even the visiting Protestant bishop will have lost fifteen pounds to the local vicar.

The famous last scene of *The Quiet Man* has been derided as another element in the film's idyllic fantasy about an Ireland that never existed. Father Lonergan organizes the villagers of Inisfree to "cheer like Protestants" as the bishop is driven through the village, thus convincing him that the Reverend Mr. Playfair has a much larger congregation than the two or three people who constitute his actual flock. Yet *The Quiet Man*'s vision of benign and mutually respectful relations between Catholics and Protestants belongs also to its festive theme, and in particular to the notion that violence, when it has occurred within a more fundamental context of communal values, may have the power to bring about a redemption or reconstitution of community.

In *The Quiet Man*'s world, where Irish freedom has been achieved and the violence of the recent past is even now undergoing transformation into a half-mythologized national memory—the point of Michaeleen Og Flynn's irrepressible stream of IRA jokes, which would not be jokes if the War of Independence were still going on—not even the deep antagonisms of politics and history are immune to the general mood of festive reconciliation.

The Quiet Man *in Cultural Memory*

In a recent collection of essays, the cultural critic Stanley Crouch remembers what it was like to have seen John Ford's *How Green Was My Valley*, set in a Welsh coal mining village, while growing up in an African-American neighborhood in the United States:

> There was something in the tale that spoke to the world surrounding me ... even though the people, superficially, were so different.... I can see my younger brother ... that street and those people ... rise into asphalt, concrete, fences, lawns, bricks, homes and life once more.... I am back there just as the boy was in *How Green Was My Valley*, and nothing is dead, nothing is gone, all is made perpetual through the regeneration of memory.

The cinematic depth of Ford's storytelling, Crouch says in the same essay, "gave me one of my earliest experiences of the universal achieved through aesthetic form."[40] As perhaps goes without saying, *The Quiet Man* has drawn just this kind of response among viewers who return to it again and again, and who see in it, as does Crouch in *How Green Was My Valley*, a story that looks through or beyond its Irish setting to a more universal level of human experience.

It is *The Quiet Man*'s perceived universality that constitutes a major problem for those who have been unable to see in the film anything more than (in Luke Gibbons's phrase) "a dreamworld of stage Irishry and nostalgic sentiment."[41] The key to that universality lies, it seems to me, in the archetypal comic pattern I have attempted to describe, the pattern of saturnalian release that gives *The Quiet Man* so strong a resemblance to such Shakespearean comedies as *As You Like It* or *A Midsummer Night's Dream*. For viewers in all ages and all societies are subject to the imposition of social control that must sometimes be felt as repressive or intolerable, and the collective longing for occasional release from the sober restraints of duty and responsibility and moral rectitude is no doubt as universal as any other human emotion one could name.

So where a certain critical mentality is able to see in *The Quiet Man* and various other Ford films only an irresponsible tendency to escapism —"the prettification of a lie," in David Thomson's deliberately hostile phrase[42]—those convinced of Ford's cinematic genius will instead see in *The Quiet Man* evidence of his enormous power to visualize, as Northrop Frye says in speaking of the archetypal power of literature, "the world of desire, not as an escape from 'reality,' but as the genuine form that human life tries to imitate."[43]

This is to see *The Quiet Man*, in short, as belonging to a comic tradition going back through Shakespeare to Plautus in ancient Rome and Aristophanes in classical Greece, one that invokes the holiday or festive spirit of misrule, as Barber puts it, both as "release for impulses which run counter to decency and decorum, and the clarification about limits which comes from going beyond limits."[44] The special claim of *The Quiet Man*, perhaps, produced against the massive resistance of a Hollywood geared to the making of profits, incorporating the ethos and rituals of Ford's film family into the very texture of its story, and lingering lovingly on its image of Ireland as a green world so far magically exempt from the remorseless economic individualism of the America in which Sean Thornton killed an opponent for a piece of the purse, is that it is a festival for our own time.

In an age of American cultural hegemony and accelerating global consumerism one may perhaps say about Ford in *The Quiet Man*, as Evelyn Waugh once did about P.G. Wodehouse, not simply that "he has made a world for us to live in and delight in," but that "he will continue to release future generations from a captivity that may be more irksome than our own."[45]

Notes

1. Gerry McNee, *In the Footsteps of The Quiet Man* (Edinburgh: Mainstream Publishing, 1990), 128.
2. McNee, *In the Footsteps*, 89.
3. McNee, *In the Footsteps*, 100.
4. Harlan Kennedy, "Shamrocks and Shillelaghs," in James MacKillop, editor, *Contemporary Irish Cinema: From The Quiet Man to Dancing at Lughnasa* (Syracuse, NY: Syracuse University Press, 1999), 2.
5. James MacKillop, "The Quiet Man Speaks," in MacKillop, editor, *Contemporary Irish Cinema*, 169.
6. Kennedy, "Shamrocks and Shillelaghs," 2.
7. Kevin Rockett, "Migration and Irish Cinema," quoted in Lance Pettit, *Screen Ireland: Film and Television Representation* (Manchester, UK: Manchester University Press, 2000), 54.
8. Luke Gibbons, "Romanticism, Realism, and Irish Cinema," in Kevin Rockett, Luke Gibbons and John Hill, eds., *Cinema and Ireland* (London: Croom Helm, 1987), 196.
9. Terry Byrne, *Power in the Eye: An Introduction to Contemporary Irish Film* (Lanham, MD: The Scarecrow Press, 1997), 65.
10. Gibbons, "Romanticism, Realism, and Irish Cinema," 195.
11. Gibbons, "Romanticism, Realism, and Irish Cinema," 195.
12. Yeats, *Essays and Introductions*. Quoted in Gibbons, "Romanticism, Realism, and Irish Cinema," 209, in the course of Gibbons' fine discussion of Irish romantic nationalism.
13. Scott Eyman, *Print the Legend: The Life and Times of John Ford* (New York: Simon and Schuster, 1999), 327.
14. Andrew Sarris, editor, *Interviews with Film Directors* (New York: Bobbs-Merrill, 1967), 181.
15. Eyman, *Print the Legend*, 161.
16. Gibbons, "Romanticism, Realism, and Irish Cinema," 241.
17. Harry Carey, Jr., *Company of Heroes: My Life as an Actor in the John Ford Company* (Lanham, MD: Madison Books, 1994), 32.
18. MacKillop, "The Quiet Man Speaks," 169.
19. Dan Ford, *Pappy: The Life of John Ford* (Englewood Cliffs, NJ: Prentice-Hall, 1979), 240.
20. McNee, *In the Footsteps of* The Quiet Man, 79.
21. Eyman, *Print the Legend*, 561.
22. Eyman, *Print the Legend*, 426.
23. Northrop Frye, *The Anatomy of Criticism* (Princeton, NJ: Princeton University Press, 1957), 1982.
24. F.M. Cornford, *The Origins of Attic Comedy*, cited in C. L. Barber, *Shakespeare's Festive Comedy: A Study of Dramatic Form and its Relation to Social Custom* (New York: Meridian Books, 1963), 7.
25. Barber, *Shakespeare's Festive Comedy*, 5.
26. Barber, *Shakespeare's Festive Comedy*, 5.
27. Quoted in Barber, *Shakespeare's Festive Comedy*, 22.
28. Barber, *Shakespeare's Festive Comedy*, 26.
29. Barber, *Shakespeare's Festive Comedy*, 23.
30. Barber, *Shakespeare's Festive Comedy*, 90–91.
31. Barber, *Shakespeare's Festive Comedy*, 223.
32. Eyman, *Print the Legend*, 397.
33. Alwyn Rees and Brinley Rees, *Celtic Heritage: Ancient Tradition in Ireland and Wales* (London: Thames and Hudson, 1961), 267.
34. Molly Haskell, *From Reverence to Rape: The Treatment of Women in the Movies* (New York: Holt, Rinehart, and Winston, 1974), 269–70.

35. Nerys Thomas Patterson, *Cattle-Lords and Clansmen: The Social Structure of Early Ireland* (Notre Dame, Indiana: Notre Dame University Press, 1994), 288.
36. Patterson, *Cattle-Lords and Clansmen*, 296.
37. Barber, *Shakespeare's Festive Comedy*, 8–9.
38. Luke Gibbons notes that "Red Will Danaher, the 'jumped up' progressive farmer ... who passes himself off as a squire," is an embodiment of "acquisitive ideology." (Gibbons, "Romanticism, Realism, and Irish Cinema," 238)
39. W.G. Wood-Martin, *Traces of the Elder Faiths of Ireland*, cited in Rees, *Celtic Heritage*, 268.
40. Quoted in Eyman, *Print the Legend*, 244.
41. Gibbons, "Romanticism, Realism, and Irish Cinema," 233.
42. David Thomson, *A Biographical Dictionary of Film* (New York: Alfred A. Knopf, 1995), 257.
43. Frye, *The Anatomy of Criticism*, 184.
44. Barber, *Shakespeare's Festive Comedy*, 13
45. BBC broadcast, quoted on back cover of P.G. Wodehouse, *The Code of the Woosters* (Harmondsworth: Penguin Editions, 1972).

The Quiet Man and the Boxing Film: Allusions and Influences

Leger Grindon

Years ago I began work on a study of the Hollywood boxing film. My intention was to explore American cinema by investigating a particular genre. I figured that exploring a genre, such as the boxing film, would lead me in unexpected directions and toward unknown films that would open to me fresh perspectives on American cinema. I can now report that I have met that objective. However, among the unexpected directions prompted by my study has been a surprising encounter with John Ford. In retrospect it should not be surprising because most in-depth studies of the American cinema lead one to Ford, a luminous presence in the history of our national cinema. But at the start of my project, the boxing film seemed to have nothing to do with him. However, by the end I found that Ford played a significant role in this popular genre. I understand that role as one of allusion to the conventions of the boxing film and influence upon the boxing films that followed. Ford's *The Quiet Man* (1952) is the pivotal point in this process of allusion and influence.

My attention was drawn to *The Quiet Man* because between 1952 and 1954 three popular and Oscar-winning motion pictures featured the retired boxer as their protagonist: *The Quiet Man*, *From Here to Eternity* (1953) and *On the Waterfront* (1954). Each of these films portrays the boxer after he departs from competition, but more importantly, his experience as a fighter is central to the drama. A similar plot device appears in modest productions from the same period including *99 River Street* (1953) and two television productions, "The Battler" (1955) and "Requiem for a Heavyweight" (1956). The model plot of the boxing genre provides a crucial foundation or "backstory" for these films. In reply they develop an illuminating extension of the genre tradition. This series of films about the retired boxer testifies to a development of the internal structure of the boxing film genre. In many respects, *The Quiet Man, 99 River Street, From Here to Eternity, On the Waterfront* and "Requiem for a Heavyweight" bring the dramatic conflicts distinguishing the boxing film to a resolution and mark the culmination of the genre as Hollywood's classical studio period (1920–60) comes to a close. Furthermore, these productions anticipate the eclipse of the boxing film, for after a final flurry of releases in 1955–56 the boxing film remained nearly dormant for twenty years. I have called these films the "after the ring" cycle in the boxing film genre.

Taken together these films employ the boxer and the conventions of the boxing film genre in a variety of ways. Nonetheless, common patterns emerge. In each case boxing harbors a tormenting past with which the protagonist must be reconciled. In the tradition of film noir, boxing in the "after the ring" cycle evokes a forceful, dark psychological experience. Not simply a memory, the ring career has become a disturbing state of mind lodged in the subconscious and crying out for rectification. In boxing noir the flashback was a widespread form, but in the "after the ring" cycle a variety of modes are employed to portray the past trauma and set the stage for its reconciliation. In these films the boxer must recall and acknowledge his fall and in a symbolic manner return to the ring, often literally to fisticuffs, in order to initiate a rebirth. Typical of the imagery surrounding the boxer, the ex-prizefighter is a loner, an individual struggling not so much against a rival as to overcome a personal inner torment. In so doing he ends his isolation by establishing a bond with others, thus reformulating his social position.

Though limited, in each case the agony of the ring animates the psychic conflicts motivating the drama. Two historical experiences motivate the crisis of masculinity embodied by the screen boxer—the ethnic commoner threatened by the Depression, and the returning World War II veteran struggling to find his place in peacetime society. Boxing can refer to both market competition heedless of human fellowship and/or warrior experience and the violence of combat. These two widely shared social phenomena continue to characterize the boxer during the "after the ring" cycle. However, these films assume a more introspective, thoughtful stance. The torment generated by ring memories provokes reflection upon the ethics of violence and the meaning of suffering. The former boxer in *The Quiet Man, 99 River Street, From Here to Eternity, On the Waterfront*, and "Requiem for a Heavyweight" uses his physical experience to ponder and reconcile a crisis of the spirit. The animating conflicts of the genre serve as themes for these dramas and each film works toward a distinctive resolution of these problems. Now let us turn to the particular case of *The Quiet Man*.

In *The Quiet Man* the scars of boxing are psychic rather than physical. Sean Thornton (John Wayne) leaves the ring tormented and subdued. He returns to his bucolic birthplace to forget his brutal profession. In this romantic comedy the ex-prizefighter has to reassert his masculinity in order to realize a successful marriage. This film allows for an optimistic union of the couple, but first the masculine trials represented by boxing need to be overcome.

The Quiet Man was a personal project of director-producer John Ford, a stalwart of the old Hollywood, who for years had been nursing a pet story of an Irish romance, but he found no interest among the studio chiefs. Finally Herbert Yates at the minor Republic Pictures agreed to finance *The Quiet Man* with John Wayne and Maureen O'Hara if Ford would feature these stars in a Republic Western first. The cavalry picture *Rio Grande* (1950) was a hit—earning $2,250,000 on a production cost of $1,238,000—and so *The Quiet Man* received a green light. The film became the highest grossing release in the history of Republic Pictures and among the box office leaders of 1952 earning $3,800,000 on a production cost of $1,750,000.[1] In addition to being an audience favorite, the film enjoyed wide critical acclaim and received Academy Awards for Best Director and Best Color Cinematography. It continues to remain a favorite for home viewing on television and video.

The romantic comedy portrays the Irish American Sean Thornton upon his return to his home village of Inisfree after spending years in the United States. He purchases the cottage where he was born and is smitten by Mary Kate Danaher (Maureen O'Hara) who returns his affections. However, her older brother Will Danaher (Victor McLaglen) objects to the union because he covets the cottage purchased by Sean and takes offense at the newcomer. Sean backs away from fighting the burly Irishman, but local custom will not allow the couple to marry over the objections of a maiden's older brother. In response the community leaders, including the village matchmaker as well as the Catholic and Anglican priests, concoct a scheme leading Will to believe that the reluctant Widow Tillane (Mildred Natwick) will consent to marry him, if he allows for the union of Sean and Mary Kate. At the wedding party of Sean and Mary Kate, Will discovers the ruse and in anger retains the bride's dowry and knocks the groom to the floor with a roundhouse punch. The blow triggers Sean's memory as presented in a nightmare–like flashback.

In the vision Sean recalls killing his opponent in the ring as the prizefighter "Trooper Thorn." The episode lasts sixty-seven seconds and portrays the boxer's reaction to his opponent's collapse after being knocked out. Sean's tormented stare at the fallen fighter begins and ends the flashback. The scene is divided into three phases: in the first phase Thorn, the referee, a cop, and Trooper's trainer and manager gaze at the fighter knocked unconscious on the canvas; in the second phase a doctor enters the ring and places a towel over the head of the dead boxer; in the third phase a group of photographers flash their cameras at the dead man and then turn to focus on the victorious but shocked Thorn. The sequence is presented in the manner of a silent film. There is no dialogue. The only sound is an ominous, melancholy music and the muted noise of an off-screen crowd. The montage of eighteen images is composed of carefully posed body shots—largely close-ups of isolated, staring faces—which highlight limited movement in stillness, such as Sean bowing his head to his gloved hand or the trainer chewing vigorously as he looks. The men are strongly foregrounded in the shallow, high-contrast compositions that use glaring lights and darkness to eliminate any background beyond the ring. The style presents the flashback in a mode reminiscent of German Expressionist cinema. The entire sequence assumes a marked contrast with the bright, expansive, pastoral imagery of the balance of the romantic comedy.

The sequence presents no boxing, only its aftermath. Shock, guilt and fear characterize the vision and reveal the motive behind Sean's restraint when challenged by the bullying Danaher. These emotions also portray Thornton's clouded background in America. The prodigal son has gained his fortune by prizefighting his way out of Pittsburgh, the smoldering pit of modern industrialism. Sean's apparent disregard for money, demonstrated when he commands Mary Kate to leave her dowry and come home, arises not simply because he has the resources to care for them both, but also because the shadow of fighting (and killing) for cash haunts the man. The world of boxing is presented as grotesque, heartless and brutal, a world in contrast to the bucolic Irish community of Inisfree.

A familiar Expressionist motif, the double, is apparent in the transition from Sean's body, fallen on the floor of the wedding party, to his face staring down at what first seems to be himself, but we soon find it to be directed at the dead boxer. The doubling alludes to Sean's consciousness divided between guilt at killing another, fear of his own death, and apprehension at what he is capable of doing if he strikes back at Danaher. Boxing is presented as a film noir nightmare haunting Thornton. The visual isolation of the figures from the crowd and from each other expresses the loneliness and alienation of the ring. The other men in the vision—the referee, cop, doctor, cameramen, and Thorn's seconds—go about their tasks detached and uncaring. Only Sean blames himself for the killing. At the close of the scene the flashing cameras incriminate the boxer, but they also valorize his prowess. One imagines the pictures of "Killer" Thorn in the sports pages the next morning. The multiple photographs also indicate the permanent impression this experience had left on Sean's consciousness. It cannot be forgotten.

With the end of the flashback Sean revives flanked by the matchmaker, Mary Kate and Pastor Playfair (Arthur Shields). "Steady, Trooper, steady," cautions Playfair as Sean, rises indicating that the Anglican priest knows of Thornton's history as a boxer. Like his conscience, the Pastor tries to calm the man and contain his rage. John Ford has said, "What interests me are the consequences of a tragic moment—how the individual acts before a crucial act, or in exceptional circumstances. That is everything."[2] So in *The Quiet Man*, Sean responds to his crisis in the later scene with his visit to Playfair's home in an effort to reconcile his past as a boxer and the troubles plaguing his marriage. Mary Kate refuses to consummate their union until Sean secures her dowry from Will Danaher. The former boxer finds himself prodded into a physical battle that he dreads. Playfair reveals that he knows of Sean's history as a heavyweight who quit the ring after a fatal knockout. In response, Thornton seeks his advice.

John Wayne, center, in the boxing ring scene from ***The Quiet Man***, 1952 (with the permission of Dan Ford; courtesy Lilly Library, Indiana University, Bloomington).

Prizefighting represents for Sean a ruthless competition, fighting to the death for money. This is what Sean came to Ireland to escape: the "dog eat dog" struggle in the marketplace. But Playfair explains that for Mary Kate the dowry "means more to her than just the money." Her fortune signifies her standing in the community, her equality with her husband, and her connection to her past and her family. "Is your wife's love worth fighting for?" Playfair asks. These two attitudes toward money, wealth earned from beating others as opposed to a token of dignity, self-worth and independence, divide the couple. Finally, Sean's realization of the dowry's significance in this traditional culture helps him to put aside his brutal past and see that fighting Danaher embodies a necessary expression of male aggression. Pastor Playfair encourages Sean's coming brawl with his blessing and assures him that Danaher can protect himself.

The Quiet Man resolves Sean's masculinity crisis with a reassertion of his fighting skills. The display of aggression seals his marriage and allows him to enter his extended family, becoming part of the traditional community. At the climax Sean drags Mary Kate, followed by a crowd of villagers, back to her brother, while Will gathers his harvest in the fields with his crew. Thornton declares that the marriage is off unless Will comes up with the dowry. Reluctantly Danaher pays. Sean takes the cash and throws it into the flames of a harvester's furnace while Mary Kate holds open the door. The couple walks away hand in hand, and as they pass, Will throws a punch at Sean, who ducks and strikes back with a blow to the belly. Mary Kate joyfully assures Sean that she will have dinner ready when he returns home, and the brawl between the two men commences while the crowd of village spectators grows. The men continue fighting across the fields while the onlookers cheer. Eventually the brawlers pause for a drink at the pub only to resume their fight. Finally, battered and bruised, but arm in arm, they retire to Sean's cottage to share the meal Mary Kate has ready. The film treats the fight with comic brio. The battle is like child's play or harmless sport, bonding the two men together in physical comradery.

The villagers, who have witnessed the evolution of the public quarrel, encourage the battle and even the priests applaud the fisticuffs. The surrounding community protects the men from both physical and psychological harm, as if the traditional habits of male aggression can be rendered benign by its transformation into social ritual. Lane Roth, in his essay "Ritual Brawls in John Ford's Films," highlights the anthropological significance of the fight, comparing its function in Ford's work to dances and funerals. He argues persuasively that these "brawls are secular rituals that promote social cohesion and integration of the individual into the community."[3] Fights, such as the climax of *The Quiet Man*, become playful ceremonies in which the entire community participates. The winner of the bout is never determined, in spite of the wagering by the spectators, for both men become brothers as a result of the pleasure they share in the battle. A key to the closing fisticuffs arises from its contrast to prizefighting. The danger of prizefighting arises from the commercialization of male aggression in which fellow feeling has evaporated and been replaced by cash competition. Just as Sean must learn that Mary Kate's dowry has a meaning apart from its market value, so too, is fighting in Inisfree distinct from boxing in Pittsburgh. The Irish village ritualizes masculine aggression and shields one from its harmful consequences. Traditional mores allow the individual to safely express his hostility as long as it is channeled into the ceremonies designated for its display. Masculinity is reborn from the crisis experienced by the noir boxer.

Contemporary sensibility, and I suspect a typical viewer in 1952, finds a husband dragging his wife across the countryside, and grown men enjoying a slugfest in the fields, offensive and simple-minded. *The Quiet Man* invites an aesthetic perspective removed from one's familiar habits. Of course, artistic license is at work and, contrary to the realist mode typical of the boxing film, *The Quiet Man* exhibits a fanciful, comic exaggeration. But that is not to dismiss its serious intent. The distance the film establishes between its vision of Ireland and modern culture is one of its prominent themes. In an earlier Celtic drama, *How Green Was My Valley* (1941), Ford also expresses the loss of tradition and a melancholia in the face of modernity. Here, another boxer, eventually blind like Samson, teaches the young Huw (Roddy McDowell) to defend himself in the schoolyard. Here too professional fighting seems a grotesque transformation of elementary skills in disciplined masculinity. In these films, boxing becomes a degenerate manifestation of modernity, expressing the corroding effects of a market system whose intensified pursuit of financial advantage has turned men and women from more fundamental and traditional values.

In *The Quiet Man* the boxer evokes the two prominent social experiences characterizing the screen pugilist, the working class ethnic on the rise and the veteran returning from war. Sean's background as an Irishman in Pittsburgh suggests the immigrant laborer in heavy industry, working with his hands to better himself in the modern economy. More specifically, the boxing flashback identifies Sean as "Trooper," suggesting military experience, and, like the combat veteran, he confronts death and wrestles with his responsibility for killing, even though his profession sanctions the taking of another's life. After retirement Sean has not simply left boxing, but departed from the urban, industrial culture crystallized by his experience in the ring. Nonetheless, his guilt lingers and the trauma of his boxing torment can only be put to rest by a series of acts marking his reintegration into traditional, preindustrial society—the purchase of his birthplace, betrothal to a village maid, the blessing of the local priest, and finally a masculine rite of passage celebrated by the community at large. Only then can Sean Thornton assert his strength, his connection to the past, and his bond to the earth. His reintegration into the pastoral community justifies his suffering and releases his torment. Trooper Thorn, the boxer, is a man alone with his guilt and his money, but Inisfree embraces the loner and absolves him in its communal embrace, exchanging his money for a wife, a home and his place in the village.

The resolution of masculinity in crisis is central in the "after the ring" cycle. *The Quiet Man* argues that the sensitivity of a single man or woman cannot substitute for the wisdom of the traditional community. Masculinity needs to be disciplined by communal practice or it will be distorted, misunderstood, and rendered harmful to both the individual and society. The visual isolation of figures in the boxing flashback may be understood to represent their personal exile from the guidance of community. Just as Sean Thornton needs to be encouraged in his expression of anger, Will Danaher needs his emotional bluster curbed. Inisfree, guided by its clergy, the Reverend Mr. Playfair and Father Lonergan, realizes harmony and reconciliation in the concluding battle between Thornton and Danaher. And both men become eligible for the marriage that has eluded them. Inisfree subordinates and disciplines masculinity and in so doing allows for its healthy expression. As a result, anger and sensitivity are given their due and justice is realized.

Sean Thornton's character is built upon the history of the screen boxer. Allusions to this prominent Hollywood protagonist allowed Ford to fashion Thornton's personal history with economy and force. *The Quiet Man* drew from the movie past and has also influenced films to come. *Raging Bull* (1980) is among the most celebrated Hollywood films of the late twentieth century. In the American Film Institute poll from the end of the century the Martin Scorsese film placed twenty-fourth among the top 100 Hollywood movies, and it is the leading film on the list from the 1980s. The boxing sequences in *Raging Bull* are among its most celebrated features. Scorsese has acknowledged *The Quiet Man* as a principal influence on his design of these sequences. My second task today is to discuss this influence.

Raging Bull highlights subjectivity and sensation in its distinctive ring battles. The boxing matches in Hollywood feature films typically replicate the experience of the fan at ringside. *Raging Bull* turns from the optimal view of a spectator to the experience of the boxer in the ring. *Raging Bull* employs an array of image and sound devices to portray Jake La Motta's emotions in the course of the fight. Most noteworthy is that the camera almost always stays in the ring with Jake rather than shooting from the side or above the ring. The film develops the sense that being inside the ring becomes equivalent to being inside Jake's psyche. Earlier boxing films such as *Kid Galahad* (1937), *Body and Soul* (1947), or *Somebody Up There Likes Me* (1956) have shots within the ring which, intercut with more distant perspectives, highlight the decisive moments of the bout; but no boxing film has designed its fighting sequences almost exclusively within the ring and employed that distinctive view as a basis for the boxer's subjectivity. Scorsese explains, "I wanted to do the ring scenes as if the viewers were the fighter and their impressions were the fighter's— of what he would think or feel, what he would hear."[4] In order to realize this design Scorsese employed storyboarding, a production technique used only for these sequences. The tight shots amplify the impact of swift camera movements and quick cuts on action to convey the intensity of the fight. As a result, the camera presents the act of hitting and the experience of being hit with a sensational immediacy.

One influential model for the design of the boxing sequences that Scorsese has acknowledged arises in *The Quiet Man* sequence discussed above. An intensification of subjectivity and sensation circulating around guilt and impotence links Ford's dream-like treatment and *Raging Bull*, but the episode from *The Quiet Man* constitutes an isolated minute rather than serving as the basis for a pattern of events throughout a film, as is the case with the boxing in *Raging Bull*. Consider La Motta's first two bouts with Sugar Ray Robinson in *Raging Bull* in order to more carefully compare the episodes with *The Quiet Man* sequence.

How has John Ford's work influenced Scorsese's design of these ring fights?

Both express the interiority of the boxer. In Ford the aim is to portray Sean's shock, guilt and fear. In these Robinson bouts, Scorsese aims for arrogance, self-confidence, and a sense of domination. However, later in the film Jake's desire for punishment becomes a factor. Both filmmakers use close-up perspectives and further isolate the boxers with a strongly lit ring in contrast to the dark background. Flashing cameras further intensify the light. The camera remains in the ring with the fighters, but the compositions are somewhat distorted by the wide-angle lens. Knockouts are given further tension with the oblique intrusion of the ropes. Stillness, and in Scorsese slow-motion, add additional tension. The editing fragments each scene, accenting the anxiety and conflicts with an unbalanced and incomplete sense of space. The sound of the crowd and the bell give a startling resonance that reverberates through the consciousness of the fighters. The towel around the fighter's neck offers a soothing touch after the fever pitch of battle. Looking becomes a focal point, whether the stares of the boxers or the more neutral gaze of the referee.

Scorsese shares with John Ford the attention to the eyes as a marker of subjectivity. Of course, there are differences as well, since Ford emphasizes the stillness of the dead whereas Scorsese presents the movement of a fight in progress. Nonetheless, a comparison illustrates how much a contemporary filmmaker learned from an old master in constructing an emotionally powerful scene that captures the feelings of his protagonist with remarkable force. Sensitive filmmakers continue to study Ford's work as a textbook for achievement in the art of the cinema.

Notes

1. Tag Gallagher, *John Ford: The Man and His Films* (Berkeley: University of California Press, 1986), 499.
2. Andrew Sarris, *Interviews with Film Directors* (New York: Avon Books, 1967), 197.
3. Lane Roth, "Ritual Brawls in John Ford's Films," *Film Criticism* 7, no. 3 (Spring 1983), 39.
4. Mary Pat Kelly, *Martin Scorsese: A Journey* (New York: Thunder Mouth Press, 1991), 132.

Ways of Knowing:
Peter Lehman and *The Searchers*

Tom Paulus

The fact that François Truffaut liked it even less than Academy voters, who preferred *Around the World in 80 Days* (1956), has not prevented John Ford's *The Searchers* (1956) from becoming one of the most discussed films in the wake of the auteur theory, which maintains that it is the director who is the artist most responsible for a movie as a completed artwork (rather than, say, the lead actor or screenwriter). The film seems to turn up at every critical juncture in the development of the academic field of film studies: from humanist auteurism to auteur Structuralism to post-auteurist Althusserian Marxism or psychoanalysis. Interest was kept alive in what was perceived as not just an aesthetically accomplished but above all a "complex" or even "ambiguous" film.[1] Complexity and ambiguity, of course, invite interpretation, and no one has done more in this direction than Peter Lehman.

Lehman's work on *The Searchers*, a remarkable project begun in the mid-seventies and far from concluded by a recent collection, *The Searchers: Essays and Reflections on John Ford's Classic Western*, has looked at the film from a wide variety of angles. At the heart of his writing, however, remains a basic auteurist query: how to differentiate a Hollywood artist and a Hollywood film masterpiece from what, in the introduction to his *Authorship and Narrative in the Cinema*, Lehman calls a "homogeneous lump" of studio/factory turnouts that do nothing more than tell a simple story and end happily.[2] The answer seems to demand fixing on a Hollywood film masterpiece that only *seemingly* tells a simple story and ends happily.

The idea that there can be more to a popular film than meets the casual eye is, of course, one of the basic assumptions of auteur Structuralism. "New Film Theory" added to this the idea that films have a social and psychic function, and that there can be a "gap" or "break" between a film's intent and effect. This effectively got rid of the first part of the problem: how to differentiate a Hollywood artist from the "lump." But it is my feeling that, notwithstanding his curt dismissal of traditional ideas of agency and author-intentionalism in his second major essay on the film, "Looking at Look's Missing Reverse Shot," Lehman did not want to get rid of the author. The essay's two-fold conclusion, that it is the greatest films that contain some of the most disturbing, out of control moments, and it is the important artists who let more into their films than they can handle, reads like an attempt to reconcile *Cahiers* pre– and post–1969 — the conception of directors at war with their materials with new notions of countercinema.[3] What Lehman calls '"psychoanalysis," therefore, is less Lacanian subject-position theory than a hearty blend of Peter Wollen's ideas on conscious and unconscious individual style from his *Signs and Meaning in the Cinema* (1969), with Jean-Luc Comolli and Jean Narboni's essay from that same year, "Cinema/Ideology/Criticism," in which they proposed a category of films that "seem at first sight to belong firmly within the ideology and to be completely under its sway, but that turn out to be so only in an ambiguous manner."[4] The *Cahiers* editorial board's application of this category to Ford's *Young Mr. Lincoln* (1939) allowed them to refine their traditional auteurist defense of exceptional filmmakers with more current ideas concerning contradictory texts.

The main influence on Lehman's psychoanalytic critique, I would argue, comes from Noël Burch's *Praxis du Cinéma* (translated into English in 1973). Burch's ideas on directorial responsibility for organizing the world of the film according to binary polarities— or "parameters"— of spatial/temporal continuity or discontinuity, his emphasis on off-screen space, elliptical editing and the "openness" of the work, are crucial to Lehman's work on *The Searchers*, from his earliest essay, "There's No Way of Knowing: Analysis of *The Searchers*," to the most recent one, "You Couldn't Hit It on the Nose: The Limits of Knowledge in and of *The Searchers*." The problem is that Burch's post–Marxist, rigorously self-conscious modernist aesthetic counterposing mainstream popular cinema is a tough fit for John Ford who made westerns. It is one thing to discuss spatial discontinuities in, say, Dreyer's *Vampyr*, but quite another to do it when you are talking about a Hollywood studio film like *The Searchers*. The hermeneutic paradigm does not apply. No wonder, then, that Lehman's conclusions have remained largely unaltered from "There's No Way of Knowing" in 1977 to "You Couldn't Hit It on the Nose" in 2004, which ends with the typical disclaimer: "[M]ost unusually, this is a film that makes clear to us the limits of our knowledge of it. We will never be able to fully draw a picture of it nor fully spell it out. We'll never be able to hit it on the nose."[5]

My concern in this essay is not with the broad epistemic problem raised (the idea that a film controls and limits the visual access we have to its fictional events, in this case the problematic revelation of narrative truth in certain characters and their actions), but with film style as a conscious answer to this problem. Style—by which we mean elements of *mise en scène*, photography, editing, and sound—is treated by Lehman as individual style, either conscious/structured or unconscious/symptomatic. To complete Wollen's useful typology of styles, we would have to say he largely forgets about collective style, in this case the tradition of classical studio filmmaking to which film and artist belong.[6]

In *Narration in Light* (1986), his standard work on point of view as a position of knowledge in relation to the fiction, George Wilson presents a reading of *The Searchers* that is largely in accord with Lehman's. Nevertheless, the theoretical context for Wilson's analysis is different in one important regard: Wilson finds it essential that we cultivate a lively sense of the subtlety, complexity, and variety, not of a single film masterpiece like *The Searchers*, but of the classical narrative tradition to which it belongs.[7] From a cultural studies perspective Richard Maltby argues along similar lines for the inherent epistemic complexity of classical Hollywood filmmaking when he says—quoting both Edward Branigan and Pauline Kael—that in every Hollywood movie there are coincidences, inconsistencies, gaps, and delays which are registered by the audience as digressions or as opportunities for an intense pleasure of movie-going. This is not to say that Hollywood cinema openly celebrates ambiguity, but rather that the Hollywood narrative is chameleon-like, adaptable, resilient, and accommodating.[8]

Lehman's zeal to present *The Searchers* as exceptional has disabled a possible way to make peace with the spirit of auteurism. *The Searchers* can be both classical *and* exceptional (never modernist though) if we take it as the perfected or even revised ("amplified") application of classical patterns. In other words, *The Searchers is* exceptional because it comes up with the most creative solutions *within* the classical paradigm. If we accept this state of affairs, we can even keep the auteur as active agent, who does not only kick in when there is an apparent breakdown in the normal functioning of things, but is a constant and concrete force for stylistic and narrative stability or change.[9]

Allowing myself to move freely between essays spanning almost thirty years—since the major points have remained largely unaltered—I shall try to present a more everyday, pragmatic view of the problem-solving process of filmmaking in the studio era. I will look at the following essays of Peter Lehman: "There's No Way of Knowing: Analysis of *The Searchers*" (1977), "Looking at Look's Missing Reverse Shot: Psychoanalysis and Style in John Ford's *The Searchers*" (1981), "Texas 1868/America 1956: *The Searchers*" (1990), and "You Couldn't Hit It on the Nose: The Limits of Knowledge in and of *The Searchers*" (2004).

The opening scene is a good place to start. Lehman finds that there is an Indian blanket on a hitching post in front of the Edwards' home in the shot of Ethan's arrival. Later it is seen on another post at another part of the house, in the same frame with Debbie. Then Ford cuts to a long shot of the house itself and we no longer see a blanket on the post from an opposite angle. This "violation of spatial and temporal continuity"—in other words, a continuity error—brings on the suggestion that a formal link is created between Ethan, Debbie and the Indians.[10]

If we look at the production notes for the film (on record at the Lilly Library at Indiana University, Bloomington), we find that the first part of the sequence, with Ethan riding in, was shot on location in Monument Valley on June 16, 1955 (this is an added scene, not included in the final shooting script). Of the other players featured in the sequence only Walter Coy was present at this date. The part with Aaron stepping out to meet Ethan belongs to the same master. The shot that begins the sequence and opens the film, of Martha looking out, and the shot of Aaron coming out and stepping to the foreground, followed by the masterfully staged shot of the rest of the family stepping onto the porch, were photographed at a later date, on July 8. The reason for this delay is that the female players were only expected on call at the rough Monument Valley location near the very end of shooting.

Lehman says that the blanket has disappeared from the post when we get an opposite angle on the house in long shot. In fact, it was never there: the post (one of two actually) we see, is not the same as the one in the earlier shots, which is clearly located much further from the house. The second continuity error in this case is not a moving or disappearing blanket, but either ill-matched shots that create a confused space or a "cheat" to elide both the distance Ethan has to cross to get to the house and the distance Aaron has to cross to meet Ethan halfway. The blanket does re-appear rather magically, since it is absent from the preceding shot. Given that this is, after all, a wide-screen film, and that many directors of the early fifties were terrified of leaving empty corners in the wide frame, I would suggest Ford put it there for reasons of compositional balance.

Ill-matched shots, or "violations of spatial and temporal continuity," are often a consequence of location shooting. Besides obvious logistical and lighting problems, two factors make it more difficult to control the process of making films involving location work. One is that such films are necessarily shot out of continuity, increasing the likelihood of matching problems or errors that can not always be resolved by retakes on the sound stage or the studio back lot. Such problems become even more likely if filmmakers cannot have their daily takes printed because of the location's distance from main traffic routes or airports. Filmmakers simply had to rely on their experience to know how the film would look and cut without seeing the dailies. Ford relied on his experience a great deal more than most other studio directors: his habit of shooting without "protection," getting only those shots he needed, gave him greater control over his film but also increased the risk of shots not matching. In his entertaining memoir *Company of Heroes* Harry Carey, Jr. writes: "Uncle Jack never ran dailies or rushes, the scenes that were shot the previous day. He always knew exactly what he had on film."[11]

In this case there is a further reason why the sequence, while beautifully staged and photographed, can appear poorly matched. Given that Ford cut, changed or added to almost all of the thirteen scenes of the opening sequence as scripted, it appears that he was still uncertain how to begin his film when shooting started. (In production notes from January 28, 1955, Ford was still considering opening the film on a prairie scene featuring the "biggest steer, with the biggest spread of horns we can get").[12] The major changes concern the introduction of two of the three major characters, Martin and Debbie, rather clumsily achieved in the screenplay. (An early, very emphatic medium shot of Debbie is withheld and the scene in which Ethan first notices Martin when he fears this "half-breed" might steal his horse was cut). Martin's introduction was moved from original scenes in the script to what was shot as an added scene. This scene was shot on July 9, one day after the filming of what is now the opening shot of the film. Both unscripted scenes/shots are striking for their visual composition (more on this later).

Another problematic moment in the film for Lehman involves a perceived spatial discontinuity in the "cavalry sequence." What happens is that Ethan, who has started slaughtering buffalo, and Martin, who tries to stop him, hear the sounds of a cavalry bugle. They stop what they are doing and stare off-screen left in the direction from which the sound comes. Ford cuts to several shots of the cavalry crossing a river, then cuts to Ethan and Martin riding down a snowy hill. They move right to left, and by every convention of Hollywood cutting patterns, Lehman points out, we expect Ethan and Martin to approach the cavalry. Instead the camera pans to reveal dead bodies and burned tepees in the foreground of the frame. We are in a village the cavalry has just destroyed.

What has happened here? The scene of the buffalo hunt was shot by the second unit — headed by associate producer Patrick Ford (and Ford's son), with assistant director Wingate Smith — on location in Edmonton, Canada, late March. A production memo from Patrick Ford, dated March 22, reveals that the second unit had no idea where the sequence would fall chronologically. In the memo Ford suggests getting footage of the buffalo (property of Elk Island National Park) grazing, a couple of angles of two doubles for John Wayne and Jeffrey Hunter riding toward the herd in the mid-distance, the essential "story shot" of the doubles taking their rifles and firing on the herd, and some closing shots of the stampeding herd. All these shots are in the film. The memo also suggests that the second unit shoot some coverage of Martin snatching the rifle from Ethan's hand, but this part of the scene was eventually photographed on a sound stage on the final day of shooting (resulting in what is perhaps the least inspired moment in the film, both from director and star).

The shots of the cavalry crossing the river, the destroyed Indian village and the Indian Agency where the soldiers take the captives were shot mid–February by the same unit on a different location in Gunnison, Colorado. The Gunnison footage again was filmed to Patrick Ford's specifications elaborated in a memo dated February 15, which suggests that Ethan and Martin "drop down into a stream bed ... to find a shambles of dead horses half-buried in snow and still-smouldering tepees."[13]

The same matching problems apply as in our previous example (notice the jump cut between the relevant shots in the footage of the dropdown into the stream bed; the camera has moved back slightly to allow for the pan towards the village). Furthermore, since Wayne and Hunter were not at the Gunnison location, there can be no shots of Ethan and Martin riding and moving to intercept the column and asking a young officer about Debbie, as scripted. We are given a short glimpse at doubles for Ethan and Martin riding at the back of the column (again to Patrick Ford's specifications: "It is highly probable that in the sequence we will grab some shots of Ethan and Martin's doubles riding down the column towards its rear"), but our main view of both protagonists during the scene comes from more uninspired studio shots, ill-matched to further Gunnison footage of troops riding into the Agency.[14]

On the subject of the "cavalry sequence" and what he sees as Ford's "abandonment of classical editing conventions," Lehman offers that our confusion in situating the relation between the spaces we have seen would vanish if Ford had faded out on Martin and Ethan and then shown them in the village. The fade would indicate the passage of time and a new locale.[15] The suggestion comes from Lehman's 1990 essay, "Texas 1868/America 1956: *The Searchers*." In his 1977 essay, "There's No Way of Knowing," the suggestion would have seemed out of place, given that the sense of spatial confusion that Lehman reads as critically significant is related to the striking number of dissolves. In nearly all of the dissolves (approximately fifty according to Lehman, forty-two according to Peter Stowell's more precise tabulation), movement is in conflict.[16] The scene in which the search party breaks up and Martin, Brad and Ethan decide to go on alone is given as an example of "directional conflict" conveyed by the dissolve.[17] We see the three ride toward the lower right of the frame as the line of Rangers moves right to left in the rear of the frame. According to Lehman, Ford then dissolves to an extreme long shot of the three crossing a river, moving right to left. In fact, there is no dissolve but a cut to the searchers crossing the river (which makes this a poorly chosen example). The dissolve comes on the following shot of them crossing the desert.

The point concerning "directional conflict" thus becomes extremely confusing itself: if there were a dissolve, and the dissolve is indeed the dominant transition device between *scenes*, then the shot of the three crossing a river is a new scene and therefore does not have to adhere to the screen direction established in the previous scene of the group splitting up. But there is a cut. Does this mean that we are still in the same scene? Well, presumably, since the essay claims that only at one point in the film are cuts used between scenes: in the "letter" sequence, to which these shots or scenes do not belong. Lehman's main concern, however, is with the "larger pattern of these dissolves." Yet what we find about the second of the dissolves mentioned in the example—from the river crossing to a long shot of the three walking left to right—is that, rather than emphasizing a conflict of directional movement, it conforms to classical editing patterns. In this shot we see the searchers wearily crossing the desert, after what we can assume is a considerable chunk of story time ("They gotta stop some time!" Brad despairs). By zeroing in on screen movement, the main function of the dissolve—i.e., to indicate time passed—seems to have been forgotten.

Before we look at the film's mainly consistent editing patterns from a temporal point of view, let us briefly take one more example of perceived spatial discontinuity, where there *is* a dissolve between scenes ("interscenic") but the point made is that the dissolve occurs *within* the scene ("intrascenic").[18] We get a long shot of the Reverend Captain Clayton from within as he leaves the Edwards' home, dissolving to an exterior shot of him leading the men who await outside. At this point it is important that we get our definitions right of what a scene is. If we take it to mean a segment in a narrative film that takes place in one time and space, then it is clear that the shot of Clayton leading the men who wait outside comes at the beginning of a new scene since it takes place in a new space (exterior rather than interior). Is there a new temporal frame for the scene as well? According to Lehman, going from Clayton inside to him leading the men who wait outside is one continuous moment, and therefore it would have been more traditional to cut to an exterior shot of Clayton emerging, mounting his horse, etc. Even if we suppose that the moment in time is continuous, do we really need to see Clayton emerging, mounting his horse, etc., especially given that there is so much to tell in this section?

Compare this to a similar moment later in the film, when Martin asks Laurie for a horse to ride after Ethan who went after Futterman: Laurie pushes Martin (who suffers his first fall over the chest) and storms outside; there is a dissolve to an exterior shot of Laurie presenting Martin with her best pony. Would it have been more traditional to cut to an exterior shot of Laurie emerging, getting the pony, then back to Martin getting up and going outside, etc.? This, of course, is a dissolve between two scenes, but so is the example Lehman mentions of broken continuity. As in the scene with Martin and Laurie, superfluous story time has been elided in a very traditional way. (We have lost another bit of time here: a scene of Debbie running after

Martin was scripted but not shot; at several points in the film the dissolve seems to "mask" these deleted scenes, some of which were shot but edited out.)

Throughout the film, the dissolve is used as a standard punctuation shot: to omit time for narrative economy's sake, and to indicate long time lapses, emphasizing the "epic" nature of the narrative. The ellipsis serves linear progression, often, as Tag Gallagher has mentioned, suggesting cause and effect, the cinematic equivalent of the literary: "And so it came to pass that...."[19] Overall, the consistency of editing patterns is strong. A first major departure from the formal dissolve pattern would be the sequence of the murder raid on the Edwards house. Surprisingly, Lehman finds exception in the end of the sequence — the shot of Scar blowing his horn to begin the raid does not dissolve but fades to a totally dark screen — and not, as Peter Stowell does, in the beginning: a medium close-up of a brooding Ethan wiping the lather off his horse leads into the sequence and is followed by a cut, where you would expect a dissolve as in most of the other transitions up to that point.[20] Let me first say that the full fade-out at the end of the sequence signals a major break in the story and serves fairly standard dramatic purposes. Furthermore, it is not the only fade in the film: there is a combination fade/dissolve to the swamp scene and to another night scene with Brad reporting that he saw Lucy. The cut that Stowell finds so unusual that it leads him to consider what follows as a product of Ethan's consciousness has a more standard dramatic use, in my view.

It is my hypothesis that Ford felt that suspense and drama were best served by crosscutting to present the scenes as occurring more or less simultaneously. A dissolve, or a wipe as suggested by the script, would emphasize time passing between the moment of Ethan realizing the threat and it actually becoming real. The cut, on the other hand, suggests no such temporal interval and presents the threat as real *immediately*. Although Ethan's realization and the slaughter itself do not seem to be occurring at the exact same time, they are pretty close if we reconstruct the chronology: we saw the rangers leaving the Edwards house in the early morning and Ethan and Martin arrive back at daybreak, which means that they were about ten to eleven hours away from home. This would place Ethan's realization around early evening, moments before the threat became real. *Immediacy* and *urgency* seem to have been the key motivators for the crosscut instead of the less pressing dissolve. Of course there is no switching back and forth between the more or less simultaneous actions in the film, but there is in the script where cuts — either wipes or dissolves — are suggested between the actions of the Edwards house preparing for attack and the posse splitting up and riding towards the ranch. There is no need therefore to hypothesize an explicitly subjective imagining (which, ironically, would have been preceded by a dissolve within the classical paradigm, as in a flashback or a dream).

Both Lehman and Stowell mention the "letter" sequence as another instance in which the rare cut as transition seems to highlight the subjective nature of the narration. The argument is that since great spatial and temporal leaps are made during this scene, one would have expected dissolves to be the transitional punctuation.[21] I would say that the "letter" sequence is not opposite to conventional continuity logic. In fact, there are four dissolves in the sequence, all instances of temporal ellipsis: from Martin unwittingly acquiring his new bride to the searchers riding, followed by Look; from Look's frightful reaction to the mention of Scar to the arrow trail she left in the morning; from the discovery of Look's body in the village to the marching cavalry; from the cavalry doctor's delay, "one minute," to Ethan and Marty entering the chapel where the captives are held. All these dissolves occur within the frame of the story told in the letter and are balanced by straight cuts when the film returns to the main temporal frame of Laurie reading the letter.

The reason for the cuts becomes pretty obvious when we look at the first dissolve to occur outside the letter frame: Charlie McCorry sings, "Gone again, skip to my Lou," and Laurie stares wistfully at the sunset, after which we get a dissolve and the main story time picks up;

what we next see of the searchers is suggested to occur *after* the reading of the letter. What is in the letter is the narration of past events, of what came *before*. As we have seen now on numerous occasions, the dissolve in this film suggests a temporal ellipsis. The use of the dissolve from Laurie reading to the events she reads about would create the false impression of events *progressing* in the story, whereas the point of the letter is that these events are past. Dissolves would have been highly confusing. As the cut to the massacre scene evoked relative simultaneity, the cuts to the frame narration in the letter scene suggest something other than succession or cause and effect narrated by the dissolves. Again, there is no need to make the case for subjective narration in this sequence (Laurie's, Martin's), since the letter merely serves to integrate major aspects of what we are to accept, according to standard continuity rules, as really happening at home and as having happened on the search.

Nevertheless, the letter sequence as a whole and one moment of spatial and temporal discontinuity in particular, have become the central tenet of Lehman's epistemological argument as laid out in the more recent essays, "Looking at Look's Missing Reverse Shot," "Texas 1868/America 1956" and "You Couldn't Hit It on The Nose." The moment is not so much a scene as a "missing reverse shot." This moment occurs (or rather, does not occur) when Martin kicks Look down the hill and she rolls out of the frame. We do not see her again until after the action of the fall is completed. But the need to not look at Look falling raises a problem: how to get Martin over to Ethan's space? When Ford resolves the problem by cutting from Martin running down the hill to him swiftly entering Ethan's frame from the right, a moment in space and time goes missing. The obvious Hollywood convention, would be to follow the action (for example, there could be a reverse shot showing Look roll down the hill, or, at the very least, a panning shot which would follow her movement). The fact that Ford chooses not to follow the obvious convention and show Look's fall leads to all sort of conclusions concerning "racial tensions" and "dangerous, repressed, sensitive material" having been let into the film.[22]

In "Looking at Look's Missing Reverse Shot" it is granted that the entire sequence in which Look's fall occurs is riddled with continuity problems and that they may not all be related to the main point. Therefore three kinds of "absences" are considered, which appear to echo Comolli and Narboni's different categories of texts from "Cinema/Ideology/Criticism": 1) absences which are structured and thus partially controlled; 2) wildly out of control absences which are profoundly ideologically symptomatic; 3) trivial absences which point to little more than carelessness.[23] An example of the third kind is the scene that comes after Look's fall and starts on a shot of Ethan kneeling down by the rocks. In this scene there is a mismatch between the boots Ethan is wearing in the first shot and the moccasins he seems to be wearing in the second shot. Likewise, the log that we see in the first establishing shot is not even close in shape to the one that we see Ethan sitting against throughout the rest of the scene.

Look's missing reverse shot, on the other hand, appears to be both structured absence and out of control absence: structured because it reveals Ford's *intention* to place temporal and spatial discontinuity at the heart of the moment; out of control because he does not acknowledge what he has done, namely that he let too much "dangerous, repressed, sensitive" material into the film.[24] Let us compare this moment to the earlier example of the disappearing Indian blanket. This was presented by Lehman as a clear case of structured absence: the ideological point of the missing blanket was to suggest a formal link between Ethan, Debbie and the Indians. We found that the disappearing blanket was a trivial absence resulting either from the fact that the sequence was shot out of continuity, or from a "cheat" to elide the space between Ethan and the house. Likewise, I would consider Look's missing reverse shot as either minor continuity error or the result of an energetic match on action to ensure narrative flow.

Lehman is right to point out that although the scene looks simple enough, it is actually quite tricky. Look at the production reports: we find that the "night camp" sequence (shot on

July 1) necessitated ten additional "scenes" (or "shots"). The problem Ford has to solve is that, in the script, we start with a full shot of Look with her blanket folded over her arm standing not far from where Ethan is and where Martin is spreading his own bed roll. In the film Martin makes his bed on a hill, because Ford needs the steep angle to "send her sprawling." Obviously, Ethan cannot be on the hill with him because in that case it would appear that they are sleeping side by side (which would let in even more dangerous content!). At the same time, Marty needs to reach Ethan rapidly because Ford wants to get the dialogue going and keep the momentum of the joke. So Ford cheats.

The whole scene, in fact, is structured around Ethan's reaction to the comic business with Look: when Martin exits frame right to go find his bed roll (seen in the top right corner of the establishing shot), we get a cutaway to Ethan (who has shifted his position slightly so that the eyelines match), followed by a new set-up with Martin on top of the hill. Space has clearly been elided in relation to the establishing shot, but the point of the scene is not the climbing of the hill but Ethan's anticipation of Martin's "wedding night" with Look. Neither do we need to see Martin running or Look falling down the hill, since the point is Ethan's reaction. Ford could have gone directly from another cutaway to Ethan's reaction, to Martin entering the frame, but since the framing is too close, he needs to go back momentarily to Martin storming down the hill, before he can cut to a medium shot of Ethan and Martin. If we take it that the scene is constructed around Ethan — there are three reaction shots of Ethan during the sequence — it becomes clear that the space elided between certain shots is similarly motivated by narrative flow.

Style is only rarely discussed by Lehman in connection with what is actually on the screen and mostly concerns "things which we don't see," like missing reverse shots, disappearing blankets or even discontinuous editing.[25] A rare example of Ford's style discussed that does not directly involve "absences" involves openings, namely doors and caves. The point — the one emphasized in all the essays — is that time and again we see Ethan framed through doorways and related compositions (like caves or tepees). Immediately Lehman gives these shots hermeneutic weight as '"visual clues" and made to fit the broader epistemological framework of inquiry. For example: "There is a constant tension in the film between Ethan and interior spaces; he does not fit in anywhere."[26] Or: "I have always believed that the combination of the motifs explains Ethan's actions, since the shot of the cave is a reminder of his atavistic regression."[27] He pays no attention to the history of film style as a pattern of continuation and change, or to the problem-solving process of filmmaking.

The question is: do we really need a theory about "womb imagery" or "atavistic regression" when we find this type of "aperture" framing in Ford's earliest surviving features, *Straight Shooting* (1917) and *Hell Bent* (1918), and in many American films from about 1909 onwards? Or would it be a more useful and verifiable hypothesis to say that this type of image — doorways, windows, etc. framing a character or gesture and thus channeling the viewer's attention — made a comeback with the cultivation of new techniques for achieving depth of field during the thirties, and with the emergence of widescreen formats in the fifties? The prominence of depth compositions (often as aperture framings) in *The Searchers* can be explained by pointing to the VistaVision process in which the film was shot: VistaVision created not just horizontal expanse but greater depth of field (through the introduction of lenses of shorter focal length) as well, especially compared to earlier anamorphic widescreen formats like CinemaScope, that gave a more shallow playing zone. Inversely, aperture framings can also be said to function in *The Searchers* as what Elia Kazan called "inner frames," their function to break the wide picture frame into chunks that can be more readily grasped.[28] Yet another line of reasoning might take off from what Eileen Bowser says about the "open door" shot producing a pictorial effect much sought after by certain filmmakers in the early days of the American film industry, wanting to argue the position that movies were art.[29] (For more on Ford's stylistic techniques in his early silent westerns, see my other essay in this same volume, entitled "'If You Can Call It an Art...': Pictorial Style in John Ford's Universal Westerns [1917–18.]"

Since Lehman nowhere treats this "visual motif" as an instance of *symptomatic* ideological meaning, we can at least assume that it was Ford's intention to get these shots (if we take intention to mean, as Paisley Livingston does, that the author has done something to make the target hypothesis the *least bit accessible*).[30] Nevertheless, we immediately have to distinguish a *degree* of intention: while it is mentioned in the script that Martin and Ethan ride toward a cave for protection, there is no mention of any door opening or closing at the beginning and ending of the film.

The scene at the cave was filmed on the second day of shooting in Monument Valley on June 17. In the order of shooting it came before the opening scene, shot on July 8, or the ending, shot on July 3. Bazin would have recognized the cave shot as an example of "decoupage" inserted into the realism of the sequence shot, showing the key ingredients of the scene (the escape and the place of safety) in the same shot. (Eileen Bower also mentions, in relation to American cinema from the mid-teens, that the aperture framing, or "open door" shot, could serve to highlight action occurring in two different spatial areas within the same shot).[31] I do not take there to be anything more to the shot. Despite an obvious resemblance, I do not consider the shot to be a reference to Maurice Tourneur's 1920 *Last of the Mohicans*. When Ford stole, the source was sometimes D. W. Griffith or sometimes his brother Francis, but mainly himself. In his memoir Harry Carey, Jr. writes: "When Ford falls in love with an image, he never lets go of it."[32] The fact that Wayne grabs his right arm in an homage to Harry Carey in the final added scene, shot three days before the ending, shows that Carey Sr. and the silent days were high on the minds of both star and director. So when Ford was stuck for a better ending than the one scripted (a rather unexciting fade-out on Martin and Laurie riding slowly after Ethan and Debbie toward the house), further homage to Carey and *Straight Shooting* must have seemed like a good idea.

I mentioned that Ford also appears to have been unsure about how to start the film, given that he cut, changed or added to almost all of the thirteen "scenes" of the opening sequence as scripted. The famous opening scene (and its iris-like function of gradually opening up the playing field) was eventually shot three days after the new ending, further emphasizing a parallelism that is already in the script by having Ethan return to the desert from whence he came. On July 9 the scene of Marty arriving at the Edwards' house was shot to substitute for the deleted scene with Ethan looking suspiciously on the "half-breed" who might steal his horse. The remaining aperture framings—the tepee where Ethan and Marty find Look's body and the cave where Ethan lifts Debbie—were shot on the penultimate days of production, August 11 and 12. I will not argue that Ford was still thinking about *Straight Shooting* when he shot the tepee scene on the soundstage (the aperture framing in this instance is clearly circumstantial, since the tent flaps mask the fact that a part of the Indian village was rebuilt in the studio), but I will say that the choice of the secondary location in Bronson Canyon, part of Hollywood's Griffith Park, for the crucial scene between Ethan and Debbie, is significant.

If it were Ford's intention to use doors, caves, tepees, not as a pictorial effect or an ad hoc solution to staging or dramatic problems, but as a visual motif that "makes apparent the dimension with which the film is really concerned" (as George Wilson would phrase it), then he would have shot the scene with Ethan and Debbie at the same cave as that shown in an earlier scene.[33] This would have made perfect sense in the story space since earlier we saw Ethan and Martin fleeing from the Indian camp to the cave, exactly as we see Debbie do later. There is no mention of a cave in the scripted scene, so it is improbable that the Griffith Park location was considered at the start of production. It is more probable that there was more uncertainty about this crucial scene, and that an ad hoc parallelism through aperture framings yet again seemed like the best solution to the problem: the scene as shot on August 12 thus recaps ideas from the first and last days of location (the first cave scene shot on June 17, the last door shot filmed on July 8) and the first day of studio shooting (Ethan picking up Debbie at the beginning of the first scene in the Edwards house).

This, of course, is only a revisable hypothesis. What it offers is a plausible context for understanding the day-to-day mechanics and the problem-solving process of filmmaking. To conclude, here is another hypothesis regarding the doorway shots that bookend the film, based on a telegram from production manager Lowell Farrell to the production office, sent from Flagstaff, Arizona on June 23, 1955: "Tell [art director Frank] Hotaling I don't think it advisable to count on doors, etc., for exterior Edwards home. He should build them there."[34] A line comes to mind from Howard Hawks' *His Girl Friday* (Hildy Johnson providing an economic rationale for a seemingly irrational act): "Production for use."

Notes

1. From the introduction to the most recent collection of essays devoted to the film: "[A]mbivalence and complexity are what give the film much of its enduring fascination." See Arthur M. Eckstein and Peter Lehman, Introduction, in Arthur M. Eckstein and Peter Lehman, eds., *The Searchers: Essays and Reflections on John Ford's Classic Western* (Detroit: Wayne State University Press, 2004), 2.

2. Peter Lehman and William Luhr, Introduction, in William Luhr and Peter Lehman, eds., *Authorship and Narrative in the Cinema* (New York: Capricorn Books, 1977).

3. Peter Lehman, "Looking at Look's Missing Reverse Shot: Psychoanalysis and Style in John Ford's *The Searchers*," in Jim Kitses and Gregg Rickman, eds., *The Western Reader* (New York: Limelight Editions, 1998), 266.

4. Jean-Luc Comolli and Jean Narboni, "Cinema/Ideology/Criticism," in Bill Nichols, ed., *Movies and Methods: An Anthology* (Berkeley: University of California Press, 1976), 25–27.

5. Peter Lehman, "'You Couldn't Hit It on the Nose': The Limits of Knowledge in and of *The Searchers*," in Arthur M. Eckstein and Peter Lehman, eds., *The Searchers: Essays and Reflections on John Ford's Classic Western*, 262.

6. See Peter Wollen, *Signs and Meaning in the Cinema* (London: British Film Institute, 1969), 163–65.

7. George M. Wilson, *Narration in Light: Studies in Cinematic Point of View* (Baltimore and London: The Johns Hopkins University Press, 1986), 11.

8. Richard Maltby, "'A Brief Romantic Interlude': Dick and Jane Go to 3½ Seconds of the Classical Hollywood Cinema," in David Bordwell and Noël Carroll, eds., *Post-Theory: Reconstructing Film Studies* (Madison: University of Wisconsin Press, 1996), 438.

9. David Bordwell, "Contemporary Film Studies and the Vicissitudes of Grand Theory," 3–37, and Noël Carroll, "Prospects for Film Theory: A Personal Assessment," 37–71, in Bordwell and Carroll, eds., *Post-Theory: Reconstructing Film Studies*.

10. Peter Lehman, "There's No Way of Knowing: Analysis of *The Searchers*," in William Luhr and Peter Lehman, eds., *Authorship and Narrative in the Cinema*, 121.

11. Harry Carey, Jr., *Company of Heroes: My Life as an Actor in the John Ford Stock Company* (Lanham, New York, London: Madison Books, 1994), 6.

12. Production note dated 28 January, 1955. The John Ford Papers in the Lilly Library, Indiana University, Bloomington, Indiana. Box 6, Folder 20.

13. Memo dated February 15, 1955. The John Ford Papers, Lilly Library, Box 6, Folder 21.

14. Memo dated February 15, 1955. The John Ford Papers.

15. Peter Lehman, "Texas 1868/America 1956: *The Searchers*," in Peter Lehman, ed., *Close Viewings: An Anthology of New Film Criticism* (Tallahassee: The Florida State University Press, 1990), 394.

16. Peter Stowell, *John Ford* (Boston: Twayne Publishers, 1986), 128–29.

17. Peter Lehman, "There's No Way of Knowing: Analysis of *The Searchers*," 111.

18. Peter Lehman, "There's No Way of Knowing: Analysis of *The Searchers*," 111.

19. Tag Gallagher, *John Ford: The Man and His Films* (Berkeley, Los Angeles, London: University of California Press, 1986), 398.

20. Peter Stowell, *John Ford*, 139

21. Peter Stowell, *John Ford*, 140; Peter Lehman, "There's No Way of Knowing: Analysis of *The Searchers*," 112–17.

22. Peter Lehman, "Looking at Look's Missing Reverse Shot: Psychoanalysis and Style in John Ford's *The Searchers*," 264.

23. Peter Lehman, "Looking at Look's Missing Reverse Shot," 266.

24. Lehman, "Looking at Look's Missing Reverse Shot," 264.

25. Lehman, "Looking at Look's Missing Reverse Shot," 261.

26. Lehman, "Texas 1868/America 1956: *The Searchers*," 397.

27. Lehman, " 'You Couldn't Hit It on the Nose': The Limits of Knowledge in and of *The Searchers*," 254.

28. See David Bordwell, *On the History of Film Style* (Cambridge, Massachusetts, and London: Harvard University Press, 1997), 242.

29. Eileen Bowser, *The Transformation of Cinema: 1907–1915. History of the American Cinema Volume 2* (Berkeley, Los Angeles, London: University of California Press, 1990), 239–40.

30. Paisley Livingston, "Characterization and Fictional Truth in the Cinema," in David Bordwell and Noël Carroll, eds., *Post-Theory: Reconstructing Film Studies*, 167.

31. Eileen Bowser, *The Transformation of Cinema*, 239

32. Harry Carey, Jr., *Company of Heroes: My Life as an Actor in the John Ford Stock Company* (Lanham, MD, New York, London: Madison Books, 1994), 179.

33. George M. Wilson, *Narration in Light*, 60.

34. Telegram dated June 23, 1955. John Ford Papers, Lilly Library, Box 6, Folder 20.

Populist Motifs in John Ford's Films
Roy Grundmann

Introduction: Ford and Populism

Critical discourse on John Ford has long acknowledged a certain duality in the director's vision and works. Many of Ford's films cherish the colonialist master narrative of the virgin West being settled by peaceful Protestant farmers. The stories they tell are of a deeply agrarian universe determined by a white Protestant ethos of self-help and self-governance, guarded and maintained by frontier values of individualism, good neighborliness, and a belief in the equality of opportunity. They uphold fantasies of a non-exploitative society untroubled by its colonialism and they conceive of the body politic as a clear-cut, well-ordered construct, basically correct, and impervious to larger, systemic flaws.

Then there is another side to Ford's films: the moral shading of their dramatis personae tends to undermine the hermeticism and righteousness of Protestant belief and underscores Ford's ambivalence towards individualism. The *mises-en-scène* or visual composition of many of his films stresses groups over individuals and feature troubled, failing, or ailing leaders over superheroes. Ford's style bears the indelible mark of German expressionism, which he frequently deploys to convey either the burden of responsibility or the dread of failing one's own people. More often than not, the Western films' rosy pastoral ideals are tinged by the director's own Eastern provenance, his Irish Catholic background, and the fact that he was the son of second-wave immigrants who came after—and who were often rejected by—the white Protestants who handed America its dominant myth.

Ford's artistic complexity is reflected in his limitations no less than in his achievements. While critics have widely acknowledged the director's unwillingness to conceive of American Indians as anything other than savages (and, later, noble savages), they frequently fail to note that this racism has eclipsed a further unwillingness—likewise found in Ford's westerns—to express the underdog status of the Irish in America through anything other than caricature. The performative excess that marks the Indian warrior in a Ford film is matched only by the buffoonery of the Irish peasant. While such characters' anarchic, carnivalesque folk spirit may provide comic relief to white woman retrieval fantasies or play Greek chorus to Protestant plight and anxiety, they do remain the self-marginalizing self-deprecations of a non–WASP immigrant. As such, they obliquely inscribe Ford's Americana with a complexity that indexes modernity itself, marked as it is by industrialization, colonization, and territorial displacement—and, thus, by successive waves of immigration.

In this sense, then, Ford's work is both populist and modernist, with the former already being informed by the latter, which it nonetheless disavows in the attempt to provide a phantasmatic reprieve from modern life's nagging ambiguities and irresolvable contradictions. While the modernist components of Ford's work, as it advanced into the 1950s, may have gained prominence (partially as a response to populism's increasingly anachronistic position), modernism was already something of a coefficient in the films of the 1930s and 40s. In fact, it can be argued that the ideological contradictions that informed populism as a historical phenomenon suggest that it was but a response to modernity's bewildering and frequently traumatic political, economic, and socio-cultural shifts.[1] While populism virulently opposed socialism or any attempt at systemic top-down reform, it did, at times, take on the form of a mass movement.[2] While it promoted individualism, private property, and the profit system, it attacked unbridled capitalism and demanded economic and labor reform. While populism had strong nativist tendencies and clamored for the curbing of immigration, it was also implicitly diasporic in its preoccupation with the settlement of the West. While it opposed political and economic elites, it was deeply susceptible to charismatic leader figures and demagogues. It detested machine politics yet favored cooperative mass movements. It insisted on the power of "the people," yet consistently placed "the people" outside history and actual politics—in fact, politics as such were suspect to the populist mentality.

Thus, notwithstanding its reactionary components, populism — even in its late nineteenth century incarnation — was already a modern phenomenon, its contradictory sentiments a sign of its struggle to respond to the very modernity it was a part of. Ford's work reflects the complexity of this struggle in more than one way. To begin with, it could be argued that the sheer ability to effectively engage massive philosophical and cultural contradictions in a work of art is, in and of itself, an intrinsically modern quality. But if Ford's work is broadly characteristic of the fragmented and deeply contradictory nature of mass culture, many of his key works deploy a particular narrative element that engages specifically populist paradoxes and contradictions. At issue is a moment that recurs throughout Ford's body of work: a specific scene that shows the protagonist(s) of a given story at the grave of a parent, a lover, a friend, an extended kin, or a slain brother in arms. The grave scene is a Fordian staple. It features characters mourning the dead, but never for the mere purpose of proffering realistic portrayals of grief or to deliver requisite pathos. Ford's films invariably ideologize the act of paying respect to the dead. They show the living declaring their debt to the deceased and promising to align their own path with the course of moral justice. Enlisting successive generations in the fight against a common enemy or linking them in the epic struggle of settling the country, the grave scene appears to bridge the rifts between disconnected mythical elements and to relink diverging generations and their disparate attitudes.

But the grave scene cannot be reduced to a mere agent of mystification. It also helps Ford to create a set of decidedly modern tropes that centrally affect his protagonists: a sense of isolation that equally befalls leaders and outlaws; an uncertainty about the world or even alienation from it; a heightened psychological predisposition that takes various forms, ranging from the merely contemplative to the melancholic and from the paranoid to the psychotic; and the hero's complex, often problematic engagement with sexual difference, resulting in the suggestion of castration in various symbolic registers. The grave scene usually occurs in the first third of a Ford film — often within the first ten minutes— and its dramatic showcasing of solemn promises, vengeful wagers, and fervent resolutions has an impact on the remaining part of the plot. While narratives continue to move towards the resolution that the protagonist vows to achieve, the grave scene tends to recast the mythological sequencing of crisis— sacrifice — resolution into somewhat self-conscious terms. Its ritualistic nature divides the plot into pre-crisis and post-crisis segments, and the latter often takes on a somber tone. In addition, the causality of the plot may erode and its mythological currency may get depicted with increasing ambivalence.

This article analyzes only a small number of grave scenes within Ford's oeuvre, focusing in the main on *Young Mr. Lincoln* (1939), *My Darling Clementine* (1946), and *She Wore a Yellow Ribbon* (1949). Space limitations forced me to consign discussion of *The Grapes of Wrath* (1940), *The Battle of Midway* (1944), and *They Were Expendable* (1945) to footnotes. One key instance of Ford's later work, *The Searchers* (1956), is dealt with in closing remarks, as is *The Man Who Shot Liberty Valance* (1962), which does not technically contain a grave scene, but which can be read as an extended elegy — one feature-length grave scene, if you wish — that rounds out critical consideration of Ford's populist mentality. Just as this article makes no claim to comprehensive analysis it also defers definitive conclusions. The topic of Ford's articulation of populist sentiments across a spectrum of films and over a period of twenty-five years is complex. The primary purpose of this article is to initiate dialogue and lay some of the groundwork for further critical considerations.

Young Mr. Lincoln

Focusing on Abraham Lincoln's early law career and fledgling political activities, *Young Mr. Lincoln* mobilizes viewers' common knowledge of Lincoln's historical significance and asks them to interpret the early part of his biography as foreshadowing his historical status. The film makes audiences rehearse and mentally complete the process of historical destiny. One of its central rhetorical devices is to position the future president in relation to a set of questions, hopes, and expectations articulated or triggered by two important women, Lincoln's mother and his first love, Ann Rutledge. But their significance goes beyond their respective roles in Lincoln's life: they come to represent womanhood as such. In the Fordian universe, womanhood is mythologically equated with the advancement of civilization, which, in turn, is held to be near-synonymous with the history of America as a nation. Lincoln's indebtedness to these two female characters is thus both individual-melodramatic and historical-symbolic.

Directly following the film's opening credits, a poem of Lincoln's mother is read, asking what has become of her son. Since the film stops short of depicting Lincoln's presidency, it functions less as an aid that would help viewers answer this question than as an ideological model that determines the mode in which the question is answered. The series of scenes that lead up to the grave scene bear out this approach. We first see Lincoln as he runs for government, speaking from a porch to a group of listeners. His speech is plain, his demeanor humble; he claims that his politics are made for the kind of ordinary people with whom he identifies. A settler family, the Clays, pay Lincoln for the supplies they purchase from his store by giving him *The Blackstone Commentaries*, a set of early and important books on standard law. Thus, they really pay him for his political views and values, and although Lincoln is to lose this first election, his study of *Blackstone*'s has set the process of historical destiny in motion.

The next scene shows Lincoln lying under a tree near a river. As he reads the law books, he is joined by Ann Rutledge. Their coyly romantic conversation serves the film to summarize Lincoln's political and moral vision as well as his future plans, the fulfillment of which is anchored by his idealized relationship with Ann. Ann recognizes Lincoln's potential. She wants him to go into law but, at the same time, she urges him to retain his humbleness and common sense. In the next scene, the film's grave scene, Lincoln walks along the same river, which is now covered with breaking ice. He puts flowers on a grave that the film identifies as Rutledge's. In a soliloquy he tells her that he is still not sure about his future plans. Propping up a stick on her grave, he declares that, judging by the direction in which the stick falls, he will decide whether to stay in the village or follow her advice. The stick falls towards the tombstone, which means he is to pursue a career as a lawyer. Then he admits to having manipulated his own oracle by having tipped the stick a bit to one side.

While the grave scene conveys to us that we are witnessing a moment of historical significance, its intimacy suggests that we have landed on the backstage of history.[3] Lincoln's self-serving oracle at Ann's grave is not chronicled in any history book, but Ford's film depicts it as the decisive turning point in Lincoln's life. Film scholar Jean-Pierre Oudart interprets the tipping of the stick as an example of the "verum index sui" phenomenon: the genuine acknowledges itself as such — Lincoln follows his own destiny.[4] The film not only creates, but also at once conceals narrative causality, and it does so quite literally by naturalizing it — by presenting it as part of the flow of nature. The romantic scene that precedes the grave scene ends with Ann leaving for the village and Lincoln throwing a pebble into the river. The ripples it causes suggest a transition fraught with historical significance. The succession of seasons (summer, winter, spring) between the two scenes and the contrast that is created between life and death add to this effect.[5]

The succession of seasons is overlaid with a chain of metonymic substitutions, depicted through a series of highly compressed events that commences with Lincoln lying under a tree by the river and reading the law book, and that ends with his soliloquy at Ann's grave the following spring. Lincoln summarizes the contents of the book — a reference to populist ideology. Then the film proceeds, according to the *Cahiers du Cinema* Editors' analysis, to endow Lincoln with "a mythological dimension through the displacement pattern law — woman — nature." The law itself derives from nature and Lincoln "naturally" communicates with it. Ann's arrival superficially functions to distract Lincoln from his studies of the law, but *de facto* triggers her substitution *for* the law, only to have her, in turn, be substituted *by* the river, that is, by nature. He no longer thinks of her red hair, only of the higher values she embodies and of what he owes her.

But as this substitution is ultimately enacted on behalf of Lincoln himself, he too is endowed with mythic features, assuming the holy trinity of father, son and holy ghost. To the Clay sons he is a father. On an allegorical level they represent the split states of the Civil War which are united by Lincoln. To Ann Rutledge he is a prospective Adam, and to Mother Clay he is a son. While these mythological substitutions suggest the film's rigid ideological coherence, they are, as the *Cahiers* Editors have shown, articulated through a set of diegetic terms — gestures, actions, and decisions on Lincoln's part — that convey a certain ambivalence towards Lincoln's historical role on the levels of narrative, style, and character psychology and that identify the film's distinct modernist sensibility.

These diegetic terms can be traced with remarkable consistency to a master trope — the symbol of castration and various forms of de-powerment connected to it — triggered by the hero's relation to female sexuality and played out via the character of Ann Rutledge. But in contrast to a screwball comedy or film noir, where the fear of castration drives male action in a battle-of-the-sexes plot and frequently humanizes the male protagonist, in *Young Mr. Lincoln* it has a dehumanizing effect. Here, female sexuality initially signifies the personal debt Lincoln feels towards his women. And when the personal debt gets transformed into a historical debt, it elevates Lincoln to a dual position of being of and above the law, of and above the people. He loses his humanity and is turned into a populist demi-god, a supernatural dignitary that the *mise-en-scène* depicts as something analogous to a fetish. He becomes fixed by historical fate, but he also does some fixing (of problems and, colloquially speaking, of villains), and his presence is fixating all the time.

The grave scene thus signifies the loss of sexuality for Lincoln in more than one way. Ann is the archetypal female — earthy, pure, and tied to the ground — a notion also hailed by populist ideology. While she will never leave her place, she must encourage the hero to leave his, so he can follow his true calling. As with Ford's figure of the westerner, a return to her — to the original, ideal woman — is impossible. And as with the westerner, the unavailability of the woman signifies Lincoln's exclusion from the mundane aspects of civilization precisely to the extent that he becomes the protector-enabler of that very civilization. The dropping of the stick onto Ann's grave is the first in a series of symbolic castrations that befall Lincoln personally (signifying renunciation), and mythically (signifying his subjection to a much more powerful and foreboding law, the law of the father), but that also empower him in a dehumanizing way.

Lincoln's actions have a castrating impact in that they help contain basic instincts, such as aggression (as seen in the lynching scene), but they also quell romantic advances (as seen in the conversation with Mary Todd on the balcony). His subsumption under the law, symbolized by the falling stick, and his rise to the status of phallic interpreter of the law, symbolized by his commanding the lynch mob to drop their tree log, are represented as two sides of the same coin.[6] This duality constitutes the sense of ambivalence that pervades the film after the grave scene and that may be called modernist.

During the 1970s, when *Young Mr. Lincoln* was first subjected to extensive analysis by the academy, the genealogical status of its modernism was being debated as a question of authorship. This debate methodologically pitted the film's "deep structure," deemed accessible only through post-structuralist dissection, against a more conventional focus on Ford's creative agency. In their concrete application, both approaches were, however, often used side by side or in close combination. Indeed, the *Cahiers* text, while deconstructing a system of codes and subcodes that was largely deemed to be lying beyond Ford's authorship, nonetheless reattributed certain modernist moments of instability and resistance to the agency of the director.[7]

Another layer may be added by considering the impact of Ford's Catholicism on his work. One might want to look at the film's ambivalent portrayal of Lincoln's dual engagement with law and discipline — being elevated to a foreboding figure of law enforcement by being subsumed under the law itself — as reflecting the sensibility of an artist raised under a faith that has always centrally concerned itself with obedience to the law and with the consequences incurred by transgressing it. Unlike Protestantism, which likes to imagine God's will as something that Christians should want to and should be able to embrace naturally, Catholicism retains in its very rituals a sense of inherent culpability and of the never-ending struggle incurred by the dictum of having to accept divine law. For a Catholic immigrant such as Ford, this mentality would have been as powerfully present as the cultural influences of modernity that gave him the lexicon with which to articulate his world view and orchestrate his cinematic productions.

The symbol of castration in *Young Mr. Lincoln* not only becomes a signifier of the despotic status of the law, but reflects populist anxieties about the transition between two mythic concepts in American history, the pre-industrial and the modern one. If one follows Erich Fromm, one could read this transition as one from a predominantly matriarchal to a patriarchal culture, from the notion that all people are equal because they are all children of mother earth to a society ruled by Christian and patriarchal precepts.[8] The two most influential women in Lincoln's life — his mother and Ann Rutledge — become the incentive for the hero to redefine his position in an increasingly complex world, one that accepts the power of the *pater familias* and acknowledges, albeit ambivalently, the power of the intellect and its consequences. In the scene prior to the grave scene, Ann Rutledge not only advises Lincoln to go into law, but also warns him that a certain stalemating influence of civilization may deprive him of the capacity for an active life. Her comment, "reading can put out your eyes," thus links the symbol of castration (related specifically to the destruction of eyesight in Sigmund Freud's reading of *The Sandman*) to civilizational progress and historical transition. As Ann herself remains strictly hidebound to the pre-industrial world, the complexity of civilization is discussed, but the film's ambivalence towards it is only developed after the grave scene.

The film's *mise-en-scène* conveys this transition between two eras and two myths particularly through character movement. These movements form a complex subsystem of signification that additionally testifies to the film's modernism. In the scenes prior to the grave scene, the dominant movements within the frame are from right to left. Lincoln and Ann follow this direction when walking along the river, engaged in romantic conversation. Richard Abel interprets this direction as Lincoln's movement to his natural sources.[9] The river, embodiment of nature as such, signifies the first phase of myth — the pre-industrial, nature-centered myth. The river initially also flows from right to left, but with the beginning of the grave scene its current "magically" changes direction, and so do the movements of the characters in the film — as can be seen by Lincoln's ride into Springfield or the direction of the Clays' wagon, as it rides towards civilization.

Abel argues that the exceptions to the "nature rule" thus come to represent the reverse of its ideology. The lynch crowd likewise moves from left to right, misrecognizing their improper self-governance as lawful behavior. But because they are in the wrong, they are stopped by Lincoln, who would otherwise not interfere with a left-to-right movement, though his semi-divine status makes him repeatedly resume the right-to-left movements. For example, he moves through the ballroom from right to left — that is, back to the natural sources that mythically elevated him to the status of agent of civilization in the first place. According to *Cahiers'* interpretation, this movement once again signifies his castrating influence: during this scene he has no communication with other characters, the society that represents the modern age. When he visits the Clays to prepare for the trial he also moves from right to left. In this case he does communicate. Yet, he assumes the function of the mythological trinity: he again seeks recourse to forces above those of civilization. This movement pattern is another element that is structured around and given meaning by the grave scene. The grave scene in *Young Mr. Lincoln* is thus significant far beyond its immediate narrative and emotional content. It is indicative of Lincoln's dual role as a benevolent and castrating agent of civilization.

My Darling Clementine

In a manner characteristic of many Ford films, the scene that shows Wyatt Earp at the grave of his slain brother in *My Darling Clementine* is positioned early on in the narrative. Like the grave scene in *Young Mr. Lincoln*, it is crucial to the film's overall ideological structure. *My Darling Clementine* opens with the Earp brothers crossing Monument Valley en route to California to sell their cattle. They encounter the Clantons, whose below-market purchase offer they reject. We also get to witness Wyatt Earp's early, inofficial activities as an enforcer of law and order in Tombstone: he neutralizes the drunken "Indian Joe" who frightens the saloon guests. Upon returning to their camp outside of town, the Earps discover the theft of their cattle and the slain body of their youngest brother, James, which causes Wyatt Earp to reverse his decision and accept the post of marshal offered to him after he helped Tombstone rid itself of "Indian Joe."

Speaking to his dead brother at the grave, Earp promises to stay in Tombstone to make it a civilized place. By now Earp is already wearing the tin star. Thus, similar to *Young Mr. Lincoln*, at least one of the grave scene's functions is to feature the protagonist explicitly embracing a path towards historical destiny that had already been indicated by/to him in the previous scene. Again, this sense of destiny is catalyzed by a feeling of indebtedness to the deceased, enhanced by the reference to a parental figure, in this case the father, who, like Lincoln's mother, is absent from the narrative but hovers over it.

The visual organization of the scene likewise resembles *Young Mr. Lincoln*'s. Typical for Ford's films, the scene features a composition of three visual elements: the protagonist, nature, and the grave. In this case, it is Earp, a distant butte, and a wooden plank serving as his brother's grave stone. Nature once again occupies an intermediate position between the living and the dead, indicating that the protagonist's promise to the deceased is of mythological significance. A more tightly framed shot then cuts out the middle element, while Earp mentions in his soliloquy that he has written to their father and to Corey-Sue, James's betrothed. Although Earp emphasizes the father's grief over Corey-Sue's, the woman's implicit significance is at least as great. Indeed, the scene's visual organization follows *Young Mr. Lincoln*'s pattern of mythological substitution, first replacing nature with woman (Corey-Sue) and then woman with law, as Earp vows to bring civilization to Tombstone: "Can't tell — maybe when we leave this country young kids like you will be able to grow up and live safe." The musical score, the second part of the Clementine theme, solemnizes the hero's sense of loss ("Ten thousand cattle gone astray") and suggests purity of vision and character.

My Darling Clementine has often been interpreted as Ford's most elaborate, precise, and celebratory rendition of the frontier myth. This is not the least because the values that underscore frontier civilization heavily overlap with those of populism. As Peter Wollen points out:

> Ford's chief love is the old West; it is there that the roots of his populism are to be found, in the society which produced Andrew Jackson, frontiersman and Indian-fighter.... The community is organized around the church, the saloon, the barber's shop and the square-dance, the nodal points of social life and of a typically populist kind of local and direct democracy.... Authority within the community is maintained by the sheriff; disorder comes, not from internal contradictions, but from outside disruptive forces who, typically, "ride into town."[10]

My Darling Clementine engages the frontier myth's basic antinomies of civilization versus wilderness, law versus anarchy, and communal protection versus the survival of the fittest. Populism cherished the westerner precisely because he oscillated between both sets of terms, mythically resolving the irreconcilable contradictions of simultaneously being within and without the law. He acted on behalf of the community, but he came to be romanticized for his rugged individualism and loner status; he protected the weak, but was hailed for enacting the doctrine of self-help; he was assumed to help create a climate of peace and safety, but was also allowed and, indeed, expected to exercise violence as a demonstration of bravado and strength.

Most importantly, while the westerner had a crucial role, or so it would seem, in enabling civilization to prosper economically and grow socially and politically, it was his very dissociation from the complexities of communal life — the fact that he answered only to himself — that bespoke populism's preference for simple infrastructures of decision-making. In addition, if early twentieth century populism revered the westerner for his folkloric appeal (borne out by the successful show business career of Buffalo Bill), populism of the 1930s may have come to appreciate the Westerner at least partially as a crypto-fascist hero, who enacts violence for the betterment of an "over-bred" and "over-civilized" society. More broadly speaking, the westerner appealed to latter day populist sentiments because he allowed bourgeois ideology to cherish primitive violence.

While the myth of the westerner thus overlaps with the sentiments of populism in several ways, mainstream culture still needed to keep the antithetical nature of Wyatt Earp's impulses in balance, so that the contradictory character of his actions remained somewhat concealed. When we see Earp making a vow at his brother's grave to remain in Tombstone until law and order have been established, it is to assure the audience that Earp's subsequent actions will not be a mere act of vengeance but will be beneficial for the community. Earp's actions endorse an uneasy equation between force and morality that suggests personal revenge is a socially beneficial and morally pure act, submerging anarchic desire under patterns of law and order.

It is not hard to see that whenever the film shows Earp engaging in the lawful aspects of establishing civilization — that is, when he is communitarian and purely altruistic — he is, to put it bluntly, unbearably boring.¹¹ Earp's efforts may be the film's official rationale and his mythic heroism may be what the film is most remembered for, but his actions amount to little more than hollow exercises. Already in *Young Mr. Lincoln*, the plot is curiously severed from the hero's myth. It has primarily an exemplary character to foreshadow the myth. In *My Darling Clementine*, the hero has a comparatively small function in resolving the plot that leads to the final violent resolution of the conflict. The film juxtaposes the blandness of Earp's actions to the much more lively, fairly idiosyncratic, dramatic vignettes involving the film's other characters. It is no exaggeration to claim that everyone in the film is more interesting than Wyatt Earp and Clementine: Doc Holliday, Chihuahua, and even "Pa" Clanton, who whips his sons into submission with deep satisfaction.

The reason why the frontier myth in *My Darling Clementine* seems so bland in its splendid transparency is because the film, in some ways, occupies a transitional position. On the one hand, it is fairly evident that, by 1946, there was little incentive for Ford to retell it in straightforward, realist terms. On the other hand, Ford had not quite reached the next creative period, in which he achieves, in Tag Gallagher's words, "a conscious vivification of his material as mythic actuality."¹² One has to agree with Robin Wood's assessment that *My Darling Clementine* represents an abstract value system rather than concrete stages of civilization, though this value system appears particularly heavy-handed. Given that Ford, like other filmmakers, was not impervious to the rapid historical changes that befell America during this decade, Wood wonders how to best descry the link between the real world and Ford's increasingly hermetic diegeses.¹³ One answer to this question is the concept of allegory. Gallagher suggests that Wyatt Earp's former tenure as marshal of Dodge City represents America's involvement in World War One, while his new turn as law enforcer reflects the role of the U.S. in World War Two.¹⁴

This concept offers considerable interpretive opportunities, particularly regarding the film's *mise-en-scène* and *dramatis personae*. Gallagher mentions the term "noir" only in passing, and if *My Darling Clementine* cannot quite be termed a noir western, it almost can.¹⁵ More precisely, there are two parts to the film: a brightly lit vision of propriety, everything we *should* believe in, and a dark vision, everything we cannot help but admit really exists, that shows a nocturnal Tombstone of outlaws and whores, spatially confusing, expressionistically lit, and appropriately drenched by rain the moment tragedy strikes and confusion rules.¹⁶ Wood attributes a certain harmoniousness to the film's execution of its themes, but I believe this harmony is superficial. Like that other darkly tinged dirge of populism, Frank Capra's *It's a Wonderful Life* (1946), made one year after *My Darling Clementine*, the latter is finally unwilling to take back its stylistic gusto and concede its striking depiction of the real ambiguities of modern life to the presentation of the old myth. The film's most pervasive acknowledgment of the erosion of populist notions of communitarian simplicity and transparency are the characters' tight close-ups that suggest their discrete, secluded selves or subjectivities— what Gallagher calls the film's noir solipsism.¹⁷ Ford even films the gunfight at the O.K. Corral in a counterintuitive manner, opting for a *mise-en-scène* of spatial confusion (arguably allegorizing the horrors of the war he had personally helped fight) instead of rehearsing a classic topography.

However indirectly, Ford at this moment was adjusting his vision of how classic American values should be represented. Consider, for example, Ford's representation of American Indians. Earp's indignation at the fact that Tombstone allows someone like "Indian Joe" access to liquor must certainly be seen as an expression of Ford's colonialist paternalism. But judging by the actual representation of "Indian Joe" in the film, it seems that Ford was no longer really interested in depicting American Indians as a threat to white settlers. While his racist assumptions were entrenched, at this point in his artistic trajectory he was already beginning to acknowledge the marginalization of American Indians from their former habitat. No question, Ford's willingness to deal with this marginalization is evidence of the kind of awkward, misguided humanism that would culminate in *Cheyenne Autumn* (1964). However, *Clementine* also replicates this very marginalization, largely depriving Indians of what little screen presence they might have had, including whatever subversive potential depictions of racial otherness might possess. Consider that the identification of "Indian Joe" as an Indian is based entirely on the film's soundtrack, that is, on the mentioning of his name and on Earp's paternalistic analysis of why he is a "problem" for Tombstone. The starkly expressionist visuals show never more than the silhouette of a man who is dressed like any other cowboy, including the requisite hat.[18]

While the film largely drops Native Americans from its world after the "Indian Joe" episode, it also arguably constitutes an early instance of the kind of structural redesignation of "savagery" that Wollen sees occurring in Ford's later work. The scene in *My Darling Clementine* that shows the overland stage getting chased is a direct visual quote from *Stagecoach*—except that it is not the bloodthirsty "Indians" that do the chasing, but Wyatt Earp, who is after Doc Holliday, having been mislead by a woman to believe it was Doc who killed his brother. The dark forces thus no longer come from without, but are identified with white frontier folk whose own savage impulses are depicted according to the conventions of noir melodrama.[19]

While *Young Mr. Lincoln* makes Ford's ambivalent attitudes towards the populist myth converge onto a single character, namely that of Lincoln, *My Darling Clementine* precipitates it into two characters, Earp and Doc Holliday. In contrast to previous interpretations that read these two as representing reverse trajectories (one moving up into the bright light of righteous law, the other descending into decay and death), both their character arcs actually resemble one another closely in that each temporarily evolves, before reverting back to an earlier stage. Earp is domesticated to a degree (the honeysuckle perfume, his going to the dance) before reassuming his westerner mode and riding into the sunset. His dark counterpart progresses from "Doc" to Doctor (resuming his surgeon activity to try to safe Chihuahua's life) and then back again before he dies.

Doc Holliday is the more interesting character of the two not only because of his noir iconography, but also because he has more than one role to play. He is, of course, the stereotype through which the director voices his skepticism about modernity. Dark, diseased, and discontent, Doc is the opposite of everything populism stands for. Yet, Ford loves this character and he makes us love him too.[20] This is because Doc represents Ford's own failing idealism. The film's false claim that Doc was killed in the duel with the Clantons may well represent Ford's last-ditch attempt to stave off his own looming sense of disillusionment. Yet, before Doc dies, he gets to recite Shakespeare—"thus conscience does make cowards of us all"—which functions as an indirect admission of Ford's own unease about the set of sobering postwar political realities America had on its hands: the gnawing awareness that it had failed to adequately respond to the Holocaust, much less prevent it; the fact that it had set up its own domestic internment camps for Japanese Americans; the aftershock of having dropped the atom bomb; and the confrontation with massive social and economic challenges, such as reintegrating the returning veterans.

Right before the grave scene, Earp asks the town official, from whom he receives the tin star, who owns the cattle and who owns the gambling in Tombstone. While the characters at issue are stereotypes, they do represent socio-economic realities (the Clantons are, after all, business men skilled in market economics) and a realistic mindset (Doc's failed idealism is, after all, a sign that he grasps reality) that far exceed their mythic western roles and allude to the post-war present. Given the difficulty of updating the frontier myth to this present, even if it is the present of a victorious nation, it is understandable why Ford, in order to continue to depict the Old West, would henceforth "retreat" into the protected, seemingly ahistorical world of the cavalry.

She Wore a Yellow Ribbon

The second film in Ford's cavalry trilogy, *She Wore a Yellow Ribbon* is further evidence of Ford's increasing unwillingness to deal with populist myths in anything but a hermetically mythic scenario. While the film very loosely references a historical framework — the defeat of Custer's troops at Little Big Horn — it uses this moment simply as a catalyst from which to develop its elegy about the epic process of settling the west, the memory of those who lost their lives in the struggle, and the "changing of the guard" among the institution (with) which Ford now prefers to identify as the "civilizing agent": the U.S. Cavalry.

The film contains three grave scenes. The first occurs at a similar structural point as the ones in *Young Mr. Lincoln* and *My Darling Clementine*. The preceding exposition adds epic flair to the film through its montage sequence, accompanied by voice over. Its main function is not only to give the impression of a historical frame of reference (the struggle for land between white and red man in the wake of Big Horn), but also to establish the specific conflict (the decision to sequester the Cheyenne in reservations) and most of the characters and their roles— notably the aging army patriarch, Captain Nathan Brittles (John Wayne). Being six days before retirement, Brittles's life is closely linked to the cavalry's history, but he is alienated from the army's increasingly complex and ambiguous role as enforcer of civilization. His experience lends him an authority that exceeds that of his military rank. Middle management rather than top brass, Brittles is portrayed as history's unsung hero— the guy who lived through it all, yet whom no one will remember. He is also the old-time populist *pater familias*— the inofficial head of the military fort who knows all its military and civilian inmates.

The first grave scene shows Brittles visiting the grave of his wife and daughter. His soliloquy to his wife suggests that he is an old cog in the military machine who, taken out of commission, does not know how to spend his remaining years. He tells her about Custer's defeat and the death of an old friend of the family who was killed when the Cheyenne attacked a stage coach. He recapitulates how he and his friend had both wooed her. He mentions that his last assignment will be to push the Cheyenne back into their old reservations. He is interrupted by Miss Olivia Dandridge (Joanne Dru), the colonel's daughter, who visits the grave and apologizes for her foolish behavior of having flirted with two young officers. She gives Brittles flowers (his wife's favorite kind). After the young woman leaves, he soliloquizes that she reminds him of his wife.

Viewers classically get to observe the Fordian hero in a moment of intimacy. As in earlier Ford films, the narrative and ideological significance of the scene have already been prepared by earlier scenes. But unlike earlier Ford films, there is no resolution of the kind Lincoln made at Ann Rutledge's grave, one that would generate the film's narrative spine. And unlike in *Clementine*, there is no genre-specific causality between the death of any characters and the protagonist's actions (Brittles's family was not killed by the Cheyenne; his actions follow from military orders). A pattern of indebtedness to the deceased is likewise largely absent — the Fordian set of antinomies find their expression in a new way. The narrative and ideological spine of earlier films was linked to the conversion of wilderness into civilization. Yet, Brittles feels ambivalent about this conversion. He feels no desire for personal revenge and, at this point, has little professional zealousness. What the grave scene does feature prominently, however, is personal memories. The grave scene is much less burdened by the task of negotiating mythical antinomies and/or ideological tensions. *Yellow Ribbon* is a poignant film and it consistently privileges emotion over action. This preference makes the narrative wobbly, its causality tenuous.

On the one hand, Brittles embodies the image of the patriarchal leader; on the other hand, there is a sense of helplessness and redundancy about him which, ironically, is caused by his anachronistically comprehensive expertise. The younger generation that is about to replace him boasts much more narrowly defined expert knowledge (the military scout, for example, is identified as a brilliant frontiersman, but lacks military leadership qualities). They have neither an overarching vision nor the ability to look back into the past, two qualities that characterized Fordian heroes until *Fort Apache*. Typical for Ford and for Hollywood in general, the hero still stands for a larger set of values, a generation, an epoch, and so on. But lacking resolve, he is no longer spun into a dynamic process of decision-making and does not convey a programmatic ideology. Instead, he has an air of melancholy about him that suggests a general sense of loss.

Brittles's soliloquy is depicted in the same solemn and intimate style as those in *Lincoln* and *Clementine*. But it now assumes a self-serving, narcissistic function: the central feature of the scene, and of the whole film, is to indulge in this melancholy mood. The soliloquy generates spectatorial sympathy that helps promote the protagonist to the realm of tragedy. John G. Cawelti notes that, as post-war American culture recognized a rift between pre-war values and post-war realities, its new westerns registered a shift in the portrayal of action and heroism.[21] In the so-called adult westerns of the late 1940s and 1950s, the hero would increasingly appear as a psychologically elaborate figure showing signs of disillusionment, bitterness, a sense of guilt and a loss of personal ideals. Ford, too, tried to achieve a new balance between traditional formulae of popular culture and a new cultural context by altering the mood of his westerns, and he did so by infusing protagonists with melancholy. But this sentiment could be maintained only so long as creators and audiences found satisfaction in the elegiac treatment of the Old West and in the reluctant, ambiguous hero who remained torn between commitments.

Brittles's paternalism renders him a respectable person for settlers, cadets, and Indian chiefs alike—he is still a classic populist hero. Yet, his story is less aggressively tied to an official, patriotic one. His retreat into nostalgia even hampers any potential historical revisionism of what is, after all, technically referenced as a part of a larger historical conflict. His anachronism is kept on a strictly individual, emotional level. The western, and particularly the populist western of Fordian provenance, seems made for this melancholy mood. Ford's handling of the genre not only shows, but also exploits the fact that populist ideology profoundly lacks the capacity for self-critique as well as socio-political analysis: it is unable to assess both itself and American society. Hence, Ford's films at this time only ever state, re-state, elaborate, and amplify the discrepancy between their anachronistic ideological realm and reality.

The second part of the first grave scene in *Yellow Ribbon* likewise suggests Brittles's displacement. His relationship with the young coquette Dandridge is like a father-daughter relationship—she is not ever seriously considered as a love interest, though the film does identify her mythological function (bearer of children, domesticator of westerners) by associating her with Brittles's wife. The *mise-en-scène* thus introduces the possibility of an archetypal bond compatible to that between Lincoln and Rutledge. As she approaches Brittles by the grave, her shadow appears over the tombstone of Brittles's wife, covers the chiseled letters of her name, and rises right up to the arch that tops the tombstone. She is not posited as a potential mate but is subsumed under his memory of his deceased wife, of whom the young woman reminds him.

The second grave scene shows the funeral of the soldier and the civilian who lost their lives in the Indian raid. Brittles holds a speech at the grave, commending the heroes of war to heaven and honoring their sense of duty. The scene's narrative and ideological structure can be compared to Ford's magisterially executed World War Two PT boat drama, *They Were Expendable*. The living ones owe the dead who lost their lives in the fight for civilization. As in *Expendable* the scene stresses the role of Christianity, which serves the moral justification of war activities. It also seeks to justify the project of settling the west. Typically, the dead are enwrapped in an American flag.

This particular flag, however, is made from the undercoat of the colonel's wife and assumes a complex ideological function. The undercoat endows America with a mythological, maternalistic past, stressing that this maternalism is the well from which civilization has sprung. In addition, the soldiers, by having enforced civilization, have re-negotiated their debt to the archetypal maternal concept and thus deserve to be reunited with it. The undercoat represents the mother's womb. Taken as an isolated iconographic microcosm, the scene continues the promulgation of populist ideology and lets its underlying mythological pattern come full circle.

Yet, with regard to the film as a whole, this observation begs qualification. Brittles's melancholy is tinged with a sense of guilt about having come too late to prevent the Indian raid. In contrast to *Expendable* the protagonist voices not only a sense of indebtedness in this scene, but is half-accused of failure. And, unlike in *Clementine*, the causal link between plot and grave scene does not engender a resolution to solve the conflict and enact a certain ideology, but merely adds to showing the protagonist's displacement. Quite literally, Brittles was at another place when the attack happened. All three grave scenes in the film show the burial area as a place for *obsolete* characters, no matter whether living or deceased. The younger generation stay away from the graves. They are too busy enjoying life. Ford does not involve them in rhetorics of indebtedness, opting instead for a depiction of the kind of generation gap that would soon befall American society in reality.

The last grave scene in *Yellow Ribbon* occurs after Brittles has received the post of inspector. The scene shows him at the grave of his wife again, but it features neither dialogue nor monologue. It consists of one long shot, which has the effect of a still photograph. Its visuals harken back to Ford's depiction of military funerals, as seen in his two documentaries, and particularly in the "minor" grave scene in *Expendable*. These visuals encapsulate the dramatic hue of the film. In relation to *Yellow Ribbon*'s first grave scene, this last one represents a kind of re-unification between Brittles and his wife. The moral indebtedness of the living to the dead, which is the force behind most grave scenes in earlier Ford films, is typically enhanced by the fact that the living leave those graves behind and move on west or simply into the realm of myth or world history.[22] Because Brittles's new job of army inspector makes him sedentary, he is the first Fordian hero who will be able to have regular access to his wife's grave until his own death. Brittles is thus domesticated, which is reflected by the fact that he is spared the tragic, though heroic, separation from his loved one's grave.

The elaborate style and narrative void of the film's final grave scene marks not only the protagonist's retreat into solitude and the narcissistic celebration of nostalgia, but also his decreasing significance as a narrative agent. At this stage in Ford's artistic trajectory the grave scene as an element of the director's approach to narrative has assumed a new function. No longer a central catalyst of narrative progress and populist ideology, it now primarily conveys nostalgia. This sentiment is concomitant with the hero's changing relationship to his community. He hands leadership over to the young officers and henceforth assumes the role of consultant. The film conveys this process in a succession of sequences that constitute the structurally idiosyncratic ending of the film.

In fact, the film has three endings. The first ending is the scene subsequent to the farewell from his troops and the second one is the conclusion of his pony operation that shows him riding into the sunset again, before he is called back and given interminable employment. The film's last grave scene is the real ending. By then Brittles has become a living legend for the other characters in the film. He himself renounces the community (the dance) for his retreat to the grave, and they willingly let him go. He no longer carries much importance for their fate or for society on the whole, and his heroic paternalism is now the stuff of anecdotes. He has been put on a pedestal, frozen in history. When he enters the ball he is already an intruder, a paternalistic super-ego.

The last grave scene makes all the more clear that the retreat into nostalgia reflects populism's inability to overcome its own anachronistic position. In their baroque style and their destabilization of an already weak narrative structure, the film's three grave scenes mark Ford's registering of the widening gap between populist mentality and contemporary America. The fact that the grave scene as a narrative and ideological idiom in Ford's films is now "allowed" to recur and, in this case, to end the film, indicates Ford's shifting attitude towards the potency of the myth itself. It is almost as though the myth is what is being buried here.

The Searchers *and* The Man Who Shot Liberty Valance

The films John Ford made between 1939 and 1946 are paeans to populism. The reason these films can so effectively promote populist attitudes is because they present their heroes as being in harmony with their respective worlds. While this is a broad phenomenon that applies not only to Ford's work, specific to the latter is that the hero's main motivation is drawn from an indebtedness to the dead — articulated most clearly in the grave scene — in order to reorganize society in a way compatible with or directly expressive of populist ideology.[23] By contrast, the films Ford made from the late 1940s on reflect a shift in the director's attitude towards society and convey an increasing pessimism in his world view. The grave scenes continue to be central to the films' narratives, rhetorical structures, and overall ideological projects. But they also become, like the films they are embedded in, tinged by a gloomy mood that indicates a general sense of loss of old values and an acknowledgment of the anachronistic position and untenability of populism. Populist values in Ford's earlier films were developed in a vigorously progressive and didactic scheme; populist values in the films from the late 1940s through the early 1960s are problematized by conveying the protagonist's retreat from reality and his alienation from (or downright antagonism to) civilization.

But even within this later phase of Ford's work one can discern certain differences. Between 1949 and 1962 Ford proposes several variations on the doomed populist hero. For example, if the anachronism of an aging patriarch such as Nathan Brittles in *Yellow Ribbon* is expressed via the character's melancholy and his marginalization from the very society on whose behalf he has acted all his life, the anachronism of Ethan Edwards in *The Searchers* (1956) is portrayed as a full-blown psychosis that is directed not only against the Indians who have abducted his niece, but against his own community, from which he is alienated and excluded.

The film's grave scene assumes the traditional intermediary position between the occurrence and resolution of the central narrative crisis or conflict. But the scene differs radically from all previously discussed scenes in that it suggests a deep defect in populist ideology, conveyed mainly through Ethan's status as psychopathic avenger. Instead of featuring the protagonist at the grave of his beloved (the family of Ethan's brother who got killed by the same Indians who abducted his niece), Ethan is the intruding outsider who disrupts the funeral ceremony and precipitates its premature termination. The scene provides no visual link between protagonist and tombstone — the gap between past and present is insurmountable — nor does it feature a soliloquy. Ford no longer gives the hero the opportunity to align his personal desire for revenge with a righteous and religious vision of furthering civilization. Revenge remains deeply personal — it becomes Ethan's main obsession and it compounds his alienation from the community of settlers who, unlike Ethan, are shown to be more or less prepared to accept the loss of lives as a price their frontier existence extracts from them. In this sense, Ethan Edwards is no longer the hero of a Ford western — he is Ford's first anti-hero.

Michael Budd has noted that the frequent deployment of John Wayne's star persona in Ford's later Westerns is an index of the director's darkening mood and increasing pessimism.[24] Whereas the persona of Henry Fonda had a natural aloofness, Wayne's characters, since *They Were Expend-*

able, strained against community rules. By the 1950s, they show overt bitterness and an inability to channel emotion into constructive action. Indeed, the grave scene in *The Searchers* does not so much generate an ideologically informed, straightforward narrative as an aimless meandering on the part of this anti-hero. It gives the whole film a latent nihilism that is still absent in *Yellow Ribbon*.[25]

Nihilism is not completely absent in earlier Ford films, but when it appears, it is not attributed to populism but to the forces juxtaposed to it. The character who first comes to mind is Doc Holliday in *Clementine*. But the parallel between Doc and Ethan points to a larger similarity that suggests a central quality in Ford's work—the director's refusal to seal a main character into an image of complete otherness. With the exception of Ford's early portrayals of Indians, otherness is never a mere tool for demonization. It always carries a certain amount of complexity, it always invites a measure of identification, empathy, or sympathy with a character. Despite Ethan's psychotic hatred and the character's inadvertent capacity to allegorize wholesale the colonialist project of settling the West, the film does, of course, also seek to portray Ethan in a tragic light. He has become that very figure—the Other—that he has fought all his life; he is a threat to the very community that he also attempts to safeguard; he is doomed to wander between garden and wilderness for the rest of his life, belonging to neither realm. These qualities make it hard to completely dismiss Ethan as a vile psychotic.

Ford's work thus abjures clear-cut boundaries in favor of a kind of ambiguity that is, again, a sign of the director's modernism. In it otherness never completely congeals, but bears the (however latent) mark of its opposite. This is not to say that Ford deliberately strove for balance in the manner of the progressive social problem film of the late 1940s and 1950s. In fact, when this progressivist impulse for balance does occur, the film's voice becomes flat and unsatisfying—as is evident in the liberal project of *Cheyenne Autumn* (1964), which, in its attempt to correct earlier treatments of Indians, only ever achieves the condescending image of the noble savage. Mostly, however, Ford's complex treatment of otherness is an index of the increasing lack of suppression of the many contradictions and paradoxes that emerge when the Fordian universe unfolds through its various registers of drama, narrative, performance, and *mise-en-scène*.

While *The Man Who Shot Liberty Valance* does not technically contain a grave scene, the film's large central flashback can be regarded as being analogous to such a scene—it contains all the major elements of the previously analyzed grave scenes. At the same time, and by virtue of a curious paradox, the film suggests a continuation of the progressive draining of the grave scene's narrative contents that is evident in *Yellow Ribbon*. *Liberty Valance* centers on a funeral, but never enacts it. The death of the old Westerner Tom Doniphon (John Wayne) is the rationale for the film's story, which commences with the arrival of Ransom Stoddard (James Stewart) and his wife, Hallie (Vera Miles) to attend Doniphon's funeral. The time is the turn of the century, after the West had ceased being the Wild West. The outlaws, first and foremost the notorious Liberty Valance (Lee Marvin), are dead by now, and civilization has prevailed over savagery. However, the death of Tom Doniphon gives rise to a retelling of the story that does what the grave scenes in Ford's later films do: indulge in the past.

Whereas the film depicts the narrative present as gray, static, and artificial, the flashback is more lively, vividly conveying life in the frontierstown as the exciting heyday of outlaws like Valance and heroes like Doniphon. The film's protagonists, particularly Doniphon and Stoddard, carry associations and values that correspond to the populist universe of earlier Ford films. *Young Mr. Lincoln* implies a transition from one mythic phase of American history to another, paralleled by the evolution from agrarian to industrial populism. While Lincoln is initially associated with the first mythic phase (which also facilitates the bond with Ann Rutledge), the film insists that he has the potential for inhabiting the second phase, that is, to develop civilization in the post civil war era. In *Liberty Valance* these two eras are split into two separate characters,

Tom Doniphon and Ransom Stoddard. Tom is a Westerner in the traditional sense and therefore representing the first phase in American history. Stoddard represents the advent of civilization. He can be compared to the function Lincoln assumes as a lawyer. The duel in which Liberty Valance is shot — seemingly by Stoddard but, as a flashback within the flashback reveals — actually by Doniphon — assigns Stoddard the position of overt, visible enactor of civilization, who is primed for mythologization, whereas Doniphon is the covert but genuine initiator of civilization.

The parallel between both films also holds with regard to the female character's role of linking two mythical phases. Ann Rutledge, while firmly tied to an early, "primitive" phase, a romanticized agrarian society, is nonetheless the major incentive for Lincoln to transition to the second, more advanced phase. Hallie, the female character in *Liberty Valance*, straddles a similar mythological divide, except that she does not help any of the male protagonists to transition from one phase to the next. Instead, it is she who transitions by moving from Doniphon (the old phase) to Stoddard (the new phase). When she visits the ruins of Doniphon's house, where the latter had already started to build an annex for her, the Ann Rutledge theme is played and the parallel becomes apparent. The fact that Hallie is hardly an adequate partner for a man such as Stoddard is conveyed by their poor communication. Their bond is not a completely happy one. In an elaboration on *The Searchers*'s allusion to the forbidden longing between Ethan Edwards and his sister-in-law, *Liberty Valance* emphasizes Hallie's deep affinity for Tom.[26] Her reorientation to Stoddard precipitates Tom's decline, which can be compared to Lincoln undergoing a process of dehumanization in the second part of *Young Mr. Lincoln*, when Lincoln becomes all super-ego. Hallie's shifting sympathies not only cause Doniphon to destroy his home but also to shoot the outlaw Valance, as he feels indebted to Hallie and believes he must help the man she loves. The result is that Stoddard becomes the official hero and assumes a position of super-ego similar to Lincoln's.

Douglas Pye has argued that Doniphon's decline is determined by the shooting of Valance.[27] They have a reciprocal relationship, meaning that each cannot exist without the other. Hence, the development of civilization is not a natural consequence of their struggle, but initiated by the introduction of an external and historically recent character. Pye sees the young Easterner Stoddard, who happens to reap the glory of the shooting, as an artifice grafted onto the plot to help the director interpret the historical development of civilization as a continuous one. This continuity is a convention of the genre.[28]

However, if one regards Doniphon and Stoddard not as separate characters but as two elements of one and the same concept, Doniphon's decline is mainly marked by Hallie's recoiling from him. His deferment to her wishes represents his own succumbing to the course of civilization. The cactus rose symbolizes Hallie's significance for both men and thus links both phases of civilization. The rose is given to Hallie by Doniphon, but is taken up by Stoddard. It not only is a classical symbol of chivalry and courtship, but constitutes the entry point into another one of Ford's mythological circuits, this one linking civilization to the flow of nature and, more particularly, water.[29] The cactus rose gets discussed in connection with the irrigation bill and can thus be compared to the symbolic dimension of the river in *Young Mr. Lincoln*. Its changing current correlates with the changing values associated with the rose. Both represent transition and continuity, both provide a mythological dimension. Hence, it can also be argued that Stoddard is not introduced as a new concept that is haphazardly grafted on the course of events, but that he functions in the film as a "logical" step forward in the overall course of civilization.

Liberty Valance anchors this course of civilization in the indebtedness of the male to the female. But despite the importance accorded to the female element for the furthering of civilization, evidence of the dissatisfying or incoherent nature of heterosexual bonds is ever more striking in Ford's late work. Either the savage element inside the hero does not go with domesticity or domesticity is incompatible with a more complex civilization. With few exceptions heterosexual relationships are not acted out. Instead they are presented as past *(Yellow Ribbon)* or become prohibited. Either way, they index the protagonist's anachronism.[30] Archetypal male-female bonds are determined precisely by the fact that they remain consigned to the realm of myth — that is, unconsummated. Those bonds that do get depicted are shown to be infertile and unsatisfying (Lincoln and his wife; Stoddard and Hallie). These intimations of dysfunction not only indicate the director's struggle to present a mythic continuity of civilization in the face of a segmenting of contemporary America after World War Two. It also indicates a central problem populist ideology could not overcome: the bitter realization that it was populism itself that rendered its members obsolete by helping society develop to an unforeseen level of complexity.

In his earlier films, Ford lets the audience create the populist myth *(Lincoln),* or he ritualistically dramatizes this myth *(The Grapes of Wrath)* or presents it through overt iconography *(Clementine).* Only a deeper analysis of Ford's work of this period shows a greater ambiguity in the handling of populist mythology. In the war documentaries and in *Expendable* propaganda is the prime agenda, but already in *Expendable* one can see how Ford feels increasingly ill-at-ease with the myth. The later phase more overtly acknowledges the gap between myth and reality. In *Yellow Ribbon* the burden of living this gap is charted in terms of mood and emotion; in *Liberty Valance* Ford lets the audience witness how the gap is created and thus debunks it. Stoddard as much as York in *Fort Apache* is the big mythic token figure, and mythmaking is identified as an Eastern practice. This, however, is only half the story. *Liberty Valance* not only debunks but practices mythmaking. By disclosing who really shot Liberty Valance, the film also reinstates a "true" myth. In addition, the audience learns of Doniphon's deferment of glory to Stoddard and his selfless renunciation of Hallie through the double flashback structure. Movie audiences perceive Doniphon's eclipse as a deliberate abdication rather than an inexorable verdict of his anachronism. They register the film's final resolution: "When the legend becomes fact print the legend," but they are called upon to do the opposite: correct the legend.

Doniphon's death is a fictional solution to a problem that could not be solved, populism's inability to cope with its own anachronism. Liberty Valance idealizes Tom as a mythical figure. In comparison, *The Searchers* is more honest in depicting the flaws of populist ideology — it does not offer a solution and dares to suggest what may happen to an anachronistic populist hero who failed to find a mythic successor or had the luck to die in a saddle. He still wanders. He is disliked and disruptive, but he seems to be more real than Tom Doniphon and ideologically less programmatic. Compared to all the other mourners at Fordian graves, Ethan is the big exception.

Author's note: The first draft of this article was written almost twenty years ago, as a semester paper for a seminar on John Ford's Americana that I took with Prof. Dr. Christine Noll Brinckmann at the University of Frankfurt, Germany. I would like to thank Prof. Dr. Noll not only for her comments on this particular piece, but for her friendship and her many years of inspiring comments.

Notes

1. See Brian Neve, *Film and Politics in America: A Social Tradition* (London: Routledge, 1992). It should be pointed out first that populism's relatively confined historical period from the 1890s to the 1930s nonetheless divides into subcategories. There was, in Brian Neve's helpful explanation, "both the particular tradition based on agrarian protest and the more amorphous cluster of ideas centered around the opposition of elites and 'the people.' More particularly," Neve goes on to say, "populism in the United States has historically been associated with the land, and with agricultural communities threatened by,

and resisting, the process of industrialization and urbanization" (28). Citing the work of such scholars as MacRae and Hofstadter, Neve further explains that populism is reactionarily nativist, yet favors radical change, though never of a systemic kind and always guided by moral impetus rather than any form of intellectual analysis (29).

2. Brian Neve, *Film and Politics in America: A Social Tradition*. Notwithstanding the strong presence of communism and socialism during the 1930s, Neve points out that populism was a powerful voice to articulate American discontent with social conditions while, at the same time, reflecting America's relative class unconsciousness. On populism and classical Hollywood cinema, see also Beverly Merrill Kelley, *Reelpolitik: Political Ideologies in '30s and '40s Films* (Westport, CT: Praeger Publishers, 1998).

3. On the film's unique combination of the historical and the fictional, the interpersonal and the mythical, see Christine N. Brinckmann's thorough and lucid essay, "Fiktion and Geschichtsmythos in *Young Mr. Lincoln*," in *Die Antropomorphe Kamera and Andere Schriften zur Filmischen Narration* (Zurich: Chronos Publishers, 1997), 10–31.

4. "A Collective Text by the Editors of *Cahiers du Cinéma*: John Ford's *Young Mr. Lincoln*," in Philip Rosen, ed., *Narrative, Apparatus, Ideology: A Film Theory Reader* (New York: Columbia University Press, 1986), 462. Originally published as "Young Mr. Lincoln, texte collectif" in *Cahiers du Cinéma* 223 (August 1970), and translated in *Screen* (Autumn 1972).

5. Nick Browne has argued that the death of the two women constitutes a "*mise-en-scène* of deferred action." Lincoln is blocked from paying the original debt in kind — thus the literal debt is transformed into tokens in the course of the plot, notably the fostering of law and civilization. The focus on Lincoln's career as a lawyer is therefore a highly efficient narrative scheme, as it transforms the deferred repayment of the debt onto the plane of historical destiny. See Nick Browne, "The Spectator of American Symbolic Forms: Re-reading John Ford's *Young Mr. Lincoln*," in B. Allan, V. Almenderez, W. Lafferty, eds., *Film Reader* (Evanston: University of Illinois Press, 1979).

6. This duality likens them to the concept of the subject falling into language, as conceived by psychoanalysis. This concept's deeply inhumane neutrality is dramatized by the film as being always potentially cruel (to Lincoln as well as to others).

7. The *Cahiers* article triggered a theoretical debate on authorship that raged for much of the 1970s. See, for example, Ben Brewster, "Notes on the text 'John Ford's *Young Mr. Lincoln*,'" *Screen* 14, no. 3 (Autumn 1973). For a response to Brewster, see Brian Henderson, "Critique of Cine-Structuralism," *Film Quarterly*, 27, no. 2. For a brief introduction to the debate, see John Caughie's commentary on Jean-Pierre Oudart's concluding section of the *Cahiers* article on *Young Mr. Lincoln*, in Caughie, ed., *Theories of Authorship* (London: BFI Publishing, 1980), 183–84. See also Nicke Browne, "*Cahiers du Cinema*'s Rereading of Hollywood Cinema: An Analysis of Method," *Quarterly Review of Film Studies* 3, no. 3, Summer 1978, 406–16.

8. Erich Fromm, *Märchen, Mythen, Träume*.

9. Richard Abel, "Paradigmatic Structures in *Young Mr. Lincoln*," *Wide Angle* 2, no. 4 (1978): 20–26.

10. Peter Wollen, "The Auteur Theory," in John Caughie, ed., *Theories of Authorship* (London: BFI Publishing, 1986 [1981]), 104.

11. For a lucid and thorough discussion of Earp's character that regards his inertia as an expression of the immediate post–World War Two sensibilities of returning veterans, see Scott Simmon, "Concerning the Weary Legs of Wyatt Earp: The Classic Western According to Shakespeare," in Jim Kitses and Gregg Rickman, eds., *The Western Reader* (New York: Limelight Editions, 1998), 149–66.

12. Tag Gallagher, *John Ford: The Man and His Films* (Berkeley and Los Angeles: University of California Press, 1986), 246.

13. Robin Wood, "'Shall We Gather at the River?' The Late Films of John Ford," in John Caughie, ed., *Theories of Authorship*, 93–95.

14. Gallagher, 225.

15. Gallagher, 228.

16. In an early article on Ford, Peter Wollen's characterization of the frontier town includes the fact that it is tenuously connected to the outside world by the overland stage that brings various itinerants to town, such as quacks, actors, and so on. See Peter Wollen (Lee Russell): "John Ford," in Caughie, *Theories of Authorship*, 104. While the very concept of a frontier town would technically require every element representing white civilization to hail more or less directly from the East, the film can arguably be divided into two such levels of contrast between East and West. The first level comprises the classic frontier signifiers: there is the saloon with its cowboys and the hotel with its dining room, there is the church steeple, the dance floor, and the farmer families that stream into town for Sunday service — these are the elements that here, as in many other films, constitute the classic contrast between civilization and wilderness. However, there is also the amassing of a conspicuous mélange of Eastern signifiers, such as the saloon's French

cook, the barber shop's name, "Bon Ton Tonsorial Parlor," and its Chicago-made barber chair (the new one will be from Kansas), the figure of Doc Holliday himself, and the conspicuous emphasis of the film on the role of Shakespearean plays in general and *Hamlet* in particular. While recent critical work on Ford's and other westerns has argued that Shakespeare and the Wild West were by no means incompatible, the excessive use of Shakespeare in this case, combined with these other elements, indicates that Ford may have wanted to deliberately drive the clash between the wilderness and the encroaching civilization into an excessive register, perhaps somewhat comparable to the later Vietnam war film's depiction of the clash of East and West as excessive and, in a way, grotesque. For examples of this category, consider Francis Ford Coppola's use of Wagnerian music in the helicopter scenes in *Apocalypse Now* (1979).

17. Gallagher, 228.

18. It is possible to read Ford's treatment of "Indian Joe" as Ford suggesting that white settler society must suppress the "savage" forces its own life style may set free. (See Robin Wood's analysis of the late films of Ford.) But it is also possible to see the character's iconographic and stylistic assimilation into the noir setting as conveying the sense that savagery is a fully white problem. "Indian Joe" is no longer an Indian but has become a white savage, like all the other white savages who came from the East.

19. The resurfacing of the noir plot structure is but a sign of the hybrid nature and dislocation of generic elements in the film that, once uprooted, show up at unexpected places: when Earp catches up with Doc, they prepare to duel in what is the only classically staged showdown of the film — which does, however, end with Earp merely disarming Doc and returning him to Tombstone.

20. Even his physical beauty is acknowledged explicitly by Earp. The casting of Victor Mature, whose own physical features convey a sense of excessive, yet fragile, prettiness (particularly his distinct looking mouth) is absolutely perfect.

21. John G. Cawelit, *Adventure, Mystery, and Romance: Formula Stories as Art and Popular Culture* (Chicago and London: University of Chicago Press, 1976).

22. Lincoln moves away from his hometown and is in a *completely* different setting when the film shows him entering the stage of world history. The possibility of Earp's return to Clementine's tombstone has been widely discussed by critics (note the reference of the town's name to the major icon of the grave scene) but one is forced to conclude that the film deliberately leaves the question open in order to pay tribute to Earp's status of a Westerner. The Joads' departure from Grandpa's grave in *The Grapes of Wrath* most clearly shows that the living need the spatial distance from the dead in order to find their future.

23. Ford's war documentaries and his feature film set on the Pacific battle field are a variant of this phase: they more or less directly disseminate pro-American propaganda. The involvement of the United States in the war is presented as justified and patriotic values are affirmed. The grave scenes in both documentaries and in *They Were Expendable* make audiences feel indebted to the heroes of war, applying rhetorical strategies and structures from other Ford films.

24. Michael Budd, "Genre, Director and Stars in John Ford's Westerns," in *Wide Angle* 2, no. 4 (1978): 52–61.

25. On the meandering narratives and decreasingly coherent plots of Ford's late films, see Jean-Louis Comolli, "Signposts on the Trail," in John Caughie, ed., *Theories of Authorship*, 109–116. On Ethan Edwards's nihilism, see Kevin Stoehr, "When the Legends Die: John Ford and the Fading of Traditions and Heroes," in *Nihilism in Film and Television* (Jefferson, North Carolina, and London: McFarland & Company, Inc., Publishers, 2006), 97–136.

26. See William Pechter, "John Ford: A Persistence of Vision," in Leo Braudy and Morris Dickstein, eds., *Great Film Directors* (Oxford, UK: Oxford University Press, 1978).

27. Douglas Pye, "Genre and History," *Wide Angle*, 2, no. 4 (1978): 2.

28. Thomas Schatz, *Hollywood Genres: Formulas, Filmmaking, and the Studio System* (New York: Random House, 1981). Schatz notes that the affirmation of "Americanism," one of the most fundamental precepts of the formulaic narrative process of genre films, is also accomplished by establishing a sense of continuity between past and present and to eliminate the distinctions between them.

29. See the discussion of the film in Joseph McBride and Michael Wilmington, *John Ford* (London: Martin Secker & Warburg, 1974), 184.

30. Ma Joad in *Grapes is* the best example: she has to serve as a mythological source and a potential mate to her son as no younger woman seems to be around who could live up to the function. Rosasharn's potential maternal role is neglected in the film.

Heroism, Faith, and Idealism in *7 Women* and Other Films by John Ford

Kevin L. Stoehr

Introduction: The Later Ford

Ford's final feature film *7 Women* (1966) is an example of how we might evaluate an artist's later work in terms of its broader context, that of his entire career of narrative and stylistic concerns—much as we might appreciate, say, Shakespeare's *The Tempest*. In the Bard's final play, the author imagines characters, scenes, and themes that invite reflection on those from his previous works. He opens up a realm of fantasy that is nonetheless grounded in the soil of everyday humanity and that is enriched by a sense of the drama's, as well as the author's, cumulative and synthetic power. With an implicit echoing of more than a few of its author's past creations, *The Tempest* presents dramatic figures who appear almost archetypal in their embodiment of fundamental emotions and ideas, ones that resist being defined fully by any one particular situation or story.

Following a similar logic of appreciation, the final film of director John Ford reflects several characters, scenes, and themes from his earlier movies. The setting of *7 Women* is also as self-enclosed as that of *The Tempest*, presenting a concentrated attunement to a dramatic situation with clear-cut boundaries, ones that help to disclose as well as to limit and conceal. And the characters of *7 Women* are likewise diverse and enigmatic, not capable of revealing their full complexities and individual histories through actions that can be limited to a single stretch of narrative. Yet these dramatic figures also evoke general ideas about the struggle and triumph of what it means to "be human." These characters are therefore representative of human nature in its everyday commonality as well as in its profound individuality and mystery.[1] A recognition of the retrospective power of this film, within the context of Ford's entire body of work, reveals an artist who, while working in the twilight of his career, had gained a sense of his total achievement and who had sought to use the occasion of a new story to weave together, whether consciously or unconsciously, the threads of old visions and concerns. Joseph McBride tells us in his epic biography *Searching for John Ford* that this movie is the "most provocative of the late films in which Ford undertakes a searching reassessment of his own cinematic mythology.... [A]mong the most fascinating aspects of *7 Women* is the way it inverts and inflects patterns from the director's earlier films, revisiting familiar Fordian themes in a fresh and often startling manner."[2]

In the last chapter of McBride's earlier book *John Ford*, co-written with Michael Wilmington, the co-authors illuminate many of these "inversions," "inflections," and "revisitations" in their analysis of *7 Women*. And in his section on the movie in his book *John Ford: The Man and His Films*, Tag Gallagher also traces some of the conspicuous as well as subtle parallels that can be drawn between Ford's final feature movie and several of his earlier films. The present essay presents a humble attempt to complement these scholars' insights by drawing substantial parallels between aspects of *7 Women* and aspects of several lesser known Ford films including *Arrowsmith* (1931), *The Lost Patrol* (1934), *The Fugitive* (1947), *3 Godfathers* (1948), and *Wagon Master* (1950).

Ford was interviewed by director and film scholar Jean Mitry just after the release of *Mogambo* (1953). Mitry had asked Ford about his tendency to make movies about small communities of individuals caught in challenging circumstances. *7 Women* is the epitome of such a film. Ford responded that he liked to bring characters into a direct encounter with a "tragic moment" in which they can "define themselves" and "find the exceptional in the ordinary, heroism in everyday life."[3] Ford's response goes a long way in explaining the sense of moral reflection and rich humanity that makes his final movie so fascinating.

Upon its release *7 Women* was nearly neglected by its own studio (Metro-Goldwyn-Mayer) and panned by many critics. Some Ford scholars and enthusiasts like director Lindsay Anderson have viewed Ford's period of filmmaking after *The Quiet Man* (1952) as a period of gradual decline, with some sparks of inspiration here and there. Ford's final film thus winds up being viewed as little more than a mostly disappointing movie that demonstrates, as Anderson put it in his book *About John Ford*, the "artificiality" of its conception and the "banality" of its characters.[4] But my own appreciation of the film follows in the path of those like Andrew Sarris, Gallagher, and McBride who see true greatness in Ford's final film. As Sarris said in his review of this movie, included toward the end of his book *The John Ford Movie Mystery*:

> *Seven Women* is a genuinely great film from the opening credit sequence of Mongolian cavalry massing and surging in slashing diagonals across the screen to Anne Bancroft's implacable farewell to Mike Mazurki's Mongolian chieftain: "So long, you bastard." ... The beauties of *Seven Women* are for the ages, or at least for a later time when the personal poetry of film directors is better understood between the lines of genre conventions.[5]

The enigmatic quality of this film arises from its elliptical manner of delivering dialogue and plot development in concisely measured doses that nonetheless point to broader, more ambiguous existential issues lying on the horizon of the immediate storyline. But the intriguing quality of the movie for any thoughtful Ford fan derives from its reflective power as a concise drama that integrates, like a river delta, the currents and concerns of a long career of creative achievement. *7 Women* is certainly not to everyone's taste, as initial audiences and film critics proved, but Ford exhibits here the type of confidence in his own creativity and aesthetic sensibility that only a profoundly mature and masterful artist can express. To take a painterly analogy which is in keeping with the director's marvelous pictorial eye, Ford is breathlessly daring here in his effortless combination of broad provocative brush strokes and the subtle swirls and twirls that form detailed lines and shadows. His palette of many colors was always a very large and familiar one.

More specifically, *7 Women* is a fitting final testament to Ford's increasingly explicit concern over the years with the fragility of faith in the face of the darker, more primitive side of human nature. And the film revolves around the same themes of community-amidst-wilderness and struggle-against-adversity that recall Ford's classic Westerns and movies set in times of war. Despite the sunny and serene exception of *Donovan's Reef* (1963), the later phase of Ford's career is comprised of several films that give us a more critical view of human nature than his earlier movies. This is an admittedly overly generalized view, since Ford was never really void of a critical sensibility or a willingness to face the bleakness of reality. Even in his earlier years of filmmaking, while able to offer a folksy brand of optimistic idealism when it came to historical portraits such as *The Iron Horse* (1924) and *Young Mr. Lincoln* (1939), Ford was a hard-nosed realist when addressing social injustice and oppression — *The Prisoner of Shark Island* (1936), *Stagecoach* (1939), *The Grapes of Wrath* (1940), *How Green Was My Valley* (1941), and *The Fugitive*, for example — as well as the weakness of human character — *The Informer* (1935), for instance. However, several of the movies made during Ford's final decade of filmmaking tend to deal in a more emphatic way with the possibilities of existence in a grueling and even godless world. This theme of humanity's confrontation with the possibility of nihilistic despair is especially true of his final feature film.

Now this is not to say that Ford is some ideals-shattering, idols-smashing nihilist, even in his later years. If anything, the overall moral message of his films tends to be precisely the opposite as that of the life-negating Nay-sayer.[6] Ford finds some way of celebrating and affirming the power of the human spirit in nearly every one of his films. But he also frequently draws our attention to those human choices and situations that make the exceptional and the heroic possible in the first place — "heroism in everyday life," as he himself states in the earlier referenced interview with Mitry. These choices and situations are most intense and challenging, not merely when there are competing values or value-systems in play, but when there arises the very tension between the will to believe in something and the complete loss of faith altogether.

McBride quotes Robin Wood's 1971 *Film Comment* essay on the works of the later Ford, in which Wood criticized *7 Women* for its overall negative moral outlook: "The essence of the film is a thinly concealed nihilism."[7] McBride rightfully rejects this type of criticism by emphasizing the fact that the "nihilism" in question may be that of a particular character in the movie itself, but never that of the director, since the film deals with the very conflict between determination and despair. As McBride states in reply to Wood's comments: "But Ford never confuses satire with nihilism…. Ford's closest emotional and spiritual affinities are not with people who preach Christianity but with those who practice its principles in their daily lives, such as (paradoxically) the unbelieving Dr. Cartwright."[8] Indeed, it is Dr. Cartwright as the "practicing" Christian, the character who embodies Christian values even while vocally disdaining organized religion, who wins the heart of the viewer, not the "preaching" Christian, the mission leader who falls into an abyss of nihilistic despair while uttering words of dogma in an empty-hearted way.

With the growing complexity of the Fordian hero, and the increasing concern with how loss and suffering can result from the transition between one order of existence and another — as in *The Man Who Shot Liberty Valance* (1962) and *Cheyenne Autumn* (1964) — several of Ford's later films give us a more explicit view of the dramatic options between faith and doubt, community and chaos, ideals and broken dreams, heroic sacrifice and passive despair. *7 Women* is one of the most explicit of Ford's films when it comes to revealing the importance and consequences of such options.

Communities Amidst Wilderness

7 Women stars Anne Bancroft in a brash and brilliant performance as Dr. D. R. Cartwright. She is a brave but jaded woman who arrives at a mission in the wilderness of northern China, near the Mongolian border. This lone outpost is run by Miss Agatha Andrews (Margaret Leighton), an upright and uptight missionary with a devotion to God that rests on rather shaky spiritual and psychological foundations. The people in this region have been terrorized for some time by a barbaric warlord named Tunga Khan (Mike Mazurki) and his gang of marauding ban-

Production photograph from *7 Women* (1966): Unidentified man (left), actress Anne Bancroft, and Ford (with the permission of Dan Ford; courtesy Lilly Library, Indiana University, Bloomington).

dits. The mission is an isolated bastion of "civilized life" amidst a savage and dangerous region, not unlike the small settled communities in the Old West.

Cartwright and Andrews face off more than once in the film, chiefly due to the physician's clear atheism as well as her violation of the smaller rules of the religious mission, such as smoking during meals. Also newly arrived at the mission is Miss Binns (Dame Flora Robson), a missionary of a different denomination who has narrowly escaped a vicious attack on her own religious community by the sadistic Tunga Khan and his brutal warriors. Cartwright is challenged first by an outbreak of cholera brought into the mission by Miss Binns' group of survivors, then by the threat imposed by Tunga Khan himself. She is also challenged to help Florrie Pether (Betty Field) in delivering her baby amidst such atrocious conditions, especially given the further complications of a menopausal pregnancy. There is no shortage of troubles for the members and guests of this mission.

The basic plot of *7 Women* loosely parallels that of Ford's early action-adventure movie *The Lost Patrol*. It does so by focusing upon an isolated community of individuals who are shut off from the rest of civilization and who try to survive against the threat of a barbaric enemy in a setting of primitive wilderness. In *The Lost Patrol*, Victor McLaglen plays the sergeant of a British foreign legion troop that takes refuge in an oasis in the Mesopotamian desert after their commander, the only one of them to know their destination, is killed by Arab "snipers." While trying to endure their homesickness as well as the scorching sun, the soldiers must also fight against unseen desert bandits who attempt to kill them.

The heroine of *7 Women*, Dr. Cartwright, is similar to the Sergeant in *Lost Patrol* in that they are both secular-minded survivalists who must contend not only with the threat of an external enemy but also with problems that are internal to the respective communities that they try to protect. They are also ready when necessary to sacrifice themselves for those communities, though it is clear that the Sergeant is not a highly effective leader, given the disastrous consequences after he takes charge. McLaglen's Sergeant is an integral member of his group — its current leader, in fact — whose sense of military tradition and ritual makes his action in the name of his troop almost instinctual. Cartwright is also part of a heroic tradition or ritual, that of the medical profession. By way of contrast, the religious mission to which she has been assigned is not *her* community by any means, since she is a woman who, much like Ethan Edwards in *The Searchers*, but quite unlike other heroines in Ford's films, has no real home or family.

Cartwright's encounters with the increasingly neurotic Miss Andrews echo to some degree the growing tension between the Sergeant and the increasingly demented Sanders (Boris Karloff). Both Andrews and Sanders are, to a large degree, religious fanatics who find it difficult to cope with those who do not share the intensity of their faith and who suffer psychologically from their inability to overcome that difficulty. Both characters are misguided anti-heroes who, while driven by their faith in some transcendent deity, fail to do what is right because of their adherence to abstract dogma. When Sanders becomes horrified by the Sergeant's sudden ending of the scriptural recitation that serves as a eulogy for a fellow soldier, we are reminded of Miss Andrews' expression of spiritual revulsion when Dr. Cartwright shows up to the table drunk and interrupts the saying of grace. We are reminded here of Ethan Edwards' abrupt interruption of the eulogy for his brother's family in *The Searchers*: "Put an 'amen' to it!"

In both *7 Women* and *Lost Patrol*, made over thirty years apart, there is an emphasis on the idea of a community that, while facing the threat of an external enemy amidst a primitive landscape, is also torn asunder by a fundamental tension between secular pragmatism called into action and religious idealism gone astray.

The same theme of a community's survival amidst the wilderness, especially in the face of an external threat, is one that resonates throughout Ford's body of work, but we see it arise most especially in his classic movies *Stagecoach*, *Drums along the Mohawk* (1939), and *Fort Apache* (1948). In *Stagecoach*, the passengers of the title vehicle must band together in the midst of a mesa-spotted desert (Monument Valley) to fight off the attacking "injuns," while in *Apache* a cavalry troop must do likewise, venturing out at times from its outpost in the middle of nowhere. *Drums along the Mohawk* depicts brave frontier pioneers in the Mohawk Valley around the time of the American Revolution who must contend with the British as well as the savage natives.

7 Women also parallels *The Man Who Shot Liberty Valance* to some degree in that it is about a small community that is trying to forge a civilized form of existence in the face of danger incurred by those who are barbaric. Tunga Khan echoes the villain Liberty Valance (Lee Marvin) in his tendency toward primitive, irrational self-interest. Aside from Comanche chief Scar (Henry Brandon) in *The Searchers*, perhaps, these are the two most savage and murderous villains in the Ford canon. In *7 Women*, however, there is no advance toward law, order, and a political state, as there is in *Liberty Valance*. There is only the hope for sheer survival. Yet in both films there is an ultimate reliance on violent retribution in order to preserve the lives of those who deserve to live, so that society/civilization might continue. And to note yet another parallel between these movies, Miss Binns (Dame Flora Robson), like Tom Doniphon (John

Wayne), is a transitional figure: just as Tom bridges wilderness and civilization, so does Miss Binns bridge the secular and religious worlds.

Parenthetically, Ford sometimes shows us that the unity of some communities is forged in opposition to the non-human rather than human world. In Ford's earlier and underrated film *Air Mail* (1932), the isolated community takes the form of an air mail station where the battle is fought, not against threatening foes, but against the natural elements—and where daredevil pilots must risk their lives for an ordinary but necessary task that helps to keep members of civilization in communication with one another. Likewise, in *The Hurricane* (1937)—where Ford used special effects with stunning results even before there was an Academy Award for such a category—a remote island community battles against the external threat of Mother Nature. As in *Stagecoach*, there is also the clear tension that arises here out of class conflict, the conflict between a pompous colonialist governor (Raymond Massey) and the "uncivilized" island natives who must adhere to the laws that he has been assigned to enforce. Ford's isolated communities are never completely unified or harmonious, since typically there are internal as well as external oppositions that make up the basic storylines.

Ford's Heroines

In their book *John Ford*, McBride and Wilmington interpret *7 Women* as "a film without a hero."[9] But it is difficult not to view Dr. Cartwright as perhaps the ultimate female hero in all of Ford, at least by the conclusion of the film. Eventually we can see her inner strength and her faith in humanity shining through the dark clouds of pessimism so as to save her small community of fellow women from being destroyed by the threatening barbarians. Cartwright is a female version of Ethan Edwards, with a rough and tough exterior but also a genuine compassion that delivers the goods when it is called for, especially in crisis situations. (Bancroft reported later than she envisioned Cartwright as a female John Wayne, and that Ford often called her "Duke" on the set.)[10] Like Edwards, Cartwright scorns religion and authority, and both characters come to "do good" in a selfless way that religion and authority could only hope to dictate. If there is a "higher power" to which the doctor refers in her moment of heroic self-sacrifice, it is simply that of the value of humanity itself. Cartwright is a complex heroine in many ways, especially as she must learn to overcome her tendency toward being jaded about this "rotten world," as she puts it at one point, and instead express her inner faith in humanity when it really counts. Her deep-seated commitment to her profession is a constant reminder of this faith, yet given her pragmatic realism, Cartwright veers toward a pessimistic demeanor when she is in the presence of haughty idealists such as Andrews.

Dr. Cartwright is certainly not the only strong female character in Ford, nor is she the only female hero who sacrifices herself for others. Ford is sometimes categorized as a "man's director" who chose to make dramas that subordinate female characters and that portray them as mostly passive in contrast to the heroic male protagonists of the film. This, however, is far from true, and is certainly not the case in his final feature film.

Among Ford's heroines there is the resilient and inspiring Ma Joad (Jane Darwell) in *The Grapes of Wrath*, echoed by the brave mother of the Morgan clan (Sara Allgood) in *How Green Was My Valley*, who marches out into a snowstorm to defend her husband's dignity from those who would criticize it. Both of these characters are archetypal mother-heroes and defenders of the faith in family, and Cartwright, though far from being an instance of motherhood, does care maternally for her patients and even tells Andrews at one point that the missionary leader should have had sons to raise and nurture. And though she is far from purely heroic, the morally complex mother Hannah Jessop (Henrietta Crossman) in Ford's earlier *Pilgrimage* (1933) does manage to redeem herself while demonstrating a will that is hard as iron but still able to listen to conscience after a time.

As for other independent-minded and self-sufficient female characters in Ford's oeuvre, ones who anticipate the figure of Cartwright, one thinks certainly of Mary Stuart (Katharine Hepburn) and Queen Elizabeth I (Florence Eldridge) in his historical drama *Mary of Scotland* (1936). When watching the face-to-face confrontations between Cartwright and Andrews in *7 Women*, one can not help but think of the final meeting between Mary and Elizabeth, wanting to reach out in the spirit of sisterly comradeship and yet driven ultimately to enmity due to their competing values and ambitions. Ford, as we now know, was close to Hepburn after making this film, up until his very death, and she joins Ford's wife Mary and mother Barbara in being among those strong-willed females in the director's life, individuals who must have had a profound influence on his views of women.

Even in a somewhat atypical Ford film like his highly underrated dark comedy *The Whole Town's Talking* (1935), the place for the female protagonist was far from being the kitchen. Jean Arthur plays Miss Wilhelmina "Bill" Clark, a woman who is as brash and independent as the male protagonist Arthur Ferguson Jones (played by Edward G. Robinson) is meek and subservient.[11] There is also the determined Lana Martin (Claudette Colbert) in *Drums Along the Mohawk*, who must summon her inner reserve of strength when taken by her husband (Henry Fonda) into the wilds of the Mohawk Valley during the American Revolution. In that same film we witness one of the most charismatic and commanding of Ford's female characters, Mrs. McKlennan (Edna May Oliver, in a wonderful though caricatured performance), who does not even flinch when she turns to find a towering and hostile "savage" in her bedroom, ready to attack.

Among the strong-willed female characters in Ford's Westerns, three stand out. There is the brazen yet compassionate prostitute Dallas (Claire Trevor) in Ford's landmark *Stagecoach* (1939), a woman with a swagger as well as a heart of gold, expressing her courage in the face of social prejudice as well as her maternal instincts in the delivery of Lucy Mallory's (Louise Platt) baby. In *My Darling Clementine* (1946), there is the title character (Cathy Downs), the prim lady from the East who nonetheless braves the wilds of the West to find her lost love "Doc" Holliday (Victor Mature). And in the final installment of Ford's famous Cavalry trilogy, *Rio Grande* (1950), Maureen O'Hara plays Mrs. Kirby Yorke, the resolute wife of Lt. Col. Kirby Yorke (John Wayne). She contends stoically with the emotional distance from her duty-bound husband, a man whose military obligations required him at one point to burn his wife's beloved plantation to the ground. She is anything but passive or subordinate, particularly while trying to retrieve her son (Claude Jarman, Jr.) who has enlisted in the Cavalry and who has been assigned to his absent father's troop.

O'Hara was the most regular and prominent of Ford's leading ladies. One of the most memorable of her performances — and not merely because it occurred in one of Ford's most popular films — is the tempestuous Mary Kate Danaher in *The Quiet Man* (1952). Mary Kate might bow to Irish custom but she is not afraid of making her point clear in no uncertain terms to her tyrannical brother (Victor McLaglen) and to her sometimes uncomprehending suitor (John Wayne). Mary Kate is a woman whose dignity comes first, and though some critics might despise Ford's "chauvinism" for portraying her in less than noble terms (dragged through the mud by her man, in fact, while most of the township follows and cheers), she is as tough and independent-minded as any of the male characters in the film. She ultimately upholds her belief in the honor that is afforded to her by the ancient customs that lend special symbolic significance to her material possessions. If Mary Kate appears subordinate, it is only for the moment. Her character is echoed to some degree by that of Minne Wead, also played by O'Hara, in *Wings of Eagles* (1957), Ford's film biography of the life of aviator and screenwriter Frank "Spig" Wead. Minne, as Gallagher describes her in his book on Ford, "is the only Ford service wife unwilling to accept her subservient role."[12]

There are other strong female characters in Ford's films, all of whom are echoed by Cartwright to some degree. There is the sultry and brash Eloise Kelly (Ava Gardner) in *Mogambo* as well as the courageous and altruistic Deborah Wright (Carroll Baker) in *Cheyenne Autumn*. There is also Hallie (Vera Miles) in *The Man Who Shot Liberty Valance*, a waitress-turned-senator's wife who affirms her love for the fledgling attorney Ransom Stoddard (James Stewart), even at the expense of breaking the heart of doting Tom Doniphon (John Wayne). Hallie follows the life-course that she sees as the best possible path to her own happiness, which means that she follows her heart. She does not surrender to Tom even though he is the strongest and most heroic of her suitors, nor does she do so because he so desperately loves her.

Dr. Cartwright of *7 Women* is the epitome of the strong and heroic female, though quite distinct from the maternal heroines of *The Grapes of Wrath* and *How Green Was My Valley*, despite her midwifery and advice to Andrews that she should have become a mother and had her own children to raise and nurture. Cartwright rejects religion and rules of etiquette and she admits to Andrews in a quiet moment of sincere dialogue that she does everything to excess, much as Ethan Edwards is excessive at times. But at the same time she is absolutely loyal to her medical oath to preserve human life, even when it requires her to risk and sacrifice her own. She is a creature of duty, though she does manage to reconcile duty and compassion. And though she is not religious, Cartwright ultimately practices the principles of helping one's neighbor, being true to her own heart as well as to the Hippocratic Oath, and accepting the need for self-sacrifice when called to a higher cause, that of the common good.

Ford and Faith

Ford was no stranger to religion and its complexity, as we know, since he hailed from an Irish Catholic family whose members undoubtedly expressed varying degrees of piety and faith. The filmmaker was a man whose worldview had surely been shaped by exposure to religion at a young age, but this experience had left him open to skepticism and criticism. Ford said to an interviewer toward the end of his life: "I am Irish ... thus, Catholic. This doesn't stop me from being anticlerical. One can be a fervent Catholic and hate sermons. I choose my priests like I distribute my films."[13]

The young John Feeney served as an altar boy at his family's church, St. Dominic's, in Portland, Maine, and when he was still a toddler the family at one point traveled several miles each Sunday from the Spurwink section of Cape Elizabeth where they lived to the church on the other side of the Fore River. McBride relates that the director's childhood service as an altar boy must have helped to "imbue him with a love of ritual and ceremony."[14] As a boy in Portland, Ford gained a glimpse of religion's capacity to unite people as well as to instill a sense of duty and humble respect. He also witnessed religion's ability to provoke tensions and conflicts, since he was made aware as a youth that, even in a quiet little coastal community like Cape Elizabeth or Portland, some religious groups did not get along with others. McBride suggests that one reason why the Feeney family may not have completely enjoyed their "garden of paradise" in their beloved farmhouse on the Spurwink shoreline was because of the anti-Irish and anti–Catholic prejudice of the English Protestant families whose children went to school with the Feeney children.[15] Ford, it seems safe to say, had gained at least a general recognition of the complex nature of religion by the time he headed to California to join his brother Francis in the world of filmmaking.

By the conclusion of *7 Women*, Dr. Cartwright's secular/atheistic humanism triumphs,

Ford (center) in line to meet Pope Paul VI, who bestowed upon Ford the jewel and cape of the Knighthood of Malta in November 1965 (with the permission of Dan Ford; courtesy Lilly Library, Indiana University, Bloomington).

while Ford also shows us a woman, Agatha Andrews, who falls into delirium and despair because of her adherence to religious dogma and whose own sacrifice of personal happiness for a "higher cause" results not in compassion but in self-absorbed madness, mainly as a result of the obsessive repression of her true inner being. This does not mean, however, that Ford's final film concludes with a critique or even an indictment of religion, since he also presents us with a heroic Miss Binns, a missionary whose own spiritual faith keeps her strong as well as compassionate.

As in nearly every movie by Ford, there is an affirmation of the human spirit and the value of human life, but not without a corresponding sense of what awaits those who ultimately fail to affirm that spirit and value. It is this tension that makes possible the genuinely heroic choices that must sometimes be made in order to rise above a given crisis and to transcend one's own inner weaknesses and contradictions. Many of Ford's characters—such as Ringo and Dallas (*Stagecoach*), Ethan Edwards (*The Searchers*), and Tom Doniphon (*The Man Who Shot Liberty Valance*)—end up acting redemptively by affirming the life of the community, even though they are outsiders. Other characters, however, are not so lucky and either fall headlong into an abyss of misery, despair, and even oblivion or else they totter at the edge of the void. Young Huw (Roddy McDowell), the narrator of *How Green Was My Valley*, opts for the dreary existence of a coal miner in a death-filled village rather than for an education and life in the wider world. Brad Jorgensen (Harry Carey, Jr.) in *The Searchers* rushes off suicidally toward the Comanche encampment in irrational, self-destructive fury; he is a man for whom the universe has suddenly become a cold, absurd place of pain and sorrow. Captain Wessels (Karl Malden) in *Cheyenne Autumn* adheres so blindly to duty that he sacrifices his intelligence and compassion.

And even Tom Doniphon in *Liberty Valance*, after assisting in the raising of a new democratic order, fades away into anonymity and obscurity, "out desert way."

In *7 Women*, Ford gives us a character who clearly falls into the void of her own confused existence: Agatha Andrews, for whom even God is "not enough," as she confesses to Cartwright in their revelatory dialogue beneath a tree in the mission courtyard. Of all Fordian characters, Miss Andrews most clearly embodies the extreme alternative to heroic survival, since she is portrayed at the end of the film as mad and hateful, no longer conscious of her faults and weaknesses, clinging fearfully to empty words while her spirit dwindles away, a woman who is so cowardly, self-repressed, and self-centered that she can not even bring herself to offer assistance in Florrie's birth, just as she could not find the strength to pray when pondering the possibility of Emma's (Sue Lyon) death.

While *The Man Who Shot Liberty Valance* shows us the chaotic and savage wilderness that underlies the roots of civilized society, and while *Cheyenne Autumn* reveals an absurd and indifferent cosmos in which an entire people suffers and an entire culture is destroyed at the hands of unsympathetic politicians who are bent greedily on territorial expansion, *7 Women* gives us a singular and concrete character, Agatha Andrews, in all of her irreducible individuality, who comes to symbolize that nihilistic realm of chaos, absurdity, and indifference. She does so despite the ironic fact that she spends her life trying to maintain a rigid faith that might serve as an invulnerable fortress against such a realm of meaninglessness—just as the barred gates of her mission are meant to keep the savage enemy at bay, despite her repeated statements that Tunga Khan will not dare to harm them since they are *American* citizens. As we learn, no wall is ever thick enough to guarantee ultimate protection and stability, whether it is the wooden gates of a mission or the emotional fortress around one's heart. The mission is eventually overrun and conquered by Tunga Khan, and Andrews falls into the whirlpool of her own fear, self-delusion, and lost sanity.

Cartwright, however, despite having called this world a "rotten" one when scolding Andrews about her intentional neglect of the dangers facing Florrie and her expectant child, presents us with the type of faith in humanity that had eluded poor Agatha. While the conclusion is a tragic one for the heroic doctor, it demonstrates her dutiful affirmation of life. She does not need religion for such an attitude, but only her own strength and compassion. The doctor sacrifices her own life for the lives of others, out of appreciation for the value of life itself and because of her medical obligation to save lives. If Ford's *7 Women* expresses an overall moral lesson, it has to do with the worth and beauty of faith in oneself and in one's fellow creatures, not to mention the corresponding dangers of the despair and absurdity that await us if we do not appreciate this value and beauty. What is criticized or even rejected in Ford's final feature is a faith in abstractions, dogmas, and empty ideals, a faith that is fragile at best and that gets in the way of an enriching life in the here-and-now.

In his final film, John Ford gives us one of his most emphatic illustrations of the tension and choice that concerned him throughout his career: that between faith (whether in ideals, traditions, duties, or divinities) and the consequences of losing that sense of conviction, particularly in a situation that demands heroic determination and moral fortitude. Cartwright and Andrews embody these polarities and possibilities, not as caricatures but as nuanced, unique, partially enigmatic *persons*. The fact that we see them sharing their deepest feelings on a few rare occasions demonstrates that faith is fragile, that human nature is diverse, and that the opposition between conviction and despair is a necessary tension that is embedded within our common humanity.

7 Women emphasizes the importance of faith in humanity, even when faith in God is absent. In this light his final film echoes a predominant theme underlying most of his films: a fundamental belief in the power of human nature to transcend itself for the sake of another — whether that "other" be a deity, a nation, an army, a township, a family, or a beloved individual. Few of Ford's earlier films, however, came as close as *7 Women* to the idea that one can sacrifice one's entire being for the sake of humanity *per se*, but without specific ties to any community, institution, or beloved individual. This is precisely Dr. Cartwright's brand of faith. She does not merely demonstrate an adherence to the duties and oath of her medical profession in sacrificing her life for that of others. She reveals an inner belief in and compassion for her fellow human beings, at least those fellow humans who do not take the form of threatening enemies, and it is this belief and compassion that no doubt drove her into the medical profession in the first place, even though we can only guess at this through her actions after a tragic moment has emerged to test her inner strength. Otherwise we know little about Dr. Cartwright's past; we can only infer a bit of the big picture from her decisions and deeds in the present moment.

Another of Ford's movies that deals explicitly with the theme of religious faith is his beautifully photographed *The Fugitive*. Like *7 Women*, the storyline revolves in part around a religious representative—in this case, a priest—whose faith is tested in less-than-civilized conditions. The movie is based loosely on Graham Greene's novel *The Labyrinthine Ways*, with the alternate title *The Power and the Glory*, and scripted by Dudley Nichols, though Ford allegedly deviated substantially from the screenplay that he and Nichols had crafted. It deals with a fugitive priest (Henry Fonda) in an unnamed land (the film was shot in Mexico) where religion has been outlawed. The priest recognizes the urgent need to escape and nearly does so twice but is consistently called back into dangerous service to the Lord when he is summoned to offer rites and blessings at times of both birth and death.

Hunting the priest is Don Rafael (Pedro Armendariz), the police lieutenant who "becomes religious" in his obsessive endeavor to rid his country of all remnants of organized religion. In preaching to his own people about why they must suffer this strictly enforced code of anti-clericalism, he identifies himself with them by mere ethnic categorization while immediately negating that vocal identification by his very extremism. He offers them in a patronizing manner the kind of utopian language and idealistic hyperbole that comes easily to the lips of religious as well as political extremists: "I'm an Indian like you are…. I want to give you *everything*." At one point, Don Rafael laughs maniacally at shafts of sunlight cascading through the crucifix-framed window of an abandoned chapel and in doing so becomes an almost laughable caricature of an irrational fanatic driven to excess by his zeal for ideological purity. He rages against his men for acting in an undisciplined manner in the presence of a dancing woman (Delores Del Rio) who is none other than Maria Delores, his ex-mistress whose infant has been abandoned by its father, the lieutenant.

Don Rafael's neglect of his infant son is a clear indication that he is, ironically, an anti-religious man who has nonetheless forsaken earthly realities for the sake of abstract dogma and oppressive idealism. In this sense he is a peculiar kind of precursor to Agatha Andrews in *7 Women*, since his fanaticism aims at the destruction rather than maintenance of organized religion. But the movies' lessons about the dangers and limits of adhering obsessively to an idealistic ethos are nonetheless very similar. Likewise, the outcast priest provides an unusual anticipation of Dr. Cartwright's character, though he is religious and she is anything but. Both ultimately demonstrate their faith in the name of human compassion rather than in the name of some transcendent deity or impersonal political formula.

Fonda's priest actually comes to acknowledge a humbling lesson of self-knowledge when he evades danger for a while and seeks refuge with a friendly doctor (John Qualen). He attains the very insight that seems to escape the police lieutenant and that is quickly repressed by Agatha Andrews after she has admitted to Cartwright, in an almost subconscious manner of self-revelation, that "God is not enough." The priest likewise confesses to the physician in *The Fugitive*: "It wasn't courage, Doctor, it was only pride… I began to think I was a brave man … a martyr.... I was building a fine lie, wearing it like a proud cloak.... [But] when the first real test came I couldn't measure up."

The Fugitive is a gorgeously styled movie, thanks to Ford's pictorial eye and Gabriel Figueroa's splendid black-and-white photography. As a Ford film it has earned praise as well as harsh criticism, and while the director himself chose it as one of his favorites, it is indeed a movie that, perhaps a bit like a film by Godard or Antonioni or Kubrick, emotionally distances but visually and intellectually engages the audience. The two main characters, the priest and the lieutenant, are too much like caricatures or even archetypes to allow the viewer to empathize to a substantial degree, even with a man (the priest) who has come to recognize his faults and limitations. Gallagher argues that the abstract, formalized, and even "theoretical" style of the film — and particularly its expressionist use of formalized landscape and subjective camera angle — was quite intentional on Ford's part, especially if one interprets the movie as a symbolic attempt at depicting the characters' psychology, morality, and spirituality through external means.

In discussing the religious elements of various films by Ford we must also mention here his less famous but nonetheless masterful westerns *3 Godfathers* and *Wagon Master*, both of which center upon religious themes explicitly, unlike most of Ford's other westerns.

3 Godfathers revolves around a very Christian theme — the three "wise men" who watch over an infant that enters the world in primitive circumstances — and which features a reading from Christian Scripture when all is nearly lost. The saving of the infant here is repeated in *7 Women* and also echoes the famous scene of the baby saved from a "wagon stampede" in *3 Bad Men* (1926) as well as the scenes focusing on the delivery of newborns in *Stagecoach* and *The Horse Soldiers* (1959). *3 Godfathers* is a re-make of Ford's earlier 1919 silent version of the Peter B. Kyne story, *Marked Men* starring the elder Harry Carey. In this later version of the same story, Harry Carey, Jr. sings "Shall We Gather At the River" over the newly dug grave of the mother (Mildred Natwick) who entrusted her newborn to the three outlaws who had discovered her. His cowboy colleague Robert Hightower (John Wayne) asks if there are any more words to the song. In this scene we get the feeling that nothing more can be said in terms of the kind of faith that will keep these men on the path of their newfound spiritual mission, that of protecting the infant from the harsh desert world that surrounds them.

The three "wise men" are actually the type of "good bad men" that Ford liked to use often, outlaws or outsiders who take it upon themselves to perform heroic acts in the interest of others. Their moral ambiguity as lawbreakers who nonetheless have hearts of gold, clearly shown in parallel fashion by Ford's earlier *3 Bad Men*, for example. They come to recognize the need for redemption as emphasized by the old Western ballad, "The Cowboy's Lament," based on an even older Irish ballad that became known as "The Streets of Laredo." William sings this song as he cradles the baby in his arms and strolls about, using the song as a kind of lullaby to put the infant to sleep: "For I'm a young cowboy and I know I've done wrong."

These three cowboys redeem themselves by attempting to save the baby, even as they try to escape from the law, though these goals become increasingly incompatible. Along the way they come to use the Bible as a geographical guide through the rugged and even lethal external world of rock, sun, and sand. Ultimately they rely upon Scripture as a moral guide through the inner world of their own virtues and vices. It is Pedro (Pedro Armendariz) who first finds the Bible ("biblia" or "bible book," as he calls it) and who later attempts to use it as a source of guidance after they have found the helpless baby and its dying mother, placing his faith in the words of God (or "Mr. Señor," as he calls his idea of the Divine). Robert Hightower is skeptical, at least at first, in putting their trust in a mere book of words, and he seems to opt initially for the idea of raising the child according to national rather than universal values when he scolds Pedro for speaking Spanish as they try to diaper the baby: "Cut out the Mex lingo around the kid, will ya, Pete? First thing you know he'll be talkin' it. We've got to raise him with good old American *habla*, like his Ma."

But Robert finally comes around to putting his faith in faith, so to speak, especially after young William (aka "the Abilene Kid") interrupts a loud quarrel between Pedro and Robert by quoting scripture. They pay close heed due to the solemnity of William's words, as if he had suddenly been transformed from a naïve young outlaw into a worldly wise sage.[16] *3 Godfathers* summons the need for faith in Divine Providence, that sense of God-driven destiny that is evoked in the words of young William as he holds the Bible above the baby who depends upon these men for his survival.

7 Women questions, and perhaps even rejects, the need for such a faith in Providence, and most especially a faith that derives from any one bible or religion (Miss Binns, for example, is of another denomination, and Dr. Cartwright is an outright atheist). But Ford's final film allows for the type of faith that *3 Godfathers* also exhibits nonetheless: a faith in the redemptive capacity of humans, even of outlaws, to do good and to sacrifice themselves when they are called upon, and thus to act heroically in tragic circumstances. The same type of "humane spirituality" is embodied by the religious figure of Miss Binns and is echoed by the cardinal (Donald Crisp) and the bishop (Basil Ruysdael) in Ford's political drama *The Last Hurrah* (1958). These are characters whose religious commitment does not stand in the way of their basic humanity, but rather expresses it, unlike the repressive religious idealism of Agatha Andrews.[17]

Following this underlying theme of the fusion of spirituality and humanism in Ford's films, *Wagon Master* depicts the hard struggle of a Mormon clan seeking to reach the promised land, faced with rough terrain and persecuted by those who do not respect their ways, as well as by those who do not do good at all — the Clegg clan, who brazenly echo the Clanton clan in *My Darling Clementine*, down to the patriarch's lonely and stubborn stand at the end of each movie. When asked about those of his films that were his own favorites to watch, Ford repeatedly chose *Wagon Master* in later years, along with such other "small" and "personal" films as *The Fugitive* and *The Sun Shines Bright* (1953). McBride describes *Wagon Master* as "one of Ford's masterpieces"[18] and Lindsay Anderson praises it as one of Ford's "most purely lyrical" films.[19]

Wagon Master is as idealistic as any of Ford's movies, particularly in terms of its optimistic expression of humanity's potential for inner strength and goodness in the face of evil. But at the same time, due to the director's natural gift for recognizing dialectical truth in the realms of heroic as well as ordinary lives, the movie demonstrates that a substantial degree of the evil that we confront lurks within the human heart itself. Most of all, *Wagon Master* reveals the limitations and rough edges of idealism, not merely in opposition to human evil, but also in the realization that spiritual faith must sometimes be compromised for the sake of that faith's survival. Those who can not tolerate the use of violence due to their very faith in human reason or the goodness of God must eventually turn to those who are not afraid to use a gun in order to save themselves from the threat of evil and to reach their goal of "the promised land." This is not unlike *Liberty Valance*'s Ransom Stoddard who comes to recognize the need for a gun in his desire to move his community from a Hobbesian state of nature (savage wilderness) to a law-governed state of civilization (cultivated "garden").

As for other Fordian characters whose lives are based on some form of unconditional belief in a higher power or cause, there is Mr. Gruffud (Walter Pidgeon) in *How Green Was My Valley*, a man who prioritizes his love of God over his love for a woman. But he learns that this sacrifice brings unhappiness at the end of the day, even if it might bring salvation in some future world. Gruffud does come to reveal doubt, not in terms of any loss of faith in God, but in the form of his criticism of the ways of the church elders after their sanctimonious piety overwhelms any compassion for a church member in need. He comes to scold the deacons for their cruel dogmatism in banishing an unmarried pregnant woman, even though he can not bring himself to forsake his duties to the church so that he can fulfill and consummate his one true love.

There is also the gaunt-faced Casey (John Carradine) in *The Grapes of Wrath*, a man who surrenders his vocation of preaching due to a loss of faith. Yet he easily risks his life when he gains a newfound faith in a secular social cause, that of helping his fellow migrant workers in their struggle against oppressive capitalists. Casey — like Mr. Gruffud, Miss Binns, Elder Wiggs (Ward Bond) of *Wagon Master*, the outcast priest (Henry Fonda) of *The Fugitive*, and the title characters of *3 Godfathers*—comes to acknowledge a more authentic and inherent faith, one based on the value of humanity itself.

Finally, as for religion-oriented scenes in other movies by Ford, there is a colorful Christmas celebration in *Donovan's Reef* where a collective commemoration of the nativity becomes a multicultural feast and ritualistic ceremony in which various nations and faiths are honored and in which comedy and the seriousness of religious belief are fused. Other religious scenes include those in *The Searchers*, one in which a funeral ceremony for Ethan's family is disrupted by Ethan himself so that the men can get on with their mission to find Scar as well as little Debbie, and one in which Ward Bond's character of the preacher-sheriff hands his Bible to a wounded man and advises him with deep-felt conviction: "Here, hold this. It'll make you feel *good*." Ford invokes religious themes with the graceful ballet of the church dance in *My Darling Clementine* and in the sermonizing of the stern-faced Reverend Rosenkrantz (Arthur Shields) in *Drums Along the Mohawk*, echoing to some degree his role as a fire-and-brimstone church deacon in *How Green Was My Valley*. There is also a religious element in the final scene of *The Informer*, the film that really established Ford as a genuine artist in the Hollywood filmmaking community. The iconic shot of the self-haunted Gypo Nolan (Victor McLaglen) collapsing before the cross in the church and begging for God's mercy, a victim of his own guilt and weak moral character, was later inserted by Martin Scorsese into another film about informants, *The Departed* (2006).

Idealism Gone Wrong

In Ford's early talkie entitled *Salute* (1929), with John Wayne and Ward Bond as two young midshipmen, a naïve cadet (William Janney) at Annapolis Naval Academy strolls through campus with his girlfriend, telling her that he feels the need to quit. He says rather reflectively that he must end his education at the Academy because "it's bigger than me." He admits that he is not quite up to the larger task at hand, that of surrendering himself to the Navy and ultimately to his country. His girlfriend disapproves of his decision, one she admits as a lack of strength and conviction, particularly when a higher cause is at stake.

It is intriguing by way of comparison to consider Miss Andrews' speech to Dr. Cartwright, a speech containing an unintended personal revelation, as they convene under a tree in the mission courtyard. Andrews speaks of needing something "bigger" than God Himself to fill her life. Andrews does not surrender her desire to "fill herself" with something "bigger than me." But since she declares almost unconsciously that "God is not enough," despite her continued clinging to her religious dogma, she has implied the possibility of a "something bigger" that is "bigger" even than God, even though that would sound like sacrilege to anyone with pious ears. Agatha commits herself, nonetheless, to an ideal or cause that does not fulfill her human needs but rather denies them.

There are certainly many examples of the theme of idealism's hard limits or utter wrong-headedness in Ford's body of work. In *Pilgrimage*, a mother's idealistic devotion to her son turns into bitter resentment and even destruction as she sends him off to war — and his eventual death — due to his refusal to end his relationship with a woman whom his mother views as competing for her son's love. In *The Hurricane*, the idealistic Governor De Laage (Raymond Massey) attempts to impose the civilized rule of law on the natives of an island, but he does so in a way that clings to rules based on power and resentment rather than pragmatic reason, like some demonic version of Ransom Stoddard of *Liberty Valance*. In *Stagecoach*, the members of the Women's Intolerance League force the prostitute Dallas (Claire Trevor) out of town with puritanical fervor, branding her as a whore in the same way that Miss Andrews later brands Cartwright as a harlot for offering herself to Tunga Khan. In *Fort Apache*, Lt. Col. Owen Thursday (Henry Fonda) clings to his militaristic code of duty, even to the point of sending his men off to their certain deaths, putting principle over practicality. In *Rio Grande*, Kirby Yorke (John Wayne) adheres so faithfully to his military mission and duty that he comes close to losing his wife and son forever, although he has already chosen a life in which his loved ones have very minor roles to play. In *The Searchers*, Ethan Edwards is so obsessed with the ideal of racial purity that his anger about little Debbie's possible defilement by the Comanche chief Scar drives him on for years in searching for her — not to save her, but to destroy her, so that she will no longer suffer in this world for her having been made "impure." In *The Last Hurrah*, Mayor Skeffington (Spencer Tracy) learns the limitations of his old-fashioned political idealism and even feels forced to play dirty when faced with the changing times and the turn to televised politics. And in *The Man Who Shot Liberty Valance*, Ransom Stoddard must learn to reconcile his abstract political idealism with the grim realities of the Old West. He learns, in fact, that he must use a gun to vanquish the enemy if his once treasured law books are to have any use in bringing about needed social and political change.

As a pragmatic idealist, Dr. Cartwright sacrifices her own life in order to preserve the lives of others because of her belief in the importance of adhering to her medical oath and profession, a sense of duty that is undoubtedly based upon some inner compassion toward her fellow human creatures. As Miss Binns explains after she has realized that Dr. Cartwright has traded herself to Tunga Khan so that the others might live, Dr. Cartwright has taken an oath to preserve human life. Dr. Cartwright's duty to her medical oath evokes the idea of the hero as a medical practitioner whose mission is to save lives through the art and science of medicine, despite great risk to his or her own life.

In Ford's work, the "medical hero" is not a one-time phenomenon. There is Dr. Mudd (Warner Baxter) in *The Prisoner of Shark Island*, a physician who gave assistance to John Wilkes Booth after this presidential assassin was wounded while trying to escape after the shooting of Lincoln. The prominent theme of the film is that of Mudd's humanity and dignity in the face of his unjust imprisonment, and his humanity and dignity are most evident when he attempts to save his fellow prisoners, not to mention prison guards, from an outbreak of the plague. Further instances of the heroic physician in Ford's body of work include Will Rogers in *Doctor Bull* (1933), Arthur Shields as the cavalry doctor in *She Wore a Yellow Ribbon* (1949), "Doc" (William Powell) in *Mister Roberts* (1955, directed by Ford and Mervyn LeRoy), Major Hank Kendall (William Holden) in *The Horse Soldiers*, and "Doc" Dedham (Jack Warden) in *Donovan's Reef*.

One can not speak of Fordian medical heroes and the theme of idealism-gone-wrong without discussing an early Ford talkie that was surprisingly nominated for Best Picture despite its glaring flaws in narrative logic, dramatic flow, and overall visual coherence: *Arrowsmith*, based on the Sinclair Lewis novel of the same title. Quite unlike the novel, Ford's film depicts Dr. Arrowsmith, played in an unfortunately stilted performance by Ronald Colman, as a man who is so hell-bent on his medical career and "the Truth" that he coldly neglects his wife (Helen Hayes), even after having chosen life with her in her hole-in-the-wall hometown over the promise of becoming a world-renowned medical researcher.

This neglect is intensified when he brings his wife to a distant, tropical land to deliver an experimental serum to hundreds of natives who are dying of bubonic plague. The situation of an epidemic is not only echoed in *7 Women* and the above-mentioned *Prisoner of Shark Island* but also arises in *Doctor Bull*, in which Will Rogers plays yet another Fordian physician with a serum and a burden to bear. Dr. Arrowsmith leaves his wife behind in a remote village as he ventures deeper into the jungle to treat the natives and, under instructions from his mentor Dr. Gottlieb (A. E. Anson), administers the serum only under the conditions of a placebo trial so as to see how effective it really is. Before leaving her, he stupidly and almost carelessly leaves a series of test tubes in their villa, filled with enough of the plague virus to wipe out an army. He tells his wife to dump the tubes into a pan of boiling water so as to dispose of the virus, but not before one tube tips accidentally and saturates a nearby cigarette that Mrs. Arrowsmith later smokes, infecting herself and sending her to a certain and most horrible death as she waits and waits and waits for her husband to return from treating the natives as well as conducting his large-scale medical experiment.

It would appear that this medical "hero" cares more for the pursuit of scientific knowledge than for his own loving and devoted wife Leora (Helen Hayes), and his reaction to her death when he discovers her lying on the floor of their villa after his return is rather cold and mechanical — though that might be due to Colman's mostly robotic performance and Ford's failure to elicit from him the type of relaxed emotional responses that he could elicit from other actors in other films. It is not until her death and his corresponding, over-the-top drinking binge in trying to deal with her demise that Arrowsmith finally opts out of his placebo trial and decides to give all of the natives the serum rather than only half. As he later states, it was the humane thing to do, though the world is also no worse off in terms of progress in medical science, since the serum obviously resulted in a cure that is celebrated back in the States when news breaks of the drug's effect. In fact, as Gallagher has pointed out in his book on Ford, Arrowsmith's placebo trial is inherently illogical, due to the very fact that there is no "control group" and that it is never clear how Arrowsmith can distinguish between those natives who have been injected with the real serum and those who have been given the placebo.[20] But by the end of the film, everyone gets the serum. Arrowsmith still feels that he has betrayed Gottlieb and his idea of a placebo trial, despite the fact that everyone now knows of the drug's success. His wife is dead due to a neglect that is based on an almost perverse sense of the medical mission, and the film concludes when Arrowsmith runs off with his newfound love (Myrna Loy) to do private research in the backwaters of Vermont, having rejected fame and fortune after such a discovery.

The movie does imply a critique of Arrowsmith's idealism, and it shows the human suffering that can result when a faith in abstract ideals and an adherence to professional duty turns obsessive, even fanatical. We see the same type of suffering caused by Agatha Andrews's turn to religious idealism, and eventually fanaticism, in *7 Women*. Interestingly, it is the "medical hero" in *Arrowsmith* who exemplifies the negative consequences of such fanaticism while it is the "medical hero" in *7 Women* who must contend bravely with similar consequences of an idealism gone wrong. Also interestingly, Arrowsmith prays to God for guidance and strength, and yet also prays to God to permit him to search for cures and life-saving techniques that will not depend solely upon God or blind faith, but rather upon scientific knowledge. What kind of prayer is this, in fact? It is the last line of his prayer that shocks, since in a way it is a paradoxical relinquishing of God' power, even as he invokes God and thanks him implicitly for his gifts as a doctor. Here is Arrowsmith's prayer:

> God give me clear eyes and freedom from haste.
> God give me anger against all pretense.
> God keep me looking for my own mistakes.

> God keep me at it till my results are proven.
> God give me strength not to trust to God.

A Fordian brand of spirituality is a faith that must eventually and always return from God to humanity. In *7 Women*, as seen in the foregoing, we are witness to a crystallized and cumulative expression of Ford's recurring lesson that heroism and idealism can take a wrong turn when they are grounded in any belief that tears us away from the human realm of earthly compassion.

Notes

1. In his pioneering book *About John Ford*, Lindsay Anderson draws a loose parallel between the late works of Shakespeare and the narrative, spirit, and tempo of John Ford's sublimely serene, rambunctiously rollicking, and intentionally hokey later film *Donovan's Reef* (1963). As Anderson [Anderson, *About John Ford*, New York: McGraw-Hill Book Company, 1983, 166] states after summarizing the storyline of Ford's later movie: "It is an elaborate, far-fetched plot, though perhaps hardly more fantastical than *The Tempest* or *The Winter's Tale*, whose themes of conflict and eventual harmony, all in a remote, idyllic setting, it to some extent echoes. There is indeed a kind of late-Shakespearian expansiveness about *Donovan's Reef*, a fairy tale humor and eccentricity that is refreshing in a cinema from which the easy-going and the poetic seem to have been mostly squeezed out."

2. Joseph McBride, *Searching for John Ford: A Life* (New York: St. Martin's Press, 2001), 663 and 664.

3. Tag Gallagher, *John Ford: The Man and His Films* (Berkeley: University of California Press, 1986), 302 (Gallagher's translation from the original French).

4. Anderson, *About John Ford*, 168

5. Andrew Sarris, *The John Ford Movie Mystery* (Bloomington and London: Indiana University Press, 1975), 184–85.

6. For a detailed interpretation of several of Ford's major films as a response to the idea of nihilism, see my chapter on Ford, "When the Legends Die: The Fading of Heroes and Traditions in the Films of John Ford," in my book *Nihilism in Film and Television* (Jefferson, NC: McFarland & Co. Publishers, Inc., 2006).

7. McBride, *Searching for John Ford*, 671.

8. McBride, *Searching for John Ford*, 671–72.

9. Joseph McBride and Michael Wilmington, *John Ford* (New York: Da Capo Press, 1975), 199.

10. McBride, *Searching for John Ford*, 664.

11. Jean Arthur, interestingly, lived for a time in Ford's own hometown of Portland, and so there was a special point of nostalgic connection between the director and the actress. She had her film debut in a bit part in Ford's 1923 silent film *Cameo Kirby*. John Ford points to this hometown connection in his interview with his grandson Dan regarding the film *The Whole Town's Talking*: "About Jean Arthur, it was a very peculiar coincidence. Jean for a time in her life lived in my hometown in Portland, Maine. She came West and I directed her in her first picture.... She was a fine girl, very nice family in Portland...." (John Ford Papers, Lilly Library, Box 11, folder 29, Misc) Arthur later became famous as a leading actress for Frank Capra in his classic films *Mr. Deeds Goes to Town* (1936) and *Mr. Smith Goes to Washington* (1939).

12. Gallagher, *John Ford: The Man and His Films*, 351.

13. John Ford interviewed by Claude-Jean Philippe (1966), "*Télérama's* Exclusive Interview with John ford in the Flesh," in Gerald Peary, editor, *John Ford Interviews* (Jackson, Mississippi: University Press of Mississippi, 2001), 97. Originally published in *Télérama*, July 31-August 6, 1966.

14. McBride, *Searching for John Ford*, 56.

15. McBride, *Searching for John Ford*, 40–41.

16. William's words, as taken directly from the film dialogue: "It says right here where we're to go, just like it's told everything about all this. You fellas don't understand. You think this is all just chance, just accidental like us comin' here this way, finding the mother, helping her, infant in the manger, star so bright last night? I ain't talkin' out of no fever sweat, Bob, honest I ain't. You think we've had anything to do with what's happened? No sir, we didn't, no more than you had anything to do with throwin' the book so it opened in the place where I'm going to read, where it tells where we're going to next. Listen, I'll read it.... 'And when the days of purification were accomplished according to the law of Moses, they

lifted up the child and brought him to Jerusalem to present him to the Lord.' It says 'Jerusalem' right here in the book...."

17. Ford scholar Charles Silver touches upon the theme of spirituality in *3 Godfathers*, but also in regard to Ford's work in general, and the same lesson that he draws here can certainly be applied to *7 Women*: "God, while not a total stranger to Ford's films, was generally an ambivalently treated guest for a director who protested that whatever profound meanings others might see in his movies, to him they were just "a job of work." ... There is a God here [in *3 Godfathers*], not so much hidden as diffused and disguised, or infused with the peculiar spirituality found in the humane values that emanate from the works of John Ford — a nineteenth-century romantic artist transcending a twentieth-century technological medium...." Charles Silver, "3 Godfathers," in Mary Lea Bandy and Antonio Monda, eds., *The Hidden God: Film and Faith* (New York: The Museum of Modern Art, 2003), 58, 62.

18. McBride, *Searching for John Ford*, 495–96.

19. The inner tension between, and eventual synthesis of, the realistic and the idealistic in *Wagon Master* is evoked by director and Ford scholar Lindsay Anderson in his appreciation of this film. It is a film whose poetic power lies in its emotional pull as well as its ethical viewpoint, as he tells us:

> This kind of poetry is not separable from its moral statement. Although Ford is a Catholic by religion, and certainly no scorner of the world, it is clear that there is much to him that is attractive as well as admirable in the Puritan ideal. The little Mormon world of *Wagonmaster* is shown with warmth — self-sufficient, disciplined and contented, moved by inspiring ideals of charity and labor. Ford himself is not exactly a part of this world (his relationship to it is very much that of the two affable horse traders); he can see humor in it as well, and he can relish contrasting human eccentricities.... (Anderson, *About John Ford*, 128)

20. Gallagher, *John Ford: The Man and His Films*, 76.

About the Contributors

Matthew Jude Barker is a genealogical and historical researcher and part-time research librarian at the Maine Historical Society in Portland. He is a lifelong resident of this city and has published many articles on local history, focusing especially on the Irish community. He is author of "The Irish Community and Irish Organizations of Nineteenth-Century Portland, Maine" in *They Change Their Sky: The Irish in Maine*, edited by Michael C. Connolly.

Peter Bogdanovich is one of our most accomplished living filmmakers in addition to being an actor, television director, and prolific film historian. He is the director of such film classics as *Targets, The Last Picture Show, Paper Moon,* and *Mask,* and he is the author of *John Ford, Who the Devil Made It, Who the Hell's In It,* and *Peter Bogdanovich's Movie of the Week,* among other books on cinematic art and cinematic history. He is also the creator of the documentary film *Directed by Ford* and has appeared in several documentaries on Ford.

Michael C. Connolly is an associate professor of history at Saint Joseph's College in Standish, Maine, and the editor of a collection of essays on the history of the Irish community in that state entitled *They Change Their Sky: The Irish in Maine*. He has published numerous articles on Irish history and culture as well as Maine history. He is a lifelong resident of the same Munjoy Hill neighborhood in Portland, Maine, in which John Ford was raised and educated.

William C. Dowling is professor of English literature at Rutgers University and the author of several books on literary history and literary theory, including *Language and Logos in Boswell's Life of Johnson, The Senses of the Text: Intensional Semantics and Literary Theory,* and *Literary Federalism in the Age of Jefferson*.

Scott Eyman is the books editor of *The Palm Beach Post* and a prolific film historian. His books include *John Ford: The Complete Films; Print the Legend: The Life and Times of John Ford; Ernst Lubitsch: Laughter in Paradise; Mary Pickford: America's Sweetheart; The Speed of Sound: Hollywood and the Talkie Revolution, 1926–1930;* and most recently *Lion of Hollywood: The Life and Legend of Louis B. Mayer.* He has appeared in several documentaries on Ford.

Dan Ford is the director's grandson, his first biographer (*Pappy: The Life of John Ford*), and the producer of the television documentary *The American West of John Ford*. He has appeared in several documentaries on John Ford.

Leger Grindon is the director of the Film and Media Culture Program at Middlebury College. He is a film scholar and the author of *Shadows on the Past: Studies in the Historical Fiction Film* as well as a forthcoming book on the boxer in Hollywood cinema. His essays and reviews have appeared in journals such as *Film Quarterly, Cineaste, Cinema Journal, Film History,* and *The Velvet Light Trap.*

Roy Grundmann is professor of film and television at Boston University, an expert on multimedia art, and the author of *Andy Warhol's Blowjob: Culture and the Moving Image.* Before coming to the United States, he studied literature and film at the Universities of Muenster and Frankfurt in Germany and at Exeter University in England. He has taught film at New York University and for the past decade has served as one of the editors of *Cineaste* magazine, for which he is now a contributing editor

Margaret Feeney Lacombe is a genealogist and expert on the Feeney (Ford) family history. She lives in Augusta, Maine, but she was born and raised on Munjoy Hill in Portland, Ford's home neighborhood. She is a relative of John Ford on her mother's side of the family and invites any and all Feeney relatives to contact her at mlacombe@megalink.net.

Kenneth E. Nilsen is chair of the Department of Celtic Studies at Saint Francis Xavier University in Nova Scotia where he teaches Scots-Gaelic and Irish language courses and collects oral interviews in these two Celtic languages. He is the author of numerous journal articles on Irish language, literature, and culture including "Thinking of Monday: The Irish Speakers of Portland, Maine," in *Éire/Ireland* 25, no. 1 (spring 1990) and "'The Language that the Strangers do not Know': The Galway Gaeltacht of Portland, Maine in the Twentieth Century," in *They Change Their Sky: The Irish in Maine.*

Tom Paulus is professor of film studies in the departments of Communication Sciences and Literary Studies at the University of Antwerp in Belgium. He is the former curator of the Antwerp Film Museum and publisher of the film/media quarterly *AS/Andere Sinema*. He has published in such journals as *Film International* and *Scope*. He is the editor of the forthcoming book *Another Slapstick Symposium: Early American Film Comedy*, and his recent essay "*The Quiet Man* and Technicolor" will appear in a new collection of essays on the Ford classic.

Robert C. Sickels is chair of the Department of Rhetoric and Film Studies at Whitman College as well as a professor of American Film and Popular Culture. He has written numerous articles on film and is the author of *The 1940s*, a volume in the Greenwood Press series *American Popular Culture through History*.

Charles Silver is director of the Celeste Bartos International Film Study Center and associate film curator at the Museum of Modern Art in New York City. He is a Ford expert, film historian, and author of *The Western Film* as well as *Charles Chaplin: An Appreciation*.

Kevin Stoehr is associate professor of humanities at Boston University. He is the author of *Nihilism in Film and Television* (McFarland) and the co-author of *Jung's Psychology as a Spiritual Practice*. He is the editor of *Film and Knowledge: Essays on the Integration of Images and Ideas* (McFarland) as well as *Philosophies of Religion, Art, and Creativity*. He has also published several essays in Open Court Press's Philosophy and Popular Culture Series. He was born in Portland, Maine, and lives in Boston, Massachusetts.

Works Cited

Abel, Richard. "Paradigmatic Structures in *Young Mr. Lincoln*." *Wide Angle* 2, no. 4 (1978): 20–26.

_____. "The 'Imagined' Community of the Western, 1910–1913." In Charlie Keil and Shelley Stamp, eds., *American Cinema's Transitional Era: Audiences, Institutions, Practices*. Berkeley, Los Angeles, London: University of California, 2004.

Akenson, Donald Harman. *The Irish in Ontario: A Study in Rural History*. Montreal: McGill-Queen's University, 1999.

Anderson, Lindsay. *About John Ford*. London: Plexus, 1999.

Band, Benjamin. *Portland Jewry: Its Growth and Development*. Portland, ME: Jewish Historical Society, 1955.

Barber, C.L. *Shakespeare's Festive Comedy: A Study of Dramatic Form and its Relation to Social Custom*. New York: Meridian, 1963.

Beatty, Jack. *The Rascal King: The Life and Times of James Michael Curley (1874–1958)*. Reading, MA: Addison-Wesley, 1992.

Berlin, Isaiah. *The Roots of Romanticism*. Princeton, NJ: Princeton University, 1999.

Bogdanovich, Peter. *Alan Dwan: The Last Pioneer*. New York: Praeger, 1971.

_____. *John Ford*. Berkeley: University of California, 1978.

Bordwell, David. "Contemporary Film Studies and the Vicissitudes of Grand Theory." In *Post-Theory: Reconstructing Film Studies*, Bordwell and Noël Carroll, eds. Madison: University of Wisconsin, 1966.

_____. *On the History of Film Style*. Cambridge, Massachusetts, and London: Harvard University, 1997.

_____, and Noël Carroll, eds. *Post-Theory: Reconstructing Film Studies*. Madison: University of Wisconsin, 1996.

_____, Janet Staiger and Kristin Thompson, eds., *The Classical Hollywood Cinema: Film Style and Mode of Production to 1960*. London: Routledge, 1996.

Bowser, Eileen. *The Transformation of Cinema: 1907–1915. History of the American Cinema Volume 2*. Berkeley, Los Angeles, London: University of California, 1990.

Boyle, Harold. *The Best of Boyle*. Portland: Guy Gannett, 1980.

Brewster, Ben. "Notes on the text 'John Ford's Young Mr. Lincoln'." *Screen* 14, no. 3 (Autumn 1973): 29–43.

_____, and Lea Jacobs. Theatre to Cinema: Stage Pictorialism and the Early Feature Film. Oxford: Oxford University, 1997.

Brinckmann, Christine N. "Fiktion und Geschichtsmythos in *Young Mr. Lincoln*." In *Die Antropomorphe Kamera und Andere Schriften zur Filmischen Narration*. Zurich: Chronos, 1997.

Browne, Nick. "The Spectator of American Symbolic Forms: Re-reading John Ford's *Young Mr. Lincoln*." In *Film Reader*, edited by B. Allan, V. Almenderez, W. Lafferty. Evanston: University of Illinois, 1979.

Brownlow, Kevin. *The Parade's Gone By …* Berkeley and Los Angeles: University of California, 1968.

Budd, Michael. "Genre, Director and Stars in John Ford's Westerns." *Wide Angle* 2, no. 4 (1978): 52–61.

Butler, Anne M. "Selling the Popular Myth." In *The Oxford History of the American West*, edited by Milner, O'Connor, and Sandweiss. New York: Oxford University, 1994.

Byrne, Terry. *Power in the Eye: An Introduction to Contemporary Irish Film*. Lanham, MD: Scarecrow, 1997.

Carey, Harry, Jr. *Company of Heroes: My Life as an Actor in the John Ford Stock Company*. Lanham, MD, New York, London: Madison, 1994.

Carroll, Noël. "Prospects for Film Theory: A Personal Assessment." In *Post-Theory: Reconstructing Film Studies*, edited by Bordwell and Carroll.

Caughie, John, ed. *Theories of Authorship.* London: British Film Institute Publishing, 1980.

Cawelti, John G. *Adventure, Mystery, and Romance: Formula Stories as Art and Popular Culture.* Chicago and London: University of Chicago, 1976.

"A Collective Text by the Editors of *Cahiers du Cinéma*: John Ford's *Young Mr. Lincoln*." In *Narrative, Apparatus, Ideology: A Film Theory Reader,* edited by Philip Rosen. New York: Columbia University, 1986, 444–82.

Comolli, Jean-Louis. "Signposts on the Trail." In *Theories of Authorship,* edited by John Caughie, 109–16.

Comolli, Jean-Luc, and Jean Narboni. "Cinema/Ideology/Criticism." In Bill Nichols, ed., *Movies and Method : An Anthology.* Berkeley: University of California, 1976.

Connolly, Michael C. "Black Fades to Green: Irish Labor Replaces African-American Labor Along a Major New England Waterfront, Portland, Maine, in the Mid-Nineteenth Century." *Colby Quarterly* 37, no. 4 (Dec. 2001): 357–73.

_____. "The First Hurrah: James Michael Curley versus the 'Goo-Goos' in the Boston Mayoralty Election of 1914." *Historical Journal of Massachusetts* 30, no. 1 (winter 2002) 50–74.

_____. "The Irish Longshoremen of Portland, Maine, 1880–1923." Ph.D. dissertation, Boston College, 1988.

_____. "Nationalism Among Early Twentieth-Century Irish Longshoremen in Portland, Maine." In *They Change Their Sky: The Irish in Maine,* edited by Michael C. Connolly. Orono: University of Maine Press, 2004, 277–96.

_____, ed. *They Change Their Sky.* Orono, ME: University of Maine Press, 2004.

Conrad, Joseph. *Lord Jim.* New York: Penguin/Signet Classics, 1964.

_____. *The Nigger of the Narcissus* in *Great Short Works of Joseph Conrad.* New York: Harper & Row, 1967.

_____. *The Shadow-Line and Two Other Tales, Typhoon and The Secret Sharer by Joseph Conrad.* New York: Doubleday Anchor, 1959.

Cooper, James Fenimore. *The Pilot: A Tale of the Sea.* New York: State University of New York, 1986.

Cumberland County Registry of Deeds, County Courthouse, Portland, Maine (Records of purchase and sale of Feeney-owned land in Cape Elizabeth, Maine): Book 514, Page 152; Book 526, Page 500; Book 528, Page 267; Book 589, Page 470; Book 609, Pages 104, 106; Book 976, Page 433.

Curley, James Michael. *I'd Do It Again: A Record of All My Uproarious Years.* Englewood Cliffs, NJ: Prentice-Hall, 1957.

Dinneen, Joseph F. *The Purple Shamrock: The Hon. James Michael Curley of Boston.* New York: W.W. Norton, 1949.

Dow, Neal. *The Reminiscences of Neal Dow.* Portland: Evening Express, 1898.

Dowling, William C. "John Ford's Festive Comedy: Ireland Imagined in *The Quiet Man*." *Eire-Ireland* 36, nos. 3–4 (Fall-Winter, 2001): 190–211.

Eagan, Eileen, and Patricia Finn. "Mutually Single: Irish Women in Portland, Maine, 1875–1945." In *They Change Their Sky,* edited by Michael C. Connolly, 257–75.

Eckstein, Arthur M., and Peter Lehman, eds. *The Searchers: Essays and Reflections on John Ford's Classic Western.* Detroit: Wayne State University, 2004.

Engel, Leonard, ed. *The Big Empty: Essays on Western Landscapes as Narrative.* Albuquerque: University of New Mexico, 1994.

Everson, William K. *American Silent Film.* New York: Da Capo, 1998.

Eyman, Scott. *Print the Legend: The Life and Times of John Ford.* Baltimore and London: Johns Hopkins University, 1999.

"Falmouth Hotel to Close Nov. 1, Says Management." *Portland Sunday Telegram,* October 26, 1958, page 1.

Ford, Dan. Interviews with John Ford. The John Ford Collection, Lilly Library, Indiana University, Bloomington, Indiana.

_____. *Pappy: The Life of John Ford.* New York: De Capo, 1998.

Ford, John. "Narrative by Comdr. John Ford, U.S.N.R., Photographic Experiences from Pearl Harbor, December 7, 1941." Recorded: August 17, 1943. Interview in Box 10 of World War II Interviews, Operational Archives Branch, Naval Historical Center, United States Department of Navy.

"Former Justice Joseph Connolly Dies." *Portland Evening Express,* Portland, Maine, October 2, 1939, pages 1 and 11.

Frye, Northrop. *The Anatomy of Criticism.* Princeton, NJ: Princeton University, 1957, 1982.

Gallagher, Tag. *John Ford: The Man and His Films.* Berkeley, Los Angeles, London: University of California, 1986.

Gibbons, Luke. "Romanticism, Realism, and Irish Cinema." In *Cinema and Ireland,* edited by Kevin Rockett, Luke Gibbons and John Hill. London: Croom Helm, 1987.

Goold, William. *Portland in the Past*. Portland: B. Thurston, 1886.
Gribbin, Peter E. *The First Century of Portland High School Football*. Portland: Dale Rand, 1989.
_____. *A History of Portland High School, 1821 through 1981*. Portland High School, 1981.
Grimes, Séamus, and Michael C. Connolly. "The Migration Link between *Cois Fharraige* and Portland, Maine, 1880s to 1920s." In *Irish Geography* 22 (1989): 22–30.
Gunning, Tom. *D.W. Griffith and the Origins of American Narrative Film: The Early Years at Biograph*. Urbana and Chicago: University of Illinois, 1991.
_____. "Landscape and the Fantasy of Moving Pictures: Early Cinema's Phantom Rides." In *Cinema and Landscape*, edited by Graeme Harper and Jonathan Rayner.
Harper, Graeme, and Jonathan Rayner, eds. *Cinema and Landscape*. Detroit: Wayne State University, 2007.
Haskell, Molly. *From Reverence to Rape: The Treatment of Women in the Movies*. New York: Holt, Rinehart, and Winston, 1974.
Henderson, Brian. "Critique of Cine-Structuralism." *Film Quarterly* 27, no. 1 (Fall 1973).
Higashi, Sumiko. *Cecil B. DeMille and American Culture: The Silent Era*. Berkeley, Los Angeles and London: University of California, 1994.
"History of St. Dominic's Parish." In *St. Dominic's: 175 Years of Memories, 1822–1997*, edited by Michael and Marilyn Melody. Portland: Smart Marketing, 1997.
Ignatiev, Noel. *How the Irish Became White*. New York: Routledge, 1995.
John Ford Collection. The Lilly Library, Indiana University, Bloomington, Indiana.
Kelley, Beverly Merrill. *Reelpolitik: Political Ideologies in '30s and '40s Films*. Westport, CT: Praeger, 1998.
Kelly, Mary Pat. *Martin Scorsese: A Journey*. New York: Thunder Mouth, 1991.
Kennedy, Harlan. "Shamrocks and Shillelaghs." In *Contemporary Irish Cinema: From The Quiet Man to Dancing at Lughnasa*, edited by James MacKillop.
Kennedy, W. Sloane. *Henry W. Longfellow: Biography, Anecdote, Letters, Criticism*. Cambridge, MA: Moses King, 1882.
Kitses, Jim, and Gregg Rickman, eds. *The Western Reader*. New York: Limelight, 1998.
Langan-Egan, Maureen. *Galway Women in the Nineteenth Century*. Dublin: Four Courts Press, 1999.
Lehman, Peter. "Looking at Look's Missing Reverse Shot: Psychoanalysis and Style in John Ford's *The Searchers*." In *The Western Reader*, edited by Jim Kitses and Gregg Rickman.
_____. "Texas 1868/America 1956: *The Searchers*." In *Viewings: An Anthology of New Film Criticism*, edited by Peter Lehman.
_____. "There's No Way of Knowing: Analysis of *The Searchers*." In *Authorship and Narrative in the Cinema*, edited by William Luhr and Peter Lehman.
_____. "'You Couldn't Hit It on the Nose': The Limits of Knowledge in and of *The Searchers*." In *The Searchers: Essays and Reflections on John Ford's Classic Western*, edited by Arthur M. Eckstein and Peter Lehman.
_____, ed. *Close Viewings: An Anthology of New Film Criticism*. Tallahassee: Florida State University, 1990.
Livingston, Paisley. "Characterization and Fictional Truth in the Cinema." In *Post-Theory: Reconstructing Film Studies*, edited by David Bordwell and Noël Carroll.
Levy, Bill. *John Ford: A Bio-Bibliography*. Westport, CT: Greenwood, 1998.
"Little Ireland in the State of Maine." *Portland Sunday Telegram*, Portland, Maine, October 16, 1910, microfilm, Portland Public Library.
Longfellow, Henry Wadsworth. *The Complete Poetical Works of Henry Wadsworth Longfellow*. Boston: Houghton, Mifflin, 1883.
Lowy, Michael, and Robert Sayre. *Romanticism Against the Tide of Modernity*. Transl. Catherine Porter. Durham, NC: Duke University, 2001.
Luhr, William, and Peter Lehman, eds. *Authorship and Narrative in the Cinema*. New York: Capricorn, 1977.
MacKillop, James. "The Quiet Man Speaks." In *Contemporary Irish Cinema*, edited by James MacKillop.
_____, ed. *Contemporary Irish Cinema: From The Quiet Man to Dancing at Lughnasa*. Syracuse, NY: Syracuse University, 1999.
MacLysaght, Edward. *More Irish Families*. New York: Barnes & Noble, 1960.
Maltby, Richard. "'A Brief Romantic Interlude': Dick and Jane Go to 3½ Seconds of the Classical Hollywood Cinema." In *Post-Theory: Reconstructing Film Studies*, edited by David Bordwell and Noël Carroll.
Martin, Peter. "We Shot D-Day on Omaha Beach." In *The American Legion Magazine*, June 1964: (14–19, 44–46).
Maurois, Andre. *Ariel: The Life of Shelley*. New York: Frederick Ungar, 1952.
McBride, Joseph. *Searching for John Ford: A Life*. New York: St. Martin's, 2001.

_____, and Michael Wilmington. *John Ford*. New York: Da Capo, 1975.

McCarron, Edward. "A Brave New World: The Irish Agrarian Colony of Benedicta, Maine." In *They Change Their Sky*, edited by Michael C. Connolly, 121–37.

McNee, Gerry. *In the Footsteps of The Quiet Man*. Edinburgh: Mainstream, 1990.

Miller, Kerby A. *Emigrants and Exiles: Ireland and the Irish Exodus to North America*. New York: Oxford University, 1985.

Milner, Clyde A. "America Only More So." In *The Oxford History of the American West*, edited by Clyde A. Milner, Carol A. O'Connor, and Martha A. Sandweiss. New York: Oxford University, 1994.

Mitchell, George J. *Making Peace*. Berkeley: University of California, 1999.

Moulton, John K. *Portland Observatory*, third edition. Falmouth, ME: self-published, 1996.

Neve, Brian. *Film and Politics in America: A Social Tradition*. London: Routledge, 1992.

Nilsen, Kenneth E. "The Language that the Strangers Do Not Know: The Galway Gaeltacht of Portland, Maine in the Twentieth Century." In *They Change Their Sky*, edited by Michael C. Connolly, 297–339.

_____. "Thinking of Monday: The Irish Speakers of Portland, Maine." *Eire/Ireland* 25, no. 1, (Spring 1990): 6–19.

O'Brien, Darcy. *A Way of Life, Like Any Other*. New York: New York Review, 2001.

Patterson, Nerys Thomas. *Cattle-Lords and Clansmen: The Social Structure of Early Ireland*. Notre Dame, IN: Notre Dame University, 1994.

Pearson, Roberta E. *Eloquent Gestures: The Transformation of Performance Style in the Griffith Biograph Films*. Berkeley, Los Angeles and London: University of California, 1992.

Peary, Gerald, ed. *John Ford Interviews*. Jackson: University Press of Mississippi, 2001.

Pechter, William. "John Ford: A Persistence of Vision." In *Great Film Directors*, edited by Leo Braudy and Morris Dickstein. Oxford, UK: Oxford University, 1978.

Pettit, Lance. *Screen Ireland: Film and Television Representation*. Manchester, UK: Manchester University, 2000.

Philippe, Claude-Jean. "*Télérama's* Exclusive Interview with John Ford in the Flesh." In *John Ford Interviews*, edited by Gerald Peary.

Pye, Douglas. "Genre and History." *Wide Angle* 2, no. 4 (1978).

Rees, Alwyn, and Brinley Rees. *Celtic Heritage: Ancient Tradition in Ireland and Wales*. London: Thames and Hudson, 1961.

Roediger, David. *The Wages of Whiteness: Race and the Making of the American Working Class*. New York: Routledge, 1995.

Roth, Lane. "Ritual Brawls in John Ford's Films." *Film Criticism* 7, no. 3 (Spring 1983).

Ruskin, John. *Time and Tide, by Weave and Tyne*. In Volume 17 of *The Library Edition of the Works of John Ruskin*, 39 volumes, edited by E.T. Cook and Alexander Wedderburn. London: George Allen, 1905–1912.

Salt, Barry. *Film Style and Technology: History and Analysis*. London: Starword, 1992.

Sarris, Andrew. *The John Ford Movie Mystery*. Bloomington and London: Indiana University, 1975.

_____, ed. *Interviews with Film Directors*. New York: Bobbs-Merrill, 1967.

Schatz, Thomas. *Hollywood Genres: Formulas, Filmmaking, and the Studio System*. New York: Random House, 1981.

Schickel, Richard. *D.W. Griffith: An American Life*. New York: Limelight, 1996.

Silver, Charles. "3 Godfathers." In *The Hidden God: Film and Faith*, edited by Mary Lea Bandy and Antonio Monda. New York: Museum of Modern Art, 2003.

Simmon, Scott. "Concerning the Weary Legs of Wyatt Earp: The Classic Western According to Shakespeare." In *The Western Reader*, edited by Jim Kitses and Gregg Rickman. New York: Limelight, 1998, 149–66.

_____. *The Invention of the Western Film: A Cultural History of the Genre's First Half-Century*. Cambridge and New York: Cambridge University, 2003.

Sinclair, Andrew. *John Ford*. New York: Dial, 1979.

Slotkin, Richard. *Gunfighter Nation: The Myth of the Frontier in Twentieth-Century America*. New York: Atheneum, 1992.

_____. "John Ford's *Stagecoach* and the Mythic Space of the Western Movie." In *The Big Empty: Essays on Western Landscapes as Narrative*, edited by Leonard Engel.

Smith, Roberta. "A Memorial Remembers the Hungry." *The New York Times*, July 16, 2002, E1.

Stoehr, Kevin L. *Nihilism in Film and Television*. Jefferson, NC: McFarland, 2006.

_____. "When the Legends Die: John Ford and the Fading of Traditions and Heroes." In *Nihilism in Film and Television*. Jefferson, NC: McFarland, 2006, 97–136.

Stowell, Peter. *John Ford*. Boston: Twayne, 1986.

Tavernier, Claudine. "The Fourth Dimension of Old Age." In *John Ford Interviews*, edited by Gerald Peary.

Thomson, David. *A Biographical Dictionary of Film.* New York: Alfred A. Knopf, 1995.

Thompson, Kristin. "The Formulation of the Classical Style, 1909–28." In *The Classical Hollywood Cinema: Film Style and Mode of Production to 1960*, edited by David Bordwell, Janet Staiger, and Kristin Thompson.

Tibbetts, Margaret Joy. "The Irish Neighborhood." In the *Bethel Courier*, 5, no. 1 (March 1981). Available at the Maine Historical Society, Portland.

Tompkins, Jane. "The Language of the Western." In *The Big Empty: Essays on the Land as Narrative*, edited by Leonard Engel.

Wallace, R. Stuart. "The Scotch-Irish of Provincial Maine: Purpooduck, Merrymeeting Bay, and Georgia." In *They Change Their Sky*, edited by Michael C. Connolly.

Wilson, George M. *Narration in Light: Studies in Cinematic Point of View.* Baltimore and London: Johns Hopkins University, 1986.

Wirths, Rollie. "Moving Costs Maine Football Star." In *Portland Press Herald*, 31 August 1955, 13.

Wollen, Peter. "The Auteur Theory." In *Theories of Authorship*, edited by John Caughie. London: BFI, 1986 [1981], 138–51.

――――. *Signs and Meaning in the Cinema.* London: British Film Institute, 1969.

Wollen, Peter (Lee Russell). "John Ford." In *Theories of Authorship*, edited by Caughie, 102–8.

Wodehouse, P.G. *The Code of the Woosters.* Harmondsworth: Penguin, 1972.

Wood, Robin. "'Shall We Gather at the River?' The Late Films of John Ford." In *Theories of Authorship*, edited by Caughie, 83–101.

Woodham-Smith, Cecil. *The Great Hunger, Ireland, 1845–1849.* New York: Harper and Row, 1962.

Wood-Martin, W.G. *Traces of the Elder Faiths of Ireland*, cited in Rees and Rees, *Celtic Heritage.*

Index

Adams, Marada 51, 65
Air Mail 29, 210
Allgood, Sara 31, 210
American Film Institute 5, 12, 79, 174
American Revolution *see* Revolutionary War
American West of John Ford 36
Anderson, Lindsay 4, 19, 27, 29, 132, 140, 158, 206, 221, 222
Araner (Ford's yacht) 23, 24, 26, 27, 29, 32, 82, 104
Armendariz, Pedro 215, 216
Arrowsmith 9, 14, 72, 130, 206, 219, 220
Arthur, Jean 211, 221
August, Joseph 157

Baker, Carroll 212
Bancroft, Anne 21, 206, 207, 208, 210
Bancroft, George 144
The Battle of Midway 10, 29, 36, 62, 79, 102, 103, 105, 107, 109, 189
Baxter, Warner 219
Bergman, Ingmar 5, 19
Berlin, Isaiah 30, 33
Biograph (film company) 24, 96, 135, 136, 138
Birth of a Nation 17, 29, 97, 135, 136, 164
Bison (film company) 133, 134, 136, 137, 140
Blazing the Trail 134, 136, 137
The Blue Eagle 27
Bogart, Humphrey 8
Bogdanovich, Peter 5, 6, 7, 19, 30, 31, 33, 140, 141
Bond, Ward 22, 27, 29, 69, 122, 156, 157, 158, 218
Booth, John Wilkes 219
Borzage, Danny 157
Boston, MA 30, 51, 62, 63, 64, 76, 82, 86, 88, 91, 92, 185
Brandon, Henry 209
Brennan, Joseph 63
Broken Coin 95
Bucking Broadway 32, 129, 131, 132, 134, 136, 137

Cameo Kirby 18, 221
Cape Elizabeth (Maine) 23, 24, 42, 46, 47, 48, 52, 53, 64, 69, 75, 76, 80, 86, 88, 92, 212
Capra, Frank 5, 10, 194, 221
Carey, Harry, Jr. 157, 167, 178, 184, 185, 186, 213, 216
Carey, Harry, Sr. 8, 18, 27, 96, 97, 98, 131, 132, 137, 139, 156, 216
Carey, Olive 96
Carradine, John 145, 218
Catholicism 9, 22, 28, 31, 44, 46, 47, 48, 75, 82, 86, 156, 166, 170, 187, 191, 212, 222
Cheyenne Autumn 73, 74, 195, 200, 207, 212, 213, 214
Churchill, Berton 144
Citizen Kane 8, 10
Clemens, Samuel L. *see* Twain, Mark
Colbert, Claudette 211
Colman, Ronald 219, 220
Cooper, James Fenimore 18, 24, 28, 32, 33
Coppola, Francis Ford 204
Crisp, Donald 31, 217
Crosman, Henrietta 210
Cunard, Grace 93, 95, 133
Curley, James Michael 45, 63
Curran, Barbara ("Abby") 38, 39, 40, 43, 69, 75, 76, 83, 84, 86, 91

D-Day 29, 36, 111–113, 115–121
Darwell, Jane 21, 32, 210
December 7th 29, 62
Del Rio, Delores 215
DeMille, Cecil B. 7, 8, 11, 12, 131, 140
Democratic Party 11, 45, 63
Devine, Andy 144
Dietrich, Marlene 146
Doctor Bull 18, 219, 220
Donovan, William (aka "Wild Bill") 10, 36, 113
Donovan's Reef 26, 28, 29, 206, 218, 219, 221
Dru, Joanne 196

Drums Along the Mohawk 10, 14, 18, 209, 211, 218
Dwan, Allan 94, 140, 141

Earp, Wyatt 8, 10, 20, 72, 97, 192–195, 203, 204
Eisenhower, Dwight D. 112
Eisenstein, Sergei 5
Eyman, Scott 6, 14, 15, 32, 33, 54, 56, 62, 63, 64, 65, 66, 67, 140, 167, 168

Feeney, Daniel 82, 91
Feeney, Edward *see* O'Fearna, Edward
Feeney, Francis *see* Ford, Francis
Feeney, John A. (father of John Ford) 45, 46, 75, 76, 77, 83, 88, 91, 92, 122
Feeney, John M. *see* Ford, John
Feeney, Josephine (sister of John Ford) 77, 79, 81, 91, 95
Feeney, Martin (cousin of John Ford) 35, 38, 43, 68, 69, 71–74, 78, 88, 92, 101, 124, 156
Feeney, Patrick (grandfather of John Ford) 75, 82
Field, Betty 208
Field Photo Branch, OSS 10, 29, 36, 102, 104, 119; *see also* Office of Strategic Services
Figueroa, Gabriel 216
Fitzgerald, Barry 45, 72, 113, 223, 155, 158
FitzSimons, Charles 158
FitzSimons, James 158
Flaherty, Robert 28
Fonda, Henry 7, 10, 21, 26, 157, 199, 211, 215, 218, 219
Fonda, Jane 12
Ford, Barbara (daughter of John Ford) 11, 100
Ford, Dan (grandson of John Ford) 10, 23, 25, 36, 37, 39, 57, 58, 62, 63, 64, 65, 66, 80, 91, 93, 100, 104, 119, 124, 155, 165, 167, 172, 208, 213
Ford, Francis (brother of John Ford) 17, 24, 35, 36, 54, 56, 63,

232 Index

66, 69, 77, 78, 79, 90, 93, 94, 95, 96, 123, 124, 129, 132, 133, 134, 137, 138, 139, 140, 155, 156, 184, 212
Ford, Mary (wife of John Ford) 9, 29, 99, 100, 101, 119, 120, 211
Ford, Patrick (son of John Ford) 79, 99, 100, 124, 179
Fort Apache 11, 12, 14, 16, 27, 72, 157, 197, 202, 209, 219
Four Sons 31
The Fugitive 22, 130, 206, 207, 215, 216, 217, 218
Fox, William 98; *see also* Fox Studios
Fox Studios 18, 22, 30, 66, 67, 78, 94, 98, 101, 155, 157; *see also* Twentieth Century–Fox
Fuller, Samuel 11, 12

Gable, Clark 9
Gallagher, Tag 5, 6, 62, 63, 64, 65, 66, 74, 79, 80, 81, 91, 141, 151, 152, 175, 181, 185, 194, 203, 204, 206, 212, 216, 220, 221, 222
Gardner, Ava 9, 212
Gaynor, Janet 27
Gibson, Hoot 8, 93
Goldwyn, Samuel 133
Gone with the Wind 10
The Grapes of Wrath 5, 7, 10, 14, 18, 20, 21, 29–32, 49, 74, 113, 144, 155, 189, 202, 204, 207, 210, 212, 218
Greene, Graham 215
Griffith, D.W. 15, 17, 20, 22, 24, 94, 96, 97, 129, 184

Hall, Jon 28
Hangman's House 30, 31, 78
Hart, William S. 137, 138, 139
Hauck, Arthur 57, 58
Hawks, Howard 5, 8, 13, 19, 29, 146, 157, 185
Hayes, Helen 219, 220
Hayward, Leland 11
Hearts of Oak 27
Hell Bent 32, 97, 129, 131, 134, 136, 137, 183
Hepburn, Katharine 6, 9, 13, 211
Hoch, Winton 157, 163
Holden, William 11, 219
Hollywood, CA 5, 9, 10, 19, 20, 24, 36, 54, 56, 57, 59, 63, 66, 69, 71, 72, 73, 75, 78, 79, 90, 93, 95–99, 101, 102, 120, 130–133, 135, 138–140, 144, 153–158, 167, 169, 170, 174, 176, 177, 179, 182, 184, 185, 197, 203, 204, 218
Homer, Winslow 133, 135
The Horse Soldiers 216, 219
Hough, R.L. (aka "Lefty") 94
How Green Was My Valley 5, 7, 9, 10, 20, 21, 31, 49, 62, 64, 113,

155, 166, 173, 207, 210, 212, 213, 217, 218
Hunter, Jeffrey 179
The Hurricane 9, 28, 210, 219

Immigrants 9, 43, 47, 49, 51, 53, 55, 59, 64, 77, 82, 86, 156, 173, 187, 191
Ince, Thomas 94, 133, 139
The Informer 7, 9, 22, 28, 31, 42, 62, 72, 74, 78, 113, 154, 207, 218
Ireland (as country/nation/place of origin) 9, 24, 30, 32, 35, 36, 38, 40, 41–48, 50, 52, 53, 54, 56, 58, 60, 62, 63, 64, 66, 68, 69, 71–74, 76, 78, 80, 82, 84, 86, 88, 90, 91, 92, 94, 96, 98, 99, 100, 101, 104, 106, 108, 110, 112, 114, 116, 118, 120, 122, 124, 126, 129, 153–158, 160, 161, 163, 164, 165, 167, 168, 172, 173
Irish (as a national and/ or cultural category of people) 9, 15, 21, 30, 31, 32, 35, 36, 38, 40, 42, 43, 45, 46–49, 51, 53, 54, 55, 59, 62–66, 68, 69, 71, 72, 73–78, 79, 80–84, 86, 90, 91, 92, 96, 99, 100, 101, 111, 122, 123, 124, 126, 127, 129, 153, 154, 156, 157, 158, 161–164, 166, 167, 168, 170, 171, 173, 187, 211, 212, 216
The Iron Horse 8, 27, 30, 207
It's a Wonderful Life 194

Jack, William 51, 53, 65
Japan/Japanese 29, 72, 102–107, 111, 120
Jarman, Claude, Jr. 211
Jenkinson, Philip 65
Jewish (as a religious or cultural category of people) 54, 64, 66
Johnson, Nunnally 157
Jones, Buck 8, 98
Judaism *see* Jewish
Judge Priest 18, 21
Just Pals 18, 98

Karloff, Boris 209
Kazan, Elia 5, 183
Kennedy, John F. 13
Kentucky Pride 18
Killanin, Lord 35, 68, 69, 71, 72, 73, 124, 125, 153
Knighthood of Malta 213
Kurosawa, Akira 5, 19, 20
Kyne, Peter 98, 216

Laemmle, Carl 93, 97, 132, 133, 134, 138, 139
Laine, Linda Noe 60, 80
Lamour, Dorothy 28, 29
The Last Hurrah 14, 30, 32, 45, 62, 78, 217, 219
Lee, Anna 31
Leighton, Margaret 207

LeRoy, Mervyn 11, 219
Lewis, Sinclair 72, 219
Libby, Lucien 29, 51, 53, 54, 65
Lightnin' 18
Lilly Library (home of the John Ford Papers at Indiana University) 23, 25, 37, 39, 57, 58, 64, 65, 91, 100, 104, 119, 124, 155, 165, 172, 178, 185, 186, 208, 213, 221
Lincoln, Abraham 10, 20, 43, 189, 190, 192, 196, 201, 203, 204, 219; see also *Young Mr. Lincoln*
Llewellyn, Richard 31
The Long Gray Line 32, 62, 78, 117
The Long Voyage Home 10, 26, 27, 28, 29, 113, 119, 156
Longfellow, Henry Wadsworth 42, 51, 52, 53, 57, 59, 61, 62, 67, 89
The Lost Patrol 9, 130, 206, 208, 209
Loy, Myrna 220
Lubitsch, Ernst 10
Lucas, George 19
Lyon, Sue 214

MacDonald, J. Farrell 31, 97
Malta *see* Knighthood of Malta
Malden, Karl 213
The Man Who Shot Liberty Valance 5, 11, 16, 18, 20, 21, 35, 51, 54, 72, 144, 146, 151, 189, 199, 200, 201, 202, 207, 209, 212, 213, 214, 219
Mankiewicz, Joseph L. 11, 12
Marked Men 98, 216
Marsh, Mae 29, 135
Martin, Peter 36, 111
Marvin, Lee 200, 209
Mary of Scotland 9, 72, 74, 211
Massey, Raymond 210, 219
Mature, Victor 204, 211
Maupassant, Guy de 10
Mayer, Louis B. 10
Mazurki, Mike 206, 207
McBride, Joseph 5, 6, 19, 23, 24, 31, 33, 48, 56, 62, 63, 64, 65, 66, 75, 78, 80, 92, 140, 204, 205, 221
McDowell, Roddy 31, 173, 213
McLaglen, Victor 28, 30, 31, 69, 72, 73, 78, 156, 158, 170, 208, 209, 211, 218
Meek, Donald 145
Men Without Women 28, 29
Metro-Goldwyn-Mayer (film studio) 10, 156, 134, 206
MGM *see* Metro-Goldwyn-Mayer
Midway, Battle of 10, 29, 36, 62, 79, 102, 103, 105, 106, 107, 109, 189; see also *Battle of Midway*
Miles, Vera 200, 212

Mister Roberts 11, 26, 219
Mr. Smith Goes to Washington 10, 221
Mitchell, George 63
Mitchell, Thomas 144
Mitry, Jean 155, 206
Mix, Tom 8
Mogambo 9, 14, 206, 212
Monument Valley (Utah) 10, 14, 16, 22, 27, 32, 129, 143, 145, 146, 178, 184, 192, 209
Morris, Michael *see* Killanin, Lord
Mother Machree 30, 54, 62, 78
Mudd, Samuel 219
Munjoy Hill (neighborhood of Portland, Maine) 23, 35, 42–67, 77, 88, 89, 90, 156
Murnau, F.W. 20, 27, 28, 30
Muskie, Edmund 63
My Darling Clementine 5, 10, 14, 15, 20, 31, 72, 130, 144, 189, 192–196, 211, 217, 218

Natwick, Mildred 170, 216
Navajos 98
Nazis 111, 112, 114, 118; *see also* World War II
Nichols, Dudley 23, 32, 132, 156, 157, 215
Nimitz, Chester 102
Nixon, Richard M. 12, 13, 79
Nugent, Frank 157, 161

O'Brien, Darcy 33
O'Brien, George 8, 22, 23, 27, 28
O'Casey, Sean 62
O'Fearna, Edward (Feeney) (brother of John Ford) 77, 79, 89
Office of Strategic Services 10, 29, 36, 102, 104, 113, 117, 119, 155; *see also* Field Photo Branch, OSS
O'Flaherty, Liam 31, 78, 161
O'Hara, Maureen 9, 21, 32, 36, 69, 72, 73, 122–125, 127, 153, 155–158, 162, 165, 170, 211
Oliver, Edna May 211
O'Neill, Eugene 21, 26, 43, 156
Orono (Maine) *see* University of Maine at Orono
OSS *see* Office of Strategic Services
The Outcasts of Poker Flat 98

Paramount (film studio) 66, 139
Parrish, Robert 10
Peaks Island (Maine) 24, 77, 89, 90
Pearl Harbor 10, 102, 110, 111; *see also* World War II
Pennick, Ronald "Jack" 108, 109, 110, 119
Pidgeon, Walter 9, 217

Pilgrimage 210, 218
The Plough and the Stars 62, 78
Pope Paul VI 213
Portland, ME 9, 15, 23, 24, 29, 30, 32, 35, 36, 38–57, 59, 60, 62–67, 69, 71, 74–84, 86, 88–92, 95, 119, 120, 133, 156, 158, 212, 221; *see also* Munjoy Hill
Portland High School 29, 48, 49, 51, 53, 54, 56, 59, 64–67, 77, 79, 80, 81, 90, 92
Powell, William 219
The Prince of Avenue A 30, 78
The Prisoner of Shark Island 14, 19, 28, 207, 219, 220

Qualen, John 26, 215
The Quiet Man 5, 7, 9, 19, 21, 29–32, 35, 36, 42, 45, 62, 66–73, 78, 112, 122–130, 153–175, 206, 211

Red River 8, 146, 157
Remington, Frederic 137
Renoir, Jean 8, 19
Republican Party 11, 20, 43, 46, 63
Revolutionary War 8, 12, 14, 209, 211
Riley the Cop 31, 62
Rio Grande 9, 11, 21, 27, 29, 32, 72, 157, 170, 211, 219
The Rising of the Moon 32, 62, 78
RKO (film studio) 155
Robinson, Edward G. 211
Robson, Flora 208, 209
Rogers, Will 9, 18, 21, 28, 30, 219, 220
Romero, Cesar 29
Roosevelt, Franklin D. 63, 66, 111, 114, 120
Roosevelt, Theodore 118
Rutledge, Ann 10, 189, 190, 191, 196, 197, 200, 201

Salute 24, 27, 28, 218
Sarris, Andrew 5, 17, 19, 167, 175, 206, 221
Schickel, Richard 135, 140
Schneiderman, George 97
Scorsese, Martin 5, 130, 174, 175, 218
Scott, Sir Walter 28
Screen Directors Guild 11
The Searchers 5, 11, 14, 16, 18, 19, 21, 31, 32, 130, 146, 176–178, 180, 183, 185, 186, 189, 199–202, 209, 213, 218, 219
Seas Beneath 28, 29
Sergeant Rutledge 20
Seven Women (aka *7 Women*) 12, 21, 130, 205–222
Shakespeare, William 30, 129, 154, 158–162, 166–168, 195, 203–205, 221

The Shamrock Handicap 30, 31, 62
She Wore a Yellow Ribbon 7, 11, 14, 21, 27, 72, 130, 157, 189, 196, 219
Shields, Arthur 158, 171, 218, 219
Sinclair, Andrew 65
Smith, C. Aubrey 28
Smith, Wingate 179
Spiddal (Ireland) 35–38, 43, 46, 68, 71, 73–75, 78, 82–84, 86, 88, 91, 101, 122–124, 126
Spielberg, Steven 5, 19
Stagecoach 5, 7, 8, 10, 11, 18–20, 29, 72, 113, 129, 142–152, 195, 207, 209, 210, 211, 213, 216, 219
Steamboat Round the Bend 18
Stevens, George 14
Stewart, James (Jimmy) 151, 200, 212
Stout, Archie 117
Straight Shooting 16, 18, 97, 129, 131, 134–139, 141, 183, 184
Submarine Patrol 28
The Sun Shines Bright 158, 217
Sunrise 27, 30

Tavernier, Claudine 62, 64
Thalberg, Irving 97
They Were Expendable 10, 29, 54, 110, 189, 197, 204
Three Bad Men (aka *3 Bad Men*) 18, 216
Three Godfathers (aka *3 Godfathers*) 18, 22, 98, 130, 206, 216, 217, 218, 222
Tobacco Road 10, 113
Toland, Gregg 8, 29, 157
The Tornado 78, 95
Tracy, Spencer 8, 9, 219
Trevor, Claire 143, 144, 146, 211, 219
Turner, Frederick Jackson 142, 143
Twain, Mark 18, 20, 31, 142
20th Century–Fox 22, 67, 78, 94, 98, 101, 155, 157
Two Rode Together 72

United Artists (film studio) 56, 66, 133
United States Navy 5, 72, 102; *see also* Field Photo Branch and Office of Strategic Services
Universal (film company) 17, 18, 30, 56, 66, 77, 78, 90, 93–98, 129, 131–135, 138–140, 184
University of Maine at Orono 24, 56, 57, 58, 62, 66, 77, 78, 92

Vanier, Oscar ("Ski") 66
Vidor, King 28
Vietnam War 20–21, 204
Von Sternberg, Josef 18
Von Stroheim, Erich 18, 133

Wagner, Richard 204
Wagon Master 28, 72, 130, 206, 217, 218, 222
Walsh, Raoul 19
Walthall, Henry 136
Wanger, Walter 146
Warden, Jack 219
Warner, Jack 11
Wayne, John 6, 7, 8, 10, 11, 12, 14, 15, 18–22, 26, 27, 29–32, 54, 69, 72, 73, 78, 126, 142, 146, 150, 151, 153, 155–158, 165, 170, 172, 179, 184, 196, 199, 200, 210, 211, 212, 216–219
Wead, Frank ("Spig") 29, 211
Welles, Orson 5, 8, 18, 19, 25, 30
Wellman, William 19
West Point 27, 99, 117
Whitman, Walt 16
The Whole Town's Talking 221
Wilmington, Michael 5, 204, 205–206, 210, 221
The Wings of Eagles 9, 21, 29, 211
Wollen, Peter 176, 177, 185, 193, 195, 203
Wood, Natalie 32
Wood, Robin 194, 203, 204, 207
World War I 27, 28, 95, 120, 194
World War II 5, 7, 10, 12, 15, 19, 26, 29, 36, 67, 110, 111, 112, 170, 194, 197, 202, 203; *see also* Nazis; Pearl Harbor
Wyler, William 14

Yates, Herbert 157, 158, 170
Yeats, William Butler 154, 158, 160, 167
Young Mr. Lincoln 5, 10, 18, 19, 20, 21, 28, 29, 30, 130, 177, 189–196, 200, 201, 203, 207

Zanuck, Darryl 5, 14, 15, 67, 155

www.ingramcontent.com/pod-product-compliance
Lightning Source LLC
Chambersburg PA
CBHW081551300426
44116CB00015B/2839